THE PEOPLE HAVE NEVER STOPPED DANCING

JACQUELINE SHEA MURPHY

THE PEOPLE HAVE NEVER STOPPED DANCING

NATIVE AMERICAN MODERN DANCE HISTORIES

University of Minnesota Press
Minneapolis • London

Sections of the Introduction and chapter 8 previously appeared as "Lessons in Dance (as) History: Aboriginal Land Claims and Aboriginal Dance, circa 1999," in *Dancing Bodies, Living Histories: New Writings about Dance and Culture,* edited by Lisa Doolittle and Anne Flynn (Banff, Canada: Banff Centre Press, 2000).

Sections of chapters 2 and 9 were previously published as "Policing Authenticity: Native American Dance and the 'Western' Stage," *Discourses in Dance* 1, no. 2 (2002); reprinted with permission.

Correspondence between Martha Graham and Aaron Copland used by permission of The Aaron Copland Fund for Music, Inc.; copyright owner of the works of Aaron Copland.

Published by the University of Minnesota Press
111 Third Avenue South, Suite 290
Minneapolis, MN 55401-2520
http://www.upress.umn.edu

Library of Congress Cataloging-in-Publication Data

Shea Murphy, Jacqueline, 1964–
    The people have never stopped dancing : Native American modern dance histories / Jacqueline Shea
Murphy.
        p.   cm.
    Includes bibliographical references and index.
    ISBN: 978-0-8166-4775-0 (hc : alk. paper)
    ISBN-10: 0-8166-4775-5 (hc : alk. paper)
    ISBN: 978-0-8166-4776-7 (pb : alk. paper)
    ISBN-10: 0-8166-4776-3 (pb : alk. paper)
    1. Modern dance—United States—History—20th century.   2. Indian dance—United States—
History—20th century.   I. Title.
    GV1783.S46 2007
    792.8—dc22

2007020869

Printed in the United States of America on acid-free paper

The University of Minnesota is an equal-opportunity educator and employer.

12 11 10 09 08 07   10 9 8 7 6 5 4 3 2 1

For Richard J. Shea, in spirit

Contents

Introduction: Dance as Document · 1

Part I. Restrictions, Regulations, Resiliences

1. Have They a Right? Nineteenth-Century Indian
   Dance Practices and Federal Policy · 29
2. Theatricalizing Dancing and Policing Authenticity · 53
3. Antidance Rhetoric and American Indian Arts in the 1920s · 81

Part II. Twentieth-Century Modern Dance

4. Authentic Themes: Modern Dancers and
   American Indians in the 1920s and 1930s · 111
5. Her Point of View: Martha Graham and Absent Indians · 148
6. Held in Reserve: José Limón, Tom Two Arrows, and
   American Indian Dance in the 1950s · 169

Part III. Indigenous Choreographers Today

7. The Emergence of a Visible Native American Stage Dance · 197
8. Aboriginal Land Claims and Aboriginal Dance at the
   End of the Twentieth Century · 217
9. We're Dancing: Indigenous Stage Dance in the
   Twenty-first Century · 240

Acknowledgments · 265

Notes · 269

Index · 309

Dance as Document

———

> The truth is the Ghost Dance did not end with the murder
> of Big Foot and one hundred and forty-four Ghost Dance
> worshippers at Wounded Knee. The Ghost Dance has never
> ended, it has continued, and the people have never stopped
> dancing; they may call it by other names, but when they
> dance, their hearts are reunited with the spirits of beloved
> ancestors and the loved ones recently lost in the struggle.
> Throughout the Americas, from Chile to Canada, the people
> have never stopped dancing; as the living dance, they are
> joined again with all our ancestors before them, who cry out,
> who demand justice, and who call the people to take back
> the Americas!
>
> ▸ *Leslie Marmon Silko,* Almanac of the Dead

This book was set in motion more than a decade ago when Laguna Pueblo writer
Leslie Marmon Silko's sprawling, intense, magnum opus *Almanac of the Dead*
got under my skin.[1] I was reading and teaching and attempting to write about
it, and I saw its pronouncements, predictions, and effects everywhere around
me.[2] In one passage that I kept turning over in my head, the trickster lawyer
Wilson Weasel Tail, addressing an audience of New Age Indian wannabe holis-
tic healers, argues for the continuing effect that the 1890 Ghost Dance religion
has had in the reclaiming of the Americas. Weasel Tail's suggestion that "the
people have never stopped dancing," and that this dancing has continuing effect, even if not immediate or visible in Eurocentric worldviews—as Weasel Tail
says, "it was the Europeans, and not the Native Americans, who had expected
results overnight" (Silko, *Almanac of the Dead,* 723)—reverberated with me in
puzzling and compelling ways. It suggested complex understandings of time,
causation, ancestral connection.

About the same time, I learned that in 1930 modern dance choreographer

Martha Graham, in her heralding of "American" dance, called on "two primitive sources, dangerous and hard to handle in the arts, but of intense psychic influence: the Indian and the Negro."[3] Her comment—at least part of it—seemed to be resonating in the growing field of dance studies. All around me, scholars were citing Graham's comment and others like it, and then exploring the role of African American dance in the history of American concert dance.[4] These approaches were fabulous and inspiring, but they made me wonder, what about "the Indian"? If "the Indian and the Negro" were so vital to the development of "American" dance, what was the role of Native American dance, and of Indigenous dancers and choreographers, in modern dance history and choreography?[5] If "the people have never stopped dancing," what continuing effects might that dancing be having? Was it part of the history of modern dance I'd learned about in college? Had it influenced what I practiced as a bashful but dedicated modern dance student? Were aspects of it infusing the numerous dance pieces I had been watching for years on contemporary dance stages? And if so, why hadn't any of the dance studies works I'd been reading discussed it? If "the people have never stopped dancing," what made the divide between Native American and modern dance still so sharp? Was it true that, as dance scholar Susan Manning suggests, "there has never been a collective movement among Native American choreographers comparable to that among African-American choreographers of modern dance" ("*American Document* and American Minstrelsy," 201 n.)? And if so, why not? What were and are the ideologies of American Indian dance practices, ideologies seemingly outside of those visible to and constitutive of what has been understood as modern dance choreography? How might received definitions of both "modern dance" and "Native American" have been contributing to this unremarked absence? Might *these* ideologies illuminate the unremarked ideologies of modern dance? If "the people have never stopped dancing," what were dance scholars not seeing?

And how to even begin to deal with seeing or not seeing it?

I started to write about the Indian influence on early modern dance stages—how choreographers like Graham and Ted Shawn and Lester Horton had staged themselves as Indians and engaged with ideas about American Indian dance in their choreography—and about the lack of critical attention to just how absent discussion of Native American dance has been.

PLAYING INDIAN

As I started this work, I scoured the Native American studies shelves for books on dance. I found several on American Indian ballerinas, like celebrated Osage dancer Maria Tallchief, and some on cabaret dancers, like Penobscot Molly Spotted Elk, that raised interesting issues about what constitutes American Indian dance and dance forms.[6] I found numerous books on the so-called Ghost

Dance and many specific anthropological studies of American Indian dances.[7] Many of these were helpful, though some were also troublesome in ways endemic to early anthropology, ways that have been roundly critiqued by the field of anthropology itself. I pored through *Native American Dance: Ceremonies and Social Tradition,* edited by Charlotte Heth, which presented compelling recent writings on many Native dance practices, including modern dance.[8] I pondered the oddity of Gladys and Reginald Laubin's 1977 *Indian Dances of North America,* written by two white scholar-dancers who lived with and were adopted by a family on the Standing Rock Sioux Reservation, and who performed "authentic" Indian dances throughout the United States and abroad from the 1930s through the 1950s.[9] I devoured Philip Deloria's *Playing Indian,* which laid out in lively, astute, compelling detail just how familiar Americans' fascination with performing as Indians is.

Deloria argues that claiming American identity by "playing Indian—putting on Indian dress and image—has been a national project for centuries." He traces it from the Boston Tea Party (where colonists dressed as Indians to protest British taxes and dump tea in the Boston harbor), through Boy Scout practices (taking on Indian names and cultures), to 1960s "Powwow hobbyists" and the happy multiculturalism of New Age devotees. He argues convincingly that "the ways in which white Americans have used Indianness in creative self-shaping have continued to be pried apart from questions about inequality, the uneven workings of power, and the social settings in which Indians and non-Indians might actually meet." As such, playing Indian, he argues, has been one of the foundations "for imagining and performing domination and power in America."[10] Deloria's excellent and full analysis demonstrated how prevalent this trend of white performers "playing Indian" is and touched ways Native peoples have reinhabited and energized a slippery "Indian" identity and wrested its political, social, and economic control away from those who produced it. Yet in addressing the topic so well, it also brought home to me the limits of another book (only) about white choreographers' self-stagings as Indians, focused primarily, again, on white performers and foregrounding the problems of white cultural production, and leaving out the very voices and perspectives these performers themselves ignore.

How, I wondered, did Native American dancers and choreographers *themselves* engage with the stage? My interest in modern dancers' interest in Native American dance persisted, but I wanted to incorporate Indigenous voices, histories, and perspectives as well. I imagined possible paths for more directly addressing Native American perspectives in dance history. I could trace a history of Native American ballet, addressing the careers of more than a dozen renowned Native ballet dancers, from Maria Tallchief through Navajo dancer Jock Soto, a principal dancer for the New York City Ballet. Or I could frame a project around Native American popular dance performance and explore the contributions of Spotted Elk and Lakota dancer and Wounded Knee survivor Lost Bird (Zintka) and other "show-biz Indian" dancing on popular stages. These would be great projects. But they also would take me away from the central issues that had taken hold of me: I wanted to explore not just the history of Native dance and dancers, and not just the influence of American Indian dance on modern dance, but especially the interrelations between Native American dance and the history and development of modern dance in America.

How, though, to explore the relation of Indigenous dances, dancers, and choreographers to modern dance? I doubted I'd find much in the library. I had a growing sense that watching old dance films and reading novels and ethnographies that referenced American Indian dance, and depending on these only for my research, was not going to enable the book I hoped to write. A line at the end of Deloria's book reverberated with me; he notes that more recent acts of "playing Indian" have taken the shape of reading books, and he levels a critique of Native American scholarship that doesn't even attempt to engage with anything other than texts: "During the past thirty years, playing Indian has been as much about reading books as it has been about meeting native people" (*Playing Indian,* 189). He criticizes the way that, in the current multicultural climate, "simply knowing about Indians . . . has become a satisfactory form of social and political engagement." His words nudged me to do more than bury my nose in library clip files.

On the other hand, setting out to the reservation, or powwow, or ceremonial grounds to research American Indian dances and write a participant-observer treatise on ways they might, for example, have influenced Martha Graham or Ted Shawn didn't sit right with me, either. I feared such an approach would reproduce some of the troublesome dynamics these early modern dancers (as well as tourists and early anthropologists) were themselves caught up in (see chapters 3 and 4). I questioned the way such a project might compound ideas of certain powwow or ceremonial dances as "authentic," with the implication that others were not. I worried such an approach might still mostly shed light on how Native dance influenced modern dancers like Graham, and on me, bracketing Native dancers' modern dance expertise in its own right.

But I still wasn't sure how to address the role of Indigenous dance and dancers in this history.

CHINOOK WINDS

In January 1999, I was invited to a dance studies conference at the University of Calgary to give a paper on how Ted Shawn, in his quest to legitimate dancing for men, used Native American dance material to negotiate issues of masculinity (see chapter 4).[11] The bulk of my research had been done reading library books and watching videos, using the rhetorical analytical skills I'd developed as a literary scholar to unpack Shawn's appropriation of the Hopi Eagle Dance and other Native dance practices for his own agenda. Mine was the only presentation on the schedule dealing with Native American dance—me, a non-Native scholar, flown in from California, presenting myself as the expert on issues in Native American dance. As I arrived, passport in hand, this issue of my positioning lurked in the back of my mind as an issue to be contended with.

Before the conference, we gathered for a few days up at the Banff Centre for the Arts. When I mentioned my topic—the relation between Native American dance and modern dance history—the people from the area asked me if I knew about the Aboriginal Dance Project and offered to introduce me to Marrie Mumford and Jerry Longboat.

Marrie Mumford is a big woman with big gray hair, and she gives off a simultaneous sense of incisive outrage and warm generosity. She shook my hand, taking in my blue eyes and fair skin, giving me that "what are *you* doing talking about Native culture?" look I'd come to know through my work in Native American studies. She was not hostile, but there was a definite edge of cool in her response to me. I swallowed hard and told her how I'd just purchased and read the *Chinook Winds: Aboriginal Dance Project* book, and how excited I was to learn of all the Aboriginal Arts program work going on at Banff, and how I'd love to talk with her and Jerry Longboat about the work they've been doing. Longboat was there too and we shook hands, and they watched me as I talked.

Over the course of the day, I started to sense some tension around the issue of why Longboat and Mumford were not involved more officially in the conference. I got the sense that Mumford and Longboat had come, in part, to register their protest that Aboriginal dance wasn't included on the program, even though the Aboriginal Dance Project was flourishing only an hour away. And then it turns out there was this white professor from California (i.e., me) flown in and paid to talk about issues in Native dance. I started to wonder if Longboat and Mumford could present with me.

It took some scrambling through logistics and politics to make it happen, but after a winter-storm flight cancellation and a series of negotiations, Mumford and Longboat were invited to participate on the panel, to speak about the work they had been doing up at Banff and about Aboriginal dance today. Their presentations sparked much excitement and many lively questions from students and scholars in the audience, and presented ideas that have stayed with me ever since (see chapter 8).

The hard questions for me came up during more casual conversations. "So. What are you doing writing about Aboriginal culture anyway?" Jerry Longboat asked as we sipped beers at a bar down the street.

I told the story of how my frustration with psychoanalytically based narrative theory had lead me to Native American literary and performance theory during my PhD studies, how I'd drawn on this in various courses I'd taught, how I'd continued following Native American studies as I moved into writ-ing about dance, how I was interested in ways Indigenous worldviews chal-lenged me to see conceptions of time, space, story, words, narrative, history—among so many other things—so differently. How it felt like I was starting to see something the rest of the dance studies world hadn't yet registered, but might be open to. Longboat nodded, and we left it at that. But his question and its implications—my responsibility to stay attuned to my relation to this topic and, if I persisted, to muster all the integrity I could in approaching it—have lingered ever since.

Slowly, an approach emerged. I had seen some contemporary Native American stage dance, similar to that discussed in the *Chinook Winds* book. I'd seen the American Indian Dance Theatre perform in the early 1990s. At a con-ference in 1995, I'd seen Daystar/Rosalie Jones present a lecture-demonstration on "Dance Drama of Indian America."[12] I began to see ways these contemporary American Indian stage dance productions might themselves be theorizing the Native American dance/modern dance history breach I was seeking to explore and began engaging with them as a way of exploring the relation between Native American and modern dance history.

In June, I interviewed Daystar (Rosalie Jones) at her home in Santa Fe. In July, at Mumford's invitation, I returned to Canada to visit the Aboriginal Dance Program for a week, to watch videos, interview performers, and see that year's production (see chapter 8). These research trips were exciting and illuminating—and also hard. At Banff that week in 1999, I spent hours hov-ering about, wondering if I should go to the cultural room and try to make friends, or go into town and play tourist, or watch the videos over again, or just go off hiking. Most of the time I wanted to hide and not struggle to approach people I didn't know and who might not really want to talk to me. I parceled Silko's new novel, *Gardens in the Dunes,* out to myself so I wouldn't curl away in my room and read all the time. Being there was so much harder than reading books. And I was only there for a week, with a meal card to use at my conve-nience and a fine bed and shower and free access to the pool, and a whole tour-ist town just a ten minute walk down the hill, where I could (and did) blend in without a hitch any time I wanted. I tried to bolster my courage by feeling self-righteous about what I was doing—because Deloria is right, just reading about Native American history and culture and politics is the contemporary way of "playing Indian" without having to have any meaningful interaction with Indian people. I didn't know how particularly meaningful the interaction I was having was, really—a week hanging out and interviewing people—but it didn't feel safe and it didn't ever feel like I was Indian, and I was definitely learning things I would never learn poring over documents at my desk. I was convinced that talking to people, face to face, was more important than just hol-ing up with documents and other people's descriptions. This seemed especially true with the topic of Aboriginal dance, given what I'd learned of Aboriginal dance history and its relation to official written discourse—its absence in most dance histories, the letters and laws simultaneously invoking and outlawing it, the court findings refusing it agency. At the core of it all, I believed that what I was doing was more important than my own uncertainties.

Over the next several years, I continued traveling across North America to see productions when and where they happened—from upstate New York to Santa Fe, Brooklyn to Lethbridge, Toronto to Washington, D.C.—and to interview practitioners. Most of what I saw was by Native American and Aboriginal dancers not particularly interested in translating powwow or exhibition dances to the stage, or in staging their communities' ritual, ceremonial, or even social dance practices. All were attuned to the complexities of staging Native dance, including the protocol that would be involved in obtaining permission from elders to use family stories or ritual items, should they wish to do so. But mostly they were interested in using tools of contemporary stage dance—training in modern dance and ballet, and increasingly practices such as Butoh and yoga that are also influencing non-Native contemporary stage dancers—as they explored Aboriginal or Native American stories, worldviews, and processes (see chapter 9). In different ways, their stage practices investigate connections across species and generations, engage with healing and other transformative practices, and acknowledge political and spiritual relationship to histories of racism, oppression, and land loss.

The dancing I saw and the interviews I conducted raised questions about what makes stage dance Aboriginal or Native American, and provided some answers. It compelled a shift from seeing Native American stage dance only in exhibition dances, marked by a narrow band of visual and rhythmic markers visually recognizable as Indian.[13] They instead suggested a recognition that Native American dancing can take many forms, take place on multiple stages, make use of varied, including contemporary modern dance, idioms. They suggested attention not to what *looks* Indian, but more so to the stories the dancing tells, the theories of embodiment and enactment the dance work investigates, the familial and tribal connections, processes, dedication, and intention with which the dancing is made.

METHODOLOGIES

As I undertook this analysis, I gave special weight to the stated intentions of the choreographers and performers, as explained in conversations, interviews, e-mails, pre- and post-performance talks, and program descriptions and scripts. I also circulated drafts of my writing to those I quoted, so they would have a chance to review, edit, clarify, or change what I wrote before it appeared in print. Citations in this book from interviews I did, as well as much of the description and analysis of particular dance pieces, have been circulated for review—and sometimes clarified and edited—by those who spoke, danced, or choreographed the pieces I describe.[14]

At the same time, my goal was not to present a neutral view. Instead, I tried to attune myself to the effects the performances I saw had on me and, as best I could discern them, on others participating as audience members in the productions. My intention was to acknowledge our involvement as participants in these events and the effects they have, and to refuse the distanced observer stance that spectacle impresarios, government policies, academic inquiry, and soft, squishy seats in darkened theaters may seem to invite.

Recognizing this reframing of an audience member's role led me to engage a different way of watching Native American stage dance. Rather than focus on the power of the gaze to objectify, as a visual studies model might, I followed more of a dance studies model, with its attention to corporeality and the energies and agencies engaged by bodies moving, within particular frames and contexts, in time and space. On the one hand, audience members at these productions are present and important as witness/participants, involved in, feeding, and fed by the energies dance calls up, its articulations and negotiations of public space, geographic location, land, spirituality, and embodiment. On the other hand, the dances, understood in this context, really aren't about the predominantly non-Native viewers watching, though they do acknowledge viewers' roles as witnesses and participants; they are about the performers' actions and their representations of themselves, their peoples, and their histories.

ARCHIVES

As I followed these contemporary dance pieces, I started to notice certain historical refrains. The tapes from the first year of the Chinook Winds Aboriginal Dance Project, for example, included pieces that confronted head-on the relation of Indigenous peoples and dances to histories of corporeal colonialism. In *Buffalo Spirit,* choreographed by Alejandro Roncería in 1996, for example, a dancer moves slowly across the stage as a voice-over reads an official 1921 Canadian circular directing Indian affairs officials "to use your utmost endeavors to dissuade the Indians from excessive indulgence in the practice of dancing." *Residential School for Boys,* also choreographed for that year's program by Roncería, both records and responds to the oppressive history of Canada's Residential School system for Aboriginal children (see chapter 9). Other pieces I'd seen addressed histories of U.S. and Canadian colonialism as well. Daystar/ Rosalie Jones's *No Home but the Heart: An Assembly of Memories,* as I discuss below, traces the effect of federal dictates and land policies on the bodies of her grandmother, mother, and herself, and ends as she stands on stage reading an official notice about her federally recognized relation to this lineage. This history of corporeal control likewise emerged in the way some dancers voiced trepidation about their own engagements with disciplining institutions,[15] and others told me of their hesitations at the conventions of Western theater, with its focus on product more than process, its training methods, the shape of its stages. A history of federally imposed corporeal control was carried as well in the stories dancers told on and off the stage about learning (and not learning) dances from their elders, and about the emotions and memories awakened through the physical, bodily explorations that dancing requires.

As I watched these contemporary dances and heard these concerns, I realized I needed to brush up on all of this history, and particularly on the antidance policies the dances referenced. I figured I would address them, briefly, in the footnotes, to give dance readers some grounding in U.S. and Canadian Indian and Aboriginal history. Yet as I began to glimpse the violence and the continuing impact of the rhetoric at play in the late nineteenth-century United States and Canada, and the ideologies that it mobilized, I came to understand that this book's explorations couldn't even start without addressing, full-on, this part of the story.

I turned back to history books and to archived documents. These included hundreds of letters sent to the U.S. Bureau of Indian Affairs in response to federal anti–Indian dance edicts from the 1880s through the 1930s, now held in the U.S. National Archives in Washington, D.C. I read through thick stacks of onionskin paper, teasing apart the rhetoric of these governmental restrictions, glimpsing flickers of support for the dancing that continued in and around them (see chapter 3). Close analysis of this official historical record, including these letters as well as history texts, legislation, Indian agents' reports, and materials from other archives, came to comprise a central contribution of this study.[16]

DANCE AS DOCUMENT

Gradually, an understanding of dance as not just recounting history or expressing emotion, but as itself a form of knowledge and history—as itself capable of enacting effect—emerged through these letters, performances, and conversations. Some dancers and choreographers talked about the transformations they experience on stage when dancing as animals or other beings (see chapter 8). Others talked about dance as a way of connecting with ancestral practices and ancestors, and of their own bodies as sites of blood memory accessed through danced exploration (see chapter 9). My post-structuralist antiessentialist graduate school training leaped out waving warning flags when I first started hearing this talk of blood memory. Yet over time, I began to hear its meaning in a very particular, practical, and political way, related to a particular history of land loss, to the keeping hidden of documented practices, the taking underground of ceremonies and dances.[17] Indigenous dancers' bodies, despite the physical effects of colonization, are a location of ways of being and knowing, held in bodies and everyday movements. And movement practices—including contemporary movement practices—are a tool for locating and unearthing these ways of knowing.

The ways many contemporary Native American dance pieces and practices directly challenged scholarly conceptions of valid history and historical markers (i.e., history documented through letters, decrees, facts, dates) likewise supported this understanding of dance's agency. Rather than only recounting history through dance, this choreographing and choreography also presented *itself* as historical research tool and document. In this way it suggested that contemporary Aboriginal stage dance functioned both as a way of researching, an epistemological "way of knowing," with theoretical insight and historical legitimacy, and as itself embodied documentation, with archival value. This in turn challenged a familiar divide that sees art making, such as choreography, as separate from the acts of historical documentation and of theorizing usually attributed only to scholars writing about art.

This understanding was familiar to me from dance studies, which as a field has been built around the idea that dance theorizes. As dance scholar Susan Foster has articulated so vigorously, dance studies has had to fight the "movement is ephemeral" reified mute body thing from day one, including both the romanticized idea that dance expresses something absolutely untranslatable so how can you write about it, and the related idea that dance itself is just dance (beautiful, pretty, but dumb) and scholars will do the theorizing about it. For years, Foster has brilliantly described how it's not that there's the dance, and then there's the scholar theorizing about the dance—it's that the dance itself is theorizing, the body is thinking, commenting, critiquing, investigating.[18]

Yet usually this is at least a new articulation, an illuminating insight—if not a heated discussion (although it is, happily, becoming more widely articulated in performance studies of late).[19] I was instead struck by how most of the Native American choreographers I spoke with proceeded from this notion as a given: that learning dance, investigating through dance, is a scholarly and theoretical, as well as political and historical, act. They articulated their dance making as a way of connecting to ancestral histories and practices and lands, as a way of knowing history and countering historical oppression/colonization levied through guns, poverty, and disease as well as through circulars and letters found in the National Archives.[20]

RELIGION AND TIME

This dancing also led to conceptions of religion quite different from those put forth by the predominantly Christian focus of North America, where faith and belief form the basis of religious involvement, and by those inscribed in modern dance, with its focus on individual expression and interiority. I began to sense and trace this difference while researching the project's historical sections, where time and again, the force of this compulsory Christianity (see chapter 1) disconnected with the force of Native American ceremonies and dances in ways that suggested foundationally different conceptions of what religion entails. While Christian missionaries seemed to understand religion in terms of practitioners' faith, the Native American and Aboriginal dancing instead articulated a sense of religion engaged with through the acts of dancing themselves. Jace Weaver's writings on religion proved helpful in explaining what I sensed here. Weaver writes, "Native religious traditions are very different in character from Christianity and Western religions. First, they are not primarily religions of ethics, or dogma, or theology. Rather, they are religions (if one may even use such a term with regard to Native traditions) of ritual practice. Further, they are not only religions of ritual observance, but they also permeate every aspect of daily life and existence."[21]

Although most of the Native American dance I've witnessed is not connected to Christian conceptions of faith and belief, virtually all *are* explicitly connected to religious/ritual approaches and spiritual understandings. In other words, they articulate a non-Christian, but also a nonsecular, approach and worldview. *BONES: An Aboriginal Dance Opera* engages in its story and staging with spirit people and a spirit world; *Miinigooweziwin . . . The Gift* portrays renewal through increasing awareness of spirits and with ritual (see chapter 9). These depictions differ from the explicit or implicit Christian ideology undergirding much early modern dance (see chapters 4 and 5). Nor, on the other hand, is it in keeping with seemingly secular depictions and conceptions of much contemporary postmodern dance. As Native studies scholar Arnoldo C. Vento notes, postmodern theories of modernization and secularization for the most part do not account for the persistence of religion such as that articulated through many Native worldviews and practices.[22] He writes, "The arguments with respect to existence of spirits, other intelligences outside our realm, the connection of the mind to the bioplasmic body in a conceptual self-organizing structure, and the altering of space and molecular patterns are still gray areas in our infant scientific stage" ("Rediscovering the Sacred," 189).

This articulation of a non-Christian and a nonsecular understanding of the world in turn posed challenges to the very concepts of time and history most prevalent today. As numerous philosophers and theorists have argued, conceptions of both Christianity and secularity underscore the notions of continuous, linear time that structure modernity.[23] Postcolonial scholar Dipesh Chakrabarty exposes ways this epistemology undergirds the very study of history as it is most often undertaken today. "The code of the secular calendar that frames historical explanations has this claim built into it: that independent of culture or consciousness, people exist in historical time," he writes. "History as a code thus invokes a natural, homogenous, secular, calendrical time," he adds. "History is supposed to exist in the same way as the earth." Instead, he argues that the discipline of history, grounded in secular understandings of time, "is only one among ways of remembering the past."[24] He teases apart the problems with naturalizing "modern historical consciousness" in which "Gods, spirits, and other 'supernatural' forces can claim no agency," approached through "a sense of chronologic history," and notes the "violent jolt the imagination has to suffer to be transported from a temporality cohabited by nonhumans and humans to one from which the gods are banished" (*Provincializing Europe*, 56).

Laguna/Sioux writer/scholar Paula Gunn Allen, working directly in a Native American context, similarly explores the contrast she sees between chronological time, which she links with colonization, and ceremonial time, which, she argues, "assumes the individual as a moving event shaped by and shaping human and nonhuman surroundings."[25] To explain she turns to the description of a Hoop Dancer in her poem of that name: "The difference between these concepts of time is embodied in the function of the dances: the green corn dances, the deer dances, and the Feast Day dances are all symbolized, held, in the hoop dance I was watching in my imagination as I wrote the poem." She explains, "Dancing in the midst of turning, whirling hoops is a means of transcending the limits of chronological time and its traumatizing, disease-causing effects. . . . The hoop dancer dances within what encircles him, demonstrating how the people live in motion within the circling spirals of time and space. They are no more limited than water and sky. At green corn dance time, water and sky come together, in Indian time, to make rain."[26]

Theorists' discussions of these notions of effect, time, and religion provided help in grappling with these abstract epistemological notions. But the dances themselves were what first led me to see it. In the stage dances I'd seen, "secular history"—dates, timelines, documents—though acknowledged, no longer held such stable hegemony. The stories the dance pieces retold (from long ago, and right now), the transformative practices they engaged, and the connections in and across geographic space they performed suggested ways of remembering and understanding the past that didn't quite fit with this notion of chronological history. Instead, they envisioned a multilayered, interconnected, spiritually animated world, and inhabited the stage as a space in which to address, acknowledge, depict, and inhabit these multiple realms and layerings—including the relations of generations and of stories across time, the agency of an ever-present spirit world, and the interconnections of humans and other beings. The envisionings and stagings were, by and large, neither Christian, secular, nor themselves acts of specific religious ceremony. Rather, they engaged, in differing though particular ways, with the theater as a space in which aspects and effects of ritual religious practice—the dedication and training it requires, the renewal it brings, the states of consciousness it creates and requires—could be assumed and explored.

I AM THE LIVING LEGACY OF THE WOMAN WHO SURVIVED

Daystar/Rosalie Jones's piece *No Home but the Heart*,[27] which premiered in Santa Fe, New Mexico, in 1999, tells the stories of four generations of Native women and their struggles and triumphs in relation to two hundred years of forced displacement from land and the gendered, racist, and class violence to which this displacement led. In particular, it underscores the multigenerational effects, especially on Indian women and their bodies, of the U.S. 1892 Ten Cent Treaty and the displacement of the Little Shell Band of Chippewa. As it recounts this history in its narrative, its choreography theorizes and enacts the ways in which continued dance practices, including that of this dance piece itself, provide a flickering of redress to the violence—the dispersal, homelessness, and economic, spiritual, social, and cultural dispossession—that this treaty, and the policies surrounding it, called into being. It also intervenes in understandings of historical time, framed by dates and other linear markers, even as it registers their force and effect.

The piece narrates a history in which Native peoples were systematically and violently disenfranchised and killed through laws, decrees, treaties, and other documents of European, Canadian, and U.S. policy that attempted to categorize and contain Aboriginal peoples, lands, and worldviews. The third section of this evening-length performance opens when the piece's Narrator, performed in the production I saw, in Lethbridge, Canada, in January 2002, by Sto:lo dancer Sid Bobb, appears on stage for the first time and speaks, as his first word, the historical date of one such declaration:

> 1783. That's the year when it all got started—when things first
> got mixed up. The French king told the fur-traders that they had
> his permission to marry the women of the "new" world . . . the
> Indian woman . . . you know, the Cree and Chippewa women.

He goes on to explain how teacher and statesman Louis Riel organized the "wonderful blend" of "mixed up, blended, all-together" people born of these marriages as the "Métis"—for which the Canadian government hanged him, leading his supporters to flee across the border into the United States "in search of food. For those who fled to the Great Plains, there were slim pickings. It was the late 1880's. The buffalo were gone. What was left? Smallpox. . . . the Red Death!" At this point a shrouded, masked dancer, named in the program as the Specter of Death, strides across the stage and begins a swaying, frenzied, seductive dance, the embodiment of smallpox and smallpox victim rolled into one.

As it dances—performed in the production I saw by Siksika dancer Geraldine Manossa—this being's body is taken over by an unseen force, throat back, inhabited, and overcome. Daystar's dance piece, in this way, embodies the force of systemic disenfranchisement of Native people, through racist, sexist policies in Canada and starvation and disease in the United States, as a deathly Specter—a ghostly, powerful, violent, unseen force, hypnotic, haunting, terrified, and terrifying. This Specter also animates smallpox itself as one of the forms taken when historical policies called destructive forces into being, as an embodiment of the terror enacted by those imperialist historical decrees of categorization and containment.

This section and the one following it underscore ways that part of what animates and empowers this violence is not only the decrees and policies themselves, but also the limited understandings of time in which they are measured. The Specter of Death appears right after the Narrator introduces specific historical dates and policies, via the French king's decree. This historical date, which is how history is so often taught and conceptualized, is thus narratively positioned in the piece as part of what contributes to the unleashing of a kind of deadly force, emerging in the form of smallpox. After the Specter of Death dancer freezes into a death image, throat back, mouth gaping, the next scene names, and is named for, a U.S. federal land grab policy set in a specific notion of progressive, linear, historical time. The Narrator, standing in the middle of four rocks he's positioned down stage center, discusses the U.S. governmental policies affecting Native peoples in the plains in the second half of the nineteenth century. In the production I saw, the Narrator, struggling to recall the date of the reservation policies he's about to discuss, pulls out a pocket watch and consults it. The movement is incongruous. Why consult a watch, measuring seconds, minutes, hours—at the most days and months of the current year—to recall the date, "1863," as the time when "All the Indians who happened to be living on the United States side of the border were told they had to move onto the 'reservation'"? The action of recalling a nineteenth-century date by checking time on a pocket watch points to the limits of understandings of historical time being narrated, the ways the time under discussion is much larger than what is actually getting measured, the ways the tools being used are inadequate to the task of that measurement, however one pretends that they aren't.

The Narrator's actions and movements on stage also imply a connection between this limited understanding of history and the progressively containing land policies being described. As the narrator recounts this linear march of historical time, marked by historical policy and document, moving from 1863 to 1893 and Chester Arthur's Ten Cent Treaty, he recounts the encroachment on Native land that accompanied this progression, stepping first inside the rocks he's placed on stage until the story tells of less and less land squeezing out more and more people, and he steps outside of them. The notion of land as measurable

Geraldine Manossa, "The Specter of Death." Courtesy Daystar/Rosalie Jones.

and salable (he talks of "a people accustomed to roaming over . . . ten million acres of land being confined into 7500 acres," and then to "2000 acres"), and the violence enacted by this increasingly limiting physical containment, thus mirrors that of the temporal containments imposed by historical time, marked and retold by markers like the French king's decree. Trying to contain people used to vast tracks of land into increasingly limited parcels, like trying to explore centuries of history using a pocket watch, belie glaringly inadequate notions of time and space, history and land, to the story this dance is addressing. At the same time, these linear, containing notions of time and space, and the documents that support and uphold them, have enacted and continue to enact forces of violence that, like the Specter of Death they unleashed and are still unleashing, enact very real, very forceful, very deadly effects.

In this scene and others, *No Home but the Heart* suggests ways the destructive forces called into being by these historical documents and policies continue to affect the bodies of Native peoples. Part of this bodily inscription is the story of the biological terrorism smallpox enacted on Native bodies. Another part is embodied in the physical labor of the hotel-cleaning Mother whose story is recounted in scene eight, "The Sheet Dance." Danced by Ojibway/Mohawk performer Penny Couchie in the Lethbridge production, this Mother vigorously, furiously, with big steps and wide sweeps of her mop, shows the back-breaking labor that landlessness and disenfranchisement have written into her body and by extension into the bodies of working-class Indian people. "This mother was thinking," the narrator repeats as he tells how she flushed toxic fumes down hotel toilets fifty times a day, and she vrrrrrooms an invisible vacuum back and forth across the stage and stumbles after it, it seemingly dragging her rather than she it.

And another part of this history can be read, throughout the piece, in its dancing. This includes all kinds of moves the piece presents, and which Daystar accesses through her modern dance piece—the Great-Grandmother's doctoring and birthing movements, the Grandmother's clog dancing, the Daughter's Jingle-dress dancing. "The Remembering Dance" addresses this danced inscription of history directly. This scene opens with the Daughter remaining on stage after masked figures at an airport have pestered her with questions about her "Nationality? Race? Origin? Genetic Association? Ethnic Grouping?" The Daughter's frustration with these attempts at categorizing her, at putting her identity into manageable parcels, recalls the limits of temporal and geographic containment the piece dramatized earlier. Daystar's expanded notes on the choreography describe her fury at this categorization, and her alternative understanding of herself: "She moves about the stage, gesturing her anger at her treatment by the masked figures, mocking them." It continues:

> Gradually her movements become more expansive and free,
> expressing her own sense of self. Finally, she looks up into the
> surface of the stool as she holds it over her head, and she sees her
> own image, which she then compares to each of the photographs in
> the Panel of Ancestors. She begins to recognize them, and her re-
> lationship to them. She begins to see her own identity. With this
> realization, she calmly sits on the stool, thinking.

The Daughter then rejects this compartmentalization of her ancestry and ethnicity. "I am not 'half' anything," a recorded voice of Daystar, as the Daughter, says next. "I am the sum total of my ancestors. I am my mother. I am my father. I am my Grandmother. I am my Great-Grandmother. I am the living legacy of the woman who survived the 'Red Death' of 1837."

While the recorded voice speaks these words, the dancer's choreography explores it. Daystar's notes to the piece explain:

> The DAUGHTER, sitting on the stool, is moved by the memory,
> and reprises the dance movements of her GRANDMOTHER'S
> clog dancing. She finishes, back to the audience, and slides her
> body head first to the floor, with legs in the air, reminiscent of the
> GRANDMOTHER'S birthing dance. She rolls over onto the floor,
> facing upstage. She sees again, the Panel of Ancestors. She stands

Sid Bobb, Penny Couchie, Daystar/Rosalie Jones, "I am not 'half' anything." Courtesy Daystar/Rosalie Jones.

slowly and moves toward the center panel with the words "I am the living legacy . . ." She turns to face front after the word 1837.

As she dances in this scene, the Daughter embodies her ancestors' movements. Earlier, in a section recalling the Grandmother/Age, a recording tells of this grandmother's many births, of her sixth child's death and the "terrible headaches" that followed, of how, "when the seventh child was born, my womb had fallen." It explains that the pain of this could only be relieved when she rigged herself so she could hang upside down. "I didn't dance anymore," she says. In "The Chair Dance" that follows, the Grandmother, now sitting on a chair rather than dancing full out, nonetheless continues to inhabit these bodily experiences. She begins clogging with her legs, recalling the dancing of her youth— movements with relation to both French jigging and Plains powwow. She stretches a long piece of fabric as she writhes on the chair, and wraps it about her head, referencing the headaches and also invoking modern dance vocabulary epitomized by Martha Graham's *Lamentations*. She slides from the chair and from there, with the cloth now around her feet, struggles and rolls and lifts into a shoulder stand, her legs in the air. In this way, she herself inhabits her own history through these embodiments and the ways they are written into her body. The Daughter, in the later "Remembering Dance," sitting on a stool then sliding on the floor, herself reembodies these memories through her own movements, accessing and reinhabiting her grandmother's history in and as dance. In so doing, she not only remembers, in this "Remembering Dance," the stories of her ancestors accessed through her dancing, she also embodies them across time, by way of her own dancing of their dances. "I am my mother. . . . I am my Grandmother," she says, inhabiting them through these bodily explorations and the dances they yield up. The story the piece tells thus insists upon not linear descent, but coembodiment, how the Daughter IS her mother and father and great-grandmother. Of course, Daystar herself accesses these danced ancestral histories not only through clog dancing and physical memories of childbearing anguish, but also and primarily through her own modern dance training and practice, and that of the dancers she directs in the piece. In this way, the piece includes as part of this history Daystar's own modern dance history and choreography, set on the bodies of the piece's young Native dancers.

Throughout the six-part dance piece, as it troubles a reliance on historical time, marked by dates and treaties, and rails against the limited land tracts and limited demarcations of identity linked with this linear, containing understanding of time, it also depicts and engages the ability of dance to reframe this understanding and redress its effects. Smallpox, for example, enters this dance piece as the spectral force engendered through the violence unleashed by historical documents and policies—but it also enters in and as a dance. This understanding of the force and power of dance—to enact death, to destroy—opens up space in which to understand and embody dance as also a force of connection across time and space and generation. Dancing, in other words, itself takes on the force more commonly attributed to historical decree—to enact effect, and to accurately remember—and can be deployed in response to these documents and decrees.

Early in the piece, Daystar dramatizes the medicine practices and doctoring abilities of the Great-Grandmother, in her time, through movement, prayer, ritual. This section tells the story of a woman abandoned on the plains by her family who, after a second husband tried to shoot her and a third put out her eye, learned how to doctor. As a voice-over finishes telling this story, the stage lights go up to show the Great-Grandmother kneeling center stage amidst several rocks, rattles, antlers, and cloth and bundles. She moves the rocks into an arc around her, looks up toward the sky, picks up the rattle and antlers and speaks into them, then stands, still hunched, and begins slowly to shake them. Softly at first, she begins to move in "The Medicine Dance" of the section's title, stepping around the rocks, looking down, then up at the sky, then down again, chanting and shaking the rattle and antlers. Her chanting gets louder and stamping more frenzied around the rocks and bundles she has gathered, until finally the stage bursts with claps of thunder and flashes of red and white light.

Daystar/Rosalie Jones, Great-Grandmother, Doctoring. Courtesy Daystar/Rosalie Jones.

As the sound of rain begins, the grandmother waves a yellow cloth in thanks, wipes her brow, gathers her things, and backs off the stage.

This explicit depiction of doctoring from generations ago, acted out by Daystar with staged lighting and sound effects, is only part of the engagement of *No Home but the Heart* with medicine practices. The piece engages another in its final scenes as well, when Jingle Dancers join Daystar on the stage and "move energetically, displaying both the old-style Jingle step and the more modern version." While they dance, and the sound of the jingles fills the theater, the narrator tells of the origin of Jingle dancing and of its function as a way to pray "for all those who need healing, for all those suffering from any sickness, or from abuse or loneliness."[28] In this way, the Jingle Dance, and the sound of the jingles and live drum, performs a prayer of healing with effects for those present in the theater right then and there.

No Home but the Heart further enacts a kind of doctoring on its audience in the very event of its performance of these stories. Daystar's production brought hundreds of people, including dozens of First Nations students, faculty, and local First Nations peoples, to the theater at the University of Lethbridge to view the performance. At the question-and-answer session after one performance, several First Nations audience members thanked Jones for telling the story, for making the dance and bringing it to the theater, and said how moving it was and how it is a story that needs to be told. "There's a healing process

Daystar/Rosalie Jones, dancing in front of a picture of her great-grandmother, Susan Bigknife, in a section from No Home but the Heart *performed at the University of California, Riverside, 2004. Photograph by Matthew Blais.*

involved in just the act of telling it, of sharing it with other people," Daystar responded. "You can read a lot of documents about history, but it doesn't really have the impact that the theater has because it [theater] is a vicarious experience. You are inviting the audience to experience it with you. You experience it with the sprit as well as the intellect." She went on to explain, "If a story gets told really good, it becomes your story, your experience." After the performances, the University's Native American Students' Association honored Jones with a post-performance feast open to all. This feast itself featured dancing by a highly skilled hoop dancer who offered his dance to the gathering, explained its healing effects, and told of where he had learned, and gotten permission to use, some of the movements he incorporated into his dancing. Thus part of the Medicine Dance that *No Home but the Heart* performs comes not just in the Great-Grandmother's doctoring scenes it depicts in the historical past, but also in the effects it creates at the very moment of its production through the performers' experience of the piece, the peoples it gathers, and audience members' experiences of it. In this way, *No Home but the Heart* comes to function as itself a form of doctoring, a contemporary dance version of the Medicine Dance the

Great-Grandmother is shown doing in the second scene, creating transformative effect in the world.

Thus, even as the piece chronicles a linear, historical narrative, moving through generations, from Great-Grandmother to Grandmother to Mother to Daughter, and through historical time, from the 1800s through nineteenth-century land policies to the present day, it also suggests connections across these timelines, embodying how, for example, the Great-Grandmother's doctoring and the dance piece's doctoring, choreographed and performed in part by the Daughter, Daystar, are aspects of the same process and practice, how the Daughter is a part of her ancestors and they part of her. The dance production repeatedly explains and embodies this connection, and how it refuses linear notions of time and instead stresses connection across time.

By employing a resolutely historical trajectory, yet at the same time both suggesting and invoking connections across that history in a way that troubles and refuses a stable notion of historical time, the piece lays bare the limits of the very linear historical trajectories around which it organizes its story. In these ways, the dance-drama *No Home but the Heart* thus not only recounts the history that official historical documents tell—the date of the smallpox epidemic, the facts of the Ten Cent Treaty, the text of a BIA letter that arrives at the end, telling Daystar's mother "you have been determined to be a descendent of the Pembina Chippewa Pursuant to the Provisions of the Act of December 31, 1982, Public Law 97–463." It doesn't only suggest that we look to Indian commissioners' letters, ten-cent treaties, or proclamations of the crown to explore, address, and redress issues of political, cultural, and spiritual disenfranchisement of Native peoples. It does do this, but at the same time it shows the effects of historical proclamations on Native American bodies, in and across time. In doing so, it suggests that history can also be read and explored in the bodies of Native and Aboriginal survivors, and in their physical, embodied explorations, and especially in and through their dancing. It thus suggests dance as a historical document of sorts, prodding historians to look not only to dates and documents, but also to danced histories, in our explorations and investigations.

Part of the history this piece's dancing documents lies in the different kinds of dancing the performers engage with, including both Indian and non-Indian dance practices—the French/Cree clogging of the Grandmother, the ballroom style of the Mother, Daystar's own modern dance (and that of dancers in the piece more generally), as well as the explicit doctoring movement of the Great-Grandmother and the Jingle dress section of the end. But this dance-document does not present this history as a melting pot of multiculturalism, a "can't we all just get along" dancerly celebration. Rather, even as the piece recognizes the historical interconnections theorized in these dances, and as the dancers throughout the piece explore this "mixed up, blended, all-together" history, they also, in the course of their clogging, ballroom, and modern dancing, find movements that are recognizably Indigenous or Indian and tied to particular Native ancestors' bodily histories. Powwow and doctoring kinds of movement repeatedly break through into dance sections other than those that are explicitly based in these Indian movements. The Daughter, as I've noted, recalls the powwow moves in clog dancing as she embodies her Grandmother; the Mother, in the masked ball section, after being called a mongrel dog, begins a Round Dance step in a small circle, as the background music segues from a waltz to a Native song.

Part of what *No Home but the Heart* shows, then, is how the act of dancing—and bodily exploration through movement, including the modern dance movement of this stage piece itself—can be a tool for accessing and addressing Native American personal and political history, even as it recognizes this history's inextricable blending with other histories and worldviews. Part of what it explores is how Native American peoples like Daystar and the dancers in her pieces—the living legacies of centuries of destruction unleashed by historical proclamations and enactments—physically engage with these histories. In so doing it theorizes an understanding of dance as document, and of bodily exploration as a kind of archival research, as much as it theorizes and documents a particular Native American history inscribed in and through dance.

Much of the story the narrator tells is about land loss and homelessness—the Ten Cent Treaty and the effect of loss of land on Native peoples—how what they have left is, as the title says, "No Home but the Heart." It suggests that, given the history of Native land loss, Native peoples have no home left but in their physical, emotional, spiritual beings—the heart, both as vital, blood-pumping organ of the physical body and as shorthand for emotional fullness and presence. At the same time, the title claims the heart as a home within this history of land loss. On the one hand, this recognizes land's importance and acknowledges its loss as a visceral, physical loss. At the same time, it also reclaims the body—by finding a home in it—as a site of Native American identity that can be accessed by contemporary Native peoples without a geographic home or land base. In other words, it claims the heart (rather than any blood fraction) as a physical, quasi-geographic location from which to respond to centuries of genocide, colonization, and removal from homeland.

Through my engagements with these dances and histories and ideas over the past decade, *The People Have Never Stopped Dancing* emerged in its present form. It begins with an examination of U.S. and Canadian federal policies restricting Native dancing, moves through the depictions of the 1920s, 1930s, and 1940s of Native choreography on the modern dance stage, and concludes with a discussion of several different concert dance initiatives that celebrate the diversity of choreographic approaches that Native peoples are currently exploring.

The book's analysis presses on historical moments, topics, choreographers, and dancers where the histories of Native American dance and modern dance come into most compelling contact and most astutely illuminate both the pervasive influence of ideas about Native American dance on the development of modern dance, and the unremarked ideologies of modern dance that have left little space for recognition of Native American dance practices.

The first part of this book presents the legal, rhetorical, and military strategies used by U.S. and Canadian governmental forces, from the 1880s through 1951, to outlaw and subdue Native religious and ceremonial dancing in North America. It traces shifts in the rhetoric surrounding these restrictions: around the mid-nineteenth century, federal policies decried Indian dancing primarily as dangerous (as readying warriors for warfare), though also heathen and barbaric; toward the end of the century, when fears of Indian warfare lessened, antidance outcry focused on the so-called barbaric and un-Christian aspects of Native ceremonies; starting around this time and intensifying in the 1920s, federal governments sought to curtail Native dance also and especially because they were seen as unproductive and wasteful of Indians' time, and as affronts to self-reliance and productive capitalism. While this rhetoric shifted—from charges of inciting warfare to barbarism to wastefulness—the restrictions remained.

This first section suggests that one tactic the U.S. and Canadian governments deployed simultaneously, in their attempt to curtail Native agency, was enabling stage representations of Indians (for example, in *Buffalo Bill's Wild West*) while they restricted ceremonial dance practices. These spectacles sought to contain the force and effect of Native dance practices not by disrupting, condemning, or outlawing them, but by staging them, thereby circumscribing them in theatrical structures that officials and audiences saw as exciting, but safe. In this way, the theatricalization of dance, alongside Christianity and the rhetoric of capitalism, became a political tool for controlling Native bodies, religion, and culture, and thereby for gaining access to control of Native land. This section explores ways that, despite the strategies behind this push toward theatricalization, the theatrical disciplinary system did not effectively contain Native American agency.

These historical chapters also set up lines of discussion that carry through to the book's second section, about the relation of this history to the simultaneous development of modern dance. For example, it explores how the Christian-based movement theories of François Delsarte, whose protégé Steele Mackaye helped train the Buffalo Bill performers to act more like Indians, likewise influenced the middle-class white women who would come to develop what we today see as modern dance. It then looks at how several important modern dance choreographers—including Ted Shawn, Martha Graham, and Lester Horton—developed their modern dance projects, and self-representations on stage, by way of a fascination with the very same American Indian dances and cultures that the federal government was seeking to contain. Finally, this section analyzes Martha Graham's signature piece, *Appalachian Spring*—itself a sign of modern dance—for the ways it performs the subsequent absence of American Indians from modern dance history.

Section three's discussion of contemporary Aboriginal stage dance begins by reexamining the careers of some early Native American stage dancers and choreographers, analyzing how they negotiated their Indianness in light of federal Indian policies of their day. It compares the dances of Mexican-born, Yaqui modern dancer José Limón and of Onondaga dancer Tom Two Arrows (Thomas Dorsey) in the context of the termination policies of the 1950s. In the context of the American Indian Religious Freedom Act of 1978, it addresses the history of powwow dance–based Native American stage dance troupes like the Thunderbird American Indian Dancers, founded by Louis Mofsie in 1963, and the American Indian Dance Theatre, founded in 1987 and today directed by Hanay Geiogamah, as well as the groundswell of modern dance–based companies like Daystar: Contemporary Dance-Drama of Indian America, formed by Daystar/Rosalie Jones in 1980, and of the Aboriginal Dance Program, established at the Banff Centre for the Arts in Alberta, Canada, in 1996, and of several other Native American and Aboriginal companies and choreographers.

After outlining this history, the book explores several specific dance pieces. Through close readings of these dances and the contexts in which they were produced and performed, I demonstrate some of the different ways I see this stage dance creating—rather than only portraying—historical, political, and spiritual relationship to land; redirecting a history of compulsory Christianity; and enacting spiritual and physical connection across generations. As diverse as these contemporary choreographic approaches are, they share these common relationships to land, to enactment, to Christianity, and to theatricality.

These dances show ways that despite over a century of contestation—by everyone from the federal government, who saw the stage as devoid of agency, to modern dancers, who made American Indian dance useful and productive by translating it to the stage for their own needs, to contemporary journalists and critics who attempt to protect what they see as "authentic" American Indian dance by claiming the stage drains it of ceremonial import or effect—Native peoples continue to engage the Western concert stage as a tool for spiritual and cultural resilience and self-determination. For contemporary Native American and Aboriginal dancers and choreographers, learning to dance and the act of dancing enact a physical and spiritual connection to land, to ancestors, to other beings, and to future generations that is held and remembered in one's body. Contemporary Native stage dance, and not just dances performed off the stage in more clearly ritual contexts, inscribes and performs these historical, political, and spiritual relationships.

This recognition sheds light in two directions. For one, it provides a way of contesting prevailing stereotypes that see American Indian dance as "authentic" only when practiced in isolation from contemporary culture. Instead, it recognizes how Native peoples have long maintained cultural, political, and spiritual agency even while adapting, drawing from, and contributing to the contemporary world. And two, it challenges Western theatrical understandings of stage performance as an act. In Native and Aboriginal contexts, stage dance enacts, and doesn't merely portray, relation to ancestors, animals, and land. In these ways *The People Have Never Stopped Dancing* explores how studying Native American stage dance provides a way of rethinking understandings of representation in dance, and of recognizing the historical, spiritual, and political agency of bodies on stage. The project both explores ways that modern dance (rather like North America itself) constituted itself, in part, through the imagined absence of Native Americans, and also begins to make Indigenous stage dance visible in modern dance history.

The conceptions that this dancing articulates have deeply influenced this project throughout, in overt and subtle ways, ways that have not always been clear to me until I was deep into a chapter, idea, approach, and with which I continue to struggle to grasp and to inscribe in the structuring of this study. As just one example, although I focus throughout on specific dance productions, the dancing I explore in many ways asks for an attuned awareness not only of the production, the choreographic premiere, the one-time (or several-time) dance event, but also of the process of dancing and dance making as bodily practice, of the passing of bodily, spiritual, philosophical, theoretical, historical training from person to person, generation to generation, over time.

The conceptions of time much of this dancing articulates, in turn, have led to a differing understanding of the importance of subjectivity, self-awareness, and interiority, not ignoring these aspects of dance making but shifting their presumed central importance. The moves, stories, physical dance practices performed and theorized in these dances connect them to a larger, continuing history of Indigenous peoples' resilience, whether or not their choreographers had conscious awareness of their dances' effects, regardless of how they might have been fully exploring a self-conscious interiority through them. The fact that, for example, José Limón's connection to an Indigenous history that may have taken half a century to be legible (which is, after all, a blip in time) doesn't diminish its import (see chapter 6). When he tells young Native dancers they are being "held in reserve" for the "future of your people" he registers worldviews in which time occurs in larger spans than myopic calls for immediate cause-and-effect results might register.

These conceptions of time also rub up against the very notions and structures of history writing that form the basis of so much academic scholarship, including that of this book itself. In different ways, these dance pieces, the stories (from long ago and right now) they retell, the transformative practices they engage, the connections in and across geographic space they perform, suggest ways of remembering and understanding the past that don't quite fit with this book's linear narrative frame, moving across the century from one historical juncture, one piece of legislation, to the next.[29]

At times, these conceptions of time and the focus on process they enable have led me to call into question the very importance of writing this history. Native dance that continues as a bodily practice, passed from person to person, family to family, generation to generation, that's readable one way inside and another way fifty years outside of its chronological moment, doesn't need to be preserved by hobbyists, or documented by dance scholars, to have the effects it has. It continues to affect its practitioners, its audience members, even the children running around not paying much attention while their parents are practicing what they're going to perform. It has them regardless of whether anyone knows it'll have them, or writes about them. From this perspective, the question of whether Native dancers are legible to scholars writing or reading books about modern dance history becomes largely moot.

Becoming aware of these differing approaches has been part of the excitement of this project, and forms a cornerstone of its contribution to dance scholarship. This book may or may not have anything to do with the continuing effects of Native American dance practices, yet it offers a challenge to a dance history in which Native American dance remains too comfortably invisible. It does so out of a conviction that the field of dance, with its long recognition of the histories and theories that moving bodies enact, deserves the interventions and challenges that grappling with Native American dance history brings.

I.

RESTRICTIONS, REGULATIONS, RESILIENCES

Have They a Right? Nineteenth-Century Indian Dance Practices and Federal Policy

Have they a right to stop us if we disturb nobody?

> ▸ *A telegram to the U.S. Department of the*
> *Interior in 1893, protesting attempts to*
> *forbid Indian dancing on the Santee Agency*

Native peoples in North America have long engaged with dance's capacities to articulate in profound philosophical, spiritual, and political ways. Negotiations are intrinsic to dance, with its required attention to shifts in weight, rhythm, relation to other bodies, and available space, and to the shifting circumstances experienced, theorized, and recorded in embodied form. In thousands of different forms, locations, and ways, Indigenous dancing has tapped these capacities: Native peoples used, and continue to use, dance as a powerful tool in continuously shifting negotiations of agency, self-determination, and resilience.

This chapter explores this resilience in the face of late nineteenth-century Indian assimilation policies that targeted Indian bodies, and dancing Indian bodies in particular. It traces U.S. and Canadian restrictions on Indigenous dance in the 1880s and 1890s and discusses how this dance threatened attempts of both the United States and Canada to assimilate Native peoples. Because it posed this threat to assimilation, dance became central to the definition of "Indians" as irreconcilably different from non-Indians—a crucial move, for once difference was established it could be eradicated, further justifying European colonists' attempts to take over tribal lands. This chapter thus sets up connections between antidance policies and the acquisition of Indian land the rest of this book will explore. It suggests that Native peoples have since engaged not only with dance, but also with the rhetoric surrounding American Indian dance, as a means of asserting Native self-determination. It further explores the threat that non-Christian religious and spiritual systems, experienced and expressed through the body, posed to the compulsory Christianity of federal disciplining systems, and to U.S. and Canadian geographic and ideological hegemony.

THREATENING DANCING

At the end of the nineteenth century, the governments of the United States and Canada attempted to control, through institutional discipline and punishment of Indian bodies, Indigenous peoples who resisted state authority by continuing to exist.[1] As a central tenet of their Indian policies, U.S. and Canadian officials were seeking to economize and—in a shift from outright warfare, which was seen as too expensive—instead "kill the Indian in" Native people by disciplining Native bodies through Western institutions.[2] These included literacy and boarding school education; Christianity, marriage, patriarchy, and control of sexuality; medicine and rejection of Native healing practices; wage-labor capitalist productivity and adherence to the doctrines of private property;[3] and imprisonment. Virtually all the institutional disciplining of Native bodies was corporeally enacted, and included, for example, the physical force sometimes used to take children from their homes and send them to boarding schools, the corporal punishment of students who spoke their own languages, and the imposition of Western hairstyles and clothing on Native children. They also included the banning of physically enacted healing ceremonies and practices seen as "satanic" and/or irrationally based in "false beliefs,"[4] the imposition of Christian belief-based religious practices rather than practice-based ceremonial religious practices, and the outlawing of resource sharing among groups rather than individuals or nuclear families. Enforcement of these edicts often involved the physical imprisonment of those caught violating them.[5]

The federal governments' stated intent in all of these institutions was to "civilize"—and thereby save—a dying people by incorporating Native people (who would then no longer be Indian) into the state. Once differences between Native Americans and European Americans were eradicated, then no special land rights need be accorded Native peoples, and Native land could be absorbed into the United States or Canada and bought, sold, and regulated according to their laws. Thus, one consequence of this corporeal policing and assimilation would be the end of Indian claims to land. White acquisition of Indian lands was in this way an active, if not always overtly acknowledged, aspect of Indian policy. For example, one effect of implementing these assimilation tactics on Indian children—removing them from their homelands, forbidding them to speak their autochthonous languages, and then encouraging them to work elsewhere—was the depopulating of Indian land for white settlement. One effect of the U.S. 1887 Dawes Allotment Act's imposition of individual private property ownership on Native peoples was that, as numerous analysts and historians have noted, by the time allotment was repealed in 1934, some two-thirds of Indian lands in the United States—eighty-six million acres of what was often the richest land—had been taken from Indians and sold to white settlers.[6] In Canada, late nineteenth-century Indian policy also followed a two-pronged approach of eradication or assimilation, policies presumed even more overtly than in the United States to lead to European dominion over the land.[7]

Yet this policy of eradicating difference also posed a challenge. If difference was to be eradicated, it first had to be established. In his compelling analysis of Canadian federal antipotlatch correspondence that circulated during this period, Christopher Bracken describes how the antipotlatch debates in late nineteenth-century Canada established that Indians were, in fact, entirely different.[8] The debates served to invent an understanding of Indians that European Canadian settlers could identify themselves and consolidate their own sense of whiteness against. First, the policies worked to establish Indians as *so* irreconcilably different that they could not just be left alone. In a dizzying twist, Bracken demonstrates, the policies then served to justify the use of force to eradicate the differences the policies had just established.

Dance was at the core of this invented, irreconcilably different, Indian identity, in the potlatch debates and elsewhere, for Aboriginal dance practices threatened governmental assimilation agendas in multiple ways. Indigenous dance practices embodied ideologies counter to those the governments were corporeally enforcing. Dance practices and gatherings threatened assimilation policies based on classroom education and literacy, as they affirmed the importance of history told not in writing or even in words, but rather bodily. Praying through bodily movement and ritual practice rather than through sitting, reading, and believing threatened colonizers' notions of how spirituality is manifested. Ceremonies that included elaborate feasts and gift-giving threatened ideologies of private property and individual ownership, definitions of what constitutes work and what productive activity might include, and the value of productivity itself. They were seen as wasteful of practitioners' physical energy and time, and thus as excessive expenditures of bodily labor.[9] In short, the federal governments of North America sensed and feared the importance of Indian dance as a social, political, and ideological agent, and the threats it posed.

The governments thus focused on and fervently attacked the dance practices of Native people, as this chapter explores. U.S. officials outlawed "war" and "scalp" dances and later restricted numerous other dance practices they saw as uncivilized, barbaric, immoral, or wasteful. Canadian officials attempted to eradicate the potlatch and the dances associated with Tamanamous rituals of west coast First Nations peoples, and later banned Sun Dance and other religious ceremonies of the prairies. These attacks constructed Indian dancing as a cornerstone of what made Indians Indian (and therefore of what needed to be eradicated for assimilation to happen). Dance thus served to define Indianness on both sides of the border, with continuing reverberations today, where in children's books, films, and popular imaginings, dancing continues to define what Indians do and are. Today, in the mass-mediated imagination, perhaps the most central popular-cultural image of an Indian remains that of a dancer, or at least one who embodies white ideas of Indian dance (most often hopping around in a war bonnet). From the University of Illinois's offensive dancing sports mascot, Chief Illiniwek, to numerous children's books and movies, children and adults, when they access images of Indians in their imaginations, continue to access images of Indian dancers.[10]

ESTABLISHING INDIANNESS

The fervent need to establish Indian difference from white colonizers, and the central role of dance in this establishment, can be read in the reports made by officially appointed Indian agents on reservations in the U.S. West in the early 1880s. At the same time, the reports sent to the Commissioners of Indian Affairs in the years preceding the first official dance restrictions make it clear that agents' *ideas* about Indian dances—and not the dances themselves—served as site of irreconcilable Indian otherness. Many of the agents themselves noted they had not even seen the dances they were so stridently objecting to, dismissing as ineffectual, and insisting be banned. After decrying the "revolting barbarism," "savage barbarism," "terrible barbarism" of "purely religious" Pawnee dances and describing how at these events males performed to the "thud of the tom-tom" on which "a rude kind of time is kept," the 1881 agent explains that actually he hasn't seen any of this. He writes, "To encounter this strongest phase of Pawnee development successfully, requires the combined action of all the civilizing forces which can be brought to bear upon them. Believing this, we have never ourselves attended one of their heathenish orgies or encouraged the attendance of employés [sic]" (CIA Report, 90–91). Likewise, in 1882 the Moqui (a.k.a. Hopi) agent writes, "I have never yet attended any of their dances, and cannot speak from personal knowledge; but, judging from reliable authority, the great evils in the way of their ultimate civilization lie in these dances. The dark superstitious and unhallowed rites of a heathenism as gross as that of India or Central Africa still infects them with its insidious poison, which, unless replaced by Christian civilization, must sap their very life blood" (CIA Report, 5).

Most likely, these agents' understanding of the "savage" and "heathenish" dancing they hadn't seen but still (thought they) knew—like their recourse to familiar racist and colonialist rhetoric of the period in which exotic descriptions of the "tom tom" and "dark superstitious" rites of India or Africa figure prominently—all came from centuries of colonialist representation of Indians and other Others, and had little to do with the Indian dances taking place around them (or, for that matter, any rites of "India or Central Africa"). Instead, their imaginations were undoubtedly infiltrated by the representations of Indian dance made by European colonizers that had been circulating for centuries, in early European etchings, paintings, and descriptions. Puritan minister Increase Mather's 1684 tract, *An Arrow Against Profane and Promiscuous Dancing Drawn out of the Quiver of the Scriptures,* for example, decried the "Heathenish customs" of dance, and urged Christians in the New World to desist and condemn the practice, by pointing to Aboriginal dancing. "It is known from their own Confessions that amongst the Indians in the America, oftentimes at their Dances the Devil appears in bodily shape, and takes away one of them alive."[11] Mather's decry was itself already multiply mediated—any Indian "Confessions" he might have read in the 1680s themselves negotiated layers of translations between speaking and writing, Aboriginal and European languages, authors, editors, and publishers, and Indigenous religious practices and Christian religious presumptions signaled by the very term "confessions." Mather's tract, like other depictions of the time, provided a lens through which agents could view Indian dancing, from a safe distance of over two hundred years. It came to signal Indian dancing, like Indians themselves, as already known in the arrogant way the colonizer has of knowing through representation,[12] and in so doing to consolidate mass-mediated European *representation* of Indians as authoritative and constitutive—a practice that, as this project explores throughout, continues today.

The agents' reports also suggest, in the agents' strident refusals to watch the dancing they officially report on and seek to replace with "Christian civilization," their (however inadvertent) awareness of the vital role witnessing plays, especially in ceremonial dancing, and of the central and perhaps compromising position they would put themselves in were they to participate by watching: would it make them part of the ceremony—dangerously close to Indianness themselves—and not outside of it? Dance *does* require the active viewing of physically present audience participants, much more so than painting or weaving or writing, whose viewers and collectors and readers are almost invariably removed in time and location from the circumstances of these artworks' creation. The Moqui (Hopi) agent's identification of dance as where "the great evils" lie in "the way of [Hopi's] ultimate civilization" signals the centrality of dance in his imagining, and in the subsequent dance regulations and restrictions, a centrality that echoes throughout the CIA reports of this period. Yet his and other agents' active refusal to see these dances, and their simultaneous attempts to write their evaluations of them into the historical record (these CIA reports are published as a multivolume set and available at many university libraries), also signal another attempt at corporeal control, here, an attempt to control and replace bodily participation with written representation as mark and location of history.

These agents' reports and many others like them thus worked to establish Indian dances and dancing as constitutive of Indian "otherness," and to replace the authority of dancing practices that require the physical participation/ witnessing and active investment of not only Aboriginal bodies but also of the bodies of agents and other authorities, with authoritative written representation of it. As the quotes above suggest, the dance practices the agents didn't see were not to be understood in culturally relative terms: as alternative ways of being human, as different ways of practicing a religion, of healing, of engaging in social and recreational activities, of telling and recording personal, familial, tribal history. The dances marked Indians as radically alter.

Once white imaginings about Indian dance helped codify Indianness as irreconcilably separate from whiteness, thereby constituting Indianness in relation to dancing, the federal governments passed antidance regulations as primary aspects of Indian policy. If the government's stated goal was to "kill the Indian in" Native people, and the Indian was constituted through participation in Indian dances, then by outlawing these dances, and all the worldviews, ideologies, and histories they incorporate, the government could achieve its goal. At the same time, having established participation in these dances as constitutive of Indianness, the government and its agents could more clearly police who and what was Indian; having constructed Indianness via dancing, any shifts in the dancing could later be used to dismiss the Indianness of practitioners.

COMPULSORY CHRISTIANITY AND FEDERAL POLICY ON INDIAN DANCE

As this history and the rhetoric of these agents' reports suggest, with their horror at imagined superstitious rites and calls for the need of "Christian civilization," Christianity lay at the core of federal constructions of Indianness. This compulsory Christianity formed the explicit base of not only religious education and practices imposed on Native peoples by missionaries and religious leaders, but in fact on virtually all federal institutional disciplining of late nineteenth-century Indian bodies in North America. The Indian schools were Christian. Agents and missionaries policed sexuality by imposing Christian marriage ceremonies on sexual partners. Ceremonially based Indigenous healing practices were rejected by Christian missionaries, who instead tried to enforce adherence to Western medical practices they viewed as rational and scientific. In short, the central tool in state construction of Indianness and corporeal control of Native peoples in federally sanctioned disciplinary institutions was Protestant Christianity, and presumptions about Christianity's superiority and eventual triumph over savagism structured Canadian and U.S. federal Indian policies as they shifted from warfare to other forms of corporeal control.

These Christian ideologies were enforced on the bodies of Indian school children, patients, and dancers. Yet paradoxically, with their focus on individual, internal faith rather than communal ritual practice, the rhetoric Christian reformers promoted involved a devaluation of embodiment. It involved a shift from spiritual experience arising from group participation in ritual ceremonial as well as everyday practices to a focus on religious belief, or feelings and understandings experienced internally and individually.[13] While this belief might lead to physical expression of internal religious states, it did not lead to or enact external change on the environment, or communities, or create effects outside of itself.

Christian understandings about internal, individual spiritual experience had been reflected in Christian attitudes about dancing for centuries, with religious leaders expressing support only, and then only begrudgingly, for nonsexual dance as expression of internal feelings. For the most part, Protestant Christianity has opposed dancing, decrying Indian dancing with especial fervor, at least since Puritan settlers from England began colonizing Massachusetts in the 1620s. There were exceptions: some early seventeenth-century Christian emissaries to the New World described colorful Indian dances, performed by Christianized Indians in the church yard, as a way of enticing the English to wrest control of the Americas.[14] Far more famous and influential were the attitudes about dance reflected in Increase Mather's 1684 tract, cited above. In this treatise, he acknowledged that some single-sex dancing may be without sin, especially that which allows men to "shew their strength and activity," or that "Dancing or Leaping" that erupts as a "natural expression of joy" (*An Arrow,* 31). Most dancing, though, he condemned as a violation of the commandment against adultery, due to the "unchast Touches and Gesticulations used by Dancers" (32) and the sinful feelings these arouse. "The very motion of the Body, which is used in Dancing, giveth Testimony enough of evil," he writes (42). "The Scripture does expresly, and by name condemn Dancing as a vicious practice" (35). In short, he concludes, dancing was invented amongst the heathen (37); papists justify it (39); and even when it does appear in the Bible—he mentions Miriam and King David (Exodus 15:20 and 2 Samuel 6:16)—those dance examples "in these dayes Judaize more than Christians ought to do" (51). As a further example of dancing's evil, he describes, as noted earlier, how "amongst the Indians in the Americas, oftentimes at their Dances the Devil appears in bodily shape." The threat Indian dancing poses is that, unlike dancing that erupts as "natural expression of joy" but effects nothing, Indian dancing is rumored to call up something other than itself—which Mather understands as conjuring the devil.

These deep-rooted Christian-based understandings continue to influence both understandings of Native American dance when practiced on and off the stage and also understandings of modern dance developed using Native American influence at a time when Native American dancing was restricted by the government. The subtle influence of Christian ideology during the birth and development of this modern dance from the turn of the twentieth century is something the ensuing chapters delve into more fully. In the late nineteenth century, however, Christian ideology was not subtly encoded in rhetoric, but instead blatantly legislated. In the United States, despite a supposed separation of church and state guaranteed by the First Amendment to the U.S. Constitution, the U.S. government directly funded evangelical Protestantism as Indian policy until the 1880s. In 1869, President Ulysses S. Grant inaugurated a "peace policy" that placed Indian reservations, and the Indian office, under the control of Christian mission boards rather than federal military forces. Church boards, in other words, were to control the federal Indian office and federal Indian reservations. "The 'peace policy' might just as properly have been labeled the 'religious policy,'" writes historian Francis Paul Prucha. President Grant also created a Board of Indian Commissioners (BIC) whose members "were to be Christians" as Robert H. Keller Jr., writes in his astute analysis of this history.[15] In 1872, Indian agencies were apportioned among various church groups, whose missionary boards then controlled the appointment of agents and other employees (Holler, *Black Elk's Religion,* 112). Keller demonstrates how President Grant's "peace policy," placing federal offices in the hands of Christian leaders, "was not a radical departure from some imagined tradition of separation of Church and State" (*American Protestantism,* 2). Rather, it was in line with 250 years of practices and traditions, as well as beliefs of the day that saw federal, state, and local governments as "divinely created institutions obligated to assist Christianity in the moral and religious redemption of human beings" (2). Churches, Keller notes, had received federal moral and monetary support for Christianizing Indians from at least 1789 (5).[16] The policy of assigning agencies to church groups continued until 1881, when growing Catholic influence in Indian affairs made Protestant church leaders anxious, while Catholics grew dissatisfied with a system that still favored Protestant influence and so argued that the apportionment violated Indian religious freedom. But even these new, and still rare, calls for religious freedom remained mired in the rhetoric of compulsory Christianity, as the following Catholic statement demonstrates:

> The Indians have a right, under the Constitution, as much as any other person in the Republic, to the full enjoyment of liberty of conscience; accordingly they have the right to choose *whatever Christian belief* they wish, without interference from the gov-

ernment. (quoted in both Holler, *Black Elk's Religion,* 115, and
Prucha, *American Indian Policy in Crisis,* 58) (emphasis added)

This statement, with its almost comical assumptions and biased deployments
of constitutional rhetoric, indicates that not only compulsory Christianity, but
also religion experienced through *belief,* remained at the core of federal Indian
policy debates. It wasn't until 1890, when American Catholicism had grown in
size, that strict separation of church and state relations became a constitutional
doctrine upheld at least in rhetoric.[17]

By 1882, the entire peace policy was acknowledged as a failure—the Indians
were still heathens, the missionaries were factionalized and corrupt, many
thought war a better policy than peace—and Secretary of the Interior Henry
Teller effectively buried it. Although the official U.S. policy of granting federal
control to primarily Protestant churches thus ended in 1882, federal sanction of
Christian influence and presumptions was implicitly transposed to the policies
that followed. Teller, a Methodist, retained Hiriam Price, a devout Christian
and a lay leader in the Methodist Church, in the position of Indian commissioner. Price's annual reports stressed the importance of cooperation with
Christian religious societies.[18]

Together, in this Christian-influenced federal environment, Teller and Price
instigated the first official federal strictures on Native American dance practices.
On December 2, 1882, Teller addressed a letter to Price directing him "to formu-
late certain rules . . . to abolish rites and customs so injurious to the Indians"
(Kvasnicka and Vida, *Commissioners of Indian Affairs,* 175) and stressing, as its
first point, the dangers of Indian dance:

> I desire to call your attention to what I regard as a great hindrance
> to the civilization of the Indian, viz, the continuance of the old
> heathenish dances, such as the sun-dance, scalp-dance &c. These
> dances, or feasts, as they are sometimes called, ought, in my judg-
> ment, to be discontinued, and if the Indians now supported by
> the Government are not willing to discontinue them, the agents
> should be instructed to compel such discontinuance. These
> feasts or dances are not social gatherings for the amusement of
> these people, but, on the contrary, are intended and calculated
> to stimulate the warlike passions of the young warriors of the
> tribe. . . . Active measures should be taken to discourage all feasts
> and dances of the character I have mentioned.[19]

On April 10, 1883, Price went ahead and did what Teller told him to do: he directed Indian agents around the country (each reservation had a federally appointed agent overseeing it) to establish "Courts of Indian Offenses." These were

courts to be staffed by "civilized" Indians who would rule on Indian cultural practices that the U.S. federal government deemed offensive.[20] The very first Indian offense named in 1883, and again in the 1892 reissued Rules for Indian Courts, is dancing. The dance restriction is outlined as follows:

> 4. (a). Any Indian who shall engage in the sun dance, scalp dance, or war dance, or any other similar feast, so called, shall be deemed guilty of an offense, and upon conviction thereof shall be punished for the first offense by the withholding of his rations for not exceeding ten days or by imprisonment for not exceeding ten days; and for any subsequent offense under this clause he shall be punished by withholding his rations for not less than ten nor more than thirty days, or by imprisonment for not less than ten nor more than thirty days. (Prucha, *Documents,* 187)

The other offenses listed are plural or polygamous marriages, practices of medicine men, destroying property of other Indians, immorality (i.e., sex out of wedlock or same-sex relations), and intoxication. The punishment for infringing on these rules was bodily as well: the withholding of food and imprisonment.

In Canada, Christianity likewise instigated and undergirded nineteenth-century federal policy restricting Indian dance practices. In 1872, the Indian Branch of the Department of the Secretary of State appointed the first Indian superintendent in Victoria, British Columbia, which had joined the Canadian confederacy the year before. From this instigation of a European regulatory gaze in British Columbia, calls for restrictions on "great medicine feasts" held by First Nations of the northwest coast—which came to be referred to under the general term "potlatch"—began circulating in official federal records and missionary correspondence (Bracken, *Potlatch Papers,* 35). Meanwhile, the Indian Act of 1876 consolidated the Canadas into a nationwide framework and imposed an elective system on Native bands.[21] Bracken references the active role that Christian missionary rhetoric played in the debate. He describes how legislation leading to an amendment to the Indian Act, which banned the potlatch along with dances associated with Tamanawas rituals, was brought to the House of Commons in 1884 after the Roman Catholic missionary at Cowican decried "the heathenish practices of 'Potlatching' and 'dancing,'" and begged "the Indian Department to have a law to stop the disastrous practice of 'Potlatching' and especially dancing as it is carried on by the Indians of Vancouver Island" (*Potlach Papers,* 81–82). The agent to whom this missionary's letter was sent in turn recommended to the Superintendent of Indian Affairs for British Columbia that he prevent "the foolish, wasteful, and demoralising custom of 'potlatching' and [call] for the punishment of any Indian allowing a Tom-an-oes dance to be held" in his home (82). This recommendation, and what the superintendent called other "strong representations from both agents and missionaries" (83), led antipotlatch and Tamanawas legislation to be introduced before the House of Commons. This legislation, which came into effect in 1885 and was included as Section 114 in the Revised Statutes of Canada, reads:

> 114: Every Indian or person who engages in or assists in celebrat- ing the Indian festival known as the "Potlach" or the Indian dance known as the "Tamanawas," is guilty of a misdemeanor, and liable to imprisonment for a term not exceeding six months and not less than two months.
>
> 2. Every Indian or person who encourages, either directly or indi- rectly, an Indian to get up such a festival or dance, or to celebrate the same, or who assists in the celebration of the same, is guilty of a like offense, and shall be liable to the same punishment.

In other words, in Canada, as in the United States, missionary and governmental regulatory rhetoric combined to create a climate that led to restrictions on these dance practices. In Canada, there was no policy of governmental appointment of explicitly Christian reformers akin to the U.S. "peace policy." Some historians have suggested this difference might be due to the less overt warfare and vio- lence in Canada during this period, and the subsequently less strident involve- ment in Indian policy by Christian reformers there. Nonetheless, Indian policies in Canada remained, if anything, more overtly tied to a Christian context than they did in the United States.[22]

SHIFTS IN RHETORIC AND FEDERAL POLICY, 1880S–1910S

In the United States, a directive listing dance as a federal "Indian Offense," pun- ishable by fines and imprisonment, remained on the books for over fifty years, until its repeal by Commissioner John Collier in 1934. Aspects of the restric- tions, including the ban on "torture" as part of the Sun Dance, continued as de facto restrictions until around 1952.[23] Canada's antidance restrictions remained on the books until 1951. Throughout this period, the rhetoric surrounding antidance policies shifted in subtle and significant ways. In the United States, the threat that Indian dancing was perceived to pose moved from warfare to the more subtle threat to European dominion of barbarism. For example, the earlier restrictions focus on the military threat that Indian dancing was per- ceived to pose. In the 1882 U.S. restrictions listed above, claims that the dances "are intended and calculated to stimulate the warlike passions of the young warriors of the tribe" serve to explain the ban. Teller argues that the dances (the "scalp dance" and "war dance" were explicitly named as offensive) are not "social gatherings for the amusement of these people," and thus presumably harmless, but rather "heathenish" and dangerous. This stricture on war dances is repeated in Commissioner of Indian Affairs Thomas J. Morgan's 1892 reissue of the Rules for the Courts of Indian Affairs.

Less than a decade later, however, the tenor and rhetoric of official federal restrictions on Indian dances shifted. Explicit restrictions on "war dances" disappeared from the 1904 "Regulations of the Indian Office," which again outlined "Indian offenses" the courts were to rule on.[24] Instead, these 1904 regulations focus on the Sun Dance—which was widely described as "barbaric" at the time—and call into question the religious status of Indian dances and ceremonies. It reads:

> The "sun-dance," and all other similar dances and so-called
> religious ceremonies, shall be considered "Indian offenses," and
> any Indian found guilty of being a participant in any one or
> more of these "offenses" shall, for the first offense committed, be
> punished by withholding from him his rations for a period not
> exceeding ten days; and if found guilty of any subsequent offense
> under this rule shall be punished by withholding his rations for
> a period not less than fifteen days nor more than thirty days, or
> by incarceration in the agency prison for a period not exceeding
> thirty days.[25]

In other words, the antidance rhetoric shifted from a primary concern about Indian dancing as prelude to warfare, with a focus on scalp and war dances, to a primary concern about Indian dancing as barbaric and immoral, with a focus on what officials called the Sun Dance.

Attitudes toward the dances as religious acts shifted during this period as well. When the 1881 Pawnee agent decried the "terrible barbarism" of dances and feasts he hadn't seen, he did so by dismissing the dances as "purely religious." Seeing the dances as "purely religious" seems meant to imply that they are not harmless social dances, but dangerous and powerful religious acts outside the realm of Christian civilization. On these grounds they are to be condemned by a country that saw itself as Christian. By around the turn of the century, however, the religious aspects of the dances were being roundly discounted by U.S. officials. "The dances of *alleged religious enthusiasm* disturb the moral training of boys and girls," wrote Commissioner of Indian Affairs W. A. Jones in his 1903 report (emphasis added). To substantiate his position, he quoted an "inspecting official, in a very recent report upon a Middle West tribe of Indians," who writes, "I have attended one of [two medicine dances held]; and while they claim that it is a religious ceremony I hardly think it should be encouraged" (CIA Report, 9).[26] As the 1904 official regulations cited above indicated, they too were revised at this time in such a way that discounts any religious import of the ceremonies: the new restrictions prohibited certain dances and "so-called religious ceremonies," where "so-called" serves to question any valid religious purpose to the practice.[27] The explicit federal dismissal, at this time, of Indian dances as religious ceremonies signals a shift in federal rhetoric regarding religion and Native Americans. It suggests that some have raised the issue of respect for the dances as religious practices and claimed federal protection for them on freedom of religion grounds. At this point, then, federal rhetoric dismisses any "so-called" religious import to the dances and instead focuses on their immorality. Readable in this shift is the way a presumption of Christianity as the only acceptable religion has lost some hold on official U.S. federal policy regarding Indian dance, although Christian rhetoric and assumptions continued to infuse Indian policy.

During this period, Canada's antidance restrictions also underwent frequent revision as missionaries and government officials found ever-new aspects of Aboriginal dances objectionable and Aboriginal peoples found ever-new ways of ignoring, circumventing, and reframing governmental attempts at censure. The most frequently rehearsed argument against the potlatch, Bracken notes, was that its giveaway practices left families destitute. After focusing on the potlatch of west coast First Nations people, Canada's antidance anxieties next moved to the prairies, where missionaries and government officials sought to restrict Indians' "Heathenish customs," in particular, the Sun Dance of the Blackfoot and Thirst Dance of the Cree.[28] While gift giving comprised part of these practices, as it did potlatching, what officials found disconcerting at first was not what they saw as the economy of waste it produced. Rather, they objected to certain aspects of the dance they viewed as torture, and to the opportunities for gathering and history-sharing they provided, and ways they might "excite" the Indians. At first, as in the United States, fears of overt warfare and rebellion fueled the objections. Especially in the aftermath of the so-called Riel Rebellion of 1885 and while rumors of a "messiah craze" that followers of Sitting Bull were reported to be spreading in the west circulated in the late 1880s, these gatherings were seen as potentially unsettling to European stability on the prairies. One superintendent of the mounted police, after visiting the Sun Dance of the Bloods, wrote in 1889 that during the festival "old warriors take this occasion of relating their experience of former days, counting their scalps and giving the number of horses they were successful in stealing. This has a pernicious effect on the young men; it makes them unsettled and anxious to emulate the deeds of their forefathers."[29] U.S. officials had similar worries. The Santee agent in Nebraska noted, in his 1894 report, "These dances are not civilizing, but a step backward. It is no benefit to a school boy or girl during holiday to hear the old-Indians recite their bravery at the massacre at Redwood, or tell how many horses they have stolen from white men, or how many women they have stolen. I believe these dances should be put a stop to as soon as they become citizens" (CIA Report, 193).

As worries of rebellion faded, the rhetoric bemoaning the waste that accompanied dancing recurred, invoking capitalist concerns about productivity.[30] In Canada in the 1880s, this rhetoric arose particularly around what was seen as the waste of time that occurred when Sun and Thirst Dance participants spent from four to six weeks in the summer gathered for these festivals, when officials thought they should have been farming (Titley, *Narrow Vision,* 165). In response to these concerns, Canadian officials tried another tactic, revising Section 114 of the Indian Act in the summer of 1895 to broaden its applicability to Aboriginal dances of the prairies as well as the northwest coast. It included prohibitions on the giving away of "money, goods, or articles," a prohibition implied in the earlier version, and also a new proscription outlawing "the wounding or mutilation of the dead or living body of any human being or animal" (Titley, *Narrow Vision,* 166). Prison sentences again ranged from two to six months.

Throughout this period in Canada, most missionaries and other Christian religious leaders were steadfast in their outrage and opposition to all aspects of Indian dancing and, as in the United States, worked closely with government officials. In 1903, one priest, the principal of the industrial school at Qu'Appelle, wrote a letter decrying the effects of dancing on school graduates and bemoaning dance's ability to "transform a promising youth into a shiftless unreliable Indian." He described the dancers as "nearly nude, painted and decked out in feathers and beads, dancing like demented individuals and indulging in all kinds of debauchery" and proclaimed his conviction "that Christianity and advancement, and paganism and indolence, cannot flourish side by side."[31] In 1906, a group of Presbyterian ministers expressed their opposition to what they perceived as leniency after agents approved picnic gatherings at which, the ministers felt, "the Indians would likely try to include some of their dances in the program," Titley writes. "They feared that in the excitement generated by powwows, missionaries might be driven from the reserves" (*Narrow Vision,* 170). In 1908, Roman Catholic missionaries met to discuss ways of suppressing the Sun Dance, then outlined their objections and sent them by way of their Bishop to the superintendent general. The multiple ways that First Nations peoples engaged with this missionary and governmental rhetoric—as Bracken suggests, using white institutions to serve and reframe their own interests—further supports the centrality of Christian discourse in this federal disciplinary process.

ENACTING INDIAN AGENCY

Despite these fervent joint missionary/official attempts and collusions, Native peoples refused, in multiple ways, to accommodate the rhetoric of either absolute difference or absolute absorption and instead continued to engage with the communal use and sharing, healing, religiosity, and history telling and making of dancing, much to the dismay of agents, reformers, and missionaries.

This is not to deny the real violence the dance restrictions and their enforcement psychically and physically enacted on Native peoples caught dancing, whose perceptions and consciousness were berated and attacked and who were sometimes imprisoned, kept hungry, forced to wear Western clothing and cut their hair, and otherwise forcibly disciplined. Descriptions of the disciplinary violence inflicted on Native dancers, for dancing, appear throughout federal reports in both the United States and Canada. The 1888 agent at the Yankton Agency in Dakota reports:

> Wakea, the expert dancer of the tribe, one of the wildest Indians
> on the reservation when I came, and for his misconduct I had to
> put him in jail, has had his hair cut, has given up dancing, and is
> living nicely on his little farm. (CIA Report, 65)

E. Brian Titley recounts an 1889 incident in which a zealous agent arrested a Kwawkewlth man and sentenced him to six months' imprisonment for engaging in a potlatch (*Narrow Vision,* 163). In 1897 and 1904, zealous agents arrested dancers from Thunderchild's reserve and the Fishing Lakes (167, 168). The implementation of these regulations was in some ways as brutal as the violence inflicted in overt warfare. Their effects were pervasive and at times catastrophic, and resulted in unfathomable losses of cultural, spiritual, and religious knowledge developed over multiple generations. They also undoubtedly affected the practice of dances and ceremonials that did survive. As Andrew Brother Elk, chair of the Native American cultural center in San Francisco and director of Earth Dance Theater at the time, noted, knowledge of federal governments' literal and spiritual genocide of Native Americans—and of the subsequent loss of Native dance practices—is still much too often dismissed or ignored in academia, from elementary school curriculum on.[32]

Yet these disciplinary measures were not a fraction as successful as a cursory reading of the agents' representations of them would at first suggest. Even as the reports list the disciplinary measures taken to suppress dancing and argue—repeatedly—that the practices are just about to die out, Native peoples' subtle and not so subtle refusals of agents' categorizations and restrictions bubble up throughout. Agents' exasperated tones and frustrations with continuing dance practices, as well as their recurring assurances, repeated year after year, that the dances will soon be a thing of the past, demonstrate the multiple ways Native dancers refused, rejected, and reframed the prohibitions in ways that allowed dancing, and the validating of worldviews they embodied and affirmed, to continue.

One tactic used in the face of this legislation, though by no means the only, was outright defiance. Some Native dancers, as well as some government officials, refused to obey or enforce the regulations. In his discussion of the anti-potlatch legislation in Canada, Bracken notes how "the majority of British Columbia's aboriginal people responded to the new law by actively defying it" (*Potlatch Papers,* 84). When focus shifted to bemoaning and restricting dances on the plains, officials tried to curtail participation by requiring Indians to get a pass to leave their reserve, and then confining dance gatherings to Indians of one reserve. But Indians frequently ignored this, and in 1892 the courts let police know they couldn't enforce pass requirements (Titley, *Narrow Vision,* 165). Sometimes, even when defiance was punished and restrictions enforced, it backfired as various law enforcement factions enforced punishments differently, and their contradictions made for bad press. After the zealous agents mentioned above arrested the Kwawkewlth man for engaging in a potlatch, a sympathetic judge released him on a technicality. Mounted police likewise released dancers from Thunderchild's reserve and the Fishing Lakes, arrested in 1897 and 1904, after discovering they were elderly men whose health might be injured by months in prison—followed by publicity embarrassing to officials (167, 168). In the United States, after the establishment of "Courts of Indian Offenses," enforcement also became a problem. Some simply refrained from doing what agents and missionaries wanted them to, much to the exasperation of the officials involved. In his 1883 report, the Pine Ridge agent in Dakota complains that the Northern Cheyennes "have remained in their normal condition of general worthlessness." He adds:

> [N]one have built houses, none have adopted civilized costumes, none have engaged in freighting, but have passed their time in dancing, wandering around the country, and occasionally making a raid on the agent's office to inform him that they are guileless children of nature; that the "Great Spirit" gave them this land; that they are constitutionally opposed to labor, &c. I sometimes suggest to them that some day when the "Great Father's" storehouses become empty of rations, they may have to try the experiment of sitting on a hill and howling to the "Great Spirit" for something to eat, and patiently await a fall of heavenly manna. (CIA Report, 34)

This report, almost comical in its exasperation, signals the blatant refusal of the Northern Cheyennes at Pine Ridge, as well as the agent's interpretation of dance or ceremony as ridiculous and invalid. His tongue-in-cheek recommendation that his charges try "howling to the 'Great Spirit' for something to eat" signals his own attitudes about ceremonial practices and his dismissal of the effectiveness of practices that he supposed were meant to create immediate effects, like food falling from the sky. Enforcement was difficult, as others refused to serve on the Courts or enforce punishments for "offenses." In 1883, the agent in Dakota noted:

> No nominations for judges of the court of Indian offenses have yet
> been submitted by me. I have studied over the matter, have talked
> it over with my Indians, and have not been able to select suitable
> persons for the position. From Indian stand point the offenses as
> set forth, and for which punishment is provided, are no offenses
> at all, and I doubt if one could be found willing to punish another
> for the offenses set forth in the rules governing such, and if will-
> ing or inclined would have the moral courage to do so. In my
> judgment the checking of the so-called Indian offenses must be
> gradual, and done, if at all, by the agent. (CIA Report, 42)

Over ten years later, in 1896, these outright refusals continued. Joseph Emery, the agent at the Klamath agency in Oregon, reported then that:

> The Christian religion which had been taught them by self-
> denying missionaries, and which the large majority had accepted
> and were taking as their guide in morals and religion, discarding
> their own idolatrous superstitions and degrading practices, was
> scoffed at and derided by at least one chief authority, and their
> churches and schoolrooms turned into dance halls. I find a spirit
> of insubordination among some of the would-be leaders of these
> Indians that will take a strong hand to correct and hold in check.
> (CIA Report, 274)

This "insubordination," or refusal to participate in the prohibitions—to follow them or aid in enforcing them—formed part of the way in which Native dancers actively rejected the worldview government officials attempted to enforce on them.

Another tactic successfully deployed to curtail the effects of the antidance laws during this period was the taking underground of dance. When dances were forbidden by law and the laws were enforced by agents and police, practitioners moved the events to locations away from the agents' surveillance.[33] The success of this tactic makes it, by definition, hard to trace in agents' reports, though the continuing practice of the dances, and occasional discoveries by agents, substantiate it. In 1884, the agent at Rosebud reports discovering the "younger element . . . traveling the camps, 'presenting the pipe,' committing all to a participation in this barbarous ceremony" of the Sun Dance. By removing the practices from agents' regulatory gazes, dancers successfully created spaces in which agents' surveillance tactics proved ineffectual.

A third, complex and pervasive, relation to the antidance regulations involved a complicated cooperation that worked both with and paradoxically against the restrictions and served to redirect their intended effects. This response included a variety of tactical evasions of the letter of the law, and other legal and rhetorical means by which some worked the system to continue practicing according to the laws of both U.S. and Canadian governments, and of their society. It also included the adoption of Christian-based antidance rhetoric and adherence to its doctrine—yet in a way in which this doctrine was to be self-administered, policed, and controlled.

Opposition to federal antidance policy was by no means universal among Aboriginal and Native peoples and dancers. Even before the official governmental regulations were in effect, many Aboriginal peoples voiced support for the restriction of them. Bracken, for example, mentions an 1881 petition sent to the Indian Superintendent by the bishop of Victoria, written by Catholic missionaries speaking on behalf of local Salish people who had adopted European practices. The petition bemoans the loss of industrious habits and the return of "the degrading practice of the Tamanwas dances" among the Salish people. Bracken also references an 1883 petition, signed by Coast Tsimshian and Nisga'a chiefs and sent to the Department of Indian Affairs, "praying that the system of Potlatching as practiced by many Indian Tribes of the Coast of British Columbia may be put down" (*Potlatch Papers,* 78). Bracken notes that other scholars have surmised that the petition was "transparently inspired and written" by Methodist and Anglican missionaries. He, however, suggests that this support might itself have been a tactic of self-governance. He notes the possibility that "the petition of 1883 was perhaps an effort by aboriginal people to use a white institution to serve their own interests rather than an heavy-handed attempt by white missionaries to erase aboriginal cultures from the map of a young nation." He argues that "the aboriginal people of nineteenth-century British Columbia were never passive victims of government policies, and they never stopped trying to control their own destinies" (79).

The most dramatic instance of this "cooperation against" restrictions might be found in the development and deployment of the so-called Ghost Dance in the years of the enforcement of antidance regulations. With possible exceptions of the Sun Dance and Hopi Snake Dance, which held for white audiences and ethnographers a morbid fascination, the Ghost Dance is the most well-known and oft-cited example of Indian dance. As numerous scholars have explored, the spread of the "Ghost Dance religion" involved the adoption and redirection of various Western colonizing institutions. Most obviously, its rhetoric was infused with Christianity.[34] At the same time, as Ronald Niezen has argued, the Ghost Dance movement also engaged with and deployed literacy—a cornerstone of Indian school education plans—as a tool both to spread word of the movement and to instruct Ghost Dance practitioners. "The prophet Wovoka, a Paiute of the Mason Valley in Nevada, placed great emphasis on the visionary quest but was fully aware of the communicative uses of alphabetic literacy, making good use of dictated letters to spread his doctrine," he writes (*Spirit Wars,* 131). Niezen notes how the rapid spread of the movement was facilitated by those who had experienced boarding school education and references a "messiah letter" outlining dance instructions written by a young Arapahoe man, Casper Edson, who had learned to read and write English at the government Indian School in Carlisle (132). Here, then, is a prime example of how Native peoples adopted and engaged with colonizing institutions—Christianity, literacy—as a way of redirecting their colonizing effects. This tactic posed perhaps the greatest threat in the way it refused a neat separation between "Native" as stable and identifiable and "white" as another.

Some adhered to the letter of the laws, yet did so in ways that redirected their intended effects. These tactical evasions read, at times, like a comedy of errors, with dancers finding ever new loopholes in which to continue their practices while evading the disciplinary effects and rhetorical intentions of the law, and agents and missionaries scrambling to convince officials to rephrase the law and close the loopholes. For example, dancers used the distinctions made between different dances to legally continue dancing even during periods in which certain aspects of ceremonial dance gatherings were proscribed. In the United States and Canada, there was a generally accepted continuum as to the relative evil of Indian dancing, with the Sun Dance at one end, as always barbaric, and dances such as the Grass Dance at the other, as possibly just a harmless social gathering. Dance restrictions were most directly aimed at the dances seen as "barbaric," such as the Sun and Snake Dances, and not necessarily at all dance gatherings. All the same, the struggles that emerged over these differences make it clear that not just dancing seen as "barbaric" but in fact all dancing threatened colonial powers. In 1893 U.S. Agent James E. Helms was outraged at continuing Grass Dance events at which Santees slaughtered a number of cattle and gave away heads of horses to visiting Winnebago. Helms, decrying the "degrading" and "heathenish custom," writes how in 1892 he threatened to arrest participants for disorderly conduct, and how in 1893 he posted a bulletin saying he "did not want any Santees to engage in the old Indian dance." In this bulletin, he also threatened to write to the commissioner and endeavor to have the annuities of those who persisted in engaging in the dance withheld. In response to this bulletin, Helms writes, a "half-breed agitator" wrote in protest to the Department of Indian Affairs (DIA):

> The Indians have dances for pleasure and help each other to put
> in their crops, and we saw a notice at the agent's office door to

stop these dances; if they don't stop we will stop scouts' pay. The
scouts want to dance till July 4, because Cleveland was elected.
Have they a right to stop us if we disturb nobody?

This letter brilliantly manipulates the rhetoric of U.S. ideology and nationalism toward its own goals. The Indians dance, this writer implies, for pleasure and to help each other be productive farmers—both supportable activities—and even more so, in this instance, they want to dance to participate in heralding the most overt figures and celebrations of U.S. nationhood: Cleveland's election and the 4th of July.[35] In asking "Have they a right to stop us if we disturb nobody?" the writer further engages a rhetoric of rights familiar to American political and legal ideology. To prohibit the Indians from dancing, the writer implies, would be downright unpatriotic, as it would threaten their rights to free assembly and to freedom of expression, which they wish to exercise in order to perform their allegiance to the United States. Especially at a time when Indians' construction as U.S. citizens was being corporally enforced in numerous institutions (even as Native peoples did not have universal citizenship), this desire to perform allegiance to the United States could hardly be denied. Indeed, the DIA supported this protestor and, in a June 14 letter, advised Helm to allow the dances "so long as they are conducted for pleasure, and are not such as are interdicted by existing regulations." Helms was infuriated by the DIA response. "In the very nature of things harm must result from these gatherings," Helms wrote. "Old traditions are revived, battles fought over again, and old Indian customs brought to the front." That July 4, the Grass Dance went on as planned. Helms writes, "I did all in my power to compel them to go home, but they claimed that they were citizens, and so long as their dances were not disorderly and they did not violate the law, that they could not be compelled to go home." He adds, "I consider the pecuniary loss to this tribe, which is no small amount, as the least of the evils arising from allowing these dances to take place" (CIA Report, 1893, 202).

In Canada, Aboriginal dancers found similar spaces within the official restrictions in which to continue dancing. When Indian Department personnel tried to restrict dancing by requiring tribal people to have a pass to leave the reserves, Indian people largely ignored the passes. Nichols writes how "Once the tribal people met relatives and friends at the reserve boundary and held the ceremonials there" (*Indians in the United States and Canada,* 233). Although the 1895 revision of the law expressly forbade the wounding and giveaway aspects of dance festivals, it did not proscribe dancing itself, a distinction Aboriginal practitioners soon explored. Again, the struggles that followed laid clear missionaries' and officials' anxieties not just about the gift-giving and wounding/endurance aspects of the Sun Dance and Thirst Dance, but about Aboriginal dancing itself. One "agitator" was arrested and imprisoned for three months in 1903 for what the newspaper called a "crafty effort" to circumvent the law after he started "circle dances" and gave away a meal (Titley, *Narrow Vision,* 168). In that same year, Canadian Superintendent General Sifton, presented with objections of missionaries to fears of continuing dance practices, was convinced that the Indian Act ought to be amended again to facilitate the suppression of dancing, not just the wounding and giveaway aspects of the festivals (169). Yet in Canada, as in the United States, federal government officials were less rabid about outlawing all dancing than local missionaries and agents, and nothing came of the request.

Other Native dancers, in both the United States and Canada, began using legal system rhetoric even more directly to protest and circumvent anti-dance laws. Bracken recounts how in 1885 an elder in the Cowichan village of Comeakin, named Lohah, presented his community's legal system as argument in favor of holding a final potlatch to distribute property owed. "It cannot be wrong to pay what we owe," Bracken cites Lohah writing in a letter to the department. "It is one of our laws that these payments should be done in public" (*Potlatch Papers,* 85). Bracken notes how Lohah argues that his people's legal system was in conflict with the legal system imposed by the Canadian government, thus adopting the rhetoric of lawfulness to counter the legal system imposed. In the United States, dancers similarly engaged with U.S. legal and democratic practices to forward their positions. Acting U.S. Agent William H. Beck, in his 1896 report to the Commissioner of Indian Affairs, for example, told of how Winnebagos under his charge circulated petitions to thwart any disruption of their medicine dance, which Beck writes "is claimed by the Indians to be a religious observance, and which the older Indians cling to with tenacity." He writes, "Immediately after the last occasion upon which I spoke against dancing the whites alluded to secretly told the Indians that I intended to break up their religious customs, and circulated a petition among them to obtain their signatures to protest against my alleged action" (CIA Report, 199). By 1908, some Aboriginal dancers in Canada, who knew that dancing itself was not banned, were likewise seeking legal advice in the face of restrictions on the Sun Dance. "They continued to dance, usually scrupulously avoiding the illegal features," Titley writes (*Narrow Vision,* 171).

Another way in which Native dancers effectively circumvented the anti-dance restrictions was by somehow convincing agents they had agreed to cooperate with or succumb to the new laws—and nonetheless continuing the dance practices unabated. It seems clear that before and after the establishment of the Court of Indian Affairs and the forbidding of dances, agents believed, or represented themselves as believing, that dancing was stopping—or at least, almost about to stop. The strain of almost disappeared Indian dancing repeats endlessly in CIA reports throughout the fifty years' ban. These writings, as well as those of Canadian officials during this period, demonstrate a persistent yearning for the dances' demise, manifested by an almost obsessive insistence—what Paula Gunn Allen calls white culture's "homicidal wish"[36]—that they (and with them presumably Native culture) were just about to die out. Agents writing their annual reports to the Commissioner of Indian Affairs announced throughout the early 1880s that dancing among "their Indians" was "diminishing" (Dakota, 1882, 39), "suppressed" (Crow Creek/Dakota, 1882, 25), "a thing of the past" (Dakota, 1882, 43), "almost entirely abandoned" (Dakota, 1883, 22), "slowly dying out" (Pine Ridge/Dakota, 1883, 43), and "gradually decreasing" (Pottawatomies/Kansas, 1885, 62). In 1888, the agent from the Yankton Agency in Dakota wrote how "while there is still some dancing at small gatherings on other parts of the reservation I am satisfied the custom is dying out, and will soon, among the Yanktons, be buried with many of their old heathen ways that have been dropped within the last few years" (CIA Report, 65). Even when reporting evidence to the contrary, agents insisted on their own triumph in eradicating dancing. The 1885 Rosebud agent, immediately after noting how dancing continues and all means other than force have been exhausted in trying to stop it, and how "considering the large number of people who attend these dances," using force would not be wise, nonetheless predicts its demise. He writes, "As the Indians become more interested in farming and fall more under the influence of the missionaries they gradually drop out of the dance, and in this way the numbers of those who attend is gradually decreasing" (CIA Report, 61–62). In the early 1880s, numerous agents reported the end to the "barbarous" Sun Dance, noting with triumph how dancers had agreed to abandon it.[37]

Yet these death reports occur against a back story in which Native dance practices in fact continue relatively prominently. Indeed the greatest refutation of the government's various ploys to contain Native agency by dismissing and containing Native dance lies in the persistence with which it continued. In 1885, the year after he'd reported he did not expect the Sun Dance to be revived, Rosebud Commissioner James C. Wright wrote:

> I had every reason to feel assured that the assent given last year
> to yielding up by the Indians to them the time-honored annual
> festival of the sun dance, though given reluctantly, was under-
> stood by all its abandonment for all time. In this I was mistaken,
> and when the usual time for preparation came this year it was
> again agitated, first by the elders. By a firm persuasion these
> gracefully yielded. Later, the younger element took it up, and
> were discovered traveling the camps, "presenting the pipe,"
> committing all to a participation in this barbarous ceremony. It
> required prompt and decisive action to prevent its consummation.

> Finally a very reluctant abandonment was secured. . . . I am satis-
> fied renewed efforts will be made each successive year for this
> demoralizing custom, and will require a firm and decisive stand
> to prevent. (CIA Report, 44)

In 1888, the "Farmer in charge" at the Turtle Mountain reserve in Dakota wrote how "the full-bloods . . . this summer held one of their sun dances in spite of all that lay in our power to prevent it" (CIA Report, 41). In 1903, Indian Commissioner W. A. Jones, wrote how the character of some of the "sun dance" and other dances was "obscene and degrading to such a degree as to make a description too revolting to print" (CIA Report, 8), again signaling its continuing practice.

This persistence echoes throughout the U.S. CIA reports of the 1880s. The agent in Nebraska wrote in 1888, "Last winter in West Saint Paul they held their regular Indian dance as when uncivilized" (173). In 1881, the agent from the Santee Agency in Nebraska wrote how the Santee and Flandreau Indians "have abandoned the Indian dance and paint" (126). Twelve years later in 1893, Santee Agent James E. Helms wrote how "The Poncas, as well as a certain element of the Santee tribe, are fond of indulging in the old Indian dances, especially that called the Grass Dance" (201). In 1896, the agent at the Rosebud Reservation in South Dakota, in a report co-signed with the missionary, wrote how "The Omaha dance has had a marked revival during the past year, and the old men have tried to persuade the young men and women to keep away from church services and from a final separation from their dances, which is a requirement for church membership. It has been hard for the young people to resist the home influences, and the new dance houses have run a sturdy opposition to the churches" (CIA Report, 300).

One primary reason American Indian dance wasn't successfully outlawed was because it was effective, an issue numerous Indian agents seemed perplexed to confront. John H. Bowman, U.S. Indian agent at Navajo Agency in 1885, noted how the Hopis persist in their "weird and strange" Snake Dance—which he then describes in some detail—because, unfortunately, the dances appeared to have effect. "One thing connected with the last two of these dances has been particularly unfortunate. Each of these has occurred in a very dry season, and both have been immediately followed by heavy showers. Whether this has been due to the efficacy of their supplications or was caused by the commencement of the rainy season is a matter of opinion. But one thing is certain, a hundred failures would not cause the Moquis to lose faith in the ceremony or make them forget their two successes" (CIA Report, 410–11). And when the dance bans were successfully enforced for a period, their effects were felt. In 1885, Rosebud Commissioner Wright wrote: "Since [the sun dance was prohibited], the agent is held responsible for all ills and misfortunes that have occurred or have visited this people. Sickness, death, hail or other storms would have been averted if the sun dance had not been prevented. His removal is consequently demanded" (CIA Report, 44).

By flaunting the agents' authority, by removing the practices from agents' view, these dancers evoked spaces in which Native cultural, spiritual, and political agency could continue outside of state discipline of Indian bodies. The continuing and effectual practice of dance in these spaces itself serves as a sign of the power the dance evoked.

TWO

Theatricalizing Dancing and Policing Authenticity

I was limber at this time and I could dance many ways.

> ▸ Black Elk, *remembering how he danced*
> *before Queen Victoria during the tour of*
> Buffalo Bill's Wild West *to England in 1887*

In the mid-nineteenth century, French music and drama teacher François Delsarte developed ideas about the body as expressive instrument that would come to profoundly influence the development of modern dance in America.[1] Delsarte's system of dramatic expression purported a mystical science of applied aesthetics, or what modern dancer and choreographer Ted Shawn would call the "laws of expression."[2] This system found universal human correspondences between inner emotion on the one hand, and movements, gestures, facial expressions, and vocal behavior on the other. At the core of this system was a faith in the truth of an "interior aspect" or "inner inspiration" that people expressed in outward gesture (Shawn, *Every Little Movement,* 25). "Delsarte devoted his entire life to discovering this eternal truth about the nature of man, and how it is expressed in gestures and speech," Shawn explains (26). "His lifetime of study convinced him that there is an inner world of ideas and principles, and an outer world of visible, tangible manifestations of these ideas and principles in material manifestation" (22). Shawn quotes Delsarte, "'Every mental state has its outward expression'" (60).

As numerous scholars have noted, Delsarte's understanding of the body and of bodily movement's relation to an immutable "real" and "natural," and the system he developed based on this understanding, is explicitly grounded in Christian thought.[3] "'Man, made in the image of God, manifestly carries in his inner being, as in his body, the august imprint of his triple causality,'" Shawn quotes Delsarte as having said (*Every Little Movement,* 24). "'Art is not, as it is said, an imitation of nature,'" Delsarte wrote. "'It is the application, knowingly appropriated, of the sign to the thing'" (23). In this system, there is a direct correspondence between sign (or in movement terms, gesture) and thing (or in Delsarte's approach, an inner "truth" or "nature"). "'Gesture is the direct agent of the soul,'" he writes (25). As the body is made in the image of God, and all bodies have a soul, when the body moves it expresses the inner, immutable truth of that soul. Therefore, dancers performing particular movements and actions were not heathens accessing spirits, ancestors, or devils outside of themselves. Delsarte's theories on the link between Christian spirituality and movement as manifested in dance were thus in direct opposition to earlier claims by Christian ministers, such as Increase Mather, that dance was a non-Christian manifestation of the devil. Delsarte's system implicitly dismissed this notion of bodily movement's capacity to actually effect change or conjure something outside of itself. Instead, as Delsarte promoted it, bodily movement expressed the godlike universal "truth" of inner selves. The meaning Delsartian movement and gesture evoked, then, represented a Christian religious "truth"—and as such was hardly threatening in a Christian country.

What role did this shift in Christian conceptions of bodily movement, from fears of it enacting effect to celebration of it as tool for accessing an inner truth, have on the policing of American Indian dance—and vice versa? This chapter first explores the historical and ideological connections between late nineteenth-century Delsartian conceptions of bodies, theater, and dance and U.S. institutional and popular treatment of American Indian dance during the same period. During the 1880s, the government deployed, as a tactic in its attempts to "other" and subsequently erase Indians, the increasing codification and policing of what an Indian could be. It enacted this codification on two fronts: in the rise of fervent pronouncements, by Indian agents and other non-Indian authorities, denouncing the "authenticity" of Native religious dances and decrying its practitioners as "fakes"; and in the staging of "real" Indians in theatrical arenas such as *Buffalo Bill's Wild West*. This policing of Native religious ceremonial dancing as fake and the simultaneous promotion of real Indians dancing in arenas—following Delsartian theatrical practices—sought to do the work that more direct attempts at imposing Christian ideology had done in previous decades: control and contain its force and effect. This chapter's argument thus places Delsartian bodily discipline in relation to the late nineteenth-century codification of the Indian as a visually identifiable, yet (supposedly) militarily, spiritually, religiously, and politically ineffectual, entity. Second, it analyzes ways that despite various practical and ideological attempts at deploying the theater of the "Wild West" as a disciplinary institution, Native performers took possession of and danced (and have since continued to dance) actively and effectively in the space the arena provided. In the meantime, the relation to a natural real that they were seen, however erroneously, to be performing in their stage dancing opened up a space in which women dancers—similarly seen as natural—could begin to develop the field of modern dance.

DELSARTE AND THE UNIVERSAL CHRISTIAN NATURAL

Having developed a codified system of correspondences between inner truth and outer expression in the 1830s, Delsarte for twenty years taught actors, artists, opera singers, lawyers, clergy, and other prominent and politically and socially eminent people lessons in "applied aesthetics," which included lectures and recitals in singing, speaking, and pantomime. This system flourished in the United States first in the teachings of Steele Mackaye, the only known American student of Delsarte, who studied with him in France for eight months in 1869–70. Shawn writes that Delsarte saw Mackaye as "the one on whom his mantle would fall, and the one best fitted to carry on his science to future generations" (*Every Little Movement*, 18). Mackaye added to Delsarte's system a greater emphasis on physical gymnastics and expressive body movement "designed to prepare the student physically to apply and use Delsarte's laws of gesture" (18). Mackaye's "Harmonic Gymnastics" in turn influenced "American Delsartian" proponent Genevieve Stebbins, who studied with Mackaye from 1876 to 1878, helped propel Delsartianism into a wildly popular movement, particularly among middle- and upper-class white women, and most directly influenced the development of early modern dance.[4]

As dance historian Nancy Ruyter notes, during the mid-nineteenth century, arts and entertainment were gaining "their first widespread acceptance as an integral and socially acceptable part of the American scene." This acceptance came largely, she notes, "through the efforts of the liberal clergy" who "came to the belief that art was a moral activity" (*Reformers and Visionaries*, 12). Later in the century, artists, suspicious of formalism (such as that codified in ballet), were "eager to find and to base their work on what was—or seemed to be— real" (14). Delsarte's system—an explicitly Christian bodily practice focusing on expressing the "real"—came into popular acceptance within this cultural milieu.

Shawn's treatise on Delsarte's system outlines the "Meanings and Uses of Various Parts of the Body" (the head, the torso, arms and hands, etc.) according to Delsarte, and what different movements and positionings of these body parts mean. He then outlined movement possibilities (walking, bowing, falling, etc.) and the expressive uses of these. The American Delsarte system then carried forward these principles, and according to Ruyter, "developed new principles of movement based on relaxation, controlled and limited tension, easy balance, and natural flow of breath" (*Reformers and Visionaries*, 29). Shawn explained, "It was the application of a law of Delsarte which made fluid, limpid, easy, effortless, 'natural' movement possible in the dance of today" (*Every Little Movement*, 64). In other words, these movement practices (still quite familiar to modern dance students today) developed out of and underscored ideologies of movement as "expression" of an emotional interiority, as "direct agent" of a soul. The whole idea of movement as an expressive art, and of dance as "emotional expression" of an emotional interiority, is linked to these conceptions.

Both theoretically and practically, the Delsarte-Mackaye system's focus further emphasized, as the site of this inner truth expressed through movement, the individual body. Rather than stressing the accessing of meaning through group actions—ritual practices involving the bringing together of communities of people over multiple days, for example—this system located meaning in individual bodily explorations. These meanings were seen as "abstract and universal"—shared by all humans throughout time—yet distilled and available through each individual practicing alone (*Every Little Movement,* 78). In this way, while this movement practice could be (and sometimes was) taught in classes or explored in groups, it depended not on people working together, but on individuals individually exploring their inner selves, souls, and emotions. It thus theoretically, as well as sometimes practically (middle-class white women practitioners could and did study the form through private lessons), isolated individuals from group practice.

Delsartian practice also, in its focus on the exploration of each movement's meaning in itself, shifted theatrical and dramatic focus away from narrative or story. One way this manifested itself was in an interest in abstract dance movement, particularly as modern dance developed as an art form. More popularly at the time, it manifested itself in "statue-posing"—the creation, in middle- and upper-class white drawing rooms, of people posed in tableaux vivants depicting, for example, Grief.[5] Ruyter explains, "Delsartian statue-posing and pantomime—the ultimate in refinement and gentility—became the opening wedge for the entrance of respectable women into the field of modern dance" (*Reformers and Visionaries,* 29). Some (like Shawn) argued this was not true Delsartianism (*Every Little Movement,* 11), but it clearly formed a large part of what translated to the public as "The Delsarte System of Expression" that became such a craze at the time.[6] There were narrative elements to these poses and pantomimes. Ruth St. Denis described watching Stebbins perform "a series of plastiques"—moving from scene to scene—and acting out the *Dance of Day,* in which she rose from the floor, did "a light rhythmic step" to signal morning, then the "slower movements of the afternoon," then moved to her knees and into the "reclining posture of sleep."[7] Clearly these progressions have narrative elements, as do the practitioners' use of gesture and stage space. But telling a story was not the main focus of these practices' explorations of Delsartian "laws of motion."[8]

Scholars have long noted the paradox in Delsarte's attempt to develop a scientific approach to the body by studying how people expressed themselves, and then codifying this as a universal blueprint for the bodily expression of an inner truth. This paradox lies in part in the codification itself, the attempt to impose a system of universal expression. Ruyter, for example, notes the "in-

herent conflict" in revolting against formalism with another form of formalism (*Reformers and Visionaries,* 29). It also lies in the way it separates the real,
understood as an interior truth, from the expression of that truth—and yet
then understands the outward performance of that expression as itself true. In
other words, it both depends upon a separation between inner truth and bodily
performance, and at the same time understands the bodily performance as not a
learned physical action—a performance—but as itself true or accessing truth.
Dance studies scholar Randy Martin, for example, hints at the "problematic
character" of Delsartian-influenced systems that divide the "essential source"
of emotion from the activity of expressing it.[9]

Despite these paradoxes, the Delsarte-Mackaye systems of "expressive art"
sparked the interest of the American public. Ruyter writes that "there is ample
evidence that it was known and taught throughout the country and touched
a large portion of the middle and upper classes," and outlines the hundreds of
schools, teachers, books, and articles dedicated to the "Delsarte System" in the
1880s and 1890s (*Reformers and Visionaries,* 27).

POLICING AUTHENTICITY

As interest in accessing an interior real in the arts gained wider acceptance
in the late nineteenth century, a heightened fervor among federal employees
for policing what a real Indian was likewise emerged. This federal policing of
Indianness stemmed, in part, from passage of the Dawes Act, calling for the
allotment of Indian lands in severalty, in 1887. According to this act, tribally
held land was "allotted" to individual Native people, with remaining unallotted
lands sold to white settlers—legislation that resulted in the loss of two-thirds
of Indian land. It also set up a system by which the federal government then
and still today recognizes many Indian peoples, some of whom must trace their
ancestry to the "Dawes Rolls" to be considered enrolled tribal members by the
U.S. government.

In the wake of the Dawes Act, in this period of increasing focus on the real
in the arts—and in the midst of the heyday of *Buffalo Bill's Wild West*—federal
Indian agents increasingly assumed the right to police what was really Indian
dance and what wasn't, and to pronounce its authenticity. For a while, federal
rhetoric largely continued to acknowledge Native dance practices as a remnant
of Indians' "old customs," although it dismissed their religious import with
increasing vehemence. Acting Indian Agent William H. Beck's description of
the Omahas under his charge in 1896 is typical. He wrote, "They claim that
they have a right to their religious observances, which are in fact the barbaric
customs of their progenitors" (CIA Report, 198). But even this comment's acknowledgement of religious dance's connection to Native culture soon shifted.
Not long after, agents began dismissing not only the religious *import* of their

customs, but also the authenticity of their religious observances themselves, calling them "shams" and "fakes." The 1897 report of the Nez Percés Agency comments that "Sham war dances, of purely an innocent nature, and feasts of varied kinds, are frequently indulged in" (CIA Report, 132). In his 1903 report, John H. Seger, superintendent in charge of Cheyenne and Arapaho at Seger College, bemoans "the revival of the 'sun dance,' which has been brought about in the last two years," and also dismisses the religious import of several dances, authoritatively deeming them "fakes." He writes:

> This "sun dance" was once a religious ceremony, and was use-
> ful in keeping their tribal organization and the genealogy of the
> people. They have discarded it as a religion and forgotten the
> ceremony. . . . The last three "sun dances" the Cheyenne and
> Arapaho indulged in were simply fakes. They were pretending
> to be something they were not. (CIA Report, 253)

The basis for this seemingly authoritative statement is unclear, and Seger's other reports (he claims that "the majority of these Indians" see the Sun Dance as a time to gather and visit their friends and have a good time "and not that it is their religion, as some claim") are likewise uncredited (and likely based on statements tailored for him or given under duress). Yet he continues, "While I have heard scientists claim that it should be tolerated, and that the Constitution of the United States should protect them in this practice, I have also heard old representative Indians say that the 'sun dance' is of the past; it is behind us; there is nothing in it for the Indian" (CIA Report, 256). Other turn-of-the-century reports reflected similar attitudes asserting the authority to question the religious legitimacy of Indian dance ceremonies, and reading in them not the expression of Indianness but instead subterfuge for other activities.[10]

This tendency to denounce religious practices as fakery, particularly in relation to the Sun Dance, wasn't exactly new. Christian apologists had long denounced Dakota holy men and their practices as conjurers. Gideon H. Pond wrote in 1854 of Dakota "wakan men" who deceive the "ignorant savage" by "artful cunning."[11] The 1883 antidance prohibitions deemed an "offence" any one who "shall use any arts of a conjurer to prevent Indians from abandoning their barbarous rites and customs."[12] Toward the turn of the century, though, pronouncements of fakery seem to have become both more rampant and also more readily and sweepingly applied to all dance practices that didn't fit agents' understandings of both what Indians and what religious practices could be.

Conflicting ideas of embodiment and its relation to religious practice lay at the core of these denouncements of practitioners as "conjurers" and religious practices as "barbarous." What agents and missionaries considered "fake," "degrading acts," and "barbarism," rather than valid religious practices, were the aspects of the multiday Sun Dance that included piercing and the giving of pieces of flesh.[13] Some twentieth-century Native American commentators on twentieth-century Sun Dances have cited "the similarity between the crucifix and Sun Dance pole, . . . equating the sufferings of the dancers with the Christian concept of penance."[14] Yet in the nineteenth and early twentieth centuries, missionaries and agents readily denounced the Sun Dance practices of "physical torture" as contrary to "the ideas of civilization" and Christianity. The idea of connecting to, accessing, entreating the aid of, or ensuring appropriate relation to grandfather/sun, divine essence, or spirit, via these bodily acts and submissions, seems to have found no place in these earlier Christians' worldviews. It also enforced Delsartian ideas that dance practices were about relation to an internal real, not about enacting relation to gods or spirits. In this system, Indian expressive performance could access either a supposedly real identity or a supposedly fake one. Non-Native arbiters or experts (exposed to Delsartian notions of gesture as expressive culture?) saw themselves as capable of judging which was which.

Linear conceptions of time—with authentic Indianness available only in the past—circulated as part of this rhetoric as well. As the quotes above demonstrate, the reason those claiming the Sun Dance was valid were "simply fakes" was because there could be no such thing, even in 1896, as a contemporary Sun Dance. The Sun Dance was "of the past," "discarded" as a religion and forgotten as a ceremony, such that those claiming its validity "were pretending to be something they were not."

In many ways, these rhetorical moves continued earlier policies that sought to eradicate Indians, but first had to establish what Indians were.

BUFFALO BILL'S WILD WEST

During this period in the late nineteenth century, those working as Indian agents and declaring whether the Indian ceremonies on their reservations were authentic, or just pretend acts with some other duplicitous purpose, were also undoubtedly aware of another rhetoric of the real circulating at the time: that performed by *Buffalo Bill's Wild West*.[15]

The huge appeal of "Wild West" performances at this time stemmed in large part from their staging of authentic Indians for non-Indian audiences. These hyperstaged performances, circulating in a period when Delsartian ideologies claimed that bodily movements accessed interior truth, did not alert the public to Indian as a performed identity. Rather, they codified for the public for years to come what a "real Indian" was. In so doing, they authorized viewers—and non-Indian officials—as experts in judging Indian authenticity. In response, agents and officials themselves took up, as if it were accurate, not only the rhetoric of the truth of an interior real suggested by Delsarte, but also the rhetoric of the real Indian performed by Buffalo Bill, and used it as an ideological and political tool against which fake Indians and Indian dance could be judged.

From the start of the Wild West shows, the show Indians were seen to be performing not barbaric conjurings or enactments of war or healing practices, but real, exterior manifestations of their authentic Indian selves. Colonel William Cody, an enthusiastic proponent of American expansionism, an Indian scout for the U.S. Cavalry, and an Indian killer who participated in over a dozen campaigns against Indians and numerous fights with them,[16] began promoting Native performance as spectacle for non-Native paying audiences in 1883, at precisely the historical juncture when "war, scalp, sun, &c" dances were officially made offenses. For his *Buffalo Bill's Wild West,* which toured the United States and Europe through 1917, Cody hired hundreds of Pawnees from Indian Territory, Lakotas from Pine Ridge, and other Plains peoples to stage all sorts of "Winning of the West" scenarios. He and his partner "Doc Carver" opened the *Hon. W. F. Cody and Dr. W. F. Carver's Wild West, Rocky Mountain, and Prairie Exhibition* on May 17, 1883, featuring thirty-six Pawnees from Indian Territory.[17] A year later, Cody repartnered with Nate Salsbury, and in 1885 hired the Hunkpapa leader Tatanka Iyotake (Sitting Bull). In 1884, *Buffalo Bill's Wild West* included "scalp and war dances," and by 1886, "Custer's Last Fight" scenarios began with Indians moving their camps, settling in, and then holding a war dance.[18] Other events included "Attacks on the Deadwood Mail Coach," "Roping and Riding Wild Bison," "Indian Attacks," and a restaging of Custer's battle with the Lakota at Little Bighorn, performed by some of the same Native peoples who had fought in the battle itself.

A number of paradoxes lie at the core of Cody's staged presentation of "real" Indians and Indian dances. First, it was the understood theatricality of the Wild West arena—its status as theater, and *not* as reality—that enabled its War and Scalp Dance performances.[19] In April 1883, just five weeks before Cody began touring his Wild West prototype, Commissioner of Indian Affairs Price had outlawed Indian War Dances. Yet "Indian war dances" were a staple of the Wild West show. Press reviews described how the production opened when "the aboriginal Indians appeared, two tribes joining in a friendly dance," and included interludes of Indian war dances.[20] "In their real ferocity, the Indian war dances smack of primitive savagery at its wildest," another review suggested (Mackaye, *Epoch,* 86). Despite this dancing by real Indians in "their real ferocity," then, the dances were permitted presumably because they were part of a theatrical spectacle and as such understood as *not* actually stimulating "the warlike passions of the young warriors of the tribe."[21]

Yet despite this distance from a real War Dance, with actual effect, the shows' popularity depended upon their consciously cultivated relation to real Indians and Indian events. As its name suggests, *Buffalo Bill's Wild West* was infused with rhetoric that underscored its relation to an identifiable real. It was billed not as a "Wild West 'Show,'" a theatrical reconstruction, but rather as the "Wild West" itself, where audiences could experience the thrill of the frontier and watch "real Indians" in action—not actors but actual Native peoples who had fought these battles. Cody learned, one biographer writes, that it was "the appearance of real Indians, real guides, real scouts, real cowboys, real buffaloes, real bucking horses, and last but not least, real Buffalo Bill" that made the show popular.[22]

The theatrical apparatus behind the real Wild West Cody staged was further supported in 1886, when the production was moved from outside arenas to Madison Square Garden indoors, and Cody and Salsbury hired actor and dramatic producer—and Delsarte protégé—Steele Mackaye to create special effects and work with the performers. Engaged as stage manager, Mackaye transformed the Wild West into an indoor pageant called *The Drama of Civilization,* complete with dramatic lighting effects, gigantic scenic backgrounds, and a steam engine–driven cyclone that blew wind with such force it toppled riders. The first act of Mackaye's four-epoch event, called "The Primeval Forest," featured wild animals leased from a circus and Cody's show Indians; the first interlude, following this act, included Indian dances (Moses, *Wild West Shows,* 34). Mackaye's son, Percy Mackaye, writes how his father took the "great, outdoor, sprawling 'Wild West,' which up to that time had been practically devoid of imaginative or dramatic coherence," and produced a "new structure, which transformed the show's chaotic medley of elements into a dramatic unity." For this, Mackaye "devised a dramatic 'scenario' of group pantomime, structurally accompanied and interpreted, at strategic points, by a terse-spoken 'oration,' amplified in tone-volume by a projective sounding-board" (Mackaye, *Epoch,* 76). Steele Mackaye, writing to Salsbury, stressed the "method, coherency and completeness to this story" and the "historic order" it presented (77). Some bemoaned the theatrical apparatus Mackaye brought to the Wild West. "Steele Mackaye has tamed it and transformed it into a circus of living pictures," wrote one. "We hope that Buffalo Bill, the Indians, the cowboys and the bisons will be let loose in the open again and that, when they go to Europe, all of Matt Morgan's scenery will be carefully left behind."[23] Yet *The Drama of Civilization* had a successful, often sold-out run in Madison Square Garden from November 1886 until February 1887. At that point, Cody and Salsbury made preparations to take the "Wild West" to Europe, where Mackaye's work continued to influence it. In his astute study of Wild West shows, L. G. Moses writes that Mackaye incorporated much of *The Drama of Civilization* into the show outside London. Moses implies that Mackaye's influence lies, in particular, in the overt narrative of "the triumph of Anglo-American civilization over Native Americans" (*Wild West Shows,* 44). This narrative opened in England, as it did in New York, onto "the primeval forest, with wild animals in their native lairs, and the Indian as he was before the white man came. A friendly dance" (Walsh, *Making of Buffalo*

Bill, 268). According to audience member Queen Victoria, it also included War Dances; "Their War Dance, to a wild drum & pipe, was quite fearful, with all their contorsions *[sic]* & shrieks,"[24] she wrote in her journal after seeing the May 11, 1887 production. Although the Wild West show officially began in 1883, it was the Mackaye-influenced productions at Madison Square Garden, and then on tour in Europe and in the United States, that formed the core of the Wild West in the popular imagination, then and today. The enormous popularity of the show's self-conscious production of a "real" Indian in a performance with dramatic unity signals the force of this paradoxical construction and seems to have tapped into non-Indian desires for Indians as real yet contained inventions of what outside the theater would be considered threatening. Audiences and editors were excited by the spectacle of "hostile" Indians meeting "off the war path," and responded with enthusiasm to invitations to meet the "Chiefs of the Pawnee and Cheyenne Tribes of Indians" at a special event before the Madison Square Garden performances: "The demand for the 'War Dance' is unprecedently overwhelming. I must have more tickets. On with the dance!" wrote one invited guest.[25]

It seems that Mackaye brought his Delsartian training in gesture and pantomime, and its philosophies and understandings, to bear on his work with Buffalo Bill's crew. Nate Salsbury cautioned him six weeks before the opening that "in dealing with Wild West actors, you must try to get *broad* effects without burdening their minds too much" (Mackaye, *Epoch,* 76). A few weeks later, Salsbury reiterated, "It seems to me, if you enter into systematic rehearsals with the blooming Indians, you will have hell, and I repeat: Give them a broad outline of what you want done, and trust them to get up to the level you set" (80). Yet Mackaye apparently did hold regular rehearsals and work closely and directly with each performer. One Madison Square Garden administrator describes how "'Steele' took every Indian and cowboy, separately and led them through their parts, in pantomime, since there were few spoken words."[26] A reviewer attending a rehearsal of "The Great Playwright Teaching Indians" in 1886 described Mackaye's difficulties, followed by acknowledgment of his persistence and success, in training the performers. After noting how Mackaye "will employ the knowledge obtained abroad by years of study in coaching the Wild West Show," the reviewer wrote:

> Mr. MacKaye was soon busy holding rehearsal, but the Indians would have discouraged Delsarte himself. The Sioux did fairly well as "light comedians"; the Pawnees appeared to grasp some idea of the duties of "walking gentlemen"; but the Comanches were "rotten," and the Crows were simply "Hams." There was not a Piute *[sic]* in the Garden who was good enough to play "utility man" in a company of "turkey actors!" . . . Mr. MacKaye posed

and drilled the Indians, the cowboys, the old settlers and the
mules in picturesque groups. . . . Mr. MacKaye was vastly tired
when he got through the day's rehearsal.[27]

These descriptions indicate he trained the performers in Delsartian acting—
how to use gesture, walking, stance—much as ladies of the time did in their
drawing rooms. The overall success of Mackaye's work, and the change from
earlier, outdoor, productions, was noted by reviewers. "Last summer's exhibition was an odd sketchy, haphazard picture of life in the far West. That of last
night was a spectacular and spirited series of tableaus and pantomime, with far
greater dramatic interest and a stronger quality of picturesqueness," wrote one
(Mackaye, *Epoch*, 84). "In the vast auditorium, the actions of this great *Drama
of Civilization* are dramatic enough to tell the tale without any words. In their
real ferocity, the Indian war dances smack of primitive savagery at its wildest,"
wrote another (86).

This Delsartian underpinning reinforces the paradox of the Buffalo Bill
show's prescribed performance of "real" Indians and of Indian War Dances'
"real ferocity." The Cody "Indian" inhabits both these paradoxes. It codifies
and prescribes a performance of "Indian" (which in the Wild West meant Plains
Indian, complete with headdress and horses) as a universalized prototypical
American Indian, despite the diversity of Native peoples from the continent.
And it plays with the tension between a presumption of an Indian real and the
theatrical performance of Indianness—codified as a choreographed theatrical
performance, yet presented and understood as itself real. This paradox can be
most clearly read in the way, on the one hand, Indian dances are circumscribed
as pretend by way of their public staging, and thus permissible in a period
when nonstaged dances are restricted or outlawed, while on the other hand,
this public Indian dancing simultaneously banks upon performers' identities
as "real" Indians performing dances with "real ferocity," the performance of
which expresses that realness. This paradox thus serves to both construct and
celebrate an Indian that is visually and expressively recognizable, and simultaneously to contain both that construction (by staging it) and any threat to it
posed by practices that don't fit its parameters. This paradox at the core of the
Buffalo Bill presentation of "real" Indians and Indian dance is part of what allowed it to continue, by providing viewers with a presentation of "real" Indians
and Indian dance that were supposedly drained of danger.

THE AGENCY IN ACTING INDIAN

While these paradoxes might have eluded most of the show-going public, high
on its fervor for "real" Indians and "real" Indian dance, it likely was not lost on
the performers themselves. As the descriptions of Mackaye's rehearsals included

above suggest, Buffalo Bill's Indian performers seem to have found, at the very least, amusement in the Delsartian pantomime performances Mackaye worked on training them to do. Between the lines of the reporter's description of how Mackaye "posed and drilled the Indians" is evidence of the performers having a fairly good laugh at it all. The scene in Madison Square Garden this observer records includes "the Crows" acting it up as "simply 'Hams'" and "the Sioux" doing "fairly well as 'light comedians.'" The scene, in other words, is one of actors overdoing their "real Indian" act and along the way refusing whatever level of serious drama of Indianness an exhausted Mackaye was trying to get them to perform. What bemusement and refusals might have underlain the Comanches' "rotten" acting? What would the Pawnee performers' pantomime of "the duties of 'walking gentlemen'" look like? Might one not read in it these actors' clear grasp of the class and race implications of its choreography? As Jane Goodall has argued in her discussion of late nineteenth-century Australian Aboriginal performers on display in shows and exhibitions, the performance act itself provides opportunities for destabilizing narratives of victimization and capture. "As bodies engaged in performance, they had opportunities to exercise very significant forms of control in their relationship with spectators," she notes of the Indigenous Australian performers depicted in photographs of P. T. Barnum's Great Ethnological Congress.[28] She adds, "There were opportunities for parody, for the creation of ironic or contradictory impressions, and for the development of generic roles whose distance from any 'natural' human model grew to a point where serious scientific interpretation was turned back on itself in mockery" ("Acting Savage," 17).

Might not the Wild West arena have provided performers with ways of destabilizing narratives of Native political and spiritual containment and defeat?[29] This is not to deny ways these shows did function—for Cody, audience members, and the government—as narratives of capture and defeat. Nor is it to deny that some performers reported feeling disoriented during the tours, or that management, publicists, and journalists controlled much of the staging and often misrepresented the show Indians' statements and performances to the public.[30] My intent here, though, is not to focus on the function the shows held for those viewing and managing them, or to reiterate familiar paternalistic tropes of show Indians' victimization at the hands of powerful whites.[31] Instead, my interest is in teasing out how these performances held different functions for those performing than for those watching, and to explore the spaces performers found within a circumscribed Wild West set in which to access agency for themselves.

Goodall points in particular to the way dramatic narrative structure itself complicates simple depictions of "savages" as exploited victims. The theatrical gaze, she suggests, "follows a sequence of action and registers bodies as vehicles of communication rather than sights in themselves" ("Acting Savage," 18). The changing roles in which Mackaye staged the Indian performers in the *Drama of Civilization* underscore this argument. Indian performers appeared throughout Mackaye's multiepoch narrative, from "The Primeval Forest," which Moses notes ended with "a fight among Indian tribes" and an interlude of Indian dances, through "The Prairie," which included a "buffalo hunt by the Indians," through "The Attack on the Settler's Cabin," in which "gunfire and screaming Indians provided the danger" (*Wild West Shows,* 34). They reappeared to close the show. One historian writes, "Sometimes the 'Drama of Civilization' concluded with a spectacle, a battle between the cavalry and Indians, and late in the season, the Battle of the Little Bighorn ended the show" (Reddin, *Wild West Shows,* 83). For this "Custer's Last Stand" epoch, Moses writes, the show Indians fought the actor playing Custer until he lay down as if dead and the arena filled with a deafening silence—at which point Cody would gallop in with the words "too late" projected behind him. Here, then, is a narrative in which Indians—though depicted, as Moses notes, as "part of the natural environment" in the opening scene—nonetheless perform as integral, ever-changing, actors throughout the drama (*Wild West Shows,* 34). Their role is, in fact, *not* that of a static and defeated figure, connected to nature and wiped out by civilization. While they are aligned with nature in the opening, the force of nature—in the form of a cyclone—reappears later as a mighty and destructive force. Their more direct role is as dancers, buffalo hunters, and warriors who continue to perform throughout the *Drama of Civilization* as it moves through its chronological epochs, and who in the end kill Custer while the supposed hero, Buffalo Bill, arrives too late to do much about it. The very narrative of historical change, and the recurring and shifting roles of Indians in that narrative, works against any naturalized depiction of defeated, victimized natives frozen in time and on the verge of extinction. As Goodall suggests, it is in part the "sequence of action" of the theatrical act that itself enables this challenge to the depiction of a static, stoic Indian expressing an authentic depiction of interior truth.

No wonder, then, that so many Native peoples participated willingly in *Buffalo Bill's Wild West.* That they saw themselves as agents in their own performances and self-depictions—if perhaps not in the show's overall narrative or in the performances of the white actors—seems clear from the comments of some. The Lakota holy man Black Elk, the narrator of John Neihardt's popular 1932 literary interpretation, *Black Elk Speaks,* told in it (and in Raymond J. DeMallie's reinterpretation of the Neihardt manuscripts in *The Sixth Grandfather*) not of his victimization but of his pleasure performing in the show. "I enjoyed the Indian part of the shows that we put on here at Madison Square Garden, but I did not care much about the white people's parts," he recounts.[32] It seems, then, that he found in the Indian parts a space of pleasure as well as a simultaneous understanding of them as "parts" and yet as parts that carried import and weight. Black Elk does not see himself as a victim in this stage act, nor does he simply dismiss the acting as fun but fanciful theatrics; instead, he evaluates his response to the performances, implying they carried import and consequence as such. It also seems that he read the whites' performance of their "parts" as cowboys similarly—as theatrical acts, and yet as also subject to critique.

Black Elk's comments about the show's 1887 tour to England, when he was twenty-two years old, further suggest ways he and others found spaces of agency in their own self-depictions before these varied audiences. Black Elk, who describes himself as among "the best looking types of the Indians and the best dancers," is chosen to dance in a private showing before the Queen:

> We danced the Omaha grass dance then. I was one of the five
> dancers at this dance. We stood right in front of Grandmother
> England. I was a boy now and so I was a pretty good dancer.
> We danced the best we knew how. I was limber at this time and
> I could dance many ways. (DeMallie, *Sixth Grandfather,* 249)

Black Elk's comments acknowledge the literal flexibility and versatility he and the other show dancers possessed, and suggest, again, the agency they held in choosing among the "many ways" they could dance to best represent themselves in these performances. Even his choice of terms indicates ways his perspective, rather than the Buffalo Bill Show context, lies behind his performance of the dance. What Black Elk calls the "Omaha dance" is the dance referred to on Buffalo Bill's programs as the "war dance," a term anthropologist William K. Powers argues was popularized by the promotional copy for Wild West shows.[33] Today, powwow scholar Tara Browner writes, the Omaha/Grass Dance styles are generally considered to be the precursor to most men's powwow dances.[34] Powers describes this "Omaha" or "War dance":

> The characteristic features are the concentrated use of the head
> and shoulders; the full exposure of the face and chest, suggesting
> a sense of arrogance or pride; and little concern with footwork
> other than keeping time to the music. The entire upper torso
> dances; the face is alive with expression, an explicit awareness
> of enjoying the dance. (*War Dance,* 72)

An 1887 photo of Black Elk and another Oglala Lakota dancer, Elk, in London, dressed in men's Grass Dance regalia, suggests resonance between these contemporary "Traditional Style" dance features and the Lakota men's dance performances before their English audiences. The photo shows the two men standing, each with one arm interlocked and the other hand on their hip, staring directly and defiantly out at the camera. Both wear feather bustles at their waist, and feather headgear. Black Elk wears bells and feathers tied around his legs below his knees. Their chests are lifted and open, one draped in a decorated otter-fur neck piece, the other adorned with lavish shell necklaces, both suggesting the "pride or arrogance" Powers reads in contemporary "Traditional Style" dance. Elk's facial expression is stern and defiant, his chin lowered slightly toward his lifted chest. Black Elk's chin juts forward a bit, his eyes focused and bright, staring directly out. The photo is clearly staged, in front of a painted backdrop of some kind of leafy nature scene—possibly even in line with the pantomime instructions Mackaye imparted—and it is a still photo, with little indication of which of the "many ways" they knew Black Elk and Elk may have chosen to perform. Yet whatever the context, the dancers nonetheless project an impression of strength, solidarity, and pride.

The Queen's comments after the showing suggest she saw a level of degradation in it. "If I owned you Indians, you good-looking people, I would never take you around in a show like this," the DeMallie text quotes Black Elk remembering her as saying (*Sixth Grandfather*, 249). Rita G. Napier reads Black Elk's lack of discussion of this comment as evidence that "his political assessment was naïve." "Perceptive as he was, Black Elk misses the impact of that potent phrase," "If I owned you Indians," she writes, seeing him "as a man questing for salvation for his defeated and disunified people," and so "gratified by her friendliness."[35] Yet Black Elk's response registers, quite astutely, the condescension in these comments when he recounts this encounter to Neihardt nearly thirty-five years after it happened. Rather than dignify or reinforce her perspective on his dancing as a sign of his own degradation as a show Indian, he instead subtly persists in reading respect and honor in her reception of his performance. "She did not care much about seeing the white men in the show. She only shook hands with the Indians," he recounts. "All her people bowed to her, but she bowed to us Indians. We sent out the women's and the men's tremolo then," he adds. "Then we all sang her a song. This was the most happy time!" (DeMallie, *Sixth Grandfather*, 251). The disjunction between her response and his is displayed for his listeners in the 1930s and his readers today to register and consider.

Other late nineteenth-century Buffalo Bill show Indian performers also expressed desires to perform and the agency they found in it, and defended their right to do so against critics. Their reasons for performing, as Napier notes, were multiple and varied. "I came over here to see if I can make some money," she quotes Kills Enemy Alone as saying,[36] further noting that some performers "sent much of the money home to help their families." Some, Napier notes, used the shows as an entrance into a career in show business ("Across the Big Water," 383). Moses supports her claim with his comment that Rose Nelson, who toured with Buffalo Bill as a child, "later appeared professionally as Princess Blue Waters, carrying on the family show-business tradition well into the twentieth century" (*Wild West Shows*, 51). For others, including Black Elk,

Black Elk and Elk, in London while on tour with Buffalo Bill's Wild West, *1887.*
Courtesy National Anthropological Archives, Smithsonian Institution.

the opportunity to perform in the shows was seen as providing a way of under-standing the white man's world and of judging for themselves its relative merit. "I wanted to see the great water, the great world, and the ways of the white men; this is why I wanted to go," he says (DeMallie, *Sixth Grandfather,* 245). While the performers were themselves popular attractions, they also did a fair amount of their own touring in Europe, taking in sights including the Tower of London, the Vatican, and the Gallery of Machines in Paris. Napier quotes one 1887 journalist's comments on "Buffalo Bill's Red Indians 'doing' the sights of London." He writes, "They have paid several visits to popular resorts, and despite their proverbial stoicism, they are as much attracted by the curiosities on view as the public are pleased by the ornate appearance of the visitors."[37] In other words, not only were they the object of spectators' gazes, they also themselves looked at and took in the peoples and sights they encountered. Like others, Red Shirt, billed as "The Fighting Chief of the Great Sioux Nation," responded to the things he saw and experienced in Europe with the desire to share them with his people. "Our people will wonder at these things when we return to the Indian Reservation and tell them what we have seen," he said after experiencing a vision in Westminster Abbey.[38] Still others of the show Indian performers, Napier notes, "saw in exhibiting the life they knew a way of par-tially continuing the old while avoiding the fate of forced acculturation as farm-ers on the reservation" ("Across the Big Water," 385). In 1899, the acting agent at Pine Ridge reported to the Indian office his condemnation of the shows for the way they place "a premium upon barbarism" with "all the gaud of feathers, naked bodies, hideous dancing, and other evidences of savagery." He writes, "The Indian is taught that savagery has a market value and is worth retaining. The boys in the day schools know it, and speak longingly of the time when they will no longer be required to attend school, but can let their hair grow long, dance Omaha, and go off with the show" (CIA Report, 42). A similar posi-tion is supported by Black Heart during a meeting with Acting Commissioner of Indian Affairs R. V. Belt in November 1890. "We were raised on horseback; that is the way we had to work. These men furnished us the same work we were raised to; that is the reason we want to work for these kind of men," Black Heart testified.[39]

The school boys' enthusiasm and Black Heart's comments suggest the per-formers saw in their work with Buffalo Bill's and other shows an extension of, and space in which to continue, their way of life, rather than a stark departure from and containment of it. In other words, for them, even as their dancing bodies conformed to U.S.-sanctioned disciplining imposed by Cody, Mackaye, the attitude of the Queen and other viewers, and the circumscription of the Wild West set, their show dancing also continued to function as Native danc-ing. While their bodies conformed to audience expectations of how an Indian is and danced like disciplined Indian bodies do, their dancing nonetheless continued to invoke and enact cultural, political, and spiritual agency. This is not to suggest a naive oblivion to the differences between dancing, horseback riding, hunting, and otherwise practicing a way of life on the plains, and performing dances, riding, and hunting on stages and in arenas. Rather, it is to suggest that the performers, somewhat paradoxically, saw more of a connection between the stage and their own worldviews and ways of life than audience members—supposedly titillated by the performers' status as "real Indians" on stage—did. A stark separation between the stage "Indian" performances, and Native practices off the stage, then, were constructed and accepted not by the Indian performers, but by the public.

Indeed, Christian reformers and government officials—and not Native peoples—led the opposition to Indian performance in Wild West shows. These detractors read a threat to their civilizing and acculturation plans in the show Indians' stage acts. The 1899 Annual Report of the Indian Rights Association, a Christian-motivated reform group, for example, blasted government support for Indian shows. The Indian show business, the report reads, "is the foster-father of those barbarous customs, modes of life, and habits of thought which Indian education justly aims to destroy." It adds, "It is worse than folly for the government to say to the Indian child, through the school: Think, dress, act like a civilized white man; and then to say, through the show business: Think, dress, act like a savage Indian."[40] In September 1890, Commissioner of Indian Affairs Thomas J. Morgan concurred, writing how "the schools encourage Indians to abandon their paint, blankets, feathers, and savage customs, while the retention and exhibition of these is the chief attraction of the shows." Morgan notes as well the "demoralizing" effects of "their representations of feats of savage daring, showing border life as it formerly existed" and the way, through these representations, "They become self-important."[41] (Apparently Morgan failed to notice the irony of citing expressions of self-importance as examples of the shows' "demoralizing" effects.) The Indian Rights Association applauded Morgan's stand, writing in an editorial of the shows' "pernicious . . . effect upon Indian character and Indian progress upon civilization." They add:

> The nonprogressive forces in Indian life center around the Omaha
> dance, the medicine man, and the old chiefs. The expression of
> that life is found in the dance, in Indian superstition, in legends,
> in the hunt, in the memories (now happily getting to be memories
> merely) of Indian warfare, with its cruel tale of murder, pillage,
> and lust. . . . There is no agency more powerful to conserve the
> old and bad, to oppose and obstruct the new and good, than the
> Indian show business. The Indian who takes part in it must wear
> his hair long, paint his face and represent the fierce excitement,
> the savage deeds, of the old life.[42]

The very acts these reformers opposed, and which the stage required (men wearing their hair long, painting their faces, riding, dancing) served as spaces in which the performers (and the school boys wanting to "dance Omaha") found affirmation and agency, spaces in which to continue, and choose to experience honor for, their way of life.

The government's relation to the Wild West show seems to waver on this point, with officials wary to permit or encourage the stage productions—yet also, at times of crisis, willing to encourage them as a way of replacing or forestalling dancing off the stage. In the United States (and later in Canada) not only Christian missionaries and reformers but also the federal governments first decried Indian shows' demoralizing, uncivilizing, and unchristianizing effects and did what they could to curtail it. From the start of the *Buffalo Bill's Wild West* endeavor, Cody needed federal approval to hire Indians and take them off reservations. This approval was not always forthcoming, and if given was done so only begrudgingly and because no legal loophole for denying it could be found. (Officials rebuffed Cody's initial 1883 request to hire Tatanka Iyotake [Sitting Bull] to perform, but later relented [Moses, *Wild West Shows,* 26–27].) For the most part, though, government officials saw the threat the Wild West show posed not in the continuing performance of Native dance and other practices it encouraged, but rather in the milieu of vice they saw surrounding the theater. Therefore, when Sitting Bull returned from this first tour and spent his money "extravagantly among the Indians," as Standing Rock Agent James McLaughlin described it (reiterating Protestant ideologies about "wastefulness" that would continue for decades),[43] the agent withdrew his support again. Faced with this renewed opposition to rehiring Sitting Bull, Cody instead hired twenty-nine men from Pine Ridge to perform, drawing up a formal agreement designed to address concerns of those in the Indian office by promising to "protect [Indians] from all immoral influences and surroundings."[44] This agreement built on the formal relationship between the Wild West show and the Bureau of Indian Affairs initiated with Cody's hiring of Sitting Bull, and Cody promised to feed, clothe, and care for the men, who were all to be married, and their wives. It addressed concerns of Christian reformers and missionaries about the supposedly wicked and sinful enticements facing actors and performers by promising to hire "Indians all of whom shall be of the same [Christian] religious faith," and to pay a representative of that religious denomination one hundred dollars a month to accompany the group on tour and look after their "moral welfare" (Moses, *Wild West Shows,* 33). Cody's plan did not entirely quell protests.[45] Yet legal authority to restrict the Indians' participation was too questionable and Cody generally got the participation he sought (Prucha, *Great Father,* 713).

In Canada, traveling Aboriginal entertainers went to Europe in 1885[46]—and probably much earlier—and organizers of Canadian fairs and exhibitions began to invite Indians to perform their dances in the first decade of the twentieth century. Canadian Indian department officials, like their counterparts in the United States, did what they could to prevent Indian dancing at public events, citing, as scholar E. Brian Titley argues, "the demoralizing effect that these performances had on the dancers and spectators alike" (*Narrow Vision*, 172). They cited with particular alarm the dangers of the "male Indians in almost nude attire parading streets and other pubic places, giving so-called war and other dances for the edification of the wives and daughters of people who claim to be civilized and refined."[47] To curtail this, given the fact that they could not legally prevent Indian dances at exhibitions, they considered "enforcing Section 208 of the Criminal Code, which forbade indecent exposure," or using the vagrancy code "against those who loitered around town for days," Titley writes (172). At first they tried persuasion. In 1911, the Indian Department wrote to agricultural exhibition organizers in seven cities, asking them to omit Indian performances from their programs. When this had little effect (the first Calgary Stampede, in 1912, apparently included in its parade six tribes of Indians in what the *Globe* reported as "a gorgeous display of beads and coloured blankets"),[48] officials sought an amendment to the Indian Act. In 1914, Parliament passed "Subsection 2" to the Act, forbidding Indians in the four western provinces and in the territories from participating in "Indian dances" outside of their own reserves and from appearing in shows or exhibitions in "aboriginal costume," Titley writes (*Narrow Vision*, 175). The amendment was enforced with fines of $25 and imprisonment for one month "on summary conviction," and in the summer of 1915, a number of convictions were secured by agents in Saskatchewan, though this enforcement apparently had little effect on dancing in general. Titley writes that "most requests from the organizers of fairs and stampedes for permission to stage an Indian performance continued to be rejected" well into the 1910s, when government desire to enlist Indian enrollment in the war effort softened enforcement of the restrictions somewhat (175).

While government officials saw the life of the theater as threatening to their programs of assimilation and Christianization, and staging as demoralizing to participants and audience members alike, they nonetheless saw it as much less threatening than a continuation of the Indian religious ceremonies and ways of life off the stage. The story of the relation of *Buffalo Bill's Wild West* to what has been called the "Ghost Dance Religion," practiced among many groups from the plains to California in the 1880s, illustrates most dramatically the ways that despite this opposition to the Wild West show, the government ultimately viewed the stage as separate from, and as a way of containing the force of, real Indian dance. Cody's *Wild West* started presenting Indian "war dances" as theater in the mid-1880s, at precisely the moment their practice off the stage was prohibited. This staging served to assuage fears of the force of Indian dance, and to convince the powers that be that the force of the dance, once converted to spectacle, had thus been contained. Yet Cody's show apparently didn't work effectively enough, as Indian dancing continued off the stage and outside the arena. With it continued whites' fears of the agency of Native dance.

SHOW INDIANS AND THE "GHOST DANCE"

Numerous scholars have addressed at length the history of the so-called Ghost Dance Religion at Pine Ridge and the ensuing massacre at Wounded Knee in December 1890.[49] Some Native scholars have argued that this widely hyped Ghost Dance "outbreak" was, in fact, a "craze" manufactured by reporters, and that most Sioux people didn't even know about the dancing.[50] Others have argued persuasively that ethnologist James Mooney—whose writing on what he called the "Ghost Dance Religion" or "outbreak" forms the base for almost all published discussions of it—effectively invented the practice. Tharon Weighill argues that by isolating and naming one version of widespread and common Aboriginal rejuvenation practices the "Ghost" dance, Mooney played on whites' fears of ghosts as dangerous and demonic, creating an atmosphere in which to rationalize the use of force against, and thereby further deterritorialize, Aboriginal peoples.[51]

According to Mooney's widely circulated discussion, the "Ghost Dance Religion" began when a number of Lakota from Pine Ridge became interested in the message of a sacred Paiute man, Wovoka, living in Mason Valley, Nevada, around 1889, during a period of increasing famine on the reservation. Word of Wovoka had spread to the Dakotas, and messengers from Pine Ridge had traveled to see him and returned. One of those receiving these messages, Black Elk, reports that Wovoka told them to "put this paint on and have a ghost dance, and in doing this they would save themselves, that there is another world coming—a world just for the Indians, that in time the world would come and crush out all the whites."[52] Several dances were organized near Pine Ridge, one of which Black Elk joined. "I went down to my body then and I could hear the voices," he says, telling the people of the vision he experienced while dancing, and of the ghost shirts he had seen the men in his vision wearing (DeMallie, *Sixth Grandfather,* 261). As famine spread across Pine Ridge, the dancing of Black Elk and others became increasingly frequent—Black Elk writes "we were dancing nearly every day"—and caused increasing fears of "wild and crazy" dancing Indians among the soldiers and agents (257).[53]

These fears led to the identification of sixty perceived leaders of the Ghost Dance, starting with Kicking Bear, Short Bull, and Sitting Bull, and including Black Elk, who were to be arrested and confined for a time in a prison off the reservation.[54] Since Kicking Bear was in the Badlands and unreachable and Black Elk was low on the list, officials decided to arrest Sitting Bull and asked Cody—Buffalo Bill—to go to Standing Rock and induce his former employee to come in. He agreed, but when he arrived the weather was warm and agents feared it would give advantage to the Indians. Two and a half weeks later, on December 15, the Indian police did attempt to arrest Sitting Bull at Standing Rock. When they did, a shooting match erupted and Sitting Bull, seven of his supporters, and six police were killed in what some Hunkpapas believed then, and since, to be Sitting Bull's assassination.

What followed in the next two weeks is what has become known as the Wounded Knee Massacre: refugees among Sitting Bull's and other bands joined Big Foot's band and fled to the Badlands. On December 28, 1890, this group surrendered to soldiers of the seventh cavalry (Custer's regiment) and moved with the troops to Wounded Knee creek. The next morning, December 29, during preparations to disarm the people, one man refused to give up his gun and in the ensuing struggle over it shooting started. In the fighting that followed, the Lakotas killed forty-three soldiers, and the 470 soldiers killed three hundred Lakota people,[55] most of them women, children, and elders. Some had been shot in the back as they ran, their bodies found scattered and frozen to death for up to two miles from the site, though a few were found still alive three days later, after a blizzard had cleared.[56] Journalists arrived at the scene and their descriptions of the frozen contorted bodies of dead Indian women—some holding babies that had been wrapped in shawls and were still barely alive—led to a national outcry, as well as to increased fears of Indian outbreaks.

Connections between the "Ghost Dance Religion" and Buffalo Bill's show Indians extended beyond Black Elk, who joined and then led the Ghost dancing upon his return from Europe to Pine Ridge in 1889, and Buffalo Bill's aborted 1890 arrest of Sitting Bull, and Sitting Bull's death.[57] Fears of Ghost dancing Indians also quite literally garnered Buffalo Bill additional performers for his Wild West shows. After the massacre, General Nelson A. Miles, commander of military operations against the Sioux, suggested that Cody hire the men imprisoned at Fort Sheridan for Ghost dancing. Cody applied to Indian Commissioner Thomas Morgan for a renewal of his contract, writing that he would make his selection of performers among those who "might be mischievous in the Spring if allowed to remain upon the reservation."[58] Morgan—who had outlawed the performance of Ghost dancing and ordered his agents to arrest anyone defying the ban[59]—enthusiastically supported the idea that Cody hire them, although he despised the Indian shows and made sure it was clear the army, and not the Indian Bureau, had made this recommendation. Moses writes:

> Morgan reasoned that in allowing Cody to take the imprisoned Sioux, who had been described as "restless spirits" in official correspondence, any renewal of the Ghost Dance religion among the Sioux could be postponed for at least the length of the proposed tour. In that two years, Morgan believed, the religion would

cease to inspire rebellion among the Sioux. (*Wild West Shows,*
110–11)

Cody, thus supported by the U.S. government and military, hired the dancers to
be part of his production.[60] Twenty-three prisoners, including Kicking Bear and
Short Bull, toured Europe with *Buffalo Bill's Wild West* before being returned
to prison, and then eventually released (Moses, *Wild West Shows,* 106–28). In
1892, another Wild West show—*Doc Carver's Wild America,* performing in San
Francisco—likewise hired Sioux "fresh from the Pine Ridge reservation" and
employed them in dancing, among other things, Scalp and War Dances and a
"Ghost Dance by those who performed it."[61]

The hype created around this dancing thus created an atmosphere of fear
and trepidation about Indian dance that stage productions banked on—and simultaneously compounded the stage as a space in which to contain these fears.
At this historical juncture, in other words, performance institutions like *Buffalo
Bill's Wild West* claimed they would contain the force and effect of Native dance
practices not by disrupting, condemning, or outlawing them, but by staging
them, thereby circumscribing them in theatrical structures that audiences saw
as exciting, but safe. By staging these dances, transposed to a performance
arena supposedly devoid of actual danger, Cody quite literally performed
Indian dances' powerful effects as contained and conscripted, rousing—and
then assuaging—non-Native viewers' anxieties and fears of attack and replacing them with fascination and titillation at a safe distance. The shows' vast popularity signals the excitement and thrill they created for many viewers, despite
the protests of a number of reformers who saw Indian participation in the shows
as degrading and demoralizing. The government's support of the shows—often
begrudgingly granted yet enthusiastically endorsed as a way of containing the
off-stage dancing of "restless spirits"—demonstrates federal belief in the power
of the stage, and the stage life, to quell real warlike passions. As always, the fear
of warfare threatens U.S. acquisition of Indian land and resources.

THE AGENCY IN INDIAN THEATRICALITY

Theatricality was thus a disciplining institution, imposed on Native peoples
in the late nineteenth century with the collusion of the U.S. government as a
way of containing and controlling Native people's agency and stealing more
Native land. This is not to suggest that this theatrical disciplinary system did, in
fact, effectively contain Native agency, or that staging Indian dance necessarily
drains it of its political, cultural, or spiritual agency, any more than banning it
stops it or literacy contains it. It is to suggest that the government thought it
did. Indeed, the power of the dancing Native body to engage and enact in ways
inarticulatable to and unreadable by the state as anything other than theater,

inner expression, or ineffectual superstition is what kept it going throughout the fifty-year ban that superceded the Wild West phenomenon. For example, despite the Wild West show's two-year attempted containment of potentially troublemaking "Ghost dancers," rejuvenation practices continued in many places and many ways, as they do today, and as the agents themselves note in their yearly reports to the Indian commissioners.[62] It seems clear that the hiring of the Fort Sheridan Ghost dance prisoners as show Indians had, in fact, failed to contain its continuing practice. The Indian performers themselves thus took possession of and danced, actively, in the space the *Buffalo Bill's Wild West* paradox provided, finding within it ways of continuing dance practices and of exploring and transforming their relation to them in a changing world. Native peoples' participation in this theatrical space, in turn, provided an opening in which to question beliefs in the theater as a disciplinary institution and the assumption that theater structures could contain Indian agency.

As the show Indian performers engaged this paradoxical space of the arena, the effects of their staged dancing were (and continue to be) different, in many ways, from dancing performed off the stage in more clearly ceremonial contexts. Black Elk's performance of the "Omaha dance" before Queen Victoria and his participation in multiday religious rejuvenation ceremonies at Pine Ridge may not have enacted change in the same way or had the same kind of effect. Yet even given their differences, both the rejuvenation dances and the performers' active stage dancing of themselves dancing like Indians did have effects on the world. Contemporary Native American theorists have reexamined dismissals of the "Ghost Dance" as a failure, as ethnographers and historians like Mooney saw it—a naive delusion about the ability of dancing to bring back the buffalo and restore the land. Instead, as the epigraph to this volume attests, some have suggested ways the Ghost dance has been and will continue to be effective in its quest to bring Indigenous peoples, lands, and worldviews back.

Again, this is not to collapse the differences between the spiritual and political agency accessed by rejuvenation dances, and the spiritual and political agency accessed by dancing in the Wild West arena or before the Queen. Given that the purposes of these two arenas of enactment were radically different, their respective spiritual and political effects on participants, viewers, and circumstances would have differed greatly as well. Yet *Buffalo Bill's Wild West*'s theatrical staging of Indians and Indian dance, designed to contain any force Indians and Indian dance could unleash, did also invoke effective forces in the world. Some of these stage performances may have effects occurring in a time frame longer than what is seen as in keeping with the European logic of cause and effect. They may have effects in spiritual realms unreadable by the disciplining institutions of the day or of today. They may have effects in other realms entirely.

One such realm might include the invention of the Indian itself. The Wild

West performance of Indians and of Indian dance was acceptable because it was theatrical spectacle, and therefore not understood to be invoking the devil or stimulating "the warlike passions of the young warriors of the tribe"—not, in other words, affecting anything. But those theatrical productions did evince performative agency. What they called into being was not Mather's devil, but an equally powerful entity: the Indian. This imagined being held and continues to hold incredible agency in the U.S. cultural, political, and legal imagination. It also holds agency for contemporary Native people who access, as they perform, its powers.

For example, young men find a space in today's Fancy Dance powwow competitions—transformed from the Omaha dance of Black Elk's day[63]—in which to access and negotiate a contemporary, ever-changing relationship to Indian identity. Even as they conjure this identity, as Black Elk and others did, as an authentic real, they also access the agency of that which they've conjured. The Omaha Dance that Black Elk and other Wild West show dancers performed before the Queen and other audience members required and reinforced a similar awareness of both tradition and innovation. Black Elk, a limber young man and a Lakota warrior able to dance in many ways, performed a dance not of spiritual and political containment, but of Indian tradition and innovation. Clearly the dance was presented, and understood by those watching, as a spectacle and as such as devoid of agency or force. Yet as a performance, requiring choreographic choices, engendering pleasure in young, limber, good looking bodies and their abilities (Black Elk knew he was a good dancer) and projecting connection, pride, and defiance, it served a different role for practitioners than for audience members.

Of course, powwow dancing such as contemporary "Traditional" and "Fancy" dance practices has its own complex and controversial debates. Some have argued for ways the powwow arena provides a space for negotiating American Indian identity and affirming community or for the ways it engenders community conversations or allows for identity to be contested.[64] Others, though, see the powwow as always both contained by the commodified history of the Buffalo Bill arena and dangerous in its prescription and imposition on all Native peoples of what a readable Indian identity must look like.[65] Powwow dance competitions, Weighill suggests, emphasize primarily a "multiculturalized space for the orientalized gaze of a consuming audience."[66] From this perspective, both the show Indians and contemporary powwow dancers are contained by the viewers before whom and the arenas in which they perform. On the other hand, a reevaluation of the agency accessed by show Indians, in spite of the views and desires of their audience members, may provide a way to acknowledge and explore the empowerment accessed by contemporary powwow dancers. As Weighill also suggests, powwow dancers' "'hyper-real' performance of primitivism," which he sees in a "satirical framework," corporeally encodes the "painful memory of oppression" maintained by "those who held the line during the most painful experiences of colonization." Weighill writes, "As decontextualizing as it might be, powwow dancing empowers and gives agency to my folks!"[67] Thus even within the belief that Native dance has been contained by Delsartian theatricality lies evidence of the force that even theatricalized dance has to unleash change on the world. Perhaps, following Spokane/Coeur D'Alene poet Sherman Alexie who writes in his poem "Powwow," "today, nothing has died, nothing / changed beyond recognition / dancers still move in circles / old women are wrapped in shawls / children can be bilingual: yes and no,"[68] there is both a "yes and no" in the possibilities explored by Black Elk, as by contemporary powwow practitioners. Perhaps viewers, including contemporary viewers who understand themselves to be sympathetic or enlightened, tend to focus more on the act of viewing and the containment and commodification enacted through their own imperialist gazing than on the "yes" engaged by practitioners' act of dancing, with the pleasurable, physical movements and choreographic choices it engenders. Shifting one's critical gaze from the disempowerment imposed through looking to the experiences of practitioners' dancing provides a way of reframing this history. As Browner writes,

> Traditional dance and music, even when performed at large, competitive pow-wows and for a non-Indian audience, can still exist within the realm of the spiritual or sacred. It often seems as if Indian participants move in a reality set off from non-Indian observers, who tend to perceive a pow-wow as a combination carnival and sporting event. These differing sensibilities enable Indians to perform dances that, although in a commercial setting, have profound spiritual meaning for them. (*Heartbeat of the People*, 35)

REAL INDIANS AND AMERICAN MODERN DANCE

Indian show promoters, on the other hand, were highly invested in audiences *not* seeing realms of the spiritual or sacred accessible in the midst of a commercial stage setting. The Indian show banked on an understanding of an interior real merely expressed by Indian performance, not the stage as a space in which Indian participants actually engage with spiritual realms in ways outside of Christian understandings of body and soul. Cody's staging of the Indian as natural and authentic in the 1880s and 1890s was thus in keeping with Christian/Delsartian teachings and worldviews. Intertwined with what Cody's audiences saw as real Indians performing a natural display of themselves was the late nineteenth-century popularity of Christian-based Delsartian ideology, in which movement doesn't access the ancestors or spirits, but expresses inner truth.

Keep in mind that this (Delsartian) theatricalizing of Indian dance blossomed in the United States at precisely the historical juncture when overt sanctioning of Christian appointments was becoming increasingly troublesome due to the rising prominence of non-Protestant religions in the United States (especially Catholicism), leading to widespread support for what has become the modern dogma of separation of church and state. These new calls for separation of church and state made it difficult to federally outlaw Indian religious practices, and so Christianity had begun to fade as an overt tool for "othering" Indians, a rhetoric further troubled by the way some Indians adopted Christianity—yet remained threateningly Indian with ties to Native land and Native rights. At this juncture, then, theatricality—the viewing of Native dance as theater or performance and *not* as bodily threat—took on some of the role that Christianity had borne in policing the threat that Native dance was seen to make. The theatrical stagings of Indians served as state-sanctioned activities intended to remove the ideological and tactical dangers that American Indian dance practices were seen to pose to the United States, just as Christianity had earlier been engaged to do.[69] State-sanctioned policy, in other words, shifted at this point from being based on faith in the efficacy of Christian doctrine to condemn and outlaw Indian dance, to belief in the practical effect of redirecting Native dance energies from community practices toward stage acts for non-Native audiences.

The Christian/Delsartian rhetoric imposed on Cody's dancing Indians, in which their movements and attire were understood to represent their authentic and real selves, in turn reinforced Delsartian notions about how public stage movement displays an inner, individual, truth. Mackaye, schooled in the Christian-based theater training of François Delsarte, trained "natural" Indians to move in the Wild West arena like "real" Indians do. Similar rhetoric of access to a danced natural, influenced by Delsartian ideas filtered through Mackaye, was also taken up by early practitioners of modern dance and lies at the core of the birth of modern dance. Isadora Duncan, the "mother of modern dance," famously rejected ballet as an "unnatural" and "false and preposterous art" in favor of "natural" Greek-based dance that expressed "the feelings and emotions of humanity" (Ruyter, *Reformers and Visionaries,* 36). Her work continues to be associated with the idea that dance can access a true and natural relation to self, spirit, and nature.

In other words, early modern dancers banked on this understanding of the natural compounded by the Wild West shows as well, but in a different way. Rather than profiting from its paradox, as the impresarios did, or using popular conceptions of the stage as "contained" to access political and spiritual realms invisible to most audience members, as some Indian performers did, they grabbed the space of the natural and, empowered by its (Christian-sanctioned) conceptions of movement as expression of interior truth, ran with it. Ruyter argues that the Delsarte system's connection to religion made it a respectable means by which middle- and upper-class white women could engage in bodily practices and participate in physical culture. "[T]he Delsartians equated art with religion, the physical with the spiritual," and this understanding of religion, with roots in its developers' Christian understandings, enabled the "mothers of modern dance"—respectable middle-class white women like Isadora Duncan and Martha Graham—to develop what has become known as modern dance (*Reformers and Visionaries,* 29). The idea of a Christian and spiritual basis for expression "remained with it and helped make possible—and morally acceptable—experimentation that would eventually lead to a new dance art" (20). For women dancers, themselves associated with the natural and biological and as such also authentically connected to what they really were, this Christian theatrical form would have been particularly enabling in providing a model for public performance of the natural.

Likewise, the relationship between dance and public display the Wild West shows reinforced would have particular resonance for women. The public presentation of Indian dance—as a way of disempowering it—in at least this particular context authorized and promoted public dance as "safer" than private dance. The different ideologies at play in Native peoples' enforced removal from separate, tribal communities and nineteenth-century middle-class women's relegation to separate, private spheres are obviously great. Yet the Wild West shows nonetheless promoted the widespread display of "acceptable" public presentations of dance formerly seen as dangerous; this cracking open of public perceptions may have helped widen the public space into which women, shunned from the public sphere and public theatrical space in particular, might insert themselves.

Buffalo Bill show Indians and the mothers of modern dance thus both drew from Delsarte and its Christian base a socially and politically condoned space in which to dance, and ideological support for dancing understood by them or their audience as expressing a real or natural. Mackaye's Delsartian staging of "real Indians," moving in pantomimed ways that (audiences believed) expressed their "true" selves in the 1880s and 1890s—and the containing of previously condemned dance practices within these representations—helped open a space in which white women, in particular, could develop Delsartian movement practices into modern dance as a theater art that represented themselves as natural. Native dance, then, was not only affected by theatrical ideas of the expressive body that greatly influenced dance history, but also affected them. The Indian dance performers in *Buffalo Bill's Wild West* were, of course, not what enabled the development of modern dance. But these widely performed stagings of "real Indians" circulating at the time (Isadora Duncan was fourteen when *Doc Carver's Wild America* performed "real war dances" and a "Ghost dance by those who performed it" in 1892 San Francisco), combined with Christianized ideals permitting dance as "natural expression" of emotion, compounded and reinforced a nascent modern dance rhetoric that also saw dance as accessing a natural.

THREE

Antidance Rhetoric and
American Indian Arts in the 1920s

Church meeting it isn't very much different. The three
churches in this district have Christmas feast. Some of the
members of these Churches . . . leave their homes and their
stock a week before Christmas and camp around the Church
and have meetings nearly a week and neglect their stock. . . .
There are some men who are known as dancers who have
good homes, raising cattle, horses, chickens and hogs, and
are living good better than church helpers.

> ▸ *Petition signed by Claude Killspotted,*
> *Red Tomahawk, and James Allyellow,*
> *March 19, 1923, denouncing the notion that*
> *"Indians dancing" led to neglect of stock*

In the 1920s, artists and tourists flocked to a newly invented American Southwest, entranced by Indian arts and culture made increasingly accessible after
the opening of the Santa Fe railway in 1863. The railway and later the automobile transported numerous artists and intellectuals to the region, and they
formed the Taos and Santa Fe art colonies in the early decades of the 1900s.
These colonies flourished until the early 1940s, and the focus of much of their
artistic interest was American Indian culture—the buying, selling, and displaying of Indian-made pottery, jewelry, and other objects, as well as the display
of Native Americans, what Leah Dilworth calls the "aesthetic appreciation of
Indian cultures."[1] Along with these artists came hordes of tourists, likewise
drawn in large part by the proximity and accessibility of Indians, Indian arts,
and Native American culture. The Fred Harvey Company formed its own
"Indian Department" in 1902, and after the arrival of the automobile began
its "Indian Detours" in 1926.[2] Watching authentic Indian dancing was a (if

not the) primary activity of these Southwest tourists in the 1920s and 1930s, a highlight of the authentic Southwest they expected to encounter. The Indian Detours included (in the right season) a viewing of the Snake Dance and Native American social dances, which sometimes accompanied the Harvey displays of Indian artifacts (Dilworth, *Imagining Indians,* 71, 83). Artists and intellectuals also flocked to the dances. Writer and activist Mary Austin, an active member of the artistic communities, described escorting the president of Princeton University to a dance at San Felipe in 1928[3] and guest Martha Graham to the Santo Domingo Corn Dance in 1932.[4] Graham dancer May O'Donnell described a decade of car trips through the region; she and her husband would stop in and around Santa Fe to camp out near and watch Indian dances.[5] Scholar Sylvia Rodríguez referred to "gazing at Indian dances" as "probably the supreme recreational activity of the early [Taos] artists and company."[6]

Yet as this interest in watching Indians and their dancing flourished, the U.S. and Canadian federal governments issued, with renewed fervor, anti–Indian dance circulars directed at the very dances tourists and artists were traveling to see. Outlawing dances as "barbarous" was still referenced, but increasingly these edicts focused on a different anxiety: the *waste* officials claimed Indian dancing produced. Their restrictions especially bemoaned the waste of time, as Indians gathered for days, doing nothing officials and missionaries could understand as useful, during a period when (according to officials and missionaries) they should have been preparing their fields and planting their crops. This "waste of time," and of potentially productive farming labor, was compounded by the excessive waste produced by the "reckless giving away of property" practiced in "give aways," which officials claimed left Indians destitute. Further compounding these "wasteful" practices was the sexuality that the dance gatherings enabled, and that officials and missionaries decried as excessive, immoral, and a threat to the nuclear-family home life they were promoting. At times officials acknowledged a disavowal of waste and extolling of productivity as explicitly North American cultural values, especially when noting their importance in preparing Indians for U.S. citizenship. For the most part, however, these values, while clearly tied to a Protestant work ethic and to a capitalist grounding in individual private property ownership, were presented as universal.

This chapter explores the competing, and intertwined, rhetoric about Native American dancing engaged by federal officials, by Native American dancers responding to the restrictions, and by non-Native artists and intellectuals entranced by Southwest Native American culture and outraged by federal restrictions on it. Drawing from hundreds of letters and documents held in the U.S. National Archives, the chapter teases out American Indian voices responding to the antidance circulars, particularly those articulating understandings of religion in terms quite different from those of politicians. These responses indicate conceptions of dance as integral both to religious practices and to land and water rights and link attempts to curtail dancing with desire for Indian land and resources. The rhetoric surrounding the federal drive to curtail Indian dance as "wasteful" and "excessive," this chapter argues, connects to artists' promotion of it as "art" and "amusement": both hinge on a promotion of use-value in Indian dancing. Yet in both cases, dance's value is nonetheless disconnected from Indian understandings of dance as integral to religious practice. Championing Native American dance for its value as American art thus came to supplant any understanding of its political, spiritual, and religious agency so much that, as these desires for and protections of American Indian "Arts and Crafts" increased, fears of its efficacy as religious practice faded, and official federal restrictions on ceremonial dance came to an end.

In the late nineteenth century, Indian Office officials each year pronounced Native American dances to be on the verge of fading away. In the 1920s (especially in the U.S. Southwest), American Indian culture was likewise seen as always, though now tragically, about to be lost for good. Dilworth persuasively outlines the pervasive rhetoric of a disappearing Southwest Indian culture that tourists and artists invoked, a rhetoric that fueled assumptions about outsiders' need to know about Indian dances before they were lost to the world. Tourists and artists living in or coming through the region could (and did) see this thought-to-be disappearing authentic Indian dancing in numerous locations. Hundreds of tourists traveled by car to pueblos on feast and ceremonial days to witness the dances or as part of the Harvey Detours. Jill D. Sweet, in her incisive study of Tewa ceremonial performances, notes that as many as thirty cars might descend on a village during a large dance.[7] Others saw dancers who performed at fairs and exhibitions,[8] or dancers who were hired to perform at Harvey arts exhibitions or hotels (Sweet notes a 1926 hotel performance in Santa Fe by a dancer dressed in a Plains war bonnet). At the same time that it was pronounced to be disappearing, Indian dance was clearly visible—and marketed and promoted—in the region.

Sweet's study teases out some of the many ways various Tewa dance practices shifted in relation to this barrage of outsiders' interest. These included adjustments, within Anglo-organized ceremonials, to "Anglo theatre practices such as applause, a different kind of concern for performance time and space, a non-participatory audience, contracts and contests" ("Tewa Ceremonial Performances," 194). Some, but not all, of these practices carried over to public Tewa-organized ceremonials, in which "the Tewa Indians selected both the theatre practices they wanted to borrow and those they wanted to avoid," generally eschewing "Anglo conceptions of theatre space, competition or formal contracts with performers" (195). Sweet suggests that these theatrical aspects did not make their way into Tewa village rituals, which remained quite separate from the ceremonials. On the other hand, she notes numerous ways that aspects of the rituals do make their way into the public events, including participants' understandings of ways the ancestors "are out there in spirit among the dancers" in public ceremonials as in village rituals. "You have to put your whole heart and yourself into what dances you are taking part in—no matter where you are dancing," she quotes one dancer (147).

This tourist activity, and tourist and ethnographic practices of intrusive looking, recording, and questioning, fueled increasing restrictions on non-Indian activities at Indian ritual practices. The Hopi, for example, banned photography at the Hopi Snake Dance at Walpi Village starting in 1913–15, and at all Hopi ceremonies in the late 1920s.[9] The Tewa, Sweet notes, refused to answer direct questions and cultivated a climate of secrecy.[10] Secrecy, in other words, was not intrinsic to the dance rituals, but rather a response to the rude behavior engendered by tourists' presumptions about their own right to knowledge about Indian peoples, practices, and cultures (as to Southwest topography, landscape, and scenery).[11] These restrictions and refusals served to protect and control the transformative power of dancing, and of watching the dances, at a time when more and more non–Native American people were seeking out chances to experience them for their own personal inspiration and enrichment.

PRACTICAL, USEFUL, THRIFTY, AND ORDERLY ACTIVITIES: ANTIDANCE CIRCULARS OF THE 1920S

While non-Indian artists and tourists flocked to Southwest Indian dances in pursuit of their own enrichment, federal officials, seeing themselves as responsible for the well-being of their wards, focused on the harm they saw the dances causing Native peoples themselves. In dance restrictions newly reissued in the 1920s, government officials stressed what they saw as the ceremonial dances' waste of time, energy, and resources; the immorality of sexuality the dances enabled; and ways the dances were barbaric and degrading. Officials were attentive (if not sympathetic) to the artistic and touristic interests in Southwest Indian art (and the rich and influential artists and writers supporting it). They were careful to provide clauses that recognized the use-value of Indian dance as "art," which they saw as elevating and refined, as well as of the health benefits of exercise that dance provided. On April 26, 1921, for example, Commissioner of Indian Affairs Charles Burke issued a special circular to the superintendents on Indian dances. In Circular no. 1665, Burke insisted, "The dance per se is not condemned. It is recognized as a manifestation of something inherent in human nature, widely evidenced by both sacred and profane history, and as a medium through which elevated minds may happily unite art, refinement, and healthful exercise."[12] Burke focuses especially on how "useful" or "wasteful" Indian dancing could be to Native peoples themselves. Burke cautioned, however, that his acknowledgment of some benefits to some dancing, as in the healthful exercise provided, does not preclude the enforcement of his regulations. He writes how the dance "under most primitive and pagan conditions is apt to be harmful," and insists that when found to be so among the Indians, "we should control it by educational processes as far as possible, but if necessary, by punitive measures when its degrading tendencies persist." Burke continued to outlaw the Sun Dance and all other "so-called religious ceremonies" that involved

> acts of self-torture, immoral relations between the sexes, the sacrificial destruction of clothing or other useful articles, the reckless giving away of property, the use of injurious drugs or intoxicants, and frequent or prolonged periods of celebration which bring the Indians together from remote points to the neglect of their crops, livestock, and home interest.

Instead, Burke explicitly encouraged missionary activities to prepare Indians for citizenship and "a higher conception of home and family life." Burke then insisted that these regulations be enforced. He suggested each superintendent first use "patient advisory methods" to convince the Indians "to confine their dances and like ceremonials within such bounds as he may with reasonable concession approve." He writes further:

> It seems to me quite necessary to Indian progress that there should be no perversion of those industrial and economic essentials which underlie all civilization, and that therefore meetings or convocations for any purpose, including pleasurable and even religious occasions, should be directed with due regard to the every-day work of the Indian which he must learn to do well and not weary in the doing, if he is to become the right kind of a citizen and equal to the tests that await him.

Here again Burke's patronizing rhetoric, with its focus on work, tests, and "industrial and economic essentials"—and deviations from these as perversions—presumes Protestant values (and reinforces boarding school teachings) about productivity and usefulness. Only when these advisory methods have been exhausted without result, Burke stated, should superintendents enforce the restrictions. He does not explain what the "punitive measures" could or should entail.

In Canada, government officials and missionaries offered a similar rhetoric of "waste" and "productivity" in the 1920s. "Giving away" had been implicitly and then explicitly prohibited at Indian ceremonies in the 1885 and 1895 revisions of the Indian Act, but proved difficult to prosecute. In the spring of 1918—in the midst of a war effort that stressed food production and conservation as patriotic acts—Parliament amended Section 114 (now referred to as Section 149) of the Indian Act to make it easier to prosecute and try those who participated in "give away" festivals.[13] Even though World War I soon ended, this "summary conviction" clause led to a new round of repression and arrests in the early 1920s, enforced by Canadian officials, particularly Commissioner W. M. Graham, for the three prairie provinces, and deputy superintendent general of the federal Indian department Duncan Campbell Scott.[14] On December 15, 1921, Scott issued a circular similar in tone to that of Burke's April missive. Scott's letter expressed alarm at the increase of dances on the reserves, and their effects on department efforts "to make them self-supporting."[15] He directed reserve officials to "use your utmost endeavors to dissuade the Indians from excessive indulgence in the practice of dancing." He further instructed officials to suppress "any dances which cause waste of time, interfere with the occupations of the Indians, unsettle them for serious work, injure their health or encourage them in sloth and idleness." He urged federal officials to dissuade, and if possible prevent, Indians from leaving their reserves to participate in fairs and exhibitions "when their absence would result in their own farming and other interests being neglected." He added, "they should not be allowed to dissipate their energies and abandon themselves to demoralizing amusements." The focus, again, was on promoting "self-supporting" farming interests and preventing "waste of time," sloth, and idleness.

Over the next several years, Burke circulated a number of missives similarly emphasizing waste and lack of productivity in Indian dancing. These calls for the restriction of Indian dancing on the grounds that it was wasteful not only derived from Protestant ideologies, but in fact grew quite directly out of Christian missionary efforts: they are based on a 1922 letter drafted by missionaries, calling for specific time and age restrictions on dancing.[16] On February 14, 1923, Burke responded to these missionary recommendations by issuing a supplement to Circular no. 1665, in which he wrote that "the main features of the recommendations may be heartily endorsed." Clearly, overt Christian missionary influence on official federal Indian policy continued unabated. In these circulars, Burke again echoed Protestant values of thrift and hard work as (paradoxically) the key to Indian "preservation." He called on superintendents to "persistently encourage and emphasize the Indian's attention to those practical, useful, thrifty, and orderly activities that are indispensable to his well-being and that underlie the preservation of his race in the midst of complex and highly competitive condition." He proclaimed,

> The instinct of individual enterprise and devotion to the prosperity and elevation of family life should in some way be made paramount in every Indian household to the exclusion of idleness, waste of time at frequent gatherings of whatever nature,

and the neglect of physical resources upon which depend food,
clothing, shelter, and the very beginnings of progress.

Burke then sent this supplement to his superintendents, accompanied by a letter of "appeal to the Indians of all our jurisdictions" urging superintendents to give it "the widest publicity possible among the Indians."

In this message "TO ALL INDIANS," sent on February 24, 1923, Burke argued that these dances "take the time of the Indians for many days" and lead to "the neglect of stock, crops, gardens, and home interests."[17] He wrote, "and then you go home to find everything going to waste and yourselves with less work to do than you had before." The thrust of the rhetoric, again, is the value of work and the productive use of land and of time. The last sentence of each paragraph focuses on the dances as not only wasteful in themselves, but also leading Indians from being productive farmers and home tenders, again echoing a familiar tactic of using lack of productivity as justification to, ultimately, take over Indian lands and resources.[18]

Within the next couple of months, both Burke and Assistant Commissioner E. B. Meritt contacted superintendents to request reports "of any dance, feast, ceremony, or other performance which in your judgment is demoralizing or disorderly, or affords an occasion favorable to vice and crime, and particularly is a hindrance to the duties essential to self-support and industrial progress," as Meritt wrote to Winnebago Agent Frank T. Mann on April 17, 1923. "It is desired to have this data based on actual knowledge of eye witnesses and it may be supplemented by statements, confidential if preferred, by Indians disposed to cooperate for better things." At the National Archives in Washington, D.C., three thick files hold these requests, the superintendents' reports, and some of the statements elicited from "cooperative" Indians. The files also hold hundreds of letters supporting and criticizing Burke's circular messages of antidance restrictions, as well as Burke's and Meritt's responses to them. Letters of explanation, sent to anyone questioning the antidance circulars, along with the reports elicited from Indians "disposed to cooperate," were to be part of the "careful propaganda" the missionaries suggested be undertaken to educate public opinion against the dance.[19]

According to many letters held in these archives, numerous Native Americans refused to obey the dance restrictions. Some redirected the official antidance rhetoric, insisting that the tourists, not the dancers, were degraded, or pointing out the waste of time and money spent by Christians on Christmas. Other Native American leaders defended Pueblo attitudes about gender and sexuality, noting in contrast some white dances they had seen. Others ignored the circulars' claims of waste and barbarity, instead insisting that the ceremonials be recognized as valid religious practices—invoking increasingly common cries for freedom of religion circulating at the time. Still other American Indian leaders drew attention to the relation to land and water performed in dance ceremonies, and the subsequent threat to Native land and water rights the restrictions posed. They (along with some artists and Indian rights activists) argued persuasively that legal debate and rhetoric about Indian dancing was intricately tied to debates and proposed legislation about land.

FANTASTIC MOTIONS: THE ANTIDANCE FILES

When the commissioners of Indian affairs asked superintendents to elicit reports by Indians "disposed to cooperate," some government officials had a difficult time finding any willing to support the suppression of Indian dances. This did not, however, dissuade government officials from the righteousness of their mission. One letter, from Fort Yates, North Dakota, agent E. E. Mossman to Burke, sent May 12, 1923, demonstrates the racist fervor with which many approached the issue. "The screaming and ki-yi-ing of the squaws, the barbaric tomtom, the savage dress, the fantastic motions have nothing to do and are not an expression of anything in any way elevating, nor does it in any way assist or supplement what the government is trying to do for the Indian in civilizing and educating the Indian," Mossman writes. His vitriol rehearses prevalent attitudes of the day about compulsory Christianity ("I know that the dancer is a poor church member"; "I know that the missionaries are almost all against the dance"), work, property, productivity ("I know that generally he is a poor farmer. I know that he is as a rule difficult to get along with. I know he is seldom a man of property. I know that he is a reactionary. I know that when dances are not allowed for some time we get much more work done by the Indians than when they dance frequently"), and "progress" through assimilation ("I know that the Siouxs if going forward are going forward very slowly and I attribute that condition more than to any one cause to the dance"). At the same time, it inadvertently (to be sure) upholds the importance of dance practices in Indian communities by noting the central role rejuvenation dances, for example, continue to play. ("The [Tacoma] Ledger says that today the ghost dance means nothing to the Indian. The Ledger does not know. While the significance of the various dances have partly been lost to the young people, they still have enough significance that they are breeding places of reaction against the teachings of the government. The music, if it should be called music, is the same that was used in the olden days when the warriors danced before or after their forays for prisoners or plunder.") His summary neatly links these rhetorical moves, championing church, industry, assimilation, and education, and noting the threats dance poses to these.[20] Mossman attached antidance reports from his farmers, but like several other agents, seems to have had difficulty finding Indians to write in support of suppressing dance. "If I can find a few old Indians, who disapprove of the dance I will try and send in statements later," he writes.[21]

However, Indian agents from dozens of regions did comply with officials' requests, some sending in lengthy descriptions of dances gathered from farmers and eliciting letters of support from Indians who disapproved of the dance. Some of these Native peoples wrote in at the agent's request, noting their support not so much of the restrictions as of the agent in charge. In a letter sent from the U.S. Indian Field Service Rosebud Agency in Rosebud, South Dakota, on June 25, 1923, for example, a man signed High Horse wrote to say "The agent you put here is my friend. I'm with him all the work to push it long. The first thing I want to say is that the agent don't like to see us go to white celebrations and the people are doing more and far better on farming and I'm sure they will put up more hay and they be more saving, and we want to fight the booze all we can."

It is of course difficult to know exactly how, and by whom, these letters came to be penned. Some, including those both supporting and criticizing the dance restrictions, suggest collaborative authorship in their style and language, and many were obviously written with the help of non-Indian editors: missionaries, missionaries' wives, agents, or artists and activist "Friends of the Indian." On the other hand, questioning anything written clearly and eloquently as non-Indian itself rehearses familiar stereotypes about American Indians. What is clear is that when eloquent, grammatically correct letters *criticized* the suppression of dances, officials were quick to append notes dismissing them, noting the likelihood the writer had help from non-Indians in drafting them (as was undeniably sometimes the case). But when gracefully written and clear treatises *supported* the dance restrictions, no such questions arose, and officials were more than happy to circulate them as authentic examples of Indian support for their antidance campaign.

The most useful such letter for the Indian Office arrived when Burke received a copy of an article published July 28, 1923, in the *Coconino Sun* of Flagstaff, Arizona. In this letter, written in response to an article the paper published supporting the Hopi Snake Dance, a "full-blooded Hopi" named Otto Lomavitu supposedly wrote in to blast both the Hopi Snake Dance and the tourists who flock to see it.[22] "It is beyond my comprehension how a man of the intelligence of a white man can wish that the Hopis should continue in this disgusting ceremony of holding a filthy snake in one's mouth for five or ten minutes at a time," the letter states. "Has the great white man become so low that he willingly spends hundreds of hard-earned dollars just to see an ignorant Indian wriggle with his writhing god the snake?" The letter (whether actually written entirely by a Hopi named Lomavitu, or with editing help from another yet representing his sentiment, or manufactured entirely by an agent or other supporter of the government) goes on to blast the tourist, who "stretches out his covetous hands to a poor, dust-covered Hopi of the desert with assumed friendly smile only to sneer when meeting him on his own town streets." Rather than seeing contact with whites as bettering for the Hopis, as some have apparently argued, he criticizes white women's nudity and vanity, "ever admiring herself in a glass, twisting her head like a reptile, ever powdering her nose and painting her eyelids." He writes, "Tourists do not show their better side as a rule, but their blackest side to a quick discerning Hopi. Bring us better qualities and we will welcome you." Lomavitu adds, "THE SNAKE DANCE IS A FAKE!" He says the fangs of the snakes are emptied of poison and extracted. "The white man does not know this, nor any outsider. The Indian laughs in his sleeves at the poor, deluded, pompous pale face." He concludes, "They who disagree with the Commissioner of Indian Affairs in his message to all the Indians (not in Arizona alone) must stay to one side while we Hopis follow out his orders the best we can. We owe all our education and civilization to the man in Washington besides our greatest benefactor, the Almighty God. We must pay our debt by becoming better citizens."

The Lomavitu letter, while clearly rehearsing rhetoric in keeping with the government's agenda (championing education, assimilation, and civilization), also inverts the condescending and patronizing rhetoric implied in policies that saw Indian dance as lewd and backwards, Indians as victims, and whites as superior, and that suggested Indians be civilized and improved through contact with whites. Instead, the letter's tactic is to mock white tourists for their immodest behavior and demonstrate ways the Hopi themselves are the ones in control of the situation. Here, the letter aligns the white woman with what he describes as the "filthy snake" of the Snake Dance, describing her "twisting her head like a reptile." He describes the white man as the victim, a "poor, deluded, pompous pale face," and insists on the cleverness and mirth of the "quick discerning Hopi" deluding the tourists.

Burke, however, failed to read the letter's insistence on Hopi intelligence and self-assertion and instead focused on its more overt antidance stance. Clearly delighted by this letter by a "real Hopi Indian," he had dozens and dozens of photostatic copies of it made and included it—sometimes multiple copies of it—in his response to letters regarding his directive. He sent copies to a Mrs. Seymour on August 23, 1923, for her to distribute to her activist friends, writing, "It would seem as if the statement of one who is a real Hopi Indian on the subject of the Snake Dance ought to be convincing to persons who are openminded on the subject." To another writer, Stansbury Hagar of New York City—who apparently had criticized the ruling for infringing on Indians' freedom of religion—Burke wrote,

> If the Snake Dance is included in the dances you have reference to as being sacred or an essential part of a native religion, I am sorry that I can not agree with you that it should be encouraged and perpetuated. There is no better answer to this matter than a letter vol-

untarily written by a real, educated Hopi Indian to the *Coconino Sun* of Flagstaff, Arizona, and, thinking you may not have seen it, a copy is herewith inclosed *[sic]*.[23]

WE HAVE MORE TO SAY BUT WE WILL HOLD IT BACK

The decks were clearly stacked against the official record including the voices of those Native Americans who supported the continued practice of dancing. And yet, a number of letters critical of Burke's circular and policy, and references to continuing dance practices in spite of them, do make their way into the files.

Some Native peoples, according to letters from the superintendents, agents, and farmers themselves, outright refused the reissued restrictions. A "Stockman in Charge" of Indians under Mossman's jurisdiction, A. Pratt from the Porcupine Sub-Station in Shields, North Dakota, wrote Mossman on May 8, 1923, to report a dance held that May 5. Pratt reported that "Peter Black Hawk, a half negro and Albert Walker" were the "two ring leaders" who "invited all the people outside to come urging them to dance, telling them there was no one there to watch them." The organizers noted that "the policeman was in Mandan and the Farmer was in bed, so after 12 o'clock every body danced," he reports. "They danced the Grass dance and Kahomini, during which there was great shouting inside and outside, a regular savage doings." Other file materials also indicate that the dance practices continued. For example, an article in the *Sioux Falls Press* of June 20, 1923, reports on a melee that broke out when a superintendent McGregor ordered Indian office employees and Indian police to stop dancing at the Rosebud reservation. The paper reported, "Eagle Elk and two of his sons were going through one of the ancient tribal dances of the Sioux. There was no self torture, nothing indecent, degrading or demoralizing. The Indians were simply trying to portray a dream as nearly as possible with nothing to shock the sensitiveness of the most fastidious." It adds that when the police intervened, firearms were drawn, but that some of the cooler spectators prevented an outbreak. "One of the chief's sons, however, was manhandled and lodged in jail at Rosebud, where he was held for several hours." The paper notes that a meeting of the General Indian council was called and "resolutions were passed urging the Indian office at Washington to take immediate action in the matter." These and other letters and press reports, then, reference both the direct opposition to the reissued regulations[24] and the continued practice of dance in spite of them.

While these letters record ways some dancers protest the restrictions by ignoring them, other letters record ways that Native American dancers and leaders protested (like the Lomavitu letter) by turning the circular's rhetoric back on itself. A number of letters invert the circular's focus on productivity and waste. For example, the Indians under Mossman's jurisdiction (hardly the "few old Indians who disapprove of the dance" Burke hoped would write letters of support for the antidance circular) railed against the restrictions and the rhetoric surrounding them, taking up the rhetoric of "waste" and "excessive spending" levied by Christian officials and throwing it back at them. A petition received March 19, 1923, from a Committee Appointed by Council of Indians of Cannonball District of Standing Rock Reservation and signed by Claude Killspotted, Red Tomahawk, and James Allyellow pointedly denounced "Superintendents and Missionarys [sic]" who have declared "the Indians dancing" as a hindrance to civilization. These tribal leaders described the hypocrisies inherent in the restrictions on Indian gathering and dancing, given the behavior of Christians in relation to the very issues that the circular denounced. The Indian leaders pointed out that *whites* "indulged" in excessive spending, waste, neglect of stock, and spending too long traveling to and from religious holidays.

These tribal leaders focus first on the charges that Native religious practices lead to waste of time and resources, arguing (even before Christmas became the consumerist feeding frenzy it is today) that white Christians spend plenty of time and money on their religious celebrations. "The three churches in this district have Christmas feast. Some of the members of these Churches leave their homes a week before Christmas and camp around the church and especially the Protestant Episcopal Church the members leave their homes and their stock a week before Christmas and camp around the Church and have meetings nearly a week and neglect their stock. These three Churches have Christmas feast and New Year feast and their members have brought their food that they should keep at home for themselves." The writers thus astutely take up the very rhetoric of waste of time and resources (and neglect of stock) levied against their religious practices and throw it back. They show the inherent bias in the claims that Indians spend more time in religious activity than Christians do. At the same time, their rhetorical tactic, applying the claims levied against Native dance celebrations to Christian religious celebrations, subtly and ironically critiques the very categories of waste and excess bandied about so readily in federal documents.

The tribal leaders next question assertions that participating in dances necessarily leads to property loss and low farming productivity, noting that some of those who participated in Dawes Act allotment plans have fared much worse economically than those who participate in dances. For example, the "native Clergy among the Indians and Catechists who never took part in Indian dancing," they write, "got the patent fee for their land and mortgage their land, bought automobiles and other things which they have no need for. Now their lands are taken from them and are without land. Are homeless." On the other hand, they note, "There are some men who are known as dancers who have good homes, raising cattle, horses, chickens and hogs, and are living good better than church helpers." They conclude, "We have more to say but we will hold it back." These rhetorical turns directly question the claims of economic waste and excess levied against dancers and dancing. They also suggest ways that silence—the refusal to say more, the holding back of words—should be read not as compliance, but as protest.

SEXUAL "IMMORALITY" AND ANTIDANCE RHETORIC

Other Indian writers responding to the antidance circulars blasted officials' preoccupation with what they saw as sexual "immorality" accompanying Indian dances, questioning their assumptions about sexuality and gender.[25]

In this period, the Board of Indian Commissioners apparently received and produced reports claiming that Southwest Indians in particular engaged in "the vilest sexual practices." These reports decried sexual excesses among the Hopi, claiming that secret ceremonies before and after dances forced students to abandon "moral and legal restraints imposed by marital obligations," and recommending adequate supervision of all dances. In 1924, former Indian Service chief officer William E. "Pussyfoot" Johnson cited testimony stating that Zuni girls were "debauched at these dances" and claiming that at one sacred dance every female participant became pregnant. He criticized the frequent fiestas of the Southwest and condemned the Pueblo people for withdrawing their children from school in order to give them a two-year course in sodomy under pagan instructors.[26] Even at the time, Johnson's accusations were seen as outrageous, and most of the correspondence regarding these charges refuted or qualified their implications. While the dances undoubtedly did provide opportunities for young people to hook up, claims of organized sexual rituals or courses were clearly figments of officials' imaginations and fanned by the government as part of the antidance propaganda. Yet concerns about sexual immorality were pounced upon by federal officials in Washington. For example, on November 26, 1930, Burke sent a letter to the Navajo agent at Fort Defiance, asking about "the ceremonial dances of the Indians, the orgies which result from them, etc." He then wrote to seven other agents, explaining that "Information has come to the Office from different sources that the ceremonial dances of the Navajoes [sic] are being converted into orgies where liquor, gambling, and immorality are present." Yet the reports that return from these agents denied these accusations; none report orgies or anything of the like. Some report instances of "men leaving their own wives for other women"; others that "We are forced to admit that the Navajos frequently avoid white man's formality in establishing marriage relations." Yet as the agent at Northern Navajo Agency, Shiprock, New Mexico, explained, "Not many of the Indians are married according to the laws of the State of New Mexico, but almost all of them observe the native ceremonies."

While some Indians writing into the office did express concern about the sexuality that attended ceremonial dances,[27] others vociferously refuted the charges and their implications. In a petition submitted to Burke's office on January 16, 1924, signed by seventeen people from San Ildefonso, New Mexico—including the cacique, governor, and two ex-governors—the writers responded point by point to Johnson's claims. "We do not consider it vile nor degrading to own the bodies God has given us," the leaders wrote in response to charges about their regalia. "Our dances all have significance, and we Indians of San Ildefonso do not know of one that has evil significance, which is more than we can say for some of the white dances some of us have seen." In response to charges of "betraying our young girls in these dances or during our yearly ceremonials," they exclaim:

> We men of this council do not know what is meant by that. We do not force our girls to marry against their wills, and we think that the life of our pueblo will in the main prove that our women are contented with the life of our community, as the men are. Some of our girls who have left the pueblo to work in the city have voluntarily returned. They marry us because they love us and we love them. . . . The womanhood of our pueblo is as sacred to us as the symbolic dances we are trying to defend and preserve, and, for that matter, we hold our manhood sacred too.

Clearly, culturally specific attitudes about sexuality, coupling, marriage, and gender fueled government preoccupation with immorality; these writers took on and threw back at the government the biases in their own presumptions.

THIS WE DO NOT LIKE: RELIGIOUS FREEDOM AND AMERICAN INDIAN DANCE

Native people whose voices are included in the National Archive also took up, with increasing focus, questions of religious freedom, especially as freedom of religion protections were (at least theoretically) extended to Native peoples following passage of the American Indian Citizenship Act in 1924. Officials tried to keep the focus on "waste," lack of "productivity," and "barbarism." But many Indian dancers and leaders instead found in these circulars veiled and overt attacks on their religious practices and rights of self-determination. Officials were forced to respond specifically to charges their policies restricted Native peoples' First Amendment rights to participate in non-Christian religion practices.

In these responses, Burke and other officials display the narrowness of their understanding of religion. In a letter stamped May 22, 1924, from Burke to a Meade Steele, in reference to the Sun Dance, for example, Burke wrote, "Every man can think and believe as he pleases, but his actions must not disregard the rights of others or the good of society in general." He explained, "There is no purpose on the part of this Bureau to curtail the Indian's religious freedom of faith, or practice; but religious belief cannot be accepted as justifying disorderly conduct or a violation of law and the enlightened sentiment of civilization." "Freedom of faith, or practice," then, translates in Burke's understanding only into protecting ways "every man can think and believe as he pleases"—an understanding of religion based in faith and belief, rather than in safeguarding physical, corporeal, ritual practices understood in non-Protestant contexts as central to the practice of religion.

This disconnect over what could constitute "religious practice"—and therefore would fall under the U.S. Constitution's "freedom of religion" clause—was increasingly heightened during this period's intense rhetorical and legal debate surrounding the status of American Indian peoples, and especially Pueblo peoples, in relation to the United States. The status of Pueblo peoples in relation to the United States had been in a state of flux since the region became part of the United States in 1848. At that point, Pueblo peoples, like all inhabitants, were granted U.S. citizenship rights. In 1876, the Supreme Court confirmed this status, ruling that the Pueblo peoples, because of their "civilized" status as people who farmed their land, were not Indians in the legal sense. This meant that Pueblo lands were open to squatters, who encroached in droves. In 1913, the court overturned that decision and ruled that the Pueblo peoples were like other Indians and were wards of the federal government (like children and mentally ill people). The court argued that although sedentary and disposed to peace and industry, the people of the pueblos "are nevertheless Indians in race, customs, and domestic government" who adhere to superstition and fetishism, and who "are essentially a simple, uninformed, and inferior people." This meant that the Pueblo peoples were now eligible for federal assistance, but since they were not U.S. citizens, they were not protected by the First Amendment's guarantee of religious freedom.[28] In 1924, in the wake of thousands of Native peoples' active service during World War I, Congress passed the American Indian Citizenship Act, in which Pueblo and other Indian peoples were given (or imposed with) U.S. citizenship; at this point the Bill of Rights applied to Native Americans.[29]

Many Native American writers whose words are included in the National Archives directly raise questions about the restrictions on Indian ceremonial dance practices that Burke's circular imposes. In a letter received April 16, 1923, from Tama, Iowa, John Morgan (elsewhere named John Witonisee), and Sam Sissewln (elsewhere called Sam Lincoln), wrote to Hubert Work, secretary of the interior, protesting the "printed circular from the commissioner asking us to do away with our feasts and dances, and hold none unless we have permission from the Superintendent." "This we do not like," they write. "We would regard it as an injustice to us to enforce this order with us. We feel it a duty to worship as our fathers taught us and we are told that one of the great principles of this government is that people may worship as they believe to be right." They add, "We would be pleased to hear from you and the commissioner as well. And we do not want to have to ask permission of the Superintendent to hold our meetings."

Other American Indian letter writers explicitly engaged freedom of religion rhetoric, arguing both that they are as Christian as those decrying their "paganism," and that at any rate they have the constitutional right to practice their religion, whatever it may be. In January 1925, Eufracio Trujillo, the governor of the Nambe Pueblo, New Mexico, along with officers of the San Juan, Santa Clara, San Ildefonso, and Tesuque Pueblos, circulated a letter arguing that "there are some people who are trying to destroy and make us abandon our religion, which is so dear to us, as is, and will be to any other Race or Nation of the earth surface." "In fact we Pueblo Indians are Christians," Trujillo wrote,

> Those same people who accuse us of being pagans, are no more
> Christians than we are. They belong to the same church, we belong,
> and we belong to the same church they belong. And in other
> words they practice the same religion, ceremonies as we do, and
> dance as we do, which we offer to prove they are not wicked as
> they claim.

The letter stated further, "we want to keep our Religion as any other white people would like to keep his." And furthermore, it said, the U.S. Constitution "gives freedom and liberty to all the people of the U.S. regardless to the kind of his creed. . . . We think and say that we are entitled to all the rights and the same privilege as other people have in the United States . . . to keep and carry out our religion."[30]

WE WORSHIP OUR GOD IN OUR OWN WAY

Other letters from Native American leaders, rather than stressing their identity as Christians in arguing for religious freedom, instead argued for Native rights to distinctly separate religious practices. Another letter, from Santo Domingo Pueblo Governor Feliciano Tenorio, sent to the Southern Pueblo Day School Superintendent H. P. Marble, March 18, 1923, explained, "We are troubled by your letter of March 12th enclosing a letter from Commissioner Charles H. Burke. These letters threaten us about our dances and religious ceremonies. . . . And Commissioner Burke says he gives us one year to give up our ceremonies for our free will, and that if we don't he will use force which he says he has the power to do." Tenorio continues:

You tell us to send you a reply. Since as far back as our memory
goes, we have been living happily in our old ways. Our dances,
songs, and gift festivals are part of our life. They are the best
part of our lifes. They are our religion. They are not wicked and
they do not make us lazy as Commissioner Burke says. We do not
understand why this threat should be made against us. Our white
friends come and are now our guests. We do not take their money
but we are glad to have them listen to our songs and watch our
dances and processions. They tell us we do beautiful things. We
do not know whether that is true, but we know that we do not do
bad things. We worship our God in our own way.

And we have always believed that the laws of the United States
gave us a promise that our religious observances should be free.
We believe that this law gives us the same religious freedom as our
white brothers. We know that the treaty of Guadalupe Hidalgo
promised that we should not be disturbed in our religious ceremonies. . . . Now we are told that the Indian Commissioner has power
to forbid our religion. And we are threatened with force unless we
give up what is just as sacred to us as our life itself.

Government officials attempted to dismiss letters like Tenorio's by claiming it
and another similar to it "were prepared by someone outside the pueblo and
submitted to be copied and signed by the officials of the various pueblos." Yet
various other letters in the file suggest that whatever editing help "someone
outside the pueblo" may have provided in drafting some of these letters, protest
against Burke's circular was instigated by the people themselves.[31]

CEREMONIAL PRACTICE AND SELF-DETERMINATION

Still other letters of protest and records of meetings pressed particularly incisively against Burke's understandings of religion by refuting governmental
claims that the dance gatherings were harmful, and insisting instead on the importance of the relations to land and water they affirm. On June 7, 1923—during
Prohibition—Superintendent T. F. McCormick from Arizona wrote Burke with
background information on a letter written by Antonio Lopez, whom the superintendent identified as a Papago Indian from Santa Rosa. McCormick called
Lopez "an uneducated Indian," but noted his friendship with other leaders
"opposed to the government supervision" and added that he makes Tiswin,
a wine, every year. He explained how Lopez and others held that "I have no
right to interfere in their fiesta" and how he has "not sufficient Police force to
stop it." McCormick included a transcript from a conference held August 18,
1923, regarding the dance circulars and the Tiswin Fiesta, at which a number of

participants spoke out against the restrictions. At the center of this transcript, and of other records of protest, is a concern with the relation to land and water the dances enact and the restrictions interfere with. These Tiswin Fiesta participants understand their Fiesta participation to be central to the making of rain and see the restrictions on the Fiesta as a threat to that creation, with adverse affects for not only themselves and their crops, but for all in the region. For example, one speaker, Tapia, is recorded as insisting not on the harmlessness of his fiesta, but rather on its continuing religious and practical importance and effectiveness. "We have been living something that has been handed down by different people and this fiesta is given us to make it rain and raise crops for ourselves. This custom is benefit to our children, our women and ourselves and we make this tiswin to make rains for our crops," he is recorded as saying. "We are going to keep up this custom as we know this is right, because it really rains—on that account our fields are looking fine. The rains that come on account of the fiesta are benefit to every body that is here because they put in their crops and enjoy cleaning them and keeping them in shape." Another speaker, from Quajate, concurred, stating "it is true we get a good deal of benefit from these customs, because white people do not know that it really rains when we give these customs. Since I have lived here I have watched this fiesta, which was handed from God—to make tiswin. It really rains on that day . . . the white people ought to leave us alone. The white men have their own customs—this is ours and we cannot give it up."

Others at the hearing insisted even more directly on the fiesta as essential as religious practice. Anton, from Quajate, explained, "We all know there is a God. He created us in this desert and left us here. When God made this desert He left us here without rain or water. I think that God's plan was for us to get this fruit and mix it up. This is not our custom—but it is a custom set especially for us by God." He added, "If we do not raise this no one is going to help us with this food." The references to God, however, occur in the context of maintaining proper religious *practices*—which require particular actions—rather than in the context of affirming a religious *belief*.

In large part, the discussion here and elsewhere in the BIA files focuses not on rights or on religious freedom as abstract concepts, but rather on the practical and tangible effects that restrictions on the people's religious practices will have, especially practices that maintain a proper relationship to rain, to the land, and to farming.

THE BURSUM BILL AND LAND RIGHTS

As these responses suggest, tribal dancers and leaders connected the restrictions on religious practices directly to Native peoples' relation to the land and to water—both so central in the Southwest. In curtailing ceremonial practices that connected people to particular lands and ensured adequate rainfall, the dance restrictions impacted Native American land and water rights; the dance restrictions were thus (once again) tied to a loss of Native control of Indian lands and water.

The most vocal outcry connecting the antidance circulars and Indian land and water rights occurred when some Native dancers, and many Indian rights activists, saw links between this newly reissued and widely disseminated "TO ALL INDIANS" letter and legal battles over rights to Pueblo lands that were raging at the time. In 1922, a year before Burke's "TO ALL INDIANS" letter, a bill that was to address the issue of non-Indian squatters on Pueblo lands—by granting title to nearly sixty thousand acres to the squatters—was introduced in Congress and passed by the Senate. When word of the so-called Bursum Bill got out, the General Federation of Women's Clubs, the All-Indian Pueblo Council, and various other groups—including those involved in the arts and the arts colonies—successfully forced the Senate to recall the bill. Their actions led to the passage of the Pueblo Indian Lands Act in 1924, which forced some squatters to leave and provided some compensation for lost land.[32]

Non-Native artists and activists in the Southwest were outraged at the links they saw between Burke's federal Indian "dance reform" policies and the Bursum Bill they had recently thwarted in Congress. These activists saw in Burke's federal Indian "dance reform" a desire to reinstate the Bursum Bill's attempt to rob Pueblo peoples of their land. Activists argued that having failed with the Bursum Bill, the government followed a less obvious line of attack on religious practices that would "destroy the whole Pueblo system and drag from under the Indian's feet the last acre of their lands" (Philp, *John Collier's Crusade,* 55–70). They argued persuasively that legal debate and rhetoric about Indian dancing was intricately tied to debates about land ownership, and that its primary aim was not protecting Indian peoples from themselves, as the officials claimed, but rather blatant, greedy, self-interest.

DEBATING THE SHOWING OF INDIAN DANCE

Alongside these debates about ceremonial Indian dance came both protest and support for Indian dance as "public performance." As federal officials continued to restrict Native American ceremonial dance practices, including those seen by tourists in the Southwest, they meanwhile continued to permit and even promote the display of dancing in Indian exhibitions, calling them an enjoyable attraction for government officials in Washington, even as several Native dancers and leaders themselves spoke out against them in the very same terms the government used: for the waste of time they cost those participating, and the harm they caused by perpetuating images of Indians as violent. This policy of enabling spectacle dance thus, as it had in the previous decades, continued to suggest that, when disarticulated from homeland and ceremonial context, Indian dance exhibitions posed no threat to governmental Indian policy. Federal policy hereby continued to belie a governmental perception of theatrical production as entirely separate from ceremonial practice.

Several letters from Indian leaders disapproving of the shows, and distraught at the dangers they saw them engendering, made it into the National Archive files. Some approach the topic from the position of Christianized Indians adhering wholeheartedly to the "Message"—yet dismayed that the restrictions on dancing hadn't been applied to exhibitions. Eugene Standing Elk, from Tongue River in Lame Deer, Montana, wrote to Burke on May 23, 1923, decrying the participation of Indians in exhibitions—and the government's approval of it.[33] In the letter, dictated to Mrs. Petter, the wife of the missionary, Standing Elk first established his position in his community and in relation to federal policy, noting he "approved every word of Burke's 'Message.'" He added, "I was formerly a great dancer. I was proud of my position as chief in the tribe. I was proud in public speaking, I was proud in the dance, and of many other vanities. But I have changed. God who gave us His Word brought about a change in me and I thank him for it." Standing Elk goes on to explain his regret that his people "insist as much on everything that is Indian, and that they take so slowly to the higher standards of life of the white people." He then explained the reason for his letter. "It grieves me that so soon after our hearts were hushed by the import of your 'Message,' a man came here to take fourteen of our people for just such an exhibition in Washington as your letter disapproved. . . . I understand they were given leave of absence in pay and taken to Washington D.C. to do the very thing your 'Message' disapproves, a display of their old time customs at public gatherings by whites." Standing Elk then quoted Burke's "Message," noting that participation in this exhibition has led to the very "neglect of crops" Burke warned against. "One of those who went plowed his ground but did not finish sowing, one sowed without first plowing in his haste to go," he wrote. Standing Elk's position, asking the government to adhere to the spirit and letter of its own message, saw as much ill in the exhibition of "old time customs at public gatherings by whites" as the government sees in the dance gatherings held on reservations.

On May 21, 1923, writer Zitkala-Sa—signed as "(Mrs.) Gertrude Bonnin (Zitkala-Sa)"—likewise decried the public exhibition of Indian dance, here not out of a Christian worldview or explicit support for the antidance circular. Instead, she sensed danger for the public attitude toward Indians in the announcement she had seen for a rodeo featuring scalp dances, and invoked the anti–Indian dance tenor of the day to call on the government to restrict exhibition dances. Zitkala-Sa too first established her relation to her community as "an enrolled member of the Sioux Tribe of Indians" who had "devoted many years of my life in working for the betterment of conditions among all Indian people." She then raised questions about announcements in the Washington *Post* and *Star* of an upcoming rodeo said to feature scalp dances and a lecture on scalping:

> The reproduction of scalp dances now, whether for amusement chiefly or for money making purposes by the promoters, can have but one ultimate result, so far as the Indians of America are concerned, and that is detrimental to them. It will tend to rouse hatred in the hearts of the people who may witness the same and yet it is with these very same people that the Indian of today must live.

Zitkala-Sa noted that "the few pennies paid to the Indians who may take part in these proposed shows cannot begin to compensate the thousands of other Indians who may be damaged thereby," and argued further that putting on the scalp dance in this way was "a drawing card, whereby the white man will again profit." "I believe the Indians' case is entitled to the protection of its guardian," she wrote. "I therefore respectfully ask that you take such action as the urgency of the case seems to demand in protecting these wards of the Nation against this immediate and impending danger from their exploitation. If necessary the promoters should be enjoined from putting on any exhibition which is liable to result in damage to the Indian wards."

While all of these voices are preserved in the national record, none of the positions calling for restrictions on Indian dance performed for non-Indian audiences were taken seriously. The superintendent at the Tongue River Agency, who forwarded Standing Elk's letter to Burke with the usual note evaluating Standing Elk's worthiness, defended the exhibition Indians' trip to Washington. "The majority of the party went not for the pleasure that they would get out of an Indian dance, but that they might have the pleasure of a trip to Washington, and also that they might have a talk with the Office about matters pertaining to the Tribe. The office is in better position than I am to say whether there was anything harmful in the exhibition staged by Mr. Evans." In a letter to Secretary of the Interior Hubert Work the previous month (May 29, 1923), Burke himself had approved and announced the "special exhibition" directed by Evans. Burke writes how the exhibition will include "old-time teepees" in "the village which is a part of the show," and how "the Indians are mostly of the type of what we call real Indians." He adds how "the seeing of these Indians in their tepees and as they would be seen on a reservation is an attraction that I am very sure the President and his friends would greatly enjoy," and mentions his plan to "invite members of the Supreme Court and other prominent officials, including the officials of the Interior department." When Burke responds to Standing Elk's protest of this exhibition, Burke calls the letter "interesting" and says he'd like to meet Standing Elk, but sidesteps addressing his concerns. In response to Zitkala-Sa's letter, Work refused any action, writing:

> It is my understanding that the Indians to be brought here for the proposed exposition are citizens and, therefore, free to take part the same as any white citizens, and that the Government has assumed no responsibility, financial or otherwise, for their presence and participation in the program mentioned.
>
> Under these circumstances, Departmental interference hardly seems justified.

Of course, the "Message" to all Indians sent three months earlier, with veiled threats as to the continuation of dancing at gatherings or for ceremonial purposes, applied to Indians who were citizens as well. Even Lomavitu's letter, while extolled as the voice of a "real Hopi Indian" writing in support of the "TO ALL INDIANS" message, engenders no enforced attempts to curtail the tourist excursions to see the Snake Dance. The government's de facto position on the matter seems to have been that Indian dance, when performed as part of an exhibition controlled by white promoters and/or for the pleasures of white tourists or government leaders, was not only permissible but promotable.

In other words, in the 1920s as in the late 1890s, the government's policy was to promote staged and exhibition dancing—including that seen by some Native peoples as dangerous in its repercussions—while curtailing ceremonial dancing understood by the people dancing to establish relation to ancestors, land, and water. Stage dancing was not seen to pose a threat to audience members, who could continue to be exposed to real, yet supposedly ineffectual, Native peoples and dances. Instead, their display performed and confirmed this image of them as militarily and spiritually contained, and removed from relation to land. Nor did this exhibition display threaten American values of productivity. This remained true even though, as the letters of protest cited above point out, the exhibitions and festivals took Indians away from their crops for many days and led to neglect of crops even more than the reservation gatherings did. Its value as entertainment—an enjoyable attraction for Supreme Court justices and Interior Department officials—mediated against it as waste.

DO WE NOT STILL NEED OUR INDIANS? THE VALUE OF INDIAN ARTS

Indian Rights activists, who were often also part of the arts colonies flourishing in the Southwest in the 1920s, vociferously railed against the antidance circulars, decrying their infringements on freedom of religion and their disregard for Native peoples and Native culture. They scoffed at the ulterior motives they saw behind governmental claims of paternalism, and instead connected the antidance restrictions to federal land-grab legislation. While government officials stressed the supposed harm ceremonial dances posed to Native American people, the activists instead focused on the benefits the dances afforded viewers. In doing so, on the one hand, they defiantly refused continuing governmental attempts to eradicate Native culture and religion outright, insisting it be enabled and valued as part of American culture. At the same time, their well-intentioned (and, for the period, radical) activism invoked the very same rhetoric the government itself deployed. The insistence of modernist artists[34] on the use of American Indian art, music, dance—for America, for tourists, and particularly for the inspiration of white modernist artists and dancers such as themselves—invokes, however inadvertently, the same rhetoric of use-value the government deployed in decrying Native ceremonial dances' waste and in promoting exhibition dancing taken out of ceremonial context and put on display for the entertainment of government officials. It also compounds ideas of cultural material as available to all for the taking, and about the resulting artistic creations as about individual artistic expression. Just as the government saw spectacle dancing as without political or spiritual connection to ceremonial dancing, artists, gleaning inspiration from these ceremonial dances for their own expressive art works, also compounded notions of art—including stage dance—as disarticulated from potent, tribally specific religious/spiritual practices with particular effects on the world.

One of the most fervent of these artist-activists was modernist writer Mary Austin, author of, among numerous other American Indian–themed literary works, the play *The Arrow Maker* (1911) and the poetry/manifesto *The American Rhythm* (1923). This most well-known and comprehensive book of Austin's "reexpressed" Native American songs as modern free verse poetry and argued for the centrality of American Indian culture to American arts, and especially of Native American songs and ritual dances to American poetic expression.[35] Austin was particularly tireless in her devotion to Indian welfare and successful at rallying for defeat of the Bursum Bill and bringing pressure to bear on Burke. Her ardent, prolific voice on "Indian reform" exemplifies artists' rhetoric of the era.

Austin, like many other activists in this period, decried the government dance ban not only because of its infringements on religious freedom and its spurious connection to land legislation. She also, perhaps even more stridently, argued for the entertainment and artistic value of Native culture. Some suggested the value of this to Native peoples themselves. Anthropologist Frederick Webb Hodge, for example, wrote in 1923 that Indian ceremonies were useful to Indians because they often combine "religious customs and entertainment" and as such "are often uplifting to the members of the tribes performing them."[36] Others, including Austin, argued for the preservation of Pueblo culture not so much for the good it did the Pueblo peoples, but particularly for the benefits it accrued for the "average American" as diversion. In a January 17, 1923, speech before the national Popular Government League on the Bursum Bill, Austin declared:

> But there is another valuation of the Pueblenos which must not be overlooked, that is, their value to the average American. I mean their *value as a diversion, as a spectacle, as a form of entertainment, peculiarly our own,* not too easily accessible to make them common, but just far enough removed to make seeing them one of the few remaining great American adventures. . . . Is not the Indian inheritance which our children have quite as precious to them and infinitely more valuable than the European inheritance of ogres and giant killers and fairies? Do we not still need our Indians, if for no other purpose than to keep us in this annual flight from complexity to simplicity, from asphalt and machinery and wage earning to camp fire and bed and open trail? . . .
>
> All Indian life, and especially the Pueblo life, is a national asset, in much the same way that the Grand Canyon, Yosemite and the Garden of the Gods are national assets, something in which we have a stake both of pride and enjoyment.[37] (emphasis added)

In this speech, Austin echoed and promoted the era's fascination with an Indian life—like the land itself—as available for the education and entertainment of non-Indians. During the first two decades of this century, as historian Philip Deloria has incisively outlined, various Indian programs were becoming central facets of fraternal societies and summer camps and increasingly integral to the growing scouting movement.[38] Perhaps the most dramatic example of a white group's fascination with and presumptions about their own access to Indian dance comes in the 1921 creation of the "Smokis" of Prescott, Arizona. This group, founded by the town's Chamber of Commerce as a tourist event, was comprised of white men who performed an annual "Snake Dance" based on the Hopi ceremonial. When Burke's 1923 antidance letter surfaced, the outrage it engendered was, in part, on behalf of these "Smoki" snake dancers who it was feared would also have to stop their dances.[39] Its threat to white men who wished to stage themselves as Indians in a dramatic spectacle, here, is at the root of some protestors' outrage.

Rather than decrying Indian dance as wasteful and unproductive—and therefore harmful to Native peoples themselves—as the officials and missionaries did, modernist artists and activists in the Southwest argued for the dance as useful and productive, especially for non-Native artists and for American identity. This rhetoric worked strategically to counter the federal antidance rhetoric within its own worldview, where use and productivity reigned, using its tools against itself. In this way it was a savvy political move on the part of protestors. At the same time, though, the pronouncements of Indian dance's usefulness as educational, psychological, and artistic tool for both Native and non-Native Americans reflected and reinforced the officials' Christian-influenced, capitalist-based, rationalistic point of view in ways that continued to distort the worldviews held in and through the dancing.

This move to promote the use-value of Native arts—primarily to non-Native viewers and consumers—became explicit in Austin's campaigning in the late 1920s. One way to promote ceremonial dance's value, Austin suggested, would be to theatricalize it as Indian dance-drama. In a 1927 article in *The Nation,* Austin called on "creative workers" to transform Pueblo religious ceremony into aesthetic and dramatic form. Austin argues that creative workers had already begun to undertake what she called this "evolution" of Indian dance from creed and myth into drama. "Already the incursive interest of creative workers occupies itself with the separation of Indian dancing from its tribal elements in order to save it for aesthetic service, as Greek drama was saved."[40] In 1930, she repeats this view, writing "Amerind drama is ready, is trembling on the verge, for that normal progression away from religious ceremonialism toward the stage, which Greek drama accomplished so successfully." She writes, "If the American stage were opened to it, Amerind drama would flow naturally, as Negro dramatic talent flows, toward legitimate theatrical expression."[41]

On the one hand, Austin was writing against the view that Indian subjects are not adequate in and of themselves as "art." In 1926, the Northern Pueblo Agency had circulated a letter to Indian Day School teachers instructing teachers not to "place paper, pencils or water colors in the hands of Indian children and turn them loose to draw according to their own ideas." The problem with this approach, the letter states, is that "the pictures drawn are always Indians, Indian dances, horses, etc." "This is not teaching in the true sense," the letter states. "I am not in favor of this miscellaneous Indian art which is not an art, but a simple tendency of the Indian mind left to follow its own discretions." It recommends "that no pictures of Indian dances, Indian customs, warriors, etc. be permitted to be encouraged."[42] Austin repeatedly derides this approach and defends representations of Indian culture as not only adequate but essential to American art.

Yet at the same time, Austin's description is rife with problems. In writing about Indian art as a "natural expression," she rehearses images of Indians as primitive and natural. In describing a "normal progression away from religious ceremonialism toward the stage," she reiterates ideas about Native peoples stuck in the past along a linear time line, here in need of progression away from their religious practices. By arguing for the "separation of Indian dancing from its tribal elements in order to save it for aesthetic service" by "creative workers," she rehearses attitudes (including that of the day school official) that what

Indians themselves produce is, on its own, insufficient, and instead needs the intervention of artists to realize its potential.

While Austin's presumptions about staged dance-drama as part of a "natural progression" away from ceremonial dance are troublesome, she nonetheless presents an interesting perspective on the "meaning and power" Indian dancing maintains on stages. Unlike the government—and like Zitkala-Sa—Austin suggests that dance presented to audiences is more than just a "show" and has cultural, artistic, spiritual import when on stage as when off. She dismisses audience members' "sentimental paralysis" in growing tearful "over the frightful violence that is done to Indian integrity by making a public spectacle of religious drama," and chides public opinion that held that "apart from its tribal significance Indian dancing will cease to have meaning and power." Her approach is tactical: she scoffs at the "average American" for not realizing that "with his and the government's connivance, a steady propaganda has been going on for the past thirty years to overcome both the religious and the art values of Amerind drama." She derides not only "our Governmental effort to wipe out Indian culture as such" and audiences that see Indian dance as objectionable, but also "the trivial incapacity of another part of the same audience to see it only as a 'show.'"[43] She instead champions dramatic stage treatments of Indian culture. Her tactic, though, is not to promote the production of these dance-dramas by Native peoples themselves. Instead, she calls on "the Dramatic Departments of our Universities" to mine this "rich new field." The intent is, like the government's, steeped in paternalism: to protect American Indians from the loss of their culture (due to government degradation of it), American artists and universities should step in and make use of it.

Austin's second, related, tactic for promoting the use, and one that will become increasingly central to the legal and cultural rhetoric surrounding Indian dance, is to promote the marketing of Indian arts. The 1928 editorial cited above suggests, after hearing Austin's talk, that "to preserve the Indian art as something alive the museum will not do." Instead, it says, this preservation of art "can be done only through the market place, by buying and continuing to buy the product of Indian artists. And if the best is bought the best will be produced." The logic here, again, is dependent on understandings of Indian art as useful and productive within a capitalist framework. First, Indian art is important to American art because of the use that artists and enthusiasts make of authentic and natural Indian artistic production. It is important because of what it offers American artists in terms of a rhythmic expression of the land. But this use can be guaranteed if connoisseurs of Indian art buy it, for their purchase of it will encourage Indians to keep making it, so that it will be there for non-Indian artists to make use of. The successful promotion of Indian arts in the capitalist marketplace, in other words, is presented as both justification for the importance of this art and a way of perpetuating it so that it will be alive and available to collectors, enthusiasts, and artists.[44]

INDIAN ARTS AND CRAFTS

With these growing endorsements of the value of Indian arts and crafts came two important—and related—legislative moves. Following desires "to make the art work of the Indians profitable" and thereby to encourage Indians to keep producing quality products, legislation designed to promote the production and sale of Indian products was introduced in Congress. It was mired in bureaucracy and debate, but in 1935, Congress authorized creation of an Indian Arts and Crafts Board "to promote the economic welfare of the Indian tribes and the Indian wards of the government through the development of Indian arts and crafts and the expansion of the market for the products of Indian art and craftsmanship" (Prucha, *Documents,* 229). This legislation was intended to encourage production of salable objects like pots, baskets, and blankets, and not dances per se. All the same, it accompanied and influenced understandings of dance as artistic material, entertaining and available to those who might wish to make use of it, and of the curtailment of it as "artistic crime."

In the midst of this debate, a new Indian commissioner, John Collier, repealed the dance restrictions that had been on the books since 1884. On January 4, 1934, Collier issued Circular no. 2970, entitled "Indian Religious Freedom and Indian Culture." In it, he writes, "No interference with Indian religious life or ceremonial expression will hereafter be tolerated. The cultural liberty of Indians is in all respects to be considered equal to that of any non-Indian group" (Prucha, *Great Father,* 951).

The federal government, in other words, sanctioned American Indian ceremonial practices as religious practices precisely at the point when popular and federal understandings most vociferously promoted the value of Native American cultural production as art for public entertainment, inspiration, and consumption. Just as the government encouraged *Buffalo Bill's Wild West* to stage Indians as a way of curtailing the threat of "Ghost dancers" in the 1890s, in the early 1930s, activists, artists, and the U.S. government encouraged the production of Indian art—including dance—so successfully that rhetoric surrounding it as harmful and wasteful was deflected. This connection is written into the very repeal of the dance restrictions themselves: as part of Circular no. 2970's directive safeguarding Indian religious ceremonial expression, Collier writes that Indian arts and crafts are to be "prized, nourished, and honored." Collier himself thus links the acceptability of Indian religious dances with the rise of respect for Indian arts and crafts.

II.

TWENTIETH-CENTURY MODERN DANCE

Authentic Themes: Modern Dancers and American Indians in the 1920s and 1930s

The function of the artist is to use authentic themes, as seeds from which to produce an art creation of his own.

▸ *Ted Shawn,* The American Ballet

Early modern dance choreographers were outraged by the federal circulars seeking to curtail Native American dance. Ted Shawn, after reading Commissioner of Indian Affairs Charles Burke's 1923 "TO ALL INDIANS" letter, wrote:

> There has been no governmental recognition of the art of dance as being worth preserving or recording. On the contrary, the bureaucratic mind being what it is, the dancing of the Indians is looked upon as degrading, morally and industrially, and veiled threats in the form of letters from the Indian Commissioner, one of which I have read, indicate an official intention to blot out such remnants as still exist. This is nothing short of a great artistic crime. The art of the dance is the fundamental art of the human race, and it is of greater importance that we preserve and record the authentic dances of the Indians now alive than that we preserve all their other arts. (*American Ballet,* 15–16)

Shawn explains that Indian dance ought to be preserved "Now that the Indian as a physical menace is hardly more than a memory of our grandparents" (15). He adds, "This, surely, is one great charge laid upon the American dancers—to study, record and translate the dance art of the Indian to present and future generations" (20).

Shawn's and other modern dance choreographers' championing of Native American dance came at a time when other dance enthusiasts still dismissed it as savage and degenerate.[1] Their opposition directly challenged both that viewpoint and government policy that sought to restrict Native American ceremonial dance practices as wasteful and degrading. It also supported their own passions and interests as modern dancers.

During the 1920s and 1930s, the interest of Shawn and other modern dancers in American Indian dance blossomed, in particular, in relation to increasingly available American Indian dance in the Southwest. Dancers and choreographers, including Shawn and Martha Graham, visited the area and the arts colonies at Taos and Santa Fe and traveled to the pueblos on feast days to watch ceremonial dances. Arrell Morgan Gibson writes how "dancers studied Pueblo terpsichorean routines in search of fresh, innovative motions, rhythms, beats, and style to add to their dance repertoire."[2] He adds that "The mysticism and symbolism of Native American dance fascinated many of the observers, particularly the explanation that the Indian dance rhythm follows the beat of the human heart" (*Sante Fe and Taos Colonies,* 97). As Southwest Indian dance came to signal an invented authentic, but disappearing, Indianness for tourists, artists, and intellectuals, it fascinated and inspired choreographers.

For example, in 1914 Shawn toured as a dancer at station stops along the Santa Fe Railroad, where he came into contact with Native Americans. That same year, he staged himself as an Aztec youth in a narrative he'd researched by reading William Prescott's *The History of the Conquest of Mexico* and auditioned for Ruth St. Denis's company.[3] A year later, Shawn and St. Denis formed Denishawn, considered a cornerstone of American modern dance history. In 1917, Shawn premiered *Invocation to the Thunderbird,* which remained in his solo repertoire until the early 1950s. As scholar Jane Sherman has outlined, Shawn's interest in American Indian dance material continued for years and infused his entire career ("American Indian Imagery," 369). Shawn described how his second ballet, the 1923 *Feather of the Dawn,* was based on versions of eight different Hopi rituals, which he performed wearing "costumes" purchased from the Indians. In January 1924, he saw "a real and complete dance ceremony, in the pueblo of Isleta" (*American Ballet,* 16). When Shawn formed his company of Men Dancers in the 1930s, the "Indian" material he'd developed via his viewings in the Southwest opened the program. In 1931, on his first tour on his own, the program included his solo "Zuni Ghost Dance" and the piece "Osage-Pawnee Dance of Greeting."[4]

Martha Graham was likewise entranced by Native American dance in the Southwest and, like Shawn, engaged with it at the start of her career. In 1930, while driving back to the East Coast after performing in California, she came across the Penitente Indians of New Mexico. Inspired by their religious practices, she premiered *Primitive Mysteries* in 1931. A year later she received a Guggenheim fellowship that financed a summer spent watching Native American dances of the Southwest. That summer, as writer Mary Austin's guest, she was presented to Santa Fe and Taos colony members and taken to observe the Santo Domingo Pueblo Corn Dance where, Gibson writes, she was "awed at the powerful nativistic spectacle" (*Santa Fe and Taos Colonies,* 97).

Watching Southwest Indian dance inspired Erick Hawkins at the start of his career as well. He writes how in the mid-thirties he took a summer off from dancing and drove around the Southwest "ferreting out work of every dance given that summer in New Mexico and Arizona."[5] He saw Corn Dances at Zia Pueblo, a two-day Zuni Rain Dance ritual, and dances at the Hopi village of Mishongnovi. A number of his later pieces work to translate his experiences to the modern dance stage, including *Plains Daybreak, Ritual of the Descent, Black Lake,* and *Killer of Enemies.*

A lifelong fascination with American Indian culture and dance also infused Lester Horton's choreography from this early period on. He began his career working with Indian material, staging "Indian" pageants, starring himself and his dancers as Indians. Horton's major theatrical debut, in 1926, was in *The Song of Hiawatha,* a pageant based on Henry W. Longfellow's 1855 epic fantasy of Indian assimilation and disappearance. Moving from Indiana to California, he performed in and directed this pageant throughout the state in 1928 and 1929 and later directed high school pageants on Indian themes. In 1931, he presented *Kootenai War Dance (American Indian)* at the Argus Bowl and in 1932 *Takwish, the Star Maker,* based on California Indian folklore, at the Little Theater of the Verdugos near Los Angeles, where he also presented various "Pueblo Indian" dances. A program for the July 7, 1933, Horton and Dance Group performance at this venue lists a "Pueblo Indian" section including a *Corn Dance, Hoop Dance, Eagle Dance, Devil Dance* (danced by Horton), and *War Dance.*[6] In 1934 he used music by Homer Grunn—who had done the music for Shawn's *Xochitl*—in his *Painted Desert,* and in 1935 his *Mound Builders* and *Rain Quest* reprised Indigenous themes.[7] When Horton regrouped his dance theater company in 1948, he opened the program with *Totem Incantation,* a "dance based upon coming of age ceremonies among North American Indian groups."[8]

This chapter analyzes this groundswell of U.S. choreographers' fascination with Native American dance in the context of federal Indian policies of the 1920s and 1930s. On the one hand, these modern dancers provided important political resistance to blatantly racist federal circulars. Yet at the same time, they also subtly reinforced the circulars' focus on "waste" and "use" by themselves arguing for Native American dance's use-value, to them and to America, as art. This approach, the chapter suggests, is linked to passage of the American Indian Arts and Crafts Act of 1935. Just as legislating the importance of American Indian art reinforced Native American dance's value, and availability, primarily to individual non–Native American collectors, rather than focusing on it as religious, ceremonial, or healing practice for Native peoples, so too did Indian-inspired choreography primarily (though not entirely) reinforce its value outside of Native American communities. To explore the possibilities, and the problems, in the interest of early modern dancers in Native American dance, this chapter focuses on the approaches of both Ted Shawn and Lester Horton in depth. It analyzes Shawn's use of the "full-blooded masculine vigour" associated with Indian dancing, examining how he staged himself and his Men Dancers as Indians in shortened versions of the Indian dances he'd seen as a way of negotiating issues of masculinity and sexuality in an art form that faced charges of effeminacy. Despite his respect for and interest in Native American culture, he removed those dances from the physical, spiritual, and legal contexts in which they are practiced, and made use of them as source of artistic fodder in "Indian" dance pieces expressing what he saw as "natural" internal characteristics of masculinity, in keeping with Delsarte's Christian-based philosophy of movement as expression of inner truth. His career, in turn, has come to be read as central to the history of modern dance in America. Lester Horton's productions and practices also drew on his ideas about American Indian dance culture, and reflect some similar problems. Unlike Shawn, however, Horton worked firsthand with Native people and explored Native dance more in terms of what it has to offer theater process and practice than as material for accessing individual expression or agendas. Like radical and leftist dance makers also working more to affect political change than to express interiority, as more strictly modernist modern dancers of the era were doing, Horton today hardly figures in dominant understandings of modern dance history.

AMERICANIZING DANCE AND AMERICAN INDIAN CITIZENSHIP

In one way, the impulse to preserve American Indian dance seen in Shawn's outrage at Burke's letter repeated rhetoric prevalent from before the turn of the nineteenth century. In his 1929 *Gods Who Dance,* Shawn wrote, "With the mechanical device of the motion picture so marvelously adapted to preserving a record of human movement, there is now no excuse for us not to preserve the dances of all these fast vanishing tribes of our own."[9] By reiterating descriptions of "fast vanishing tribes" and "our" mandate to preserve them, and in calling for artists to "preserve and record the authentic dances of the Indians now alive," Shawn, like numerous other American officials, scholars, artists, and intellectuals, reinforces an (inadvertently wishful?) idea that Native peoples are, indeed, on the verge of extinction. Horton, too, argued for implicitly non-Native dancers to preserve American Indian dance. In a 1929 article on "American Indian Dancing," Horton writes, "If dancers would make an effort, to preserve this beauty which exists literally at our back doors, something magnificent might be born. A dance can be built upon these art forms that would be truly representative of this great country, something new and fundamental."[10]

Shawn's and Horton's moves to claim the "Indian" as "truly representative" and authentically Americanizing also took part in a shift in the twenties and thirties toward seeing Indians as validating and consolidating America through their identities as original Americans. The explicit goal of Shawn and other dancers of the era, as the title to Shawn's 1926 *The American Ballet* indicates—and as Julia L. Foulkes has recently discussed—was to validate a distinctly American dance tradition.[11] In this book, Shawn calls for an American dance tradition distinct from the ballet traditions of Russia and France, and outlines his interest in American Indian dance as an American dance form. As literary scholar Walter Benn Michaels notes, this move to see Indians as intrinsically American was characteristic of the era.[12] Rather than simply mourned as disappeared, here the Indian was instead heralded as sign of and figure for a distinct American culture, albeit one, as in the previous century, still disappearing—this time through Indians' assimilation into American citizenry. This rhetorical and legal identification with the Indian *as* American culminated in 1924 with passage of the Indian Citizenship Act, in which Native peoples were given (or imposed with) U.S. citizenship.[13] In the context of Native American history, of course, a heralding of America and a desire to consolidate American identity itself served to affirm and consolidate the successful colonization of Indigenous people and land. Shawn's and Horton's acts of "dancing Indian" were also part of an American tradition of consolidating power and identity by "playing Indian," as Deloria has persuasively demonstrated.

IGNORING ALL HINTS: PRIVILEGE AND PRESUMPTIONS ABOUT RIGHTS TO KNOWLEDGE

Behind modern dancers' interest in Native arts and dances lay assumptions about non–Native Americans' right to knowledge about Indian peoples and cultures, assumptions performed particularly dramatically at this time in relation to the Southwest. The artistic and touristic practices of the 1920s and 1930s implied not only that Southwest landscape and scenery, but also Indian peoples and practices, were available to viewers in a primarily visual capitalist economy.[14] The call for the recording and preservation of Indian dance was connected to its availability to non-Indian enthusiasts, and to its use to artists, for the edification and entertainment of, primarily, non-Indian peoples. And the call for its role as artistic inspiration, fodder for dance and other artists' creative endeavors, was connected to this belief in its availability to all. This belief was itself rooted in Christianity's assumptions about the importance of "spreading the word" about its own religious perspectives as widely as possible, and in the privilege white

Americans have historically asserted in insistently learning about and embodying others.

These beliefs fueled and were fueled by longstanding tourist and ethnographic practices of intrusive looking and recording. In his 1884 book on the Snake Dance, John G. Bourke explains how he feigned ignorance and "quietly ignored all hints" that he leave a ceremony (*Snake Dance of the Moquis,* 149). Erna Fergusson, in her 1931 book on Indian Ceremonials of New Mexico and Arizona, tells how she got around the "deep impenetrable veil falling behind [the eyes of an Indian friend of hers]" when she asked when the Parrot-dance would be happening by promising to bring presents for his family.[15]

Shawn's focus on and reproduction of the Hopi village of Walpi in *The Feather of the Dawn* serves as a case in point. From the late 1880s through the 1910s and early 1920s, Walpi was a tourist hotspot for those hoping to see a Hopi Snake Dance ceremony. It was also the site of the first official restriction of photography of a specific Southwestern Indian ceremony; photographic restrictions—limiting photography and filming to use for historic, not commercial, purposes—were enforced at a Snake Dance on August 21, 1913.[16] Shawn was not photographing or otherwise reproducing a Snake Dance; his piece includes a "Corn Dance," "Basket Dance," "Eagle Dance," "Wolf Dance," and others woven into a dramatized legend Shawn interprets. But the site of Walpi nonetheless registers a history of conflict between Hopi dance ceremonies and non-Hopi viewers and intruders,[17] a focal site of conflicting worldviews about the need or desire to preserve or document a dance, about the force and function of representation.

DANCE AS ART AND THE AMERICAN INDIAN ARTS AND CRAFTS ACT

Paradoxically, then, even as they protested government policy banning dance as immoral or implicitly sacrilegious, artists and activists participated, however inadvertently, in federal rhetoric and tourist presumptions regarding American Indian culture and dance. Shawn's taking of dance material for his own artistic use, and making them contained, shortened, productive—not too wasteful of time or effort—supports the rhetoric of Burke's 1923 letter, outlawing dance on the grounds that it kept Indians from being productive enough land dwellers. It also fell in step with 1930s U.S. governmental policy that turned the country's focus toward Native American culture's importance not for the religious and healing needs of its own communities and understandings of the world, but in American culture at large.

Official federal restrictions on Native American religious practices ended on January 4, 1934, when Indian Commissioner John Collier issued Circular no. 2970, "Indian Religious Freedom and Indian Culture." This circular reversed Burke's antidance policies and initiated an era in which Indian dance was no longer officially restricted. Congress then passed the Indian Reorganization Act, or Wheeler-Howard Act, of 1934. This bill brought to an end the policy of allotment and (albeit paradoxically) established some federally sanctioned guidelines for Indian self-government. Alongside these two 1934 legislative endeavors—and ideologically linked to them in several ways—came mounting support for the importance of Indian arts and crafts. For years, Collier had been reiterating a point he included in part of the "Indian Religious Freedom and Indian Culture" circular—that Indian arts and crafts were to be "prized, nourished and honored—and promoting a marketing scheme for Indian arts and crafts products" (Prucha, *Great Father*, 951). In 1930, a bill to create a board that would promote the production and sale of Indian products was introduced in the House. That bill died within the year, but Collier's enthusiasm did not, and in 1935 Congress passed the Indian Arts and Crafts Act. The committee promoting the bill argued that the "key to a materially wider market and materially increased income for the Indian arts and crafts lies . . . in an improved production—through improved production processes, through better products, and through better adaptation of products to American usage" (Prucha, *Great Father*, 974–75). To accomplish this, the bill established a board of five members, appointed by the secretary of the interior, to promote Indian arts and crafts and expand the market for them. Part of its charge was to create government trademarks of genuineness and standards of quality; to establish standards and regulations for the use of such trademarks; and to license, and charge a fee for, their use. It allowed for the fining and imprisonment of anyone caught using these government trademarks on goods or products that were not Indian products of the particular tribe or group (Prucha, *Documents*, 229). Like the Citizenship Act of 1924 and the Indian Reorganization Act of 1934, the Indian Arts and Crafts Act of 1935 legislated increased federal mechanisms of control over Indian lives, culture, and resources. In regulating the production of Indian Arts and Crafts often linked to ceremonial practice, this heralding of Native arts and crafts took the place of—yet in some ways continued—federal control over Native religious practices, despite Circular no. 2970's end of official restrictions on them.

Modern dance choreographers' repeated support for American Indian dance as authentic material from which they could then draw freely for their own artistic dance production anticipated and reinforced the focus of these policies on safeguarding art. Shawn, for example, protested federal restrictions of American Indian dance not because they infringed on Native American religious rights or because the restrictions were harmful to Native peoples' wellbeing, but rather, as the citation opening this chapter indicates, as "a great artistic crime." What Shawn saw as "vanishing tribes" and their dances served as a primary source of American dance, and preserving their dance material a special charge of American choreographers engaged in producing great art. By reiterating claims of dance as an art, and of the curtailment of it as an "artistic crime," in other words, these modern dancers tapped into policy that shifted focus from dance as part of religious, ceremonial, or healing practices. Like the Arts and Crafts Act, this approach reinforced dance's value, and availability, to non–Native Americans. As Michelle Raheja writes in her analysis of the act:

> Ironically, the Act didn't promote the preservation of Native American spiritual and social practices through the fostering of ceremonial, personal, and communal objects such as baskets and sand paintings, but promoted the creation of objects that could be readily sold for mass consumption in the tourist trade. The initial Indian Arts and Crafts Act, along with a host of other legal interventions ostensibly designed to protect Indian culture from non-Indian encroachment, fits hand in glove with the promotion of capitalism and Pan-Indian, not tribally-specific identities.[18]

Like other Indian-made "arts and crafts" products, dance as art (rather than as religion) was a useful commodity available to the public, and this public recognition of the value of Indian arts, the bill asserted, could better Native Americans economically. At the same time, Indian dance as art would also be adapted for the use of (implicitly non-Native) Americans.[19]

While this bill did not attempt to regulate the buying and selling of Indian dance (and debates about copyrighting dance movements and choreographies continue today), its rhetoric seems nonetheless to have influenced modern dancers with interests in Indian dance. The Arts and Crafts Act reinforced the idea that literal reproduction of dance steps or movements might *not* be allowable by non-Indian dance artists seeking to reproduce dances exactly. Shawn's disclaimers on the subject fit within this framework. Shawn describes his second ballet, *The Feather of the Dawn,* in which he stages himself as a Hopi dancer, noting, "The scene was a reproduction of the village of Walpi, and many of the costumes were authentic Hopi pieces." And yet, he explains:

> The dance writing was, frankly, adaptation. One must see the original, and become aware of its inner import as well as its visible pattern, but the literal reproduction is the function of the scholar and museum field worker. The function of the artist is to use authentic themes, as seeds from which to produce an art creation of his own. (*American Ballet,* 20)

Martha Graham's position as to the use of Indian dances is similar. "Although I have been greatly exposed to the Native American tribes, I have never done an Indian dance. I've never done any ethnic dance. I've received an excitement and a blessing and a wonderment from the Indians," she writes in her auto-biography. "The American Indian dances remained with me always, just like those haunting moments before sunrise in the pueblos, or my first view of the Hopi women in their squash blossom hair arrangements that I was to use in Appalachian Spring."[20] The focus, for both, is Southwest Indian dances as a kind of catalyst for artistic inspiration, their use in accessing and providing a sense of mysticism or style to use in their own creations.

The Arts and Crafts Act expressed anxieties about non-Indians exploiting a market for "genuine" Indian products, and explicitly forbade the passing off of artistic production by non-Indians as "Indian art." In this vein, its ideology required the kinds of disclaimers Shawn and Graham made about their Indian-influenced dances. With these comments, they adhered to the rhetoric, and eventually the law, of the day with its belief in "genuine" Indian art—and acknowledged the limits of their own abilities to produce it.

Yet the Arts and Crafts Act left space for dance artists to see spiritual or intangible aspects of dance, such as "an excitement and a blessing and a wonderment" Graham says she received from the Indians, as not protected by the act in spirit or letter. While the act underscored the use-value of Indian art, it deflected awareness of any use to the religious and spiritual aspects of American Indian dance; blessings and wonderment and religious inspiration were not understood as artistic commodities. Thus, while dance artists were quick to distance themselves from reproducing authentic dances, dance as spiritual inspiration or source of blessing could nonetheless be made unproblematically available to them for their own artistic needs.

Instead, they adhered to the idea of dance as art, and to the modernist ideal of individual artists charged with the ability—indeed the mandate—to glean from the shards of culture and history in their artistic production and, from those shards, to "make it new" and make it their own. Shawn's faith in the artist's ability to take from the "authentic themes" in Native American dance and use them "as seeds from which to produce an art creation of his own" fits firmly within this modernist ideal.

Shawn's view of the federal stance on Indian dance as "a great artistic crime," then, reflected and reinforced the growing interest of modernists, hobbyists, scouts, and collectors in Native arts and dances. For him and other dancers, Indian dance (and particularly Southwest Indian dance) served as available material to ground the Americanness of their projects, to provide a sense of awe and wonderment they could translate into their art, and (for Shawn) to negotiate issues of masculinity and sexuality, particularly for men out of the so-called heterosexual norm.

A FULL-BLOODED MASCULINE VIGOUR:
TED SHAWN'S MEN DANCERS DANCING INDIAN

In the spring of 1914, Shawn auditioned for Ruth St. Denis's company by staging himself as an Aztec youth. St. Denis's own "Orientalist" approach to American dance was in full swing at the time, part of the general passion for the exotic in dance at the turn of the century that accompanied the project of U.S. imperialism that flourished at the time (in 1898 the United States annexed Hawaii, went to war in Cuba, and seized the Philippines from Spain). Her response to Shawn's Aztec impersonation was to declare, "This is the best male dancing material in America!" and to offer Shawn then and there a position in her company (Sherman, "American Indian Imagery," 369).

In 1930, Shawn split with Ruth St. Denis, both as wife and as dance partner with whom he'd formed the highly influential Denishawn in 1915, and formed his own company of Men Dancers. His oft-stated goal in this endeavor was to foster "an acceptance of the idea of dancing as a virile and manly sport and art expression," as he wrote in his 1926 book, *The American Ballet* (97). In a 1938 lecture on "Dancing for Men," he explained, "the dance as an art is emasculated, the great stars of the dance are women and the men have taken on an effeminate quality of movement."[21] Explicitly conceived of as a way to counter these assumptions, Shawn's all-male company, Ted Shawn and His Men Dancers, premiered their first concert in April 1933, opening with two pieces based on Shawn's conceptions of American Indian dance: *Osage-Pawnee Dance of Greeting* and *Invocation to the Thunderbird*. Throughout the seven-year tenure of the dance group, these and other Indian pieces were repertory staples, performed hundreds of times in locations from London to Boston to Vancouver and San Antonio.[22]

Shawn researched some of these "Indian" dances in books by non-Native scholars and ethnographers. Yet he also traveled to the Southwest and observed dances that formed the basis for some of his own, such as his 1923 *Hopi Indian Eagle Dance* (later revived for the Men Dancers). He noted the "great mystical insight" of the Pueblo and Hopi tribes, and his awe at the dances he saw when traveling there. "It was absolutely beyond me to analyze and catch this rhythm. It was the most fascinating thing I have ever seen," he wrote in 1926. "I have seen Hopi men do the Eagle Dance. There is no living white man today (and that included all of the greatest of the Russian Ballet, as well as American dancers, including myself) who, after spending a year studying this dance, would be able to do it" (*American Ballet*, 18).

When Shawn staged his *Hopi Indian Eagle Dance*, he clearly and admittedly gave in to this failure. The Southwest eagle dance is part of a multiple-day curing ceremony. At Tesuque Pueblo, for example, the Eagle Dance ceremony begins with a four-day fast. "Though danced only by two men, it is one of the most effective of all pueblo dances, and one which white dancers always wish

Ted Shawn, Hopi Indian Eagle Dance, *1923. Courtesy Jacob's Pillow Dance Festival Archives.*

to learn," wrote 1930s ethnologist Erna Fergusson, whom Shawn references as his friend, and whom he accompanied on at least one dance outing. "After a few lessons they readily understand why the dancers must be treated with medicine water for strength before they can do it. It requires unusual skill and an amazing control of leg muscles in its stooping, swooping, and varied movements."[23] In an article on Tewa Pueblo dance (not Hopi, but nearby and probably some of what Shawn saw) Jill Sweet described similar power in Southwest dance events. "In addition to beauty and humor, Tewa dance events contain power," she writes, explaining how the experience of dancing, or even of watching dancing all day, is transformative. It often follows days of fasting and prayer, and accompanies rhythmic percussion that "creates an environment of sound conducive to trans-formation," she writes. "When the dancers take on the role of the buffalo, deer, Cloud People, or clowns, they take on the personality of the being they are im-personating. They become, in a very real sense, the animal or spirit. Hence, the experience is one of physical and psychological transformation to a heightened state of being" ("Beauty, Humor, and Power," 98).

Shawn's *Hopi Indian Eagle Dance,* however, makes no attempt to recognize the function and power of the Eagle, or of the Hopi ceremony he is embodying. In multiple ways, Shawn's two-minute piece evades the cultural, religious, and healing aspects of the Eagle Dance. For one, he stages the dance as a solo, where one dancer interrupts the line of Ponca dancers (who themselves have a solo-ist) with a giant swoop. Sweet notes how such a focus on the individual goes against the ideologies embedded in the Southwest dances she's seen. She writes how, for the Tewa, dancing in unison is aesthetically and culturally desireable: "The image of the entire group moving together should never be disturbed by someone who dances 'too hard.' In other words, a dancer who stands out from the others destroys the beauty of the group moving as one" ("Beauty, Humor, and Power," 94). Shawn also, as contemporary Blackfeet/Chippewa dancer/choreographer Rosalie Jones/Daystar has noted, completely alters Native American understandings by concluding his dance with the death of the Eagle he is impersonating. Jones writes how at the end of Shawn's piece, "Two hunt-ers enter; they draw arrows and strike the eagle; it falters, staggers, finally col-lapses, gracefully, into the arms of two hunters, who drag it off into the wings." She explains, "Within most Native American tribes the eagle is a messenger that carries prayers to the Creator because it flies higher than all other creatures of the natural world. For us, it would be out of the cultural context to portray an eagle being shot, killed, and dragged away." Jones adds, "Ted Shawn was dancing dressed as an American Indian, but the choreography was pure vintage early modern dance in the genre of Anna Pavlova's famous 'dying swan.'"[24]

Shawn's modernist use of primitive materials, like other modernist artists' uses of primitive materials of the time, was thus not about engaging with the worldviews or religious and political concerns of the people he embodied. Nor was it about allowing their dance to transform the modern dance medium, rec-ognizing it as a creative force that might alter his understanding of what dance is and does. Even less was it about sharing the stage with Native peoples or ceding them any control in the development of an American ballet. It involved no more than distanced engagement with Indian dances or dancers, or no at-

Ted Shawn and His Men Dancers, Ponca Indian Dance. *Courtesy Jacob's Pillow Dance Festival Archives.*

tempt to understand or engage the dance's roles in particular Native American worldviews.[25]

Instead, Shawn engaged this dance material, in part, to address his own concerns about masculinity and dance.[26] An anxiety about the "effeminate" and "emasculating" reputations of male dancers weighed heavy on him, as his own writing made clear.[27] Shawn's idea in creating an American ballet was to reject the preeminence of women modern dancers and argue for the need for male dominance in the dance world by proving "conclusively that dancing is and has been essentially and primarily a man's activity" (*American Ballet,* 89). Shawn argued for man's rightful domination in the field of dance by asserting that "Men have always done the big things, the important things in life, being quite willing to let the embroideries and ornamentations be the work of women" (93). He backed up his argument with references to nature, Greek drama, Roman theatre, "all the countries of the Orient," the great court ballets of Europe, and the strength, endurance, precision, accuracy, and extreme mental control that dance demands—all "generally considered masculine qualities" (92). He then assigned both dance music and subject matter to specifically "masculine" and "feminine" categories, to be performed by men and women respectively.[28]

Having strictly defined these categories, Shawn turned to American Indian dance to fulfill his ideal of masculinity. When Ted Shawn and His Men Dancers began presenting work in 1933, Indian dances opened his program. Over the years, these Indian dances came to define Shawn's Men Dancers project.[29] Shawn biographer Walter Terry writes how *Invocation to the Thunderbird,* an exultant ritual rain dance based on "aboriginal sources" that Shawn developed to a John Philip Sousa piece called "The Red Man," became "almost [Shawn's] trade mark, an American Indian dance of great virility, strength, athletic prowess, and intense sense of ritual."[30] Nor was this one biographer alone in seeing Shawn's "Indian" pieces as paradigmatic of the kind of masculinity he hoped to project. A 1935 London reviewer tells how "two or three rather 'beefy' young men in the stalls" at a performance were "obviously out for a rag," given "traditional English distrust of anything even faintly savouring of effeminacy." The reviewer notes, however, how the young men's mood changed as soon as the curtain opened on *Primitive Rhythms.* "But from the moment the curtain rose on a wild Indian devil dance there was a change of feeling," the reviewer writes. "Nothing feminine here we decided, but a full-blooded masculine vigour wholly divorced from orthodox ballet. The dancers revealed a physique which might be—and quite possibly was, envied by the beefy young men."[31] The "full-blooded" vigor and physique the reviewer reads in the Indian dance thus deflects Shawn's dancers from potentially violent charges of "effeminacy" and instead makes them the envy of male viewers.

Part of this masculine ideal, for Shawn, included display of the nude male body. He wrote how "when the creative artist dancer thinks his biggest thoughts, he instinctively seeks to dance nude," adding, "We cannot associate the cosmic Man with clothes, because clothing suggests classification—clothes would place him as to race, nationality, period of history, social or financial status" (*American Ballet,* 65). He pointed to Walt Whitman, Greek culture, and the civic benefits of public nudity—which, he argued, would force us all not to corrupt our bodies and instead to "join the Y.M.C.A., and begin to develop some muscle; thus we would build up a physically more perfect race" (77). He then used the "Indian" dances in his repertoire, in particular, to fulfill this idea. In *Osage-Pawnee Dance of Greeting,* Shawn costumed the "half-naked, tawny-skinned men in genuine beaded buckskin panels that hung fore and aft from a beaded belt" (Sherman, "American Indian Imagery," 377). Barton Mumaw, Shawn's dancer for many years, told of the trials he had getting the Men Dancers to dress for the piece in a costume with a G-string that left the bottoms mostly uncovered, and to shave their pubic hair so as not to counter Massachusetts obscenity laws.[32] A 1935 reviewer remarked how in this "tribal number, the gentlemen would have made the ordinary chorus girl feel as if she was clothed for a blizzard."[33]

Ted Shawn, "Dancing and Nudity." Study by Arthur Kales. Courtesy Jacob's Pillow Dance Festival Archives.

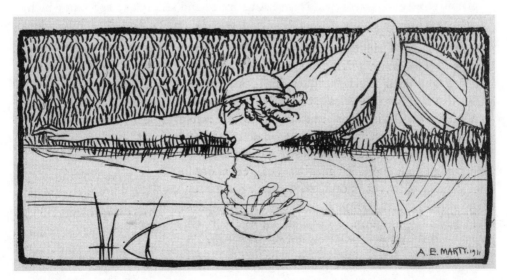

André Marty, "Nijinsky as Narcisse," 1911. Copyright 2005 Artists Rights Society (ARS), New York/ADAGP Paris.

Shawn was claiming that nudity allowed one to represent universal ideas and ideals. Yet while trying to claim that nudity provides this naturalized, dominant masculinity, unplaced "as to race, nationality, period of history, social or financial status," Shawn turned repeatedly to Indianness not only in his dances, but also in his photographic self-representations. For example, his chapter in *The American Ballet* on "Dancing and Nudity" includes not only a photo of Shawn as a nude classical statue, but also a photo of him lying naked on the bank of a river, staring at his reflection, wearing a feather headdress. All he sees in the river is head and headdress; the side of his nude body is instead displayed for those watching. Shawn, in an earlier piece on "The Defense of the Male Dancer," sought to distance himself from the Russian ballet dancer Vaslav Nijinsky, calling him "the decadent, the freakish, the feverish," and asserting instead that "America demands masculinity more than art."[34] Yet this self-portrait as Indian looking in river both references Shawn's relation to Nijinsky as a prominent male dancer and uses the Indian image to transform what Shawn saw as Nijinsky's "freakish" masculinity into a (to Shawn) more appropriate one for men who dance. In a famous print of "Nijinsky as Narcisse" from 1911, the dancer extends himself onto a river bank and gazes at his reflection, one arm bent at the elbow, hand pressing down. Shawn's image mirrors the Nijinsky print, including the crooked elbow, but replaces Nijinsky's tight cap with an Indian headdress.[35] Shawn, in other words visually encodes the importance of masculine dancing for men by donning the most visually recognizable sign of Indianness—a Plains-looking headdress—and using that image to signal a transformation from Nijinsky's "decadent" masculinity to the virile masculinity Shawn instead hopes to promote. This act of "playing Indian" both primitivized and stereotyped Native Americans, and served as a space in which to justify male nudity for, again, Shawn's own agenda.

Part of Shawn's intent in bolstering this virile masculinity was to divorce it from notions of homosexuality of the day. In many ways, he did; Susan Foster has argued compellingly that Shawn's choreography, like that of other early modern dancers, "sequestered sexuality." She writes how, "By showing the noble male body engaged in vital, virile expressive work, he begged entirely the questions of the dancers' sexual orientation" despite his many-year sexual relationship with Mumaw.[36] Shawn's Men Dancers concerts, she writes, "reaffirmed the anti-sexual stance of modern dance and defended his work against allegations of homosexuality" ("Closets Full of Dancers," 163). In her analysis of Shawn's Men Dancers choreography—its use of "relentless, repetitive, symmetrical" bodies, stiff torsos, rigid arms, clenched fists evoking images of brute strength, preference for frontal display—Foster argues that Shawn "directed attention away from the dancing body as a preconceived source of sexual impulses and towards the spatial and temporal properties of the movement" (164). Ironically, some of the very emblems Shawn deployed to deflect homosexual allegations—including dressing as exotic other as a license for nude male display—also today signal homosexuality.[37] Yet however successful Shawn's work was at closeting homosexuality (and as Foster notes, for some young men in his audiences, it didn't entirely), Shawn's Men Dancers work, with the Indian dancing the group did at its helm, was instrumental in redefining the image of gay male dance. The image of masculinity Shawn and his dancers projected was far from that of the sensual, effeminate ballet dancer epitomized by Nijinsky. As Foulkes argues, "the almost hypermasculinity of his troupe diminished the homosexual implications of the bare bodies because it did not fit into the societal framework of homosexuality as fey, effeminate inversion" ("Dance Is for American Men," 129). Shawn's work, instead, made space for "hypermasculine" ideals. Although in the 1930s this hypermasculinity was presented as implicitly heterosexual, it also served to enable and foster a new genre of male dance identity distinct from that of the effeminate ballet dancer, one that at the very least made space for gay male performers and provided possibilities for alternative masculinities in dance.

In some ways, embodying Indianness might suggest possibilities for disrupting a one-way economy of "playing Indian." Deloria, for example, writes, "The donning of Indian clothes moved ideas from brains to bodies, from the realm of abstraction to the physical world of concrete experience. There, identity was not so much imagined as it was performed, materialized through one's body and through the witness and recognition of others" (*Playing Indian,* 184). Dance is a bodily act that requires interaction between peoples: you have to go and see the dance, meet and interact with Native peoples; you can't, like Picasso, just look at masks in museums or your studio. In this way, staging such as Shawn's might have refused the distancing that enabled other modernist appropriations of primitive culture. Yet for Shawn, staging Indian dance was not about actual embodiment. It was about dressing up as—dancing like an Indian, representing and making visible Indian dance images, reinforcing what Michael Taussig has called a Euro-American privileging of vision at the expense of other sensory involvements and relations. The limitation of his project, then, is not that Shawn appropriated Native culture for his own ends (although he does do this), but that he doesn't recognize the potentially radical import for witness and redress of his dancerly embodiment, and instead borrows only visual codes of Indian dress and undress to project his ideals about dance and masculinity.

Obviously, Shawn is a white man staging the dance away from Hopi peoples, contexts, and histories, and thus might be excused for not attempting to probe its relation to spiritual and ritual healing and transformation. And yet Sweet quotes a Tewa man instructing dancers on presenting shortened dances in urban centers for non-Indian audiences. "You've still got to dance with your whole heart because the songs and dance still are sacred and bring beauty, no matter if you dance here [in the village] or out there," he says ("Beauty, Humor, and Power," 103). Shawn's dance registers none of the sacred, healing aspects of the Eagle Dance. Shawn's appropriation, then, comes not in putting on the culture of another. Although he does do that, that in itself could be seen as transformative, as some Native American dance itself is about taking on the transformative powers of another—the buffalo, wolf, deer, or eagle—by putting on regalia and recognizing one's relation to another being. Rather, Shawn's appropriation comes in his dancing Indian (and witnessing Indian dance) as if it didn't really effect any change in the dancer, audience, or world. Just as the CIA reports of the day dismissed the idea that the ceremonials had any actual effect in healing or bringing rain, so too do the artists. Shawn, for example, pokes gentle fun at the religious roles of the ceremonies he sees, writing in a tone of feigned awe of the Isleta winter solstice dances Fergusson takes him to, "And each year the ceremony is successful—the days immediately begin to grow longer!" (*American Ballet,* 17). Shawn distills an Eagle Dance he notes is "undoable by whites" for his own ideological and artistic purposes, without attentiveness to or respect for its power. In the end, his dancing supports Deloria's conclusion that the radical potential of Indian play ultimately most often "allowed one to evade the very reality that it suggested one was experiencing" (*Playing Indian,* 184).

Shawn's focus on visuality, on the one hand, is part of what marks the limits of the potential of "playing Indian," as Deloria lays it out, to not imagine but perform identity in a bodily act of witness and recognition. Yet as usual with this topic and history, any position is complicated and multivalent. In another sense, Shawn's focus on visuality was important given the racial ideologies of Indianness in America, where attempts at disappearance and lack of visibility or adequate blood quantum have long been used to dispossess American Indian peoples. Jones, for example, despite her quarrels with Shawn's renditions, nonetheless cites Shawn's importance in an essay on Native American stage dance. She sees his work as part of what signaled Native dance as invisible to American culture, and credits him with countering this cultural invisibility by helping start a historical trajectory of staged Native American dance that today includes American Indian Dance Theatre and her own company. "The American dance audience to whom he introduced it saw an Indigenous dance form that had become not extinct, but invisible in America of the 1930s," Jones writes.[38] She later explained, "I think that helped to carry on some image of the Native American at that time when the general public thought that Native Americans were a vanishing race and extinct, or about to become extinct."[39] It seems crucial to recognize and call forth not only the limits, but also the positive reverberations to Shawn's putting of Indian dance on stage as visible over sixty years ago.

In practical ways, too, Shawn's long-held interest in American Indian dance enabled the development of American Indian stage dance by American Indian dancers. As Shawn began staging public dance performances at Jacob's Pillow, the Berkshire Farm he'd purchased, he actively solicited the work of numerous Native dancers to perform there. These include multiple appearances by Indigenous dancers not necessarily promoted as Indian—including José Limón (in 1946, 1948, 1950, 1951, 1952, 1953), Maria Tallchief (1951, 1957, 1960, 1961, 1962, 1964, 1965), and Marjorie Tallchief (1963, 1964)—as well as those who were, including Tom Two Arrows (Thomas Dorsey) in 1957 and six dancers from St. John's Indian School in Laveen, Arizona, in 1965. This promotion of Native dance continued even after Shawn's death in 1972 with several appearances by the American Indian Dance Theatre in 1989, 1995, and 1998. In this way, too, as Jones remarks, Shawn's interest in American Indian dance has helped acknowledge and make visible to dance-viewing publics a tradition of American Indian stage dance.[40]

The "deep red-brown paint" Shawn's male dancers put all over themselves before donning their G-strings and dancing Indian shared more with blackface makeup than with the painted markings of animal beings Native dancers wear when preparing to take on the spirit of another through dance. At the same time, it is important not to underestimate the transformative power of the dances he engaged with, promoted, and performed to, over time, effect transformation.

MANY INDIANS ABOUT: LESTER HORTON'S DANCE THEATRE

Lester Horton's interest in and engagement with American Indian dance overlaps chronologically and rhetorically with Shawn's, and shares many of its assumptions and limitations. In his early "Indian" pageant productions, Horton's renditions rehearsed familiar tropes, and problems, of "playing Indian" similar to those of Shawn's, and likewise reflective of the legal and rhetorical positioning of Native Americans during his day. Horton's self-staging as Indian in *Song of Hiawatha,* and of himself and other non-Native dancers in these other early productions, also echoed tropes in which the white man proves a better Indian than the Indian himself.[41]

American Indian dance was also far from the sole influence on Horton and his choreography. Accounts of his life and career stress his voracious appetite for learning about all kinds of peoples and cultures, and for drawing readily on what he encountered. At the Olympic Festival of the Dance at the Los Angeles Philharmonic in 1932, along with the *Kootenai War Dance,* Horton also presented *Voodoo Ceremonial,* inspired by a W. B. Seabrook book on Haiti,[42] which included African-inspired movement motifs he was to use throughout his career. In 1929, he performed with Michio Ito, who used Japanese Noh drama as a basis and based his movement vocabulary on upper body movements, and he toured with Ito for two years.[43] Dancers note his attraction to these and a whole

variety of different materials, and his dynamic, intuitive, and bold artistic engagements with them.

Yet a passion for learning about American Indian dance and history, and for
collecting Indian drums, blankets, headdresses, masks, baskets, and numerous
other materials, nonetheless particularly inspired Horton throughout his life,
and infused his early career especially (Warren, *Lester Horton*, 6, 9). Numerous
sources cite Horton's lifelong interest in—even obsession with—American
Indian culture from his childhood days in Indiana, where he visited "mysterious Indian mounds," haunted museum displays of American Indian arts and
artifacts, and pored over descriptions of stories, songs, chants, and dances at
the public library. In some ways, his engagement with American Indian dance
provides an alternative model to the acts of "playing Indian" performed by
Shawn. Horton's work to a greater extent than others of his generation did allow
for questions about "the social settings in which Indians and non-Indians might
actually meet," which Deloria argues were so frequently pried apart from "the
ways in which white Americans have used Indianness in creative self-shaping"
(*Playing Indian*, 190). Horton's company did include Native American performers; he was interested not only in the visual or spiritual inspiration Native dance
provided him, but also in ways Native dance practices influenced the processes of theatrical production he was exploring. Rather than mocking understandings of dance as transformative—as having effect on weather patterns or
sun cycles—his "Indian" dances raised questions, however obliquely, among
his audience members about the acts of transformation they enabled. And yet,
Horton's engagement with Native American dance, and the influence it had on
him, has been much less frequently acknowledged by dance historians than
Shawn's or Graham's. While many factors may contribute to this neglect—Los
Angeles–based Horton in general is much less frequently discussed than East
Coast–based modern dance pioneers—it nonetheless raises questions about the
kinds of Native American dance influence that critics and historians have been
able or willing to see and acknowledge.

Horton apparently told the story of how his interest in dance was sparked
when he saw a Denishawn concert in 1922 that included Shawn's *Xochitl,* and
how he began to study dance the next year, at age seventeen, after seeing Shawn's
Feather of the Dawn.[44] While "that was the story he told most frequently," biographer Larry Warren notes that "In different versions he sometimes attributed
his awakening to dance to a touring wild west show which featured American
Indian dancing" (*Lester Horton*, 8). Another critic writing on Horton's dance
career cites a story Horton apparently told her about how, when "a tiny lad
about five years old," Horton went to see the circus in Indianapolis. "Of all the
wonderful sights at the circus, the most wonderful to Lester Horton were the
Indians."[45] It seems, therefore, that Horton consciously presented his exposure

to theatricalized versions of "Indian" dance as central to his very beginnings as a stage dance choreographer.

Similarly, Horton consciously cultivated an "Indian" identity for himself as a dancer. In 1929, he writes, "That the American Indians and their tribal dances have always held a fascination for me is not surprising, when one considers the fact that my grandmother was a full-blooded Algonquin Indian" ("American Indian Dancing," 9). Margaret Lloyd reprises a version of this claim when she notes that "his interest in the American Indians . . . was also in his blood, since one of his great-great grandmothers was a full-blooded Algonquin and there was another Indian strain even farther back in his English-Irish-German ancestral mixture."[46] Biographer Larry Warren throws some doubt on these claims when he opens his biography of Horton by noting how

> In one or two interviews Lester Horton, who enjoyed indulging his fantasy on such occasions, told of a full-blooded Algonquin Indian grandmother. He also spoke from time to time of an abolitionist ancestor who had worked with the underground railroad helping slaves to the North and to freedom. Probably closest to the truth was his description of his forbears as a motley collection of English, Irish, and German immigrants who had settled in the Indianapolis area without particularly distinguishing themselves. (*Lester Horton,* 4)

Regardless of how much truth lies behind Horton's self-presentation as a little bit Indian, what is undoubtedly true is that his cultivation of this identification infused his initial self-conception, and his presentation to the world, as a dancer and choreographer. For a short time early in his career, Horton used the professional name "Okoya Tihua" to publicize his appearances in the *Hiawatha* pageant, a name Warren writes was drawn from American Indian mythology (25). At points, following his interest and apparent expertise in things Indian, others would attach Indian names to him. One acquaintance, Elsie "Pellie" Martinez, at whose house Horton lived for a period in 1928 during the *Hiawatha* tour, notes how he charmed her and others from her circle of friends in Piedmont, California. "We were very interested in the Indians of the Southwest, and he knew a great deal . . . had a feel for the people," she recounted. "My husband was a wild, picturesque Mexican who was very fond of Lester and nicknamed him Quaché, the Hopi word for buddy (pal)" (Warren, *Lester Horton,* 26–27). On the one hand, Horton's insistence/invention of an "Indian grandmother" and his adoption of "Indian" names are familiar tropes, both from the 1920s when Indianness had come to signal true Americanness—so being a little bit Indian made one legitimately American—though also dating back at least as far as the

Pocahontas myth and continuing today in New Age appropriations of Indian identity. At the same time, Horton seems to have been playfully aware of the tropes and desires for Indian authenticity with which he was flirting. Warren recounts an instance, after a *Hiawatha* performance, when one of his supporters whispered to Horton "that when the wind blew against his loincloth, 'you could see white skin.' 'Don't worry, Mama,' Horton reassured her, 'it's all absolutely authentic,'" Warren writes (*Lester Horton,* 23). His playful insistence that his visible whiteness did not trump claims to Indian identity pokes fun at understandings of Indianness as visible in skin tone or blood quantum, and at ideas of authenticity.

Like Shawn, it seems that Horton initially gleaned many of his ideas about Indians from books and museums, both intensely mediated spaces whose representations of "authentic Indian" culture are always already contained by the limits and biases of their authors and curators, and by the practices of ethnographic scholarship and museum collecting themselves. At the same time, Horton, like Shawn, also traveled to see Native American dances practiced live. "Arrangements were made for several trips to Indiana reservations so that Lester could study at first hand the dances he would be performing and teaching for Hiawatha," Warren writes (*Lester Horton,* 15). Lloyd adds that while director of the Indianapolis Theater Guild in 1926, "he managed to attend any Indian ceremonial within negotiable distance. . . . He lived among the Indians, danced with them, learned their lore, and came home to create dances and costumes on the authentic base" ("Modern Dance," 279). Warren continues, "The following spring he spent several weeks in Santa Fe where . . . Lester was given the opportunity to learn from excellent Indian performers who taught him dances as well as complex chants. He claimed to have been invited to perform in public with his teachers; a rare compliment if true" (*Lester Horton,* 15). While it is hard to know in what sense he "lived among the Indians" or "danced with them" in Indiana, or who the "excellent Indian performers" in Santa Fe were, what they thought of Horton, and what actually transpired during those lessons, it seems likely that some level of actual personal engagement and corporeal interaction, rather than just distanced visual observation, did transpire between Horton and the dancers with whom he worked.

Perhaps the greatest difference between Horton's and Shawn's models lies in this danced interaction between him and Native peoples, a connection that carries over into his dance training and production practices as well. While Shawn's interaction with the Native American dance forms he reproduced on his own body seems to have been from watching them from a tourist's vantage point, Horton's interests, geographic location, and personality compelled him, throughout his life, into more sustained engagement with Native American people—as with other people from a great diversity of backgrounds. Warren notes his "easy rapport with members of minority ethnic groups living in the

Lester Horton, Pueblo Eagle Dance, *1929. Photograph by Toyo Miyatake.*

Los Angeles area," a description reinforced by the recollections of numerous dancers and company members, and attested to by the multiracial makeup of his company well before the Civil Rights movement (*Lester Horton,* 70). Most famously, his company included African American dancers Alvin Ailey, James

Lester Horton, Prairie Chicken Dance, *1929. Photograph by Toyo Miyatake.*

Truitte, and Carmen de Lavallade, Mexican American dancers such as Renaldo Alarcon, and Japanese American dancers such as Misaye Kawasumi who performed a memorial to Hiroshima in 1952—an interracial mix practically unheard of in the 1950s. Anecdotes tell of the friendly relations Horton had and

Lester Horton, Pueblo Eagle Dance, *1929. Photograph by Toyo Miyatake.*

warm welcomes he received from merchants and artists from Los Angeles's many
diverse communities, of Horton refusing bookings at night clubs that would
have required he "send all Black, Oriental, or white performing units," and
of hotels refusing the interracial company accommodations in 1953 (Warren,

Lester Horton, Prairie Chicken Dance, *1929. Photograph by Toyo Miyatake*

Lester Horton, 188). In his history of African American concert dance, John O. Perpener III notes, "Colored by its founder's eclecticism, social consciousness, and eccentricities, the Lester Horton Dance Theatre drew its material from different cultures, and Horton would not tolerate racial discrimination among its members" (*African-American Concert Dance,* 196).

Less well known, yet still in line with this policy and practice of interaction and interrelation, was Horton's inclusion of Native American performers in his Indian pageants. When *The Song of Hiawatha* debuted in California on July 2, 1928, Horton "even had a few *real* Indians in this production," Warren writes (*Lester Horton,* 22). Bella Lewitzky, who danced with Horton from 1934 through 1950, writes how "When I first came to the studio, there were many Indians about. We learned songs and dances from them. We couldn't master the falsetto that the men use, but we sang Cherokee and Navajo songs, and learned Pueblo dances."[47] She explains further, referring to Horton's studio on 7375½ Beverly Boulevard:

> In the studio were intertribal Indians, because there was an intertribal Indian center in Los Angeles. I remember a woman named Kuuks Walks Alone—a big Indian girl. Lester brought into his studio many, many of the Indians. He had a great fondness for their craft, for their culture, for their songs, their dances, and we learned them. We learned Cherokee songs and Cherokee dances. . . . Lester did the hoop dance and the eagle dance, and I think they must have been really quite authentic. Because having seen them later, if my memory doesn't serve me too badly, I think he was good at it—what he did.[48]

Both Warren and Margaret Lloyd also mention Kuuks Walks Alone, who danced with Horton during the early pageants and stayed on after as part of the group. She is listed as "Personnel of the Lester Horton Group" on the program to a piece Horton choreographed and staged in 1934 to Ravel's *Boléro,* to which, Warren notes, he'd given a gypsy setting (*Lester Horton,* 54).

Lewitzky and other dancers who worked with Horton suggest that this interest in Native American culture and dance, and this interaction with a diverse group of dancers including some Native Americans, influenced not only the specific choreography of Horton's "Indian"-themed pieces, but his technique as a whole. One site for such effect came through the involvement of such a diverse group of dancers in Horton's classes and company, and the influence Horton drew out of them in developing his technique. Company member James Truitte explains that while Martha Graham built her technique on her own body, "Lester, on the other hand, did his technique on his company, so he could work with every kind of body and therefore he could explore the anatomy more, and any kind of body can do the Horton technique."[49] Horton, then, developed his technique through the people and bodies physically present around him, including undoubtedly some of the "many, many," Indians there. Unlike Shawn, then, whose practice and process of choreographing using "Indian" material came from his visual observation of them as a tourist and who didn't create spaces for Native American performers, or enable them or the dance practices he witnessed to transform his understandings of dance or the stage, Horton's dance-making process it seems did at least allow for this participation and its influence.

That Native American dance influenced the development of Horton's technique echoes overtly and implicitly through discussions of it. A well-known video on Horton's career asserts that "his technique came out of a deep identification with the spirit of Native American ceremonial dance."[50] In her oral history, Lewitzky remarks, "he adored American Indians, and made that his leitmotiv. He came back to it again and again" (74). She then goes on to describe how "his love for a variety of cultures also penetrated his work. . . . So his influences, which were basically American Indian, oriental, African American, were all somewhere, part of what we did" (98). She recalled compositional assignments that described "form more than content," where instead of asking his dancers to move from emotions ("Do a happy dance, do a sad dance"), Horton would instead ask for "A circle dance, a square dance," Lewitzky said. "In his improvisation, he could go—I can remember one instruction he gave to the class: 'Travel across the floor like a praying mantis.' We're westerners. I never saw— I thought that was the most wonderful term, 'praying mantis.' What could that be?" (100). Her comments suggest that his approach focused on spatial direction rather than individual emotional interiority, and on improvisation initiated from imitations of other beings—and that she saw this as a non-Western instruction. Biographer Larry Warren recently asserted, "With the help of a friend who knows a great deal about movement analysis, I am nearly convinced that the technique that Lester Horton developed for training dancers, as well as his approach to movement in his choreography were considerably affected by study and performance of American Indian dance."[51]

Other characteristics of Horton's company and process also seem to overlap with some aspects of many Native American dance practices, aspects that have influenced contemporary Aboriginal dance programs and choreographers as well. Horton tended to involve large groups of dancers in his pieces—some with more training than others (often to the chagrin of his more professionally trained dancers like Lewitzky). Dorathi Bock Pierre suggests that this early interest in group work stemmed from his interest in and exposure to American Indian dances:

> Horton's dances were at first solos, and he was dissatisfied with
> this, for nearly all primitive dancing is group dancing, with an
> occasional solo figure stepping out, motivated by the group. The
> moment he felt sure of his own work, felt he was moving in the
> right direction, his ambition became to form a group of dancers,
> a group who felt as he did, that the beauty, significance, and im-
> portance of the primitive dance had an educational and theatrical
> value today. ("From Primitive to Modern," 14)

Horton's theater practice also didn't separate dance movement from other aspects of performance. Lewitzky writes, "For the Indians, singing is an important part of dancing—they don't separate the two. Lester staged works that combined both." She adds, "Today I am amused to find people saying, 'It's so new to have dancers who speak.' We all spoke, we all sang. We had total theater" ("Vision of Total Theater," 46). Part of this "total theater" approach also included involving participants in the entire process of dance making, rather than just the performance itself. "Everyone participated in all phases of the creative process," Warren writes (*Lester Horton*, 38). "Everyone was responsible for some aspect of production, and was expected to participate in the making and maintenance of costumes, props, and scenery, and in the upkeep of the studio" (14). As numerous scholars of Native American dance ceremonial practices have noted, this is also an aspect of most Native dance rituals, in which the days and weeks of preparation form as integral a part of the ceremony as the dance presentation itself.[52] Horton's interest in "choreodramas," or choreographies with strong bases in story and narrative, also resonates both with Native American ceremonial dances, which most often proceed with a narrative trajectory or purpose, if not actually based on a story, and also with contemporary Aboriginal stage dance pieces.[53] Lewitzky's discussion of Horton's development as a choreographer suggests that his development as a "narrative dance maker" followed, in part, from his interest in Native dance:

> But he also moved from Oscar Wilde and Indian lore into an area
> where he was a narrative dance maker and dropped the other
> elements except as he needed them. So that by the time I studied
> with him, he was inventing a technique. (Oral History, 78)

She implies that his strong interest in narrative dance is something that was *not* dropped from his engagement with "Indian lore" even after he no longer directly dealt with "Indian" topics.

Horton's productions also led some dancers and audience members to at least ponder the relation between dance ritual and transformative processes. Unlike Shawn's "Indian" dances, which audiences understood as purely theatrical renditions, Horton's dancing at times raised questions about their effect. Warren writes that one "dancer in the production recalled that, after one particularly stirring performance of 'Invocation to the Thunder God,' the audience was startled to hear a crash of thunder in the starry California night, followed by a few drops of rain, which was almost unheard of in that part of the country in July" (*Lester Horton*, 23).

Horton's fervent and unwavering dedication to dance, and his giving of his life to it as a practice, likewise echoes some understandings of Native American ceremonial dance. Belinda James, a classically trained ballet dancer from San Juan Pueblo living in New York City, remarked that what appeals to her about ballet is the complete dedication and training—the life commitment—ballet requires: "I respect the training. It's an honorable and amazing thing," she said. "If you're a pilot, you can't just have an off day. This is how [dance] should be—it should be that seriously taken." James connected this belief in the seriousness of dance, its importance and the responsibility of those who do it, to Pueblo rituals. "That's how the rituals are," she said, noting the honor, and the responsibility, of those who are called upon to perform tribal rituals. "You don't decide [to be a dancer or leader]—the elders come up and say. You don't have a choice." When this happens, the understanding is that "you should be honored that you're going to be part of this whole universal responsibility."[54] Of course, Horton is famous for drawing untrained dancers into his company and onto the stage (and from there, demanding they give their lives to it); nor was Horton's dedication to dance unique to him. One need only think of Graham or Balanchine for examples of other choreographers who also gave their lives to dancing, and demanded unwavering, all-consuming dedication from their dancers. Yet the intensity of Horton's dedication to dance was clearly central to him and to his project, and is noted in virtually every discussion of him and his work.[55] This approach to dancing and the demands it placed on those who danced with him—however newly arrived—seem in line with the understandings of the vital role of dance and the crucial importance of dance's work on the community and the world engaged within some Native American ceremonial dance practices.

Both Lewitzky and Warren suggest that Horton's early and explicit interest in Indian dances and cultures, engaged within specifically "Indian" movements and stories, was diffused as his technique developed over the years. Lewitzky describes ways that, even though he danced Hoop and Eagle Dances with the "many, many" Indians in his Beverly studio, Horton engaged with Indian material in his choreography in a more generalized way. "The next things that occurred [after Horton's interest in 'visual color and mass' that stemmed from his pageantry background] would be his love of Indian lore and legend, with which he took generous artistic liberties," Lewitzky said. "They were never meant to be historically accurate, nor even culturally accurate—somewhat, because he loved and respected these people." Though he "skirted around all the time these ideas" of ethnic religious and ceremonial dancing, including "a chango ceremony within the voodoo—which he called 'voudoun'—religion," and "captured some of it," Lewitzky suggests he did so,

> I think probably less successfully than in the American Indian, where he loved it better, or knew it better, or a combination of both—so that he could by moving away from what was specifically given to that society make it larger, move to a distillation of certain ideas. And that permitted him to cross the boundaries into

things not actually given to that particular community, but basically ceremonial. ("Vision of Total Theater," 110)

Lewitzky continued by describing pieces that, in this vein, sought not to reproduce particular Indian dances or ceremonies, but to move to this "distillation of certain ideas." She describes, in particular, the set of his 1948 piece, *Totem Incantation,* as "a rather generic thing" (106). "The purity was to his vision and not to the particular tribal truths" (107). She adds:

> *Totem Incantation* had a blanket dance in it, which he totally invented, and it was very, very charming. The young man—When he has come of age and chosen his maiden, they dance. It's a mix of wedding dance and, say, just a ritual dance of springtime for two young people. Again, it tends to be generic rather than authentic, but in so doing, it captured something a little larger than whatever else it would have been. (108)

Warren's description of Horton's later material is similar. "Some of the newer movement material was abstracted from his recent choreographic excursions into ethnic sources, but now, rather than the gestures and postures he had utilized in his less mature years, it was the energy of the primitive that he captured and restated in his own terms" (*Lester Horton,* 157).

On the one hand, Horton's "Indian" dances share many problems with Shawn's "Indian" pieces, and with many other dramatic representations of Indians of the period. These told narratives of Indian death or disappearance, and/or rehearsed and inscribed familiar tropes in which white men prove better Indians than Native peoples themselves. Anecdotes also suggest an exotification of Indians in Horton's performance career. For example, Lewitzky writes how in the early days, in Chicago, Horton "earned his living by dancing in nightclubs, mostly just a little loincloth and a very elaborate headdress—that would be typical of him—with joss sticks all around" ("Vision of Total Theater," 76). Horton's distillation of Indian ceremonial materials for use in his own artistic productions likewise shares some troublesome aspects with Shawn's in the way he abstracted and made use of Native materials as he needed them, divorcing these from the contexts in which they were practiced and performed.

And yet, something seems different here as well. For one, Horton engaged with Native American dance and culture not as a passing fancy, or as a tourist watching from the sidelines, but with a lifelong commitment and dedication, and as someone who actively sought out not just Native dance materials (although he did do that), but also Native peoples and teachers. For another, it seems from the choreographic descriptions available that Horton's "Indian" pieces were not antithetical to the spirit of the dances they engaged with, the way Shawn's "dying swan" Eagle Dance was. Perhaps also the way that the Indian influence on Horton's dance technique and dance making *wasn't* visible, after a certain point in his career, yet still seems to have been central to his technique and theatrical approaches was itself indicative of a long-term engagement with Native culture, and an understanding of its influence in something other than visual terms.

This is not to suggest that Horton's career was only or even primarily influenced by Native American ceremonial dance, or that it profoundly influenced contemporary Native American and Aboriginal stage dance. The influence of his interest in American Indian dance was central to his early career especially, but ultimately was only one influence of many, even during this period. His involvement with Native American dancers and peoples seems to have largely dropped out by the 1940s, and with it—perhaps appropriately—his staging of explicitly "Indian" themes and materials. At this point dancers from various other backgrounds influenced his work much more directly—and vice versa. Horton's impact, for example, on the development of African American stage dance is much more profound and overt than his impact on Native American stage dance.[56] This influence can be traced most dramatically through the career of his student Alvin Ailey. "Lester Horton turned out to be the greatest influence on my career," Ailey writes in the 1989 foreword to a book on Horton's technique. "The technique I learned from Lester has continued to affect and influence me and my work. It is an important part of the curriculum of the Alvin Ailey American Dance Center, and continues to be an inspiration for my choreography."[57] Perpener notes how, after Horton's death, "Ailey assumed the duties of company director and choreographer, moving a step closer to the artistic career that would dominate his life" and profoundly influence concert dance worldwide (*African-American Concert Dance,* 197).

On the other hand, this influence on African American stage dance, through Ailey, Carmen de Lavallade, and James Truitte among others, may itself have been charged by Horton's involvement with Native Americans and Native American dance. The first piece Ailey saw performed by the Horton company, as he watched from the wings in 1948, was *Totem Incantation,* the piece Lewitzky describes above. This piece, based upon North American Indian coming-of-age ceremonies, tells the story of a Young Man who asks a Shaman to be "conducted through the ceremony of acquiring a guiding spirit." The program for this piece tells how, when the Young Man returns from his fast in preparation for this, "the Shaman selects the eagle as the Young Man's guiding spirit." The arms for Horton's 1952 *Liberian Suite,* a piece that first featured de Lavallade and Truitte, both of whom later worked with Ailey, and which Ailey himself rehearsed—and later staged on his own company—bear a striking resemblance to those of Horton's earlier Eagle Dance poses. They also bear some resemblance to the curved outstretched arms of groups of forward-bent dancers in Ailey's signature piece, *Revelations,* arms represented in so many pictures of that piece. *Revelations* was of course much more directly based in and inspired by African American spirituals and African dance–derived movements than by any subtle and many-times mediated invocation of an Eagle Dance. Yet might not the influence of Horton's explorations of Native American dance, infused throughout his choreography and perhaps carried over into the choreography of his students, have remained, however obliquely, in their work, in ways that have not been adequately recognized? Whatever its sources, Ailey's *Revelations* formed part of the background teaching, and inspiration, for young Aboriginal dancers at the Chinook Winds Aboriginal Dance Project at Banff Centre for the Arts in 1996. In a journal entry about her experiences there, Inuit dancer Siobhán Arnatsiaq-Murphy writes:

> When I watched the videos in the evenings, I thought to myself,
> I can achieve that, I could someday be that. One of the videos we
> viewed was Alvin Ailey's *Revelation[s]*. In a lounge surrounded
> by my peers I cried three times, shielding my face from the others,
> it was only for me to know. . . . Here at this moment, I found what
> it is to be touched by a performance.[58]

It seems possible that Horton's explorations and acknowledgement of Native dance may have influenced even his later dancing, and that of his students, in specific ways, rather than simply being absorbed into a larger Americanizing dance project.

Horton's choreographic relationship to masculinity also differs from that of Shawn, and of Erick Hawkins. Shawn and Hawkins explicitly turned to Native American dance as a way of negotiating, projecting, and validating a sense of virile masculinity they worried both ballet and American modern dance troubled. Horton, however, seems to have explored both masculinity and sexuality through his choreography without engaging Native American or other ethnic dance traditions to justify his doing so. This is not to say that his choreography didn't directly investigate masculinity, nor does it mean that Horton didn't investigate sexuality and eroticism using ethnic dance material. But an overt interest in and projection of both male and female sexuality had been part of Horton's oeuvre since the early days, from the protruding papier maché bosoms worn by Elizabeth Talbot-Martin in the 1934 *Salome,* through his 1937 *Sacre de Printemps* (in which the angular and sensual movements of the dancers and the harmonic and rhythmic score startled audience members, some of whom saw the piece as "obscene"), through the sensuality of his *Liberian Suite,* which Warren called "pure Horton and, as such, . . . ahead of its time: too bold, too colorful, too physical for 1952" (*Lester Horton,* 166). "Since the late 1930s, [Horton's] designs had boldly enhanced the sexual attractiveness of the dancers," Warren writes. "Both sexes were made to look alluring and confident in their sexuality" (151). Anecdotes likewise attest to Horton's interest in men dancing with awareness of their sexuality.[59] Warren notes, "There was an aggressive masculinity to his work in both the choreographic material and the sometimes brash and clumsy but always extroverted movement material" (96). Ailey notes that it was, in part, this exploration of masculinity through dance that led him to Horton. "A friend had shown me some Lester Horton movements and they seemed exciting and masculine," he writes.[60] While Horton's sexually charged and overt pieces sometimes drew on recognizably ethnic dance material—*Liberian Suite* certainly included African-derived movement, costumes, and subject matter—in none of them did Horton seem to be using this material as a way of justifying or exoticizing his interests in exploring and projecting masculinity or sexuality on stage. Rather, this sexuality infused much of his choreographing, including not only these more clearly ethnically influenced pieces, but also those marked more in line with a Protestant sexual repression, such as *The Beloved,* a charged and erotic duet with Lewitzky and Herman Boden based on a newspaper story in which a man beat his wife to death with a Bible for suspected infidelity. In a way, Horton's refusal to assign his explorations of sexuality to ethnic movements or materials may have been, in part, what caused such controversy, even leading some of his dancers to balk at what they saw as his bawdiness when, they thought, he should have been addressing more serious leftist political issues of the day. Unlike the trajectory of "closeted sexuality" Foster traces, Horton did make dances that were overtly about sex and the pleasures, powers, and pains that attend sexuality. While they do not directly address his own homosexuality the way more contemporary choreographers address theirs, it nonetheless also refuses the narrative of "chaste dancing" that Foster notes defined so much early modern dance.

Lewitzky does suggest, however, that Horton's homosexuality was, perhaps, part of what led to his feelings of commonality with and his relationships with other peoples considered outside the mainstream, including Native Americans. "That he was outside the mainstream of society and so were all the people he loved . . . gave them common ground," she said. "He was just obviously weird," she said, asking, "who has hair down to here, curly, and this is the day of the crewcut, wears a Navajo velvet shirt with silver buttons on it open down to his navel—and this long before our singer friend [Elvis Presley] ever appeared that way in public and was loved for it—and tight pants with an Indian woven belt." Lewitzky added:

> He was outside the pale. He was also homosexual. In those days, there was no such thing as an overt homosexual . . . homosexuality was not something that the major society would have accepted. So he was an artist, a maverick, he dressed as he pleased,

quite beautifully, but in the eyes of the world peculiar, and he
was a homosexual. That's about as outside I think, as you can get
from the mainstream. (Oral History, 114–15)

This commonality as outsiders, Lewitzky hypothesized, led to Horton's "particular love—and it was truly that—and really abiding interest in almost all cultures that were exotic." She added:

> The colorful ones, the theatrical ones, appealed to Lester. Now,
> they had costume, color, legend, design elements that appealed
> to his theater sense, and I think that might have had something
> to do with why he might have, I think, been attracted to them.
> But I think more profoundly, he was welcomed by them. These
> were people outside the pale of society in those days, far more
> than they ever would be today, and Lester loved them. And they
> invited him into their world with open arms. He was always wel-
> come. (111)

Horton's approach, in other words, was not to stage himself as a scantily clad Indian (at least after his early nightclub days) as a way of masking or obscuring readings of his sexuality, as Shawn did when Shawn staged exotic visual images of Indianness so that this Indianness, and not his interest in male physicality and sexuality, would code as exotic and erotic. Horton, it seems, instead sought out peoples from cultures that were, like him, also "outside the pale"—including Native Americans from an "intertribal Indian center in Los Angeles"—and developed professional connections and friendships with them. His impulse was not to use images of other exotic cultures to mask his staged explorations of sexuality, but to find spaces of community where a colorful, talented, theatrical, driven, gay man would be welcomed and nourished.

Horton's dance company, however—like radical modern dancers working in New York during the 1930s—has been largely relegated to a minor role in the development of American modern dance.[61] Isadora Duncan, Ruth St. Denis, Ted Shawn, and Martha Graham generally comprise the primary players in narratives of early modern dance, with Doris Humphrey, Charles Weidman, and José Limón in their footsteps. Historians have attributed this neglect of Horton to his geographic location in Los Angeles, far from the dance center of New York and from its increasingly influential critics. Yet it also seems that some of his company's characteristics—including some influenced by his involvement with Native American culture and people—also made Horton's work particularly unreadable in the history of modern dance being developed and retold by historians. The size of his company, for one, made traveling financially and logistically complicated. His interest in group dancing, then, led in part to his inability to adhere to touring and scheduling conventions of the day (and continuing still). More subtly perhaps, the company's explorations of movement seem more motivated by the theatrical effects of motion, color, movement, and the intense dedication he required of dancers expected to give all to all aspects of production and to the company, and less motivated by the tropes of natural individual expressionism that characterize narratives of modern dance. His dance making thus seems less about dance as reflection of inner expression than fits with the predominant "modern dance history" narrative in which modern dance is an "expressive" art, where "movement never lies."

Explicit in the Christian-based philosophies of François Delsarte, which helped legitimize middle-class white women's explorations of bodily practice and influenced the birth of modern dance, was the way gesture and movement accessed an inner natural. This impulse for inner emotional expression was understood to come from the soul. In this way, dance could be understood as an essentially harmless expression of emotional interiority, or of joy or amusement, in keeping with Christian ideals—including Delsarte's and even Mather's decrees—rather than threatening to them. Ted Shawn's interest in staging Native American dance seems in keeping with this ideal, in which Indian dance becomes a catalyst not for effecting transformative change in the world, but for exploring what he claimed were "natural" characteristics of masculinity. His early training as a Unitarian minister and his enthusiasm for Delsarte's explicitly Christian-based teachings serve to underscore suggestions of a Christian basis to this ideology.

Horton, on the other hand, seemed less interested in harnessing Indian dance practices and movement as an expression of a universalized natural than in exploring how that movement might affect and enrich a dance theater process and practice. This interest in the effects of dancing, not for the interiority of the soul it accessed, but for the theatrical and transformative effects it created, treads near Puritan fears of dance conjuring a wicked devil, or nineteenth-century fears of Indian dance invoking warlike passions—perhaps too near. It doesn't fit with the "birth of modern dance" narrative quite as neatly as Shawn's or Graham's explorations of Indian dance do.

This book has traced how, after widespread mainstream acceptance of Delsarte's system, federal regulators of the 1920s reconciled Indian dance and Christian ideologies, not by outlawing Native dances as dangerous, but by arguing that Indian dance is essentially harmless expression of joy or amusement. Burke, in the 1920s, described Indian dance as "art, refinement, healthful exercise" and "decent amusement" for Native Americans. To address the troublesome issue of multiple-day dance ceremonies' contrast with a Protestant work ethic that reinforced capitalist doctrines of productivity, officials pushed for dances to be shortened and made useful in amusing and keeping healthy their practitioners. Any danger of their doing what the Puritans feared—effecting agency—was thus brushed off. The Indian Arts and Crafts Act of 1935 furthered this ideology by focusing on the usefulness of Indian artistic production and stressing the economic benefits that Indian artistic commodities would bring Indians, and the educational and spiritual benefits they would bring non-Indian Americans. By asserting the usefulness of Native American arts in producing health and refinement, and economic self-sufficiency, Christian-influenced fears of dance's agency could be assuaged, and Christian-infused American ethics of productivity could be upheld. At the same time, ideologies (also Christian-informed) of culture as available to all, and appropriable in an ecumenical smorgasbord of shared cultures, could be upheld.

This trajectory, however, leaves little space for Native American dance as religious or spiritual practice with effects for, primarily, the communities of people engaged with it. Nor does it provide much space for explorations of Native American dance's transformative effects. Given this narrative, then, perhaps it makes sense that Native American dancers, and Native American dance, dropped out of narratives of modern dance history following this period heralding the artistic value of Indian dance. As just one example of this, Native American participation largely dropped out of Horton's company after the 1930s. And too, Horton's company dropped out of central narratives of modern dance history.

At the same time, perhaps this absence itself speaks volumes. The following chapter argues for the recognition of Indian dance's absence from modern dance history as central to the story modern dance has told—and begins to retell a part of a version of that story.

FIVE

Her Point of View: Martha Graham
and Absent Indians

—————

> It is in no sense an Indian dance as native or folk dance. It
> is rather the memory of the MOTHER, her point of view is
> there, rather than the Indian's. . . . The INDIAN GIRL is not
> a threat but a dream.
>
> ▸ *Martha Graham, in an early script of*
> Appalachian Spring

In her autobiography, *Blood Memory,* Martha Graham notes that she originally imagined her 1944 *Appalachian Spring* would include an "episode with
an Indian girl." She writes that she first envisioned the piece to include "the
thoughts of a pioneer woman when she sees an Indian girl on whose parents'
land the frontiersmen have settled" (226). Graham adds, "She was to represent a dream, a figure always at the fence of our dream. It was the legend of
Pocahontas, the legend of American land, youth, and country" (226).

The first and second versions of the script she sent to Aaron Copland in early
1943 include this "Indian Girl" as a major character. In the "Prologue," called
"Mother and Indian Girl," an Indian Girl "emerges from the shadows and does
a dance" while the Mother (who later became the Pioneer Woman) sits. In the
first version, written between May 29, 1943, and July 10, 1943, Graham writes,
"It is in no sense an Indian dance as native or folk dance. It is rather the memory
of the MOTHER, her point of view is there, rather than the Indian's."[1] Graham
explains, "She will in no sense do Indian dancing. But she is deep in our blood
as a people" ("Copland Script," 2). She continues, "The INDIAN GIRL is not
a threat but a dream. She is a human figure standing there at the fence of our
dreams always. The legend of Pocahontas has a real hold on us and we are never
quite free from her." This Indian Girl continues to haunt the stage, though not
always visibly. "I plan to have her always on stage. Sometimes she will not be

seen," Graham writes (2). Indeed, the next scene opens, according to Graham's notes, as "The INDIAN GIRL retreats into the shadows" (6). During the next section, "Wedding Day," "The INDIAN GIRL cuts across the path of the women, and dances with the men, but is never seen by the women." In an interlude, the Indian Girl appears as the "imaginary companion" of the Children. "The others do not see her," Graham writes (9). "The play of the children is incidental and yet it is really the core of this scene," Graham adds. "The CHILDREN and the INDIAN GIRL are moving in a kind of fantasy" (9). The Indian Girl next appears in a scene of a Fugitive, described in the character descriptions as "the man who is hunted, persecuted; who becomes almost clownish in his supreme agony" and associated with the escaped slave. "As the FUGITIVE falls he rushes forward but the INDIAN GIRL is there before him and holds the FUGITIVE across her knees in a way reminiscent of the Pieta" (9). The Indian Girl's association with the Children, and as a childlike figure herself, continues as she appears next again with the Children. "Again the INDIAN GIRL is part of the scene with them. In a small way she becomes the symbolic captive in the scene they are playing" (10). Later, "The MOTHER sits and the INDIAN GIRL sits at her feet almost as though she were being told the story" (11). In the first script, the ballet closes when "the INDIAN GIRL RISES and goes back into her shadows," then "Suddenly on a simple clear line of sound the INDIAN GIRL starts to run strongly and quietly around the stage in a low beautiful free run. She stops as suddenly as she started. CURTAIN" (12).[2]

These episodes, and this Indian Girl who lurks in the shadows and appears as a fantasy of the imagination, as both captive and savior, aren't included in the final production of *Appalachian Spring*. There is no overt recognition of an Indian girl's parents' relation to the land, of an Indian girl emerging from the shadows, of an unseen Indian girl playing with children. Instead, in describing the piece as it is known today, Graham writes, "*Appalachian Spring* is essentially a dance of place. You choose a piece of land, part of the house goes up. You dedicate it. The questioning spirit is there and the sense of establishing roots" (*Blood Memory*, 231).

Where is this Indian girl, envisioned and then absented from *Appalachian Spring*? This chapter explores the role of this apparently absent Indian woman in Graham's signature piece, suggesting that Graham's impulse to acknowledge her has not been entirely erased from *Appalachian Spring*. Its most basic argument is that Native American culture and dance played an active, if not always visible, role in Graham's dance process and choreography much later than has been usually acknowledged. During Graham's choreographic career, Native American dance moved from being a marked source of inspiration (as in Graham's "Primitive" series) to being represented figurally (as in *American Document* and *El Penitente*) to emerging in the largely invisible presence that haunts *Appalachian Spring*. These moves in Graham's choreography coincide with shifts in U.S. Indian Policy, from the Indian New Deal policies enacted in the 1930s by John Collier, toward the termination policies of the 1950s. They also epitomize Native American dance's unmarked presence in most modern dance histories today. The very present absence of representational Indians in Graham's *Appalachian Spring* thus serves as both a radical and a troublesome sign of modern dance history's relation to Native American dance.

EVOKING INDIANNESS IN GRAHAM'S "INDIAN PERIOD"

Graham's interest in overtly evoking Indianness has roots in Graham's earliest Indian-influenced pieces, when her exposure to and interest in Southwest Indian dance directly influenced her choreography. As critics, biographers, dancers, and scholars have all noted, Graham was drawn to Indian dance in Mexico and the U.S. Southwest from early in her career. In August 1930, while driving back to the East Coast after performing in California, she was inspired by the Catholic religious practices of Native Americans of New Mexico. A year later, she received a Guggenheim fellowship that financed a summer in Mexico, in part watching Native dances. That summer she observed the Santo Domingo Pueblo Corn Dance and was apparently awed at the spectacle (Gibson, *Santa Fe and Taos Colonies,* 97). Throughout her autobiography, she mentions numerous other times she was in attendance at Pueblo dances, from the 1930s at least into the 1950s. "The Southwest always had a healing, nurturing effect on me," she writes (*Blood Memory,* 185).[3] In an oft-quoted passage from 1932, Graham asserts that "America's great gift to the arts is rhythm: rich, full, unabashed, virile," and discusses the rhythms of "our two forms of indigenous dance, the Negro and the Indian." She asserts that the "Indian dance" is "for awareness of life, complete relationship with that world in which he finds himself; it is a dance for power, a rhythm of integration."[4]

May O'Donnell, a member of the Graham company from 1932 to 1938 and again from 1943 to 1953, described how she and her husband shared an interest in Southwest Indians and Indian dancing with Graham and Louis Horst, and once visited with them near Santa Fe when their travels overlapped. O'Donnell explained that yearly summer visits to the Southwest, to see Indian dancing, became commonplace for both herself and her husband on car trips back and forth from New York to California over at least a ten-year period. This dancing, O'Donnell noted, involved Native people both from the Southwest and from farther east, who had come in their cars. She said the dancing involved a lot of footwork but not much arm work. "You always felt that their dances meant something," O'Donnell said. "So that what they did would be not just to be pretty, but something connected to what their dance meant to them. Maybe their Gods." She added, "When the Indians would do their pieces, their dances were dances not [for enjoyment]. Like for us, we dance because we enjoy just seeing each other dance. When they were dancing, it was partly religious. It's part of their belief, their Gods." She said, "It's almost like a sacred thing." O'Donnell added, "We had a real nice, close feeling about not only the land itself, but the people, and for many summers, we would go back and forth."[5]

Dancers from the early 1930s note the influence this exposure to Southwest American Indian land and culture had on Graham's class work and choreography. Dancer Marie Marchowsky writes of "the contraction and release principle," described as the "fundamental source" of Graham's early course work: "The exercises were primitive: legs and feet parallel, hands cupped, feet flexed as if rooted into the earth. The movement was influenced by American Indian dances—a source of inspiration to Martha."[6] Ernestine Stodelle likewise attributes Graham's early choreographic interest in repetition, in simplicity, in "an inner muscular awareness of weight and energy," in intensity, and in what Stodelle calls "purity of feeling" to Graham's interest in "the primitive" exemplified by Southwest Indian culture.[7] "The mystic in Martha found its 'skyhole' in the Southwest," Stodelle writes (Deep Song, 73). O'Donnell, too, noted this influence. "The beat of her body rhythms and movements, the search for the return to the primitive, were all part of this time," O'Donnell wrote of the early 1930s (quoted in Horosko, Martha Graham, 60). "These dances were earthy, part of the return to the primitive, getting back to the source, to a kind of rugged basis," she explained. "For instance, the primitive position, the more turned-in body, the more archaic kind of stance—they were all very contained and very powerful from within, moving inward out, and of course being the kind of dramatic dancer that Martha basically was, it had to be motivated from an inner source."[8]

Graham's interest in dance as a "rite," as Agnes de Mille described it, found its most acclaimed expression in the pieces that came most directly out of her early 1930s travels to the Southwest and in interest in the Native culture she saw there (what critics called her "Primitive" series).[9] Numerous accounts describe Primitive Mysteries as a "spiritual experience" for dancers and audience members alike.[10] "Martha has been said by her colleagues to have achieved an actual physical vibration of directed force when working. Some even suggest she gave off heat, the heat of radiance and concentration," wrote de Mille. "For those short minutes during which Martha celebrated her ritual, Christ was crucified and the Virgin was assumpted into heaven." Discussions of the piece focus as much on its preparations (noting Graham's fits of frenzy and the terror her dancers felt at her outbursts)[11] and its electrifying effect on the dancers and audience members as on its structure or movement. "The audience gathered. They witnessed. When the curtain came down they rose and screamed. They gave Martha twenty-three curtain calls," writes de Mille (Martha, 181). Ramsey Burt includes the piece in his discussion of "possession" and stage dance that includes ritual movement or movement material "that has the potential to lead to disassociational states of consciousness" (Alien Bodies, 187).

Martha Graham, "Hymn to the Virgin" from Primitive Mysteries, 1935. *Photograph by Edward Moeller. Courtesy Jerome Robbins Dance Division, The New York Public Library for the Performing Arts, Astor, Lenox, and Tilden Foundations.*

Primitive Mysteries, which critics have seen as emblematic of Graham's "Indian period," thus registered its Indianness not by mimetically representing Indians on stage. Instead, it evoked an Indian influence in its title, in Graham's frequent comments about what inspired it, in its topic, and, perhaps, in the quasi-religious fervor with which Graham approached her dance making and performing. There were echoes and suggestions of "Indian" influence in the dances. For example, Barbara Morgan's photographs of the dance show women dancers moving around a central figure, Graham, with their right elbows lifted as they jump; the circular formation suggests that of various Native American dances. Other photos show formations in the "Hymn to the Virgin" section that more specifically echo the influence of Catholicism on Southwest Indian culture. In several photos, dancers' hands and arms are placed in ways that suggest a crown-of-thorns motif such as those carved onto the Southwest "Santos" figures that Graham collected and that reportedly inspired her work in this piece.[12] In one place, dancers' forearms, bent at the elbows, radiate out from Graham's head and shoulders. In another, one dancer stands in a deep plié behind Graham and fans her fingers wide behind Graham's head, suggesting the same motif; it recurs in another Barbara Morgan photo where one dancer again stands behind Graham, fingers spread behind her head, while dancers behind in a line lift their arms and their gazes. Some commentaries of the dance suggest the dance's sounds and movements likewise evoked a Native American "feel," as Ernestine Stodelle implies when she writes "The sound of their footsteps is like a swish of twigs against a drum skin; the tempo of their walk, slow-paced, even" (*Deep Song,* 75). On the whole, though, the connection to Native American subject matter is more suggested or invoked than represented as explicitly "Indian." Critics stress that the piece was "not a direct translation, but a ritual about a ritual" as Stodelle writes (74). In 1936, critic John Martin writes, "There is nothing authentically Indian anywhere in the work, except that Louis Horst has built his beautiful musical setting on authentic Indian themes."[13] Burt notes that "The chorus of dancers wear long, tight fitting sheath dresses that do not look particularly 'Indian,' but are made of the same type of woolen jersey tubes" that Graham used for many pieces during the period. The Virgin's dress too, "did not look 'Indian' but distinctly Western," he wrote (*Alien Bodies,* 188). O'Donnell explained that Graham's interest in American Indians and the idea of the primitive was similarly unmarked; it was not something Graham spoke of explicitly to her dancers. "Martha never talked about it," she said of working with Graham on *Primitive Mysteries,* and of the Indian influence signaled in it and by its title. "Sometimes we wouldn't know until the [performance] what the title was" (interview). This, O'Donnell explained, was typical of how Graham worked. "I remember a dance we worked on in 1935. Very often she wouldn't explain much about work in progress, what her idea was, and in that piece we had no idea what she was doing or where we were going."[14]

Even in what Martin called Graham's "Indian period," then—a period best exemplified by *Primitive Mysteries*—Graham's choreography doesn't seek to represent Indians, but rather to evoke Indianness. It seeks to create the ritualistic, mystical sense that Graham felt, saw, or experienced as an audience member herself in the Southwest at the time. Scholar Mark Franko's separation of Graham's early choreography, which Franko sees as formalist, from her later, emotionally expressivist work is relevant to this interest in evocation rather than representation. Franko argues, with *Primitive Mysteries* as his primary example, that in early Graham choreography "expressive moments were consistently displaced by a formalist choreographic practice."[15] He argues that Graham's early pieces used structure to *create* meaning, not to express emotional interiority: "Primitive Mysteries was an exercise in the creation of choreographic meaning, rather than the articulation of any particular meaning in choreography" (*Dancing Modernism,* 49). He dates a later, "dramaturgical" stage of her work from 1934 to 1946.

Graham, then, like other modernist artists, understood Southwest Indians as a model or catalyst for her artistic inspiration, as a way of accessing a sense of mysticism that undergirded its aesthetic and its creation of meaning. She eschewed literal representation of Indian arts and in her "Primitive" series made no attempt to reproduce Native American dance steps, regalia, or ceremonies. At the same time, she, like others, understood aspects of Native American spirituality to be available to her for use in her own art making. Her drawing of mystical, spiritual inspiration from Southwest Indian culture to make *Primitive Mysteries*—without needing to explicitly acknowledge, let alone seek permission for this use—was thus in keeping with the cultural and political climate of the day.

THE INDIAN IMPULSE WAS SPENT

When Graham stopped discussing the Indian influence on her dances, and no longer gave them titles that overtly suggest the primitive, critics stopped recognizing any Indian influence in them. Some dancers did see a continuing relationship. O'Donnell, describing some of the first Graham choreography she saw, noted how Graham in the 1932 *Ceremonials* "had been influenced—after doing *Mysteries*—by the American Indian ceremonials; this piece wasn't a religious dance, except it did have a ceremonial quality, that same stylization" (Tobias, "Conversation with May O'Donnell," 78). Critics, though, saw Graham as moving in this piece and others of the day away from an "Indian" dance period into an "American" one. John Martin wrote in 1936 how, starting with the 1932 *Ceremonials,* "the Indian impulse was spent." Martin placed Graham's 1935 *Frontier* foremost among Graham's "American period" of dances with a "specifically American quality" (*America Dancing,* 31), writing how "'Frontier' is

Martha Graham,
"Indian Episode" from
American Document,
1938. Photograph by
Ben Pinchot.

deeply felt and simply projected." He added, "Here, one believes, Miss Graham has touched the finest point of her career, and only an audience of wooden Indians could fail to be moved by it" (21). By *Frontier,* following Martin's descriptions and Franko's stages, "America" has become the dramaturgical subject Graham's choreography represents. The "Indian" is, to a critic in the audience, but a wooden observer outside of its boundary lines.

It seems accurate that, after the early 1930s, Graham's "Indian" influence became either invisible to critics, as in *Frontier* (where an engagement with Indian land is only an implicit subject, a subtext of any "Frontier" woman's marking out of the land by fence and boundary and step), or literally representational. In the 1938 *American Document,* another cornerstone of Graham's "American period," the "Indian" is not an impulse but mimetically present, quite literally embodied by Graham, with long dark hair, draped in what looks like the stripes of a flag. Graham's 1940 *El Penitente* continues in this vein. Here Graham, inspired by the Penitente Indians she was exposed to during her travels in the Southwest, stages a dance drama in which a self-flagellating

Penitent battles with his sexual desire for a young Mary/Magdalene/Madonna figure. The piece's title makes its relation to Southwest Indians indisputable, a relation underscored in a contemporary video that introduces the dance as the camera pans the Southwest landscape with its Pueblo dwellings, "This most mysterious part of America," speaks of Graham's interest in the land "of the Hopi and Navajo Indian pueblos," shows pictures of curio figurines—and of Merce Cunningham dancing in the piece wearing a crown of thorns headpiece with lines radiating from it as in the curio figurines—and notes how "the land-scape and its people had a deep impact on Graham's spiritual life and work. Her dance, *El Penitente,* is a powerful evocation of these experiences." The choreography underscores this evocation when a vaguely "Indian" feel emerges early on in the angles and movement of the Penitent as he stomps his right leg repeatedly, his torso turned to the side, right arm outstretched and left bent in, and later as the Mary figure echoes this movement.[16] In 1942, Graham premiered a piece, *Land Be Bright,* in which Erick Hawkins appeared as James Fenimore Cooper's fictional character "Chingachgook, the friend of Leather Stocking."[17] The dance, according to biographer Don McDonagh, had "obvious structural parallels to the patriotic 'American Document,' but was not a successful dance." It was quickly dropped from her repertory just before she began work on what would become *Appalachian Spring.*[18]

Susan Manning has argued convincingly for the way *American Document* vivifies a change in American modern dance and its relation to racial representation. *American Document* is framed by and patterned after an American Minstrel show, with an all-white cast performing "episodes" that addressed and included readings by and about Puritans, Indians, Emancipation, and other aspects of American history, introduced by an Interlocutor. Manning describes how, when the piece was staged from 1938 to 1940, audiences applauded it and what she calls its "metaphorical minstrelsy"—its staging of racially marked issues and dances by white dancers in a kind of metaphorical blackface—enthusiastically.[19] By 1944, however, when Graham revived the dance for a retrospective, "critics looked askance at its reliance on metaphorical minstrelsy or, perhaps more accurately, at its layering of metaphorical minstrelsy and mythic abstraction" (Manning, *Modern Dance, Negro Dance,* 126). Manning continues, "After the war, American Document disappeared from Graham's repertory, and metaphorical minstrelsy from the representational apparatus of modern dance." In Manning's extensive description and discussion of the piece, she notes that critics in 1944 took particular issue with its staging of African American subjects. For example, John Martin wrote that Graham was "guilty of clichés" in "the actual movement of her Negro slavery section"—although in 1938, Martin had not questioned "an approximation of the style of a Negro minstrel." At the same time, as Manning notes, Martin's discomfort with Graham's references to

African American movement and style did *not* extend to her representation of Indians. "The Indian episode, however, is superb," he wrote.[20] At this point, then (what Franko would call Graham's "dramaturgical" stage), white representation of African Americans made critics uneasy, while representations of Indians on stage by white dancers did not.

Shortly following this period, however, through the choreographic process of making *Appalachian Spring*, Graham actively rejected literal representation of identifiable "Indians" in her dances and by her dancers, and instead returned to her earlier impulses to evoke the Indian as a haunting specter and spectator in American dance.

WE CAN NEVER ESCAPE THE SENSE OF HER HAVING BEEN HERE: EVOKING INDIANS IN *APPALACHIAN SPRING*

At Copland's request, Graham removed the Indian Girl from the dance that was to become *Appalachian Spring* after the second version of the script. In *Blood Memory*, Graham writes, "Somehow the ideas of the dream of the Indian girl were conveyed in the ballet through other means" (228). Indeed, from the earliest scripts, even before Copland voiced any opinion, Graham envisioned the Indian Girl as much in her absence as in her visible presence on stage. In her opening description to Copland, Graham wrote, "Certain things are alive and present for us although far in the actual past as far as time is concerned. But America is forever peopled with certain characters who walk with us in the present in a very real way." She continued, "That is why I have introduced an INDIAN GIRL. There is no reason in one sense for her to be there, that is in the purely realistic sense. And yet she is always with us . . . in the names of our cities, rivers, states, and in the play of all of us as children. We can never escape the sense of her having been here and of her continual existence as the supreme spectator of all our happenings." Throughout, this "Indian Girl" appears in the dance only to disappear into the shadows, or as an invisible, imaginary presence both there and not there, seen and not seen—yet pervasive and integral to the piece's structure and especially to its investigation of America. In other words, Graham envisioned the Indian Girl, from the start, as a haunting spectre—a kind of ghostly being present in her absence, suggested but never fully acknowledged, only visible in flits and moments, and then only to some of those watching.

This Indian Girl's absent presence—initially envisioned as emerging from the shadows, at times invisible to the women on stage, but then left out of the final version of the ballet—continues to haunt *Appalachian Spring*. She lurks in the piece, at times inhabiting the figure of the Bride, at times the Pioneer Woman, at times in the cradled imagined baby, apparent in the relation to eroticism, religion, and spirituality evoked by the piece's narrative. As with *Primitive*

Mysteries, her influence is signaled by the piece's title, by Graham's comments on the ballet, and by elements of the piece's story and structure.

One of the ways Graham signaled the Indian Girl's continuing presence in the piece is with the title "Appalachian Spring" itself. In her script, Graham explained that including the character of an Indian Girl was not unique to her exploration of America. "Certain poems have used her as the figure of the land; for example, Hart Crane, in his poem, 'The Bridge.'" The title "Appalachian Spring"—which comes from this poem[21]—was added to the ballet after the piece was largely completed, but Graham's script makes it clear that Crane's poem influenced her from the start. The section of the poem the phrase comes from, "The Dance," is itself from a subsection called "Powhatan's daughter." In this section of the poem, Crane invokes Powhatan's daughter—Pocahontas—both as the land that the narrator travels over and through and as a bride with whom he sleeps. "There was a veil upon you, Pocahontas, bride— / O Princess whose brown lap was virgin May,"[22] he writes, describing her "bridal flanks" and "tawny pride." As the narrator canoes the river, his eroticized descriptions of the land and water as the bride Pocahontas mount. "I could see / Your hair's keen crescent running," he writes. He then leaves his boat and takes "the portage climb." "I could not stop," he writes. And then, "One white veil gusted from the very top. / O Appalachian Spring! I gained the ledge." The phrase "Appalachian Spring," in other words, names the orgasmic moment—the "Appalachian Spring" is a spurting source of water—when the poet/narrator both sleeps with Pocahontas and reaches a vantage point from which to survey the land.

The trope of the land as female and sexually available to male explorers in what Annette Kolodny has called the "lay of the land" has a long history in American culture.[23] So too does the figure of Pocahontas as a sexually available embodiment of real American identity. Early colonial adoptions of the Pocahontas story stressed her marriage with a white man as a way of imagining and asserting a program of European absorption of Native cultures and lands. Scholar Robert Tilton describes how stories of the marriage of Pocahontas and John Rolfe flourished during the early eighteenth century as a model of the opportunity of intermarriage as a way of imagining and asserting the absorption of Native cultures and lands in consolidating America. By the post–Revolutionary War period, though, Tilton argues, the desire to avoid the theme of miscegenation led artists reconstituting the Pocahontas narrative to shift the focus of the tale from Pocahontas's marriage to Rolfe to her dramatic, love-inspired rescue of Captain John Smith, a focus for the tale that remains its central, Disneyfied, theme today.[24]

Even though the Pocahontas figure is visibly gone from the *Appalachian Spring* we know, it reflects the tropes of the Pocahontas story that Crane's poem evokes. The *Appalachian Spring* ballet's most basic story—that of a Bride and Husbandman "coming into their home for the first time," with the Groom stroking the house to signal his possession of it on his first entrance—echoes Tilton's analysis of the rhetoric the Pocahontas marriage story reinforces. Tilton writes how the Pocahontas/Rolfe marriage tale reinforces the story of "a white, land-owning race" with "native" rights to the land. He notes how via this marriage, these landowners (or at least their children) "would possess an Indian presence 'in the blood,' and perhaps even certain attractive Indian character traits, but would for all intents and purposes be Caucasian" (*Pocahontas,* 25). Following this analysis, then, it seems that Graham's bride, as well as the series of brides danced by Asian American women after Graham gave up the role, might well signal hints of a dark-figured Indian presence within a story of a newlywed American couple's acquisition of land in a piece that celebrates and consolidates America.[25]

Notes in Graham's notebook further reinforce the idea that Graham initially imagined choreographing a Pocahontas story, with a Pocahontas figure liter-ally represented on stage, during this period—and perhaps as part of this bal-let, as the comments in her early script referring to "the legend of Pocahontas, the legend of American land, youth, and country" represented by the imag-ined Indian Girl indicate. Graham's published notebooks, which cover dances that premiered from 1943 through 1973, contain a one-page sketch labeled "Pocahontas: Notes for a Dance Never Choreographed." The sketch outlines a piece staging Pocahontas as a court lady in London, watching European court dance. "Sarabande, Gavotte—Dance of period," Graham writes parentheti-cally. She goes on to describe a kind of showdown of gazes and visions, with Pocahontas and the women of the court transforming what they watch by way of their gazing at it, and that transformation signaled by the kind of dancing they watch being done. Pocahontas is first "seated to watch dancers," until the "women of the court eye her." Yet thus eyed by the women of the court, she her-self watches the men of the court, who, as she watches, are replaced in her eyes by "very elegant Indian warriors in ritual dances." By watching, Pocahontas thus turns them into Indian warriors and the dance they're doing into ritual dance. Graham writes next how the women of the court "eye her & seem to strip her of her court clothes & she becomes the beautiful savage again." This shift is signaled by new forms of dancing, "old dance forms, but with drums beneath," Graham suggests as a possibility. In these multiple economies of the gaze, Pocahontas can first transform the men into Indian warrior dancers by way of her gaze, but finally is herself transformed by the gaze of the London court women into "the beautiful savage" underneath the court lady attire in which she first appears. These descriptions mark the power of the gaze—especially that of the gazer at dance—in controlling and transforming what it sees. In Graham's proposed staging, the transformation would be quite lit-eral: as the "Pocahontas" figure watches, dancers depicting "elegant Indian warriors" replacing court men would appear on the stage. Presumably, in the dance Graham imagined, this section would involve a "beautiful savage" appearing on stage to dance (reflecting the scene where the women of the court eye Pocahontas, strip her of court clothes, and re-create her as the savage). In this formulation, then, the dance viewer controls the dancer and the dance, in whatever image she imagines. Graham's own viewing of Indian dance and her audience's viewing of her dance pieces are implicated in this economy alongside those watching and being watched within the staged Pocahontas narrative Graham is sketching.

In Graham's notes, the Pocahontas figure, thus transformed into "the beautiful savage again," goes on to envision the "rescue" version of the Pocahontas myth. "In her eyes she enacts the saving of John Smith," Graham writes. At the same time, Graham's notes also suggest Graham imagined a relation between this familiar John Smith rescue narrative and the less commonly represented marriage to Rolfe narrative; she ends her notes with the parenthetical comment "note—John Rolfe—his letter about marriage—His fear of damnation in marrying a strange woman—P. 128)." In this letter, Rolfe asks Governor Thomas Dale's permission to marry Pocahontas, in which he stresses that his chief intent is not "the unbridled desire of carnal affection" but instead the good of the plantation, the country, the glory of God, his own salvation, and "the converting to the true knowledge of God and Jesus Christ, an unbelieving creature, namely Pokahuntas." Rolfe's marital merger with Pocahontas—for the good of the country—is echoed here in Graham's reference to this marriage, and in the way the dancer dancing as "Pocahontas" (who would very likely have been Graham herself) merged, theatrically, with this Indian woman, for the good of American dance. As Pocahontas is sexually and politically available to Rolfe as a way of consolidating his foothold in the new world, she is culturally available to Graham who can embody her. By staging herself as an Indian (in *American Document* and then again presumably in the plans here), Graham embodies her dance as American, much like Pocahontas and Rolfe's mixed-race offspring; her dance, like the Rolfe descendants, is imagined as possessing certain attractive Indian character traits (like nobility and connection to the land, like old dance forms with drums beneath), but still being, for all intents and purposes, Western and Caucasian; it is, after all, still Graham—the descendent of Mayflower pilgrims—who would likely be the Indian, here.

All of this, of course, except for one thing: as Graham makes clear, these notes were to a dance that was *never choreographed*. Graham sketched out but then actively *rejected* this dance possibility; she did not in her choreography explicitly explore the Pocahontas narrative, that prototypical American myth. Nor did she explicitly stage a story of interracial marriage as consolidating of America and implicitly posit this merger as a trope for the consolidating of American modern dance. Instead, these notes, and the fact that this dance piece was sketched but not choreographed—and then explicitly labeled as "never choreographed"—signal Graham's serious consideration of such literal, visual representation of Indianness, and her conscious rejecting of any direct representation of Indian figures during this "American period."

Yet just because Graham rejected this literal, visual representation of Indianness does not necessarily mean she rejected the influence of American Indian culture, history, and dance on her work after this period. She herself suggests as much. "Although I have been greatly exposed to the Native American tribes, I have never done an Indian dance," she writes in her autobiography. "I've received an excitement and a blessing and a wonderment from the Indians" (*Blood Memory*, 176). The Indian Girl's continuing presence, "conveyed in the ballet through other means," registers in part in the sense of wonderment and blessing Graham saw herself receiving. It lurks too in the ways she is signaled in, but left out, of the piece.

In her autobiography, as Graham discusses the influence American Indian dances had on her career, Graham subtly *asks* readers to consider what is "left out" of artwork, as well as what is represented in it, as part of its beauty and meaning. In one passage, Graham describes beautiful, handwoven, sacred Indian rugs in which part of the rug is left incomplete: "It is made more beautiful and more mysterious by what is left out," she writes (*Blood Memory*, 176). Immediately after this comment, Graham continues. "The American Indian dances remained with me always, just like those haunting moments before sunrise in the pueblos, or my first view of the Hopi women in their squash blossom hair arrangements that I was to use in *Appalachian Spring*" (176). Perhaps one trace of this mysterious Indian Girl lurks, then, not in her overt representation, but in her corporeal absence evoked through dancers' hair arrangements. This Hopi "squash blossom" hair arrangement, with hair gathered in large buns on each side of the head, appears in Graham's dance, but has become one large bun behind the head.[26] This hairstyle serves as a reminder of the Indian Girl's lingering absent presence on the *Appalachian Spring* stage.

Another echo emerges in the Pioneer woman's choreographic connection to Native American figures and dances, or at least to the ideas of these Graham explored in her earlier pieces. Graham had stated that not only did she herself "never do an Indian dance," but even the Indian Girl, first imagined in the Copland ballet "will in no sense do Indian dancing." This figure's Indianness would instead be evoked or suggested. "She need not be dressed in the complete native sense but her belongings should have a sense of the exotic such as some of the old drawings have," Graham writes in her character descriptions. In a similar way, some of the Pioneer Woman's movement includes not literal depiction of Indian movement, but rather a subtle evocation of what seem like Indian-esque movement motifs. The Pioneer Woman's movement in this section echoes the bent-legged walking/hopping movement of the Virgin and the Penitent in *El Penitente*, as well as a vaguely Indian-dance feel to the thumps of the movement. Early in *Appalachian Spring,* after kneeling off and to the side of the Husbandman as he gazes out over the fence, the Pioneer Woman stands. Behind her, the four young women Followers dance in unison, hopping and holding the rims of their skirts up, then falling prostrate. As the Pioneer Woman begins to dance, the four Followers thump the ground with flattened hands, making a thudding sound, and the Pioneer Woman holds her right arm outstretched beside her and her left bent in and stomps her feet, the sound merging with the thumps made by the Followers, the movement evoking a vaguely Indian feel similar to that in *El Penitente.* She then kneels between the Followers with her arms outstretched above her while the followers circle her, echoing the Virgin surrounded by women in *Primitive Mysteries,* and then spreads her fingers behind each of the Followers' heads, echoing the crown of thorns made by dancers' arms behind the Virgin and by fingers spread behind the Virgin's head in *Primitive Mysteries.* The movements happen in succession, grouped together in a brief section of a much longer piece, evoking movement clearly labeled "Indian" elsewhere and thereby signaling the absent Indian Girl's fleeting, momentary emergence in the choreography.

Another echo of this Indian Girl can be heard in the way all the women in the piece negotiate a relation with Christianity as male authority, depicted by the Preacher. The Pioneer Woman's hands, returning to a prayer position in between her dances, signal that relation, as do the Followers' circling of the Preacher and their eroticized adulation of him. Like the erotic relation between groom and Pocahontas/land in Crane's poem and the tempestuous dangers it threatens, the ballet addresses the erotic desire of Bride and Husbandman, as well as between Preacher and Followers. Here, though, this erotic struggle is explored in the context of a patriarchal Christianity. As *Primitive Mysteries* and *El Penitente* demonstrate, Graham's interest in and exposure to Native American culture and dance emerged via Southwest Indian relation to Catholicism via women's experience of them. The Indian religious practices Graham explored in *El Penitente,* in particular, negotiate sexuality in relation to Christianity; the piece explores a young man's seduction by Magdalene and condemnation and salvation by the Christ figure, set in an implicitly Southwest Indian context. As numerous scholars have noted, Native religious practices of the Southwest negotiate a relation to Catholicism, with practitioners finding spaces in which to merge and continue a relation to Native culture and religion as Catholics. Similarly, *Appalachian Spring* explores the ways female sexual desire and women's artistic ambition come into tension with the imposed structures of marriage, church, and male authority. A central impulse of the dance is this tension between the authoritative Preacher and Husband, and the Bride and other women—and also between the narrative of domesticity the piece projects and the incredibly driven, uncompromising, and ambitious artistic visionary that was Martha Graham. *Appalachian Spring*'s study of relation to male authority and its strictures of women's sexuality, in other words, sounds an echo of Southwest

Indian cultures' negotiated relations to Spanish Catholicism—and the search for a space of joy and ecstasy within imposed structure in which to flourish.

Yet another "haunting moment" where the Indian Girl emerges might be in the cradled arms of the Bride and the Pioneer Woman. This cradling clearly references the Bride's imagining of a future baby. In *Blood Memory*, Graham tells how she once actively considered adopting a six-month old part-Indian baby girl as her daughter (195). "I found myself thinking of this child, thinking seriously of what it would mean to adopt her," Graham writes, ultimately rejecting the idea. The incident occurred in 1951, well after *Appalachian Spring* was choreographed. Yet Graham described it as "the most vivid reality I have had regarding a child, the most complete identification of my life with one of a child's" (195). Perhaps the vividly absent baby cradled by the two women in *Appalachian Spring* elicited this identification, and the empty-armed rocking evokes the absented Indian Girl. Critics are quick to note the biographical connections between this piece, celebrating domestic love, and Graham's passionate love for Erick Hawkins at the time.[27] Yet Graham was fifty when the piece premiered; if the possibility of parenthood this dance explored also had any biographical referent, it was most probably to an adopted child. O'Donnell explained how in making the piece, "once, right onstage (and we'd never practiced or talked about this), she suddenly gave me an imaginary baby. It was her dream child, of course, and naturally I took the 'baby' and sat down" (Tobias, "Conversation with May O'Donnell," 92). She notes that she teased Graham about it at the time. "Martha, you weren't married long enough to have a baby" (interview). Perhaps Graham's "dream child," invisible yet gestured toward, appearing in her arms on the American frontier much sooner than the Bride could have given birth to her, was the Indian baby girl that almost became "the most vivid reality" she had with a child.

Most obviously, the Indian Girl envisioned as integral to and then absented from *Appalachian Spring* lurks in the exploration of land and space, fenced off for pioneers, that the piece and its set so clearly evoke. The "thoughts of a pioneer woman when she sees an Indian girl on whose parents' land the frontiersmen have settled" are still there in the dance as a "dance of place" conceived in recognition of American land as Indian land. It seems, in fact, that Graham initially envisioned the Indian Girl as emblematic of the relation to place she saw the ballet exploring. "She is like a tree or a rock in her relationship to place," Graham wrote in her first character description of the Indian Girl. "At times we forget her but she is always with us as part of the romance of our youth as a land" ("Copland Script," 3). In the second version, Graham adds, "In the sense that she is the land she is the protagonist of all that happens here. I think we do not know how often she possesses our thoughts." Graham notes, "She is the symbolic figure of the land, the Eve of our Genesis."[28] The Indian Girl lurks then not only in these various hauntings glimpsed in the piece, but also in the sense of land, place, and American "appetite for space" the final dance so clearly explores.

These influences, however, remain fleeting and suggestive—haunting the piece, rather than overtly appearing in it. It seems that, as with her choreographing of *Primitive Mysteries* and in her choreographic process more generally, Graham in *Appalachian Spring* did not make any Indian subtext (or, for that matter, any other text or subtext) overtly clear to her dancers.[29] Instead, it remained an impulse, a "haunting moment," and perhaps the manifestation of whatever Graham understood the blessing and wonderment she received from the Indians to be.

IMPLICATIONS

In many ways, Graham was radical in her explorations and understandings of the troubles attending non-Indian representation of Indianness. In her initial script, she writes: "I realize that Indian material is hard to handle, and that it must be done with theatricality and complete design, rather than from the anthropological point of view. In that sense she is not a native Indian. She is not an Indian's Indian but a white man's Indian." Her recognition that Indianness is not (only) about the performative representation of visibly or authentically Indian markers would spark lively debate today among contemporary explorations of Native American history, politics, and identity. For one, her comment about how the Indian Girl in her initial script is "a white man's Indian" suggests Graham's awareness of her own position as a white artist representing an idea of an Indian, and of the limits of this idea. For another, it (and especially Graham's later rejection of it) signals an awareness of the limits of visual representation of "Indians" more generally. As Leah Dilworth notes in her study of representations of Indians in the Southwest, the tourist industry creates Indians as objects "caught in the trap of visibility," viewed by tourists from a "protected, removed position, rather like a box seat at the theater" (*Imagining Indians,* 107). "The tourist is always the subject," Dilworth writes, "The Indian is always the object of the gaze, a commodity to be consumed visually" (109). By rejecting visual representations of Indians in her later choreography, Graham refused her theater-goers this position of visual commodification and consumption.

Her piece's rejection of visual representation of Indianness might also be said to challenge what Chadwick Allen calls "the U.S. government's attempt to systematize and regulate American Indian personal and political identities through tabulations of 'blood quantum' or 'degree of Indian blood,'" and other challenges to the authenticity of Native people who may not appear sufficiently Indian according to visual markers of identity.[30] Allen, drawing from an analysis by M. Annette Jaimes, discusses how federal legislation that required Indians to prove one-half or more Indian blood in order to receive "Dawes Act" allotments led to a standard of blood quantum "that came to control Indian access to all federal services, including commodity rations, annuity payments, and health care. Following this history of federally legislated 'blood quantum,'" he writes, "Indians who did not 'look' Indian enough were—and are today—particularly suspected of falsifying indigenous identity" ("Blood (and) Memory," 97).[31] By conceptualizing American Indian presence in her dances as possible in terms other than visual representation as recognizable Indians, Graham sidesteps the legacy of these troublesome federal identification policies.

Graham's approach, her famous descriptions of "movement as the one speech that cannot lie," the power she saw in modern dance movement, rather than in "steps . . . too obviously learned," and her identification of Indian dance as a source of these understandings were themselves sources of inspiration to some American Indian dancers. Modern dancer Juan Valenzuela, who identified himself as an "anglicized" Aztec and Yaqui and Spanish "first-generation Mexican-Indian," noted his identification with Graham's approach and his debt to Graham at a 1972 conference on anthropology and American Indian dance.[32] Speaking as "the only Indian representing the Indian Nation at this conference," Valenzuela expressed dismay at choreographers who see "surface symbolism in our traditional and ceremonial rituals" and then "add these to their choreographic endeavors and title them Indian." He wrote, "How can they? They desecrate what we do in religious supplication to the Great Spirit" ("Roots, Branches, and Blossoms," 303–4). Yet he notes how Graham's conceptualization of modern dance in relation to rhythm and inspiration, for him, sets it apart from other modern dance techniques that have "only worked my tired aching muscles with repetition, for skill" but have "not fed my spirit or my imagination with inspiration." He wrote, "I am indebted to Martha Graham. She has been the teacher who has devastated my being with her technique, with her philosophy, and with her dances" (300). Valenzuela cites the oft-quoted passage, noted above, in which Graham writes how "America's great gift to the arts is rhythm," and identifies "The Indian Dance" as about "awareness of life, complete relationship with that work in which he finds himself" (300–301). Valenzuela begins his citation of Graham's famous passage a paragraph earlier than most, starting with her discussion of how "it is not possible for one people to understand another people entirely, or to feel with the soul of another," and the question, "How then is it possible to adopt a dance form which is the revelation of a people's soul?" Valenzuela, in this way, registers and appreciates Graham's recognition of her own inability to fully understand "another people," as well as her understanding of dance as not just about skill, but rather as something that feeds the spirit and imagination. Her drawing of understandings and inspirations from Indian dance and incorporation of these in her technique and choreography, rather than her representation of "Indians" or "Indian dance" on stage, then, struck a chord with and was a source of inspiration for this American Indian modern dancer.

At the same time, Graham's negotiations of American Indian dance in her choreographic project do support other troublesome government policies and rhetoric, such as those asserting the trope of the "vanishing American" and of a paternalistic "Great Father" looking after his children. The absent present Indian Girl in *Appalachian Spring* is, most obviously, absent; virtually no discussions of the piece in the past half century (other than Graham's own) have mentioned her influence on or place in the piece. Conceived as existing in the shadows, only fleetingly visible to those around her, as an imaginary playmate for children, as sitting at the feet of a pioneer Mother, as standing "revealed in the shadows" (which is how the second script ends), she is defined, from the start, as childlike, and through her own absence. Her presence on the stage—if indeed it is such—is gestured toward as an adoptable Indian baby. The removal of even this level of infantilized, shadowy recognition in the final production reinforces all the more forcefully these familiar tropes.

Graham's articulation of Indian presence in her choreography via a mystical, unmarked Indian "blessing" on herself has troublesome implications as well. Graham's experience of spiritual effect from watching Indian dancing echoed that of other modernist artists' interest in primitive cultures. As Dilworth notes, "Modernist primitivism was never about practicing Native American belief systems. It was, rather, about an aesthetic practice that would lead to spiritual experience" (*Imagining Indians*, 199). In this modernist aesthetic, Native American culture provided the individual artist with artistic fodder for her *own* development, rather than marked a significant relation to, recognition of, or respect for these as Native American religious practices, practiced by and for Native American peoples. As Dilworth writes, "The artist, in the role of mutable, mobile maker of meaning, retained the power of signification and subjectivity." She adds, "Indians emerge as free floating signifiers available for all kinds of signification" (209). Although Graham was perhaps radical in her eschewing of representation in her explorations of a perceived Indian blessing on her dance making, this blessing's relation to Native American peoples remains shrouded and romanticized, and understood only in relation to Graham's own individual artistic development as a dancer and choreographer. Her relation to Indian culture was thus similar, and similarly troublesome, to that of other modernist artists who developed their careers by engaging their own ideas of Indianness in their art making.

The effects of Graham's exposure to Southwest Indian ceremonial dance seem more ambivalent and complicated than her comments about receiving "an excitement and a blessing and a wonderment from the Indians" might imply, as well. Anecdotes about Graham's experiences suggest that perhaps what Graham received from her exposure to the Indians of the Southwest was, at times, less a blessing than the fallout from her presence at ceremonies she was not adequately prepared, or invited, to witness. De Mille describes an event that suggests Graham's viewing of Indian dance in the Southwest was in fact sometimes inappropriate and offensive, and led to illness and delay in her choreographic work. De Mille explains how, one July in the early 1930s, Graham and Horst got off The Chief transcontinental train in New Mexico and learned "that there was to be an important rain dance at the Zuni pueblo, to which the public was not invited." They decide to go, hop in de Mille's jalopy to drive to the pueblo, and are riveted by the dancing—but leave "precipitously, first because we were urged to get the hell out by the masked and dancing priests, and second because it had started, perhaps in response to the magic, to rain very hard. The trip home was forty miles long. The rain got harder; there was thunder, lightening, flash floods. Louis got pneumonia. His summer plans were spoiled, and so were Martha's. She brought him home and nursed him for weeks" (de Mille, *Martha*, 175–76).

The way Graham's interest in Indian culture empowers her as *American* dancer sounds familiar, and troublesome, strains as well. Through her dancing—blessed by her ideas of Indians and, particularly by *Appalachian Spring,* called "the cap of Graham's Americana period" (McDonagh, *Martha Graham,* 177)—she becomes the heir of America and of American dance, holding title "in the blood," much like the landowning titles held by the offspring of Pocahontas and John Rolfe. It is in her "blood memory" that American dance flows.[33] Her self-conception as progenitor of an American heritage, legitimized in part through her recognition and merger with an absent Indian influence, further appears in her imagining of herself as the mother of an adopted Indian baby—before such adoption practices were restricted.[34] The Indian blessing Graham saw herself receiving, in other words, enabled an American dance that displaced and replaced the very Indians whose blessing was supposedly being received, and reinforced absence as the primary trope of reference to American Indians in modern dance history without acknowledging its contribution.

This modernist move to displace and replace the very Indians whose culture and spirituality are seen to undergird its artistic contribution was also a product of its time and connected to federal policy of the day. In 1943–45, Congress was attacking Collier's reform policies and brewing new termination policies, designed, as Prucha writes, "to assimilate the Indians once and for all and thus to end the responsibility of the federal government for Indian affairs" (*Great Father,* 1013). This move to assimilate American Indians into mainstream white society reemerged with particular fervor during World War II. The war, and the active involvement of large numbers of American Indians who volunteered for military service, brought with it attitudes and expectations about Indian relation to American national identity.[35] On the one hand, this surge of Indian participation in the military reinforced stereotypical notions of Indians as natural warriors.[36] Yet even as rhetoric of the day reinforced this idea of Indian exceptionalism, it also reinforced the political identity of Indians as American citizens in a period of nationalism; it thus reinforced drives toward assimilation (1009).

The war's effect on the economy curtailed possibilities of federal recognition of Indian self-determination as well, as funding for the Indian Office was drastically cut, derailing the policies of Indian self-governance for which Collier had been pushing. Postwar economic policies that continued to call for reduction of government spending, and cold war rhetoric that distrusted communal values, compounded moves toward Indian assimilation and led to the passage of federal policies that sought to terminate Indians' trust relationship with the U.S. government—and, eventually, relationship to Indian land. These policies, which came into effect in the early 1950s, were designed to merge Native peoples into mainstream American culture, thereby decreasing the presence and visibility of Indians as Indians, just as did the staged versions of *Appalachian Spring* that toured to such acclaim while these policies were emerging.

At the time of *Appalachian Spring*'s creation and reception, in other words, World War II and its attending attitudes and policies created an environment in which Native Americans and Native American identities were once again being pushed, from various angles, to meld into and support America and a unified American identity.[37] The political environment of the 1930s, in which artists overtly drew from and celebrated spiritual and mystical aspects of Native American culture in their own artistic explorations, no longer prevailed. Instead, the Indian, as Indian, was understood to be merging into America, supporting its war effort, lurking underneath its Americanizing moves, seeking inclusion in its mainstream. Given this climate, a ballet of American identity, in which a Pioneer Woman looks out and no longer sees the "Indian girl on whose parents' land the frontiersmen have settled," is accurate to the wartime effects and policies of the time. Graham's initial envisioning of this Indian Girl as "deep in our blood as a people," and her description that "we can never escape the sense of her having been here and of her continual existence as the supreme spectator to all our happenings," is accurately embodied in this figure's representational *absence* from the stage.

What is exciting about Graham's ballet is the way her scripts and autobiography so loudly cry out for recognition of this present absent Indian, and how she haunts American modern dance. Rather than ignoring the Indian influence on Martha Graham's career—and on the development of American modern dance—what if we were to instead follow Graham and take her claims seriously when she says, "The American Indian dances remained with me always, just like those haunting moments before sunrise in the pueblos," exploring the blessing she saw herself as receiving from Southwest Indian peoples, land, and cultures, looking at the way American Indian dance haunts her career, recognizing the influence, inspiration, excitement, blessing she says she received—and also analyzing it critically in our discussions and teaching of Graham's choreography and of the American modern dance history of which it is so central a part.

SIX

Held in Reserve: José Limón, Tom Two Arrows, and American Indian Dance in the 1950s

You are being held in reserve for the contributions that you can make to the future of your people.

> ▸ *José Limón, speaking to students at*
> *the Flandreau Indian High School in*
> *South Dakota, as remembered by*
> *Daystar/Rosalie Jones*

In 1954, U.S. President Dwight D. Eisenhower inaugurated an international cultural exchange program, hoping to display the artistic fruits of freedom and democracy abroad and to thereby help fight the cold war by counter-ing Communist attacks on American culture as greedy and materialistic. The first company exported as cultural emissaries for this purpose was that of José Limón. In November and December 1954, Limón and members of his company went to South America, where they performed *La Malinche, The Moor's Pavane,* and ten other pieces. Limón's Mexican heritage and Spanish language abilities were seen as assets in his ability to appeal (and speak) to Latin American audi-ences. Yet although he staged himself as El Indio in dance pieces that emphasized Indigenous struggles in the Americas, and viewers noted his dark skin and high cheekbones, the U.S. government did not stress Limón's racial or ethnic identity, instead presenting his work as exemplary of American modern dance and of the superiority of American democracy and cultural production in the context of the cold war.[1]

Six months after Limón's trip, Eisenhower's Dance Panel raised the question of exporting American Indian dance as part of the cold war agenda. Questions about Limón's relation to Indigenous identity did not enter the picture; the search at this time was for a recognizably "Indian" dance practitioner to export. As Naima Prevots outlines, panel members first considered sending Reginald and Gladys Laubin—two white dancers who had been adopted by the Sioux and spent their lives researching and performing authentic Plains dances in full regalia.[2] The Laubins were rejected as Indian dancers because, according to one State Department spokesperson, "they are too civilized, and do not act according to the preconceived notion that Europeans have of American Indians." The Laubins were considered and rejected again in 1961, although panel member and dance critic Walter Terry protested that the Laubins were "more Indian than the Indians." Dancer and choreographer Agnes de Mille then recommended sending a Boy Scout troupe who had made an extensive study of Native Americans. The panel rejected these and other non-Indian or amateur groups, not believing them to be authentic. Instead, the State Department sent Onoda'gega (Onondaga) Iroquois dancer Tom Two Arrows on trips to India and Asia in 1956 and 1957.[3] In stark contrast to Limón, the government promoted Tom Two Arrows as an authentic American Indian demonstrating authentic Indian dances on world stages.

This chapter explores the complexities of arguing—with over fifty years' hindsight—for both José Limón and Tom Two Arrows as Native choreographers. While these dancers' State Department tours have most frequently, and accurately, been read in the context of the cold war, this chapter suggests another political agenda at work, albeit more obliquely, in the U.S. State Department's bookings of both in the 1950s: the Indian termination policies of this same period. In these domestic policies, the U.S. government sought to terminate its trust relation with Indian people and their tribes, and to abolish Indians' ties to reservation lands and cultures by coercing Indian assimilation into the cultural mainstream. This chapter suggests that in different but related ways, José Limón and Tom Two Arrows—both working within the strictures of their time—succeeded by inhabiting, however unconsciously, comfortable positions within the rhetoric of these termination-era agendas. Limón, by *not* being read as a Native choreographer, but as an American emissary of "the modern dance," fulfilled the termination-era assimilation narrative. His position as an American modern dance artist who looked but didn't act and wasn't read as Indian fit within this era's drive to Americanize Indians. If his brown body, telling the stories it told, spoke of Native identity at all, it was of an identity so assimilated as to not even register as Indian. Two Arrows, on the other hand, fulfilled the termination agenda through his billing as an identifiably real Indian, demonstrating authentic Indianness for non-Indian audiences, and *not* as a contemporary choreographer making innovative performance choices in a changing world. Both of these dancers were caught in the attitudes reinforced by the racist policies of their era, and performed within them. Yet the same time as they built their careers while maneuvering through this terrain, their choreographic choices also exceeded the termination-inspired narrow definitions of the 1950s. As Native American dancers and community members have long recognized, both made important contributions to American Indian dance history.

TERMINATION AND INTER-INDIAN IDENTITY

During the 1950s, the U.S. government actively pursued a redefinition of its political and economic relation to Indian peoples via land claims and assimilationist policies, including a de facto promotion of pan-Indian or inter-Indian identity in urban centers. This termination era began in 1946 with the creation of the Indian Claims Commission, to which tribes presented their long-standing claims concerning stolen lands and broken treaties, received monetary compensation, and thereby finalized claims settlements for lands worth more than the cash awarded, effectively ending any federal responsibility for them. In 1952, Congress established a Voluntary Relocation Program, offering counseling and guidance for Indians who relocated from reservation lands to urban centers. In 1953, Congress passed the Termination Resolution, which called for Indian equality under the law as well as the release of certain tribes from federal supervision: for terminated tribes, this meant the end of federal protection and aid, and of state tax exemptions. Indian peoples whose lands were rich in natural resources, such as the timber-rich Klamaths and Menominees, were singled out for early termination.[4] In the place of this federal aid and state tax exemption, Public Law 959, passed in 1956, made institutional and on-the-job training available to Indians, but only in urban areas, usually far away from Indian lands and homes. The relocation and termination policies of the 1950s thus worked to separate Native peoples from ties to their lands, reservations, cultures, and communities, and encroached on Indian rights of self-determination.

While many Native people refused to leave their home communities, an estimated thirty-five thousand did relocate to major urban areas in response to these policies.[5] In these new locations—which included almost every major city in the United States—new inter-Indian communities comprised of Native peoples from a diversity of backgrounds, brought together through relocation, held regular powwows. In the 1950s, these intertribal powwows served (as they continue to serve) complex political, social, and spiritual functions within American Indian communities. As Philip Deloria suggests in his discussion of "white urban and suburban hobbyists" of this era, they also began to serve a purpose for the non-Indian enthusiasts who frequented them: they became a site for the acceptable performance of "Indian" identity. Hobbyists were drawn to the "Indian" identities performed at powwows, attending them with fervent interest. Eventually, this led them to see the "Indian" identity danced at powwows as increasingly available to and indistinguishable from themselves, and they started to dance in the powwow arena themselves.[6] By disarticulating Indian peoples from particular land, the era's termination policies had helped enable this identification;

if Indians could move to urban centers, dance at powwows, and still be Indian, non-Indians who danced properly at these powwows felt they could also "consolidate a unique personal identity" through their own engagement with this Indian authenticity, Deloria recounts (*Playing Indian,* 141).

Hobbyists' drives to learn authentic Indian powwow dancing, however, required that this dancing be stable and learnable—that there be an authentic dance by way of which Indian identity was performed and to which the hobbyists could assiduously adhere. This definition left little room for understandings of Indian dance (or Indian identity) as flexible or innovative. Deloria quotes one 1961 powwow hobbyist journal's chastisement of some white hobbyists who failed to represent Indian culture accurately. "They know about three more facts and a lot more fiction about Indians than the audiences for whom they perform; and beyond that, they feel that improvising is the key to success," the article states. "This attitude may be appropriate for modern dance, but it has nothing to do with Indians" (*Playing Indian,* 145). The hobbyists, while policing themselves, thus clearly articulated the ways in this termination era (and largely since) in which choreographic explorations understood as integral to modern dance such as change, innovation, and improvisation have been seen to have "nothing to do with Indians."

A careful examination of the work of José Limón and Tom Two Arrows, however, enables a different understanding of Indian dance of the era, albeit one not readable at the time or since as part of modern dance history. While both dancers embodied national termination agendas in their staging of work on behalf of the State Department, this chapter suggests that their choreographic explorations and improvisations also worked in complicated ways to challenge those termination-era identities and agendas, and also to challenge understandings of American Indian dance that ignore their complex improvisatory contributions.

JOSÉ LIMÓN: TERRA INCOGNITA OF THE SPIRIT

In 1939, modern dance choreographer José Limón created his first major choreographic work for the Doris Humphrey–Charles Weidman company. Sequestered in a studio at Mills College, Limón embarked on what he called "the most precarious of journeys, that into one's interior, the 'terra incognita' of the spirit." He writes in his memoir, "The rare and blessed solitude I found in the improvised studio that summer gave me, such as I was, to myself. What I would find there I did not know. All I knew was that I wanted to find out who and what I was. For almost ten years I had been a pupil, disciple and follower. Now the time had come for me to assume full stature."[7] He called the piece he choreographed out of these interior explorations and improvisations *Danzas Mexica-*

nas. It included solos from what he called "five symbolic figures from Mexican history—the Indio, Conquistador, Peón, Caballero, and Revolucionario." Excerpts from it, filmed in Mexico in 1951, show Limón, bare chested, wearing the modern dance uniform of long black tights, rehearsing the "Revolutionario" and "Indio" sections: he investigates relationships between stiff angled arms and legs two-stepping in place with the quality of the body's weight that are integral to the fall and release of Humphrey technique, and to his own.[8] Limón writes that in making the piece he connected "The confrontation of the blood and the culture of the European and the American Indian, resulting in centuries of unremitting conflict," to the "cruel, heroic, and at the same time beautiful story of my native land." He writes, "It is never entirely absent from my thinking. I am certain that it has been a strong influence in shaping me into the person I have become" (*Unfinished Memoir,* 90).

Ten years later, Limón founded his own company. In the first dance he choreographed for it, Limón again staged himself as El Indio in a piece rooted in Mexican history and culture. This 1949 piece told the story of "La Malinche," identified in the program notes as the repentant spirit of an Indian Princess who had aided Cortez and who now returned to "lament her treachery" and "expiate her ancient betrayal" (Limón, *Unfinished Memoir,* 138–39). The dance, a trio, stresses the conflict between El Conquistador (Cortez) and La Malinche (an Indian woman), as well as the charged relation of El Indio—the unnamed Indian man—to both Cortez and La Malinche. In it, Lucas Hoving, a fair, Dutch, visibly white dancer playing Cortez, lifts the woman to his groin on a cross, displaying a sexual conquering and the interwoven, eroticized, relationships between colonized and colonizing men and the woman upon whom this violence is acted. The cross becomes alternately a tool of erotic dominance over La Malinche and a sword, as Hoving turns it sideways and thrusts it forth, while La Malinche turns him and the outstretched sword on the stage, directing him and his weapon, at least momentarily. When the El Indio figure emerges from the wings, on his knees, La Malinche returns as a spirit, hovering ghost-like about him, covering him with her skirt, he then pushing her away. Rather than performing stances of domination, in this section the dancers begin to move together, in sync with one another, dancing with stomping kicks and clapping, embodying elements of Mexican dance in between their leg lifts and arabesque hinge turns.[9] In its juxtaposition of the cross as sexualized weapon in the first section and the haunting, powerful spirit of the second, the piece provides comment on the compulsory Christianity of European domination, and on the force and import of an ever-present, expansive, spirit world in the face of this colonization. It also draws on the power of story, framing its investigation, as Limón's work so often did and so much contemporary Native stage dance does, in dramatic narrative.

In 1951, Limón premiered *Los Cuatro Soles* in Mexico City, dancing as Quetzalcoatl, the plumed serpent, in a piece "based on an ancient legend explaining the pre-Hispanic concept of the universe." For the same program, he also choreographed and danced as the Archangel appearing in a Mexican church in "Tonantzintla," a dance "inspired by the sumptuous and ingenuous spirit of Mexican baroque art as represented by the decoration of the name of the Indian church of Santa María Tonanzintla near Cholula." A month later, he created another piece, *Diálogos,* in which Limón dances first as an Indian Emperor (Montezuma) who surrenders to a European captain, Cortez, in 1520. Next, he appears as The Indian President—the Indigenous President Benito Juarez who, the program notes read, with "the strength and nobility of his race . . . smashes the imperialist attempt" of an Austrian archduke, the invading Hapsburg prince Maximilian, in 1867.[10] Retitled *Dialogues* when performed at Jacob's Pillow Dance Festival in the Berkshires that year, the piece reprises themes from *La Malinche,* here even more overtly addressing histories of colonization. In the first section of the piece, Limón dances as Montezuma bare chested, wearing long hair, a head piece, shorts, and ankle dressings while Hoving performs as Cortez. Limón's angular, strong movements engage with Hoving's more lyrical phrasing, Limón's long hair swirling as they touch and lift each other.[11] Here, as noted, the European conquistador prevails. In the second section, Limón is now dressed as The Indian President Juarez, in a black suit and bow tie, yet clearly also—through his regal carriage, lifted chest, and angularity, not to mention the fact that Limón is dancing both roles—an 1867 reprisal of the 1520 Indian Emperor. Hoving appears as The Archduke (Maximillian), in uniform, with epaulettes. Here, the two men dance with their backs to each other, looking out away from and almost ignoring one another. Toward the end of the piece, Limón removes a slip of paper from his pocket and holds it out, reading it, while Hoving comes forward, lowered, looking increasingly cowed. One caption to the photo reads "Lucas Hoving as the Emperor Maximilian, hears his doom read by Mexican mestizo ruler, Juarez" ("José Limón," 15). The piece ends after Limón stands legs apart, holding the paper out over his groin; Hoving falls to the floor, and Limón, still holding the paper, steps over Hoving and walks off stage. Each of these Limón pieces from the early 1950s makes overt or implicit reference to the European colonization of Native peoples in the Americas—and also displays the cultural and political strength of Native peoples and cultures in the face of this colonization.

Since he began dancing, Limón's importance has been cited as a modern dancer in the tradition of Isadora Duncan, Ruth St. Denis and Ted Shawn, Martha Graham, and Charles Weidman and, especially, in his artistic lineage as a student and protégé of modern dance choreographer Doris Humphrey rather than to any relation he might have to Mexican American or Native American

José Limón and Lucas Hoving, Diálogos, *1951. Photograph by Jacqueline Paul Roberts. Courtesy Jerome Robbins Dance Division, The New York Public Library for the Performing Arts, Astor, Lenox, and Tilden Foundations*

dance. It was not that no one noticed Limón's heritage. Critics at the time and since have been quick to connect Limón's visual appearance and his weighted physicality to an Indian background. "He had the high cheekbones and dark eyes of a Native American," writes Ann Vachon.[12] Ann Murphy writes, "José had a high, fine bone structure that looked windswept and regal. He was smoke-dark like his Yaqui ancestors, and his physical body emitted a power and weight that lent him a regal earthiness fit for an Indian leader."[13] Former Limón dancer turned critic Ernestine Stodelle described how he, "in masterful strokes, combined the sophisticate of elegance of the Spaniard with the animal vitality of the Indian."[14] Nor is it that visual and performative markers of race in modern dance didn't register during the period Limón was performing. The dance world identified and championed Alvin Ailey's interweaving of African American themes and focus with modern dance vocabulary only a few years after Limón staged these pieces, and the State Department sent Ailey abroad as cultural ambassador in 1961, in part to counter images of racism and racial unrest in the United States.

The lack of critical attention to Limón's Native identity stems undoubtedly, in part, from the fraught politics surrounding recognition of Indigenous Indian identity in Mexico, during Limón's lifetime as well as today. Limón's family, as he notes in his autobiography, "did their best to forget" the "dash of Indian blood" they, "like most Mexicans," had. "It was not considered quite nice, in those times, in respectable provincial society, to be tainted with the blood of the wild tribes of the mountains or deserts, the peons enslaved in the gigantic haciendas, or *las plebes,* the degraded and poverty stricken rabble of the cities" (*Unfinished Memoir,* 2). These complicated, class-based, racial politics in Mexico, as well as complicated relations to Indigenous identity in Mexican American communities, have undoubtedly contributed to the lack of critical discussion about Limón's relation to Indigenous identity or dance history.

Yet despite presentations of Limón as unmarked racially, Limón served (and continues to serve) as a role model for Native dancers and choreographers. Daystar/Rosalie Jones, the artistic director and choreographer for Daystar: Contemporary Dance-Drama of Indian America, wrote about the personal rapport she felt with Limón because of his mixed Indian-Spanish heritage, and the special private choreography class she had with him at Julliard in 1969 and 1970, while she was studying there on a scholarship for young Native artists instigated by Lee Udall, wife of Secretary of the Interior Morris Udall.[15] In that class, she and a Lakota Sioux student, Cordell Morsette, worked with Limón on dance composition. She and Morsette were later sent "out in the field" to the Flandreau Indian High School in South Dakota to teach. She writes that over the course of a semester "the Flandreau students created, and performed, in a theatrical modern dance context the work we called *The Gift of the Pipe,* a piece Morsette had scripted that told the story of White Buffalo Calf Pipe Woman.

Daystar/Rosalie Jones, an official from South Dakota Arts Council, Martha Hill (then director at Julliard School of Dance), and José Limón at Flandreau Indian High School, South Dakota, 1971 or 1972. Courtesy Daystar/Rosalie Jones.

Just months before his death, Limón arrived as a special guest to see the students' end-of-semester performance. Daystar writes, "Mr. Limón addressed the student body at Flandreau Indian High School. I paraphrase his remark to the student assembly. He said: 'You are being held in reserve for the contributions that you can make to the future of your people.'"[16]

Alejandro Roncería, the program director at the Aboriginal Dance Project at Banff Centre for the Arts in Alberta, Canada, from 1996 to 2001, also brought up José Limón as an important figure in the history of Aboriginal or Native American stage dance. "When José Limón started doing some of that work in the 1940s, 1950s, he was bringing already these ideas about Mexican traditional dances into the stage," Roncería said.[17] Roncería saw in Limón's choreography not just the structures of European dances like the pavane, but also the influence of Indigenous dance and culture. He noticed Indigenous structures,

*José Limón with a Flandreau Indian High School Student, Eagle Horse, 1971 or 1972.
Courtesy Daystar/Rosalie Jones.*

for example, in the choreographic interweavings of line that echoed Mexican Indigenous dances' references to the braiding of long hair. "His dances are very influenced by the structures of Indigenous dance in Mexico. All the braiding," he said, "I've seen this kind of thing in the pueblos. There are some traditional dances that are doing this." Roncería also noted an Indigenous influence in "the way you perceive the beat" in Limón's choreography.[18] Limón's work also shares many elements with much contemporary stage dance today created in explicit relation to Indigenous dance: a base in personal, historical, tribal, or mythic narrative; an engagement with the violence of Christianity; a recognition, and sometimes an invocation, of a spirit world; the use of the paper document as literal prop and historical storytelling device.

While it may seem that Limón's activity in the dance world was far removed from Native American political strife of the time, Limón's autobiography suggests important historical connections and rhetorical links to Indigenous histories. Limón writes how his family moved to the United States in 1915, two years after Limón's uncle was killed during the Mexican Revolution and as "chaos reigned over northwestern Mexico" (*Unfinished Memoir,* 4). They moved "from one northern city to another," living for a time "in the frontier city of Nogales," Mexico (6). En route in a train "replete with displaced humanity," alongside soldiers with "an astonishing number of cartridge belts crisscrossed over their chests" (6), Limón's brother Gilberto took ill and later died. Limón writes:

> At the far end of the coach someone played an accordion, sad, mel-
> ancholy, *canciones.* It was sunset. The sun set in pure fresh gore.
> My mother's face, the crying of my baby brother, my frightened
> sister Dora and little brother Jesús, the lost, lost train, the brutal
> landscape of central Sonora, harsh and arid—how the memory of
> this scene lies in ambush to assault and torment me when I least
> expect it! How I abhor the sound of an accordion!
> After an eternity the exhausted train limped into Nogales. (6)

During this period, many Yaquis in Mexico moved to Arizona, near Nogales and South Tuscon, to escape the violence of the 1910–20 Mexican Revolution just as the Limóns had. By the 1920s, there were an estimated two thousand members of Pascua Yaqui communities in Arizona.[19] In other words, Limón's Yaqui mother and her children were traveling the same route as others who crossed the border to Nogales, Arizona, and later became part of Yaqui communities there.

Limón didn't claim attachment to any Yaqui community, let alone the group in Arizona, and the public didn't know of or recognize Limón's Yaqui back-ground. His life and dancing were thus not directly affected by termination-era practices and ideologies and their effect on these Yaqui communities in Arizona.[20] Yet, in a larger sense, the Yaqui history of violence-filled migration and subsequent lack of land base were topics Limón did address throughout his career. A quarter century after the train ride to Nogales that killed his baby brother, Limón staged *Danzas Mexicanas,* dancing with crisscrossed ammuni-tion across his taut chest in the "Revolutionario" section and arched back on the floor as the Péon, choreographically addressing this episode in his and other Yaqui people's histories.

The reasons why the State Department sent Limón abroad as a pioneer of an implicitly universalized American modern dance, and not as a Mexican, mestizo, or Indian dancer, are not hard to imagine. Limón himself stressed the universalist humanism of his dance. He had a deeply impassioned interest in what we today would call abstract humanism. "We are never more truly and profoundly human than when we dance," he wrote in 1953.[21] In describing his investigations and improvisations while he was making *Danzas Mexicanas,* Limón named his spirit a "terra incognita," a Western European naming of his self as unknown land. Yet, even as he investigated these abstract humanist ap-proaches, both his comments and his choreography staged an expression of that

José Limón, "Revolucionario" from Danzas Mexicanas, *1939. Photograph by John Lindquist. Courtesy Jerome Robbins Dance Division, The New York Public Library for the Performing Arts, Astor, Lenox, and Tilden Foundations.*

interiority via an exploration of the specificity of his body as a battle ground
for European colonialism of Native peoples and Native land. To his sweep-
ing statement about being most profoundly human when we dance, he added,
speaking of dance:

> It is religion. In primitive societies it solemnizes birth, puberty,
> marriage, and death, the seasons, the sowing and the harvest, war
> and peace, and *to this day in our western world,* young boys dance
> to the Virgin before the high altar in the Cathedral in Seville, and
> the Indians in Mexico and the Southwest dance their religion.
> ("On Dance," 99) (emphasis added)

By naming dance as "profoundly human," and then turning to Spanish Catholicism, and to "the Indians in Mexico and the Southwest" as examples
of how dance functions *"to this day in our western world,"* Limón included a
present-day connection to Indians—today, not in some arcane, authentic past
or exotic culture antithetical to Western ways—as aspects of the universal that
European-based cultural values of the 1950s extolled.

His choreography embodied a similar position, exploring its grand humanist
themes through specific stories grounded in Mexico's history of colonization
and its effects on his body. In *Danzas Mexicanas,* he performed in all five sections, as Indio and Conquistador, Péon, Caballero, and Revolucionario, representing and inhabiting the tensions between these political identities via his
body. As the names and pictures of the piece show, the dances underscore these
thematic and physical positions of tension and resistance, his body taut, his fist
clenched, ammunition crossing his torso. Significantly, though, if his spirit is
the "terra incognita" of Western fantasy and exploration, and his brown body
the battleground on which colonialism is waged, he is also the Conquistador, the
explorer. These complex positionings underscore Limón's vision of himself as
both the terrain of exploration and the agent or the explorer of the "unknown
land" of his body and spirit; he was the one seeking to understand himself and
his history, via an exploration of the stories and possibilities his body told.
Limón technique famously stresses complex explorations of the parts of the
body—the weight of the head, the articulations of the ribs, chest, shoulders,
pelvis, knees, elbows, feet, hands—what he called the "voices of the body"
(Limón, "On Dance," 103). Rather than a codified movement vocabulary, Limón
technique stresses physical exploration of the isolated parts of the body and
what they speak.[22] This formulation emphasizes the agency of self-exploration
of all of one's body, including its interiority and the embodied history it tells,
resulting in a danced, self-determined representation of what one has discovered. Limón expressed this exploration of his interiority both as this abstract

universal—an understanding of art that carried the most value in mid-twentieth century America—*and* as an exploration pertinent to his particular position as a Mexican-born man with Indigenous ancestry.

In short, in these and other early pieces, despite how the government billed and exported him, and however unreadable that may have been at the time, Limón *was* explicitly performing himself as Indian in the modern dance choreography he staged. In *La Malinche* he called himself El Indio and set his brown body against another male dancer in a story of sexualized, Catholicized colonial struggle.[23] In *Dialogues,* he did so again, even more so. In *Danzas Mexicanas,* he explored multiple aspects of his embodied history. Limón had Native ancestry; according to standard, phenotypic markers, he looked Native; he danced about Native history. This was an era characterized by political and economic support for abstract art, as opposed to communist-oriented realist art that dealt with social context.[24] Yet, it was a time when the complex individual consciousness that this abstract art was seen to explore was not something the federal government acknowledged Indians to have.

It probably didn't help that the Indian themes Limón focused on told stories of European colonialism of the Americas, with an insistent awareness of struggles for sovereignty, and of the impermanence of European domination. These were certainly not themes the federal government wanted to herald as "Indian," then or now. Had he choreographed dances about El Indio's connection to nature, or about Native peoples' victimization alone, perhaps his pieces would have registered more readily as Indian. Instead, he created dances that investigated the multiple, complex stories his body voiced, that acknowledged the politicized histories of Indigenous peoples in the Americas, and that explored the complexities of this history and of this Mexican and Native and mestizo interior within the rubric of the abstract humanism of modern dance. At the time when Indian land—including that of Yaqui peoples in the United States—was being encroached upon, and Indian identity defined not through a politicized relation to land and resources but instead through public performances of recognizable Indian signifiers, these dances weren't readable as Native.

Yet the response of contemporary Aboriginal and American Indian choreographers to Limón as a Native choreographer suggests that, at least on some level, an awareness of his own mixed Native heritage was with Limón always, and readable to at least some of those watching. On the one hand, Daystar's recollections of working with Limón at Julliard suggest there was nothing particularly Native about his teaching. Although the composition class she and Morsette had with Limón in 1969 and 1970 was for these two Native American students only, Daystar writes that, as she recalls, Limón's focus was not to develop any kind of Native work. "I feel that his objective was to give us compositional techniques that we could use later, and that we should have a solid foundation in the modern dance idiom as it was being done at that time. He would present us with a 'problem' that we would then solve choreographically," she writes.[25] And yet on the other hand, Jones writes that, in retrospect, she believes his identification as a Native person was a clear part of his understanding of himself and his goals as an artist. When she was working with Limón, Jones considered him to be "a great choreographer and a phenomenal person, a very kind person, a professional person, and an artist who struggled against odds to become a dancer and a choreographer." She explains, "That passion was what inspired me. It was only later, as I grew older and more mature, that I speculated that his mixed blood heritage must have given him reason to come to terms with it for himself." She adds, "But, he was such a 'bigger than life' persona that it is my personal opinion that from the start, his identity and goal was totally clear to him."

Dancer and choreographer Juan Valenzuela, who is Aztec and Yaqui, who (like Limón) left Mexico for the United States during the Mexican Revolution, and who studied with Limón, Martha Graham, and Katherine Dunham, similarly included Limón's words and image as part of a 1972 educational brochure on "Dance with Indian Children."[26] After including short writings on "Cultural Differences: Dance" by Martha Graham and Maria Tallchief, the brochure includes a section on "Dance as Magic" by José Limón. In it Limón writes, "Magic, as you know, is very largely composed of the human will. You will, mightily, for something to happen, and you take steps and measures. I strongly suspect that American Indians have known this from time immemorial." He adds, "The dance can invoke gods, demons, angels and furies wherever they may be. It can challenge them and defy them, and propitiate and tire and deafen them with the clamor of its chants and rhythms, and perhaps they will hear us, and send us their grace and benediction, a rain to redeem us from the drought which threatens us, one infinitely more lethal than that of the arid Western plains" (8). In this passage, Limón first recognizes a difference between himself and American Indians, even as he subtly but insistently connects American Indians with what is Western as well as contemporary. But then he includes himself in the "us" that dance's invocation affects, explicitly connecting himself with the relation of dance to invocation that he has just associated with American Indians.[27] In this way his words, like his dances, speak to a relation between himself and what he sees as American Indian understandings of dance that later practitioners like Daystar, Ronceria, and Valenzuela recognized.

TOM TWO ARROWS: STRENGTHENING
FUTURE TRADITIONS OF THE HAUDENOSAUNEE

Tom Two Arrows was the professional name of Thomas Dorsey, an artist and performer of Lenni-Lenape (Delaware; "Original People") descent who was adopted by the Onoda'gegas (Onondaga; "People of the Hills," one of the Six

Nations of the Iroquois) before marrying an Onoda'gega woman.[28] During the 1940s and 1950s, Two Arrows supported his family by painting, performing, and teaching "Indian Arts and Crafts" to the public in schools, museums, colleges, and clubs on the East Coast, and by dancing at powwows.[29] He is remembered most frequently today as a visual artist. His paintings, depicting Iroquois games and dances, were first commissioned by the Albany Institute of History and Art in 1941, when he was twenty-one years old, and traveled nationally for two years. Later work was commissioned by SUNY-Albany, as murals and backgrounds at several locations including the American Museum of Natural History in New York, and to illustrate several children's books. Two Arrows's work is now represented in the permanent collections of seven museums across the United States, and in 2002 the Albany Institute reexhibited his paintings and prints.[30] His performing career, while equally impressive, remains less well known. Before performing in Southeast Asia for the State Department in 1956 and 1957, he danced and taught frequently in the New York area. In the late 1940s, he taught at a boy's camp in Maine (former campers today include a picture of him in his dance regalia on the Camp Menatoma Web page).[31] In the fall of 1950, he was on the faculty of the 92nd Street Y in New York, where he taught courses in "American Indian Dancing," including "A Study of Rhythms (Iroquois)," "Basic Iroquois Dance Steps," and a "Study of Five Dances and Their Format and Music within the Long House."[32] He presented lecture-demonstrations on "Indian Dance in the Americas" at the Y and the Henry Street Playhouse in New York that same fall.[33] In 1951, he danced Native American dances on an educational film produced by the Department of Education at the American Museum of Natural History in New York, a film "intended to teach observation and understanding by depicting the Indian as a skillful observer of nature." Later that decade Two Arrows performed for well over twenty thousand people throughout Asia while on the State Department tour. After returning, he performed at Jacob's Pillow in the Berkshires.

The work Tom Two Arrows did as both a visual artist and a performer who was explicitly promoted as Indian helped disseminate a positive image of American Indians at a time of intense racism. Two Arrows's son, Thomas Dorsey, notes that his father learned, practiced, and presented these dances, "in the midst of the termination period" when Indians were pressed from all kinds of directions, and from extreme poverty. "It was a time when you were thinking about survival, not Indian culture," he explained. Many Indians had left their home reservations and moved to cities to try and make a living. "A lot of people [in urban areas] were a generation or two removed from Indian culture," Dorsey explained, noting that even the Indians on the reservation didn't necessarily have access to cultural preservation information. "At the time, Indians were another dirty dark-skinned minority down the road," he said. "That was a time when it wasn't very romantic to be Indian. If you went into town shopping, you'd be sure to go in a big group." He explained, "During the fifties, most of the European American world knew little and cared less about the Indian world. It was apparently sufficient for them to believe that we were all extinct save a few archaic examples in the western United States." At a time when positive depictions of Native Americans were largely absent from public view, Dorsey stressed, his father "was a well recognized and well respected member of our Native community and valued for portraying Native people to the general public in a realistic and sensitive fashion."[34]

While Limón has, until recently, been ignored as an Indigenous choreographer, Tom Two Arrows, although well known within his community and in East Coast American Indian artistic circles generally, and despite his successful State Department tours, has until recently been largely ignored entirely in American dance history. When Tom Two Arrows died in 1993, the brief mention in an Albany paper noted his career as a renowned Indian artist who "also made two trips to Asia for the U.S. Information Agency representing the American National Theater and Academy."[35] By and large, dance scholars remain ignorant of Two Arrows's performing career, undoubtedly due in part to our dependence on archival records and material, which are largely unavailable in Two Arrows's case. While dozens of hours of footage of Limón exist in various libraries and archives, the nine-and-a-half-minute educational film held at the American Museum of Natural History, which the filmmakers interspersed with scenes from nature and voiced over with stereotypical rhetoric about Indians, is what remains of Tom Two Arrows's legacy in the official archive of dance history. Its singular presence alone speaks volumes about the continuing absence from contemporary dance history of American Indian dance that was promoted not as choreography but as demonstrations of authentic material. It thus provides a glimpse into both what was literally and figuratively recordable as real Indian dancing during this period (these demonstrations), as well as a record of how this definition itself limited dance history's consideration of Native American dance (and thus how limited archival research dependent upon such records is). Placing this footage alongside the few other snippets of reference to Tom Two Arrows's public dance career available archivally, as well as discussions with Two Arrows's son, however, provides the possibility of considering the agency of the dancing he did that both has and hasn't been recorded or discussed as part of dance history.

The *Indian Dances* video is designed for school children, and at the time—1951—its focus certainly presented a more positive image of Native peoples than others available to children at the time. The film intersperses clips of Tom Two Arrows dancing in a studio with outtakes from photographer Edgar Monsanto Queeny's film *Sunrise Seranades* to show that, according to its catalog description, "American Indians observe birds and animals in nature, and these observations influence Indian dances."[36] Although Two Arrows was necessarily changing, adapting, and improvising as he danced alone, in a studio, before a camera, the Natural History film was intended not as a document of Two Arrows's innovative choreographic choices, but rather as an educational film about how Indian dance relates to nature. It begins with the camera panning a diorama from the Natural History Museum's "Hall of North American Birds" and then shifts outdoors to the "ordinary everyday hidden dramas that take place" in nature. It then cuts to footage and sound recordings of the sharp-tailed grouse on a prairie and continues with a discussion of how "long ago at sunrise on the great northern prairies, the Plains Indian would hide to watch a strange drama," the sharp-tailed grouse performing their courtship dance. "The Indian was fascinated by this ceremony, and would crouch for hours watching. To the Northern Indian, the moves of this ceremonial dance were especially appealing. In fact, he imitated them in his own courtship dance," the film explains. From here, the film cuts to a black screen with a young Tom Two Arrows dancing bare chested, with fringed leggings and a loin cloth, bent forward, rocking a feather roach on his head forward and backward, hands on his hips and elbows out, moving rhythmically and gracefully. His movements don't quite match the beat of the Indian music that has clearly been added later as a soundtrack.[37] The film next turns to a discourse on the American eagle, "whom the Indian observed carefully and admired. . . . The Indian would watch him circle, and then dive to pounce upon his prey. And later, some of them, like the Iroquois, imitated him in the sacred feather dance." The screen then fades from the eagle flying to Tom Two Arrows moving from an upright to a crouching position, in front of a white circle of light with a tied feather bird lying in its center. His torso is bare and his arms stretched out with grace and strength, and a single feather roach on his head moves as his head swoops down and forward, his arms reaching back, his feet in place on the circle's edge. In one hand he holds what looks like a rattle, in the other what appears to be a feather staff. He moves in, chest leading, arms back, head bobbing, then hops in one step, bends forward, and with his mouth picks up the feather bird and stands and stretches his arms up and outward while the scene fades again to a nature panorama. The film goes on to show Two Arrows demonstrating two more dances, a "Pueblo deer dance" and a "Plains Buffalo hunting dance," all filmed in the same studio against the same black, decontextualizing backdrop. It concludes, "Yes, the Indian was a close observer of the drama of Nature. His very life depended directly upon what was happening in the world around him."

In this film and elsewhere, Two Arrows's dancing was presented not, as Limón's was, as an example of ever-changing and innovative choreography created because the dancer made conscious improvisational choices and responses to structures, limits, and situations he faced. Instead, the film's clumping of all Native peoples into broad statements that speak about what the Indian did (and its representation of dances from four distinct tribal traditions by the same

Indian dancer), its repeated stereotypical descriptions of this Indian as "silent," "hidden," and "crouching," and its relegation of all Indians to the past tense (despite its presentation of Tom Two Arrows performing very much in the present) bespeak familiar romanticized images. The production and promotion of Two Arrows's dancing thus underscored non-Indian ideas of Indian dance as being about the demonstration of traditional forms (as it was to powwow hobbyists). The film presents Indian dance as both "sacred" (as the Iroquois feather dance is described in the film) and available, given a skilled practitioner willing to demonstrate it to interested public audiences. It does not suggest dance as a tool for creating, navigating, or investigating Indigenous cultural, political, or spiritual meaning-making.[38] Two Arrows himself likely had nothing at all to do with the editing of this film; his engagement with its production undoubtedly ended after he was filmed dancing in a studio. Given the acceptability of this kind of image of Indians in the 1950s, it is perhaps not surprising that this depiction of Tom Two Arrows, and of "Indian Dances," is what remains in the public record. Nor is it surprising, given the termination era's agenda of assimilating and invisibilizing Indians, that Tom Two Arrows, with this one recording of his dancing publicly available, has had almost no place in the annals of U.S. dance history.

This absence illuminates the limits of what has been seen as American Indian dance's relation to modern dance history all the more given the ways that some modern dance institutions in the 1950s concert dance world *were* trying to create space for and interactions with American Indian dance. Tom Two Arrows, invited to these stages, actively inhabited these openings as a dancer who was, in fact, negotiating and investigating multiple complex meanings in the choreographic choices he was making. In the summer of 1957, just months after returning from his State Department tours, Two Arrows presented three pieces at Jacob's Pillow Dance Festival. On a program that also featured two Balanchine pas de deux performed by Osage Ballerina Maria Tallchief, Two Arrows performed an *Eagle Dance,* described as "a legend of a young man who learned the dances of the sky world and how to use them for ceremony"; a *Husk Face Dance,* described as "a society dance of oddly masked folk who act as keepers of the door during long house ceremonies"; and a *Hunters Dance,* "a story telling dance, also used for prayer and for good luck on the trail." Dorsey described how the dances his father presented publicly at Jacob's Pillow were selected from "very traditional forms of dance." He explained, "We don't have a good range of dances, there were just a few." These three, he explained, were all ceremonial dances, some of them fairly secretive. The Husk Face dance masks, he said, were made of cornhusks and were related to (but, significantly, not exactly the same as) wooden False Face masks used in the False Face ceremony, masks that are "part of a fairly secret healing ceremony." He explained, "Now, we don't allow those masks to be held by non-Indians. We've asked for them to be repatriated." The Eagle Dance and Hunter's Dance, he explained, also involved ceremonial objects that today would be much more carefully guarded—both by the community and by the federal government (which, for example, restricts use of eagle feathers). Today, he said, "you really wouldn't want to use the turtle rattle—but it was important to be able to preserve that."[39]

It's impossible to know exactly what and how Two Arrows danced at Jacob's Pillow, or on the State Department tours. It seems likely that at Jacob's Pillow, Two Arrows presented versions of some of the same dances he had just returned from presenting abroad, perhaps in versions that drew more fully on story or legend than the performances more directly billed as "presentations" did.[40] The context of dancing on the renowned Jacob's Pillow concert stage undoubtedly created different expectations than performing as a cultural ambassador or in an educational children's film for the Natural History Museum. From its founding, Jacob's Pillow has actively supported Native American dancers and provided a space of openness and respect for American Indian dance that presenters today continue to remark. For example, Hanay Geiogamah, the artistic director of the American Indian Dance Theatre, noted the genuine interest, openness, and respect with which people at Jacob's Pillow approached AIDT, and spoke of how much he and the company appreciated the supportive atmosphere they felt performing there. He added that the place's gentle, laid-back atmosphere added to the sense of open interest and receptivity he experienced on four separate occasions in the 1980s and 1990s. "I didn't feel like I was there as a folk dancer," he said. "They were interested in what we were doing."[41] When Two Arrows performed and participated in workshops at Jacob's Pillow in 1957, it's quite possible he was met with a similar receptive interest. He was also flanked by dance theatre dancers such as the celebrated ballerina Maria Tallchief—recognized as Native American even as she inhabited the prototypical Western ballet format—adding to the framing of his dancing in a theatre dance context, and to an openness to considering his dancing as more than just demonstration. The Sunday after his performances, Two Arrows participated in a Walter Terry "Dance Laboratory" on "Dancing for Men—Ballet, Modern, Ethnic, Jazz." Two Arrows's participation in this laboratory also placed him in a situation in which not just informational presentation, but also choreographic exploration of what Native American stage dance might include was likely enabled.

On the one hand, Tom Two Arrows's publicly presented Native American identity reflects the ideologies of this termination era, as well as of a long history of historical interrelationships, trade routes, and cultural borrowings between Native peoples. His stage name (like that of Penobscot dancer Molly Spotted Elk) reflects the propensity of the public to read as authentic only Indians with Plains-sounding names. As Dorsey noted, the choice to publicly present dances that today would be more carefully guarded served, in part, as an active intervention within the cultural milieu of termination and disappearance the government was promoting at the time, rather than out of disregard or ignorance of these issues.[42] Two Arrows's own pre–termination era writings demonstrate his passionate understanding of the continuing vibrancy of Haudenosaunee ceremonies, games, and dances, and of Haudenosaunee sovereignty. In notes to an exhibition of his paintings commissioned by the Albany Institute of History & Art in 1942, he writes forcefully of the Haudenosaunee as "a powerful and sovereign political force in America today," and insists that the dances he depicts be seen as contemporary:[43]

> Although the style of these paintings appears to present an old fashion culture long-since disappeared, the fact remains that the Haudenosaunee still conduct these ceremonies, play these games, perform these dances, and sing these songs wearing modern clothes while doing them. . . . Traditional life goes on behind the scenes away from media attention, although not immune to it. The Haudenosaunee can be adept at living in today's predominant culture when they need to, although this often brings them enormous problems. But they will find their own way to persist, and so the traditions of the Haudenosaunee will be strengthened in the future.[44]

He adds, "The sense of community and beauty evoked by the music of a singer, his drum, and the dancers can be very powerful. As the Haudenosaunee say, 'We do not pray—we dance.'" These words, displayed beside Two Arrows's paintings several years before the termination legislation that sought to undercut Haudenosaunee sovereignty and promote an urban pan-Indianism, underscore the awareness Two Arrows held of these issues and show them to be under active debate at the time. As they recognize and affirm Haudenosaunee sovereignty and the appropriate separation of certain ceremonies from non-Haudenosaunee view, Two Arrows's paintings and words also underscore the need for Haudenosaunee to find "their own way to persist" in the face of enormous problems wrought by living in "today's predominant culture."[45] They foresee termination-era policy attacks on Haudenosaunee sovereignty and implicit (as well as explicit) drives for Indian assimilation, signal awareness of the need for Haudenosaunee peoples to ride out this era with persistence and creativity, and also predict the way that, over time, Haudenosaunee traditions will continue with strength and vibrancy.

In 1942, when John Collier's "Indian New Deal" reform policies were still largely policy, the atmosphere in the country seems to have been one in which statements like Two Arrows's about the Haudenosaunee as a "powerful and sovereign political force in America today" and noting the appropriate separation of most Haudenosaunee ceremonies from public view could and did hang

alongside commissioned art exhibits. By 1957, though, termination-era legislation attacking Iroquois self-governance, and the termination era's effect on
Native peoples in the United States more generally, had shifted the atmosphere
surrounding Native Americans and Native American art and culture. Tom Two
Arrows's Indian dance presentations emerged most visibly on public stages
during and in the aftermath of this period, as the federal government targeted
Indian tribes within New York for termination.[46] During this time, Two Arrows's
performances seem to have referenced, for his non-Indian audiences and State
Department promoters, a stable, recognizable Indian. This Indian representation he successfully performed implied continuity with the past, a connection
to nature, and a culture available to all who wished to learn about it regardless
of the body they had or the histories it held. Aspects of Two Arrows's performances played to these understandings: he appeared in Indian regalia; he spoke
willingly with interested audiences; he communed with birds and nature. In a
photo, he looks like an Indian figurine, posing with his arms out yet frozen in
place, friendly, smiling, upright, and open, the culture-sharing pan-Indian his
funders wanted him to be.

Part of why this recognizable definition of "Indian" was and is so appealing to the federal government is that it works, ultimately, to disappear Indian
agency and culture—and therefore any right to Indian land—which was the
termination policy goal. If American Indian identity is about authenticity and
not choreographic invention or skillful improvisation, it's quite easy to discount or dismiss. All one need do is prove another is not authentic enough,
and as the markers that made him or her Indian are discounted, so too is that
person's political agency as Indian in the eyes of the government. Indianness
(and Indian land) can then be available to whites (like the Laubins); even dismissal of Indian dancers as inauthentic representations of the Indian image (as
the too-civilized Laubins were) serves an agenda where the government is the
one defining and policing Indianness.

And yet, however much the government promoted Two Arrows as a static,
recognizable, authentic Indian performer, he wasn't static: he was dancing.
His dance performances themselves undoubtedly told different stories than
that of the pan-Indian, Plains-style, culture-sharing nature lover the government seems to have been pursuing. For one, his dances weren't Plains powwow
dances familiar to hobbyists schooled in authentic Plains culture; they were
specific, Onoda'gega dances with a base in Onoda'gega culture, drawing from
Onoda'gega tradition and ceremony in ways that helped ensure their continuation yet also undoubtedly altering them for public display (as the Husk Face
masks perhaps referenced, without invoking, the False Face ceremony).[47] At the
same time, his dances, performed in villages in Southeast Asia and on stages in
the Berkshires, were far removed from the ceremonial Onoda'gega contexts in
which they were traditionally practiced. While the powwow article cited above
decries "improvising" as "appropriate for modern dance" but having "nothing

Tom Two Arrows. Photograph by John Lindquist. Courtesy Jerome Robbins Dance Division, The New York Public Library for the Performing Arts, Astor, Lenox, and Tilden Foundations.

to do with Indians," Tom Two Arrows's performances were undoubtedly inventive. Far from the Long House, performing primarily alone, he was necessarily creating a choreography within the structures and strictures available to him, conscientiously drawing from Onoda'gega ceremonial dances yet altering and adapting them to these public contexts, playing and supporting himself and his family by presenting these culturally specific Iroquois dances to paying, non-Indian, audiences. In this way, within the termination-era context, Two Arrows paradoxically invented a static image of himself as Indian for his funders and audience members, much as Indian performers have done for years.

And at the same time that Tom Two Arrows constructed this authentic Indian for his funders and audience members, his performances also, in interesting ways, refuted and complicated the era's notions and categorizations about Indians.[48] For one, he continued to perform these very specific Onoda'gega traditional dances. He continued learning them, continued practicing them, continued teaching them not only to these non-Indian audiences, but also to the family members traveling with him and to other Native peoples he sought out, and who began to seek him out, in between his public performances. Two Arrows's son stressed the long-term effects of his father's dance practices for his family, nation, and the larger East Coast Indian community. What he and other cultural preservationists of the day did, Dorsey explained, was "Cultural preservation through a time of cultural dissipation in the Indian community." "Pop also was extremely knowledgeable. He had a depth of Indian knowledge," Dorsey said. "There were a lot of local, family and tribal people who would seek out my father for mutual cultural association." Dorsey added, "A number of the performers around here were mentored by my father," explaining further that his father provided a link to Indian culture for people trying to make a living off the reservation. "That was also a time when the reservations back East were losing a lot of the traditional element, ceremony, dance, even the language was in severe decline. Dad, making bows, crafts, dancing, maintaining traditional crafts, and painting were a repository for Indian traditionality for me that lots of reservation residents didn't have," he explained. There were "a number of people who he would urge to persist in Indian culture. He was well known all over the east," from the Passamaquoddy to the Seminole peoples, Dorsey said. Even Dorsey himself—who did not grow up on a reservation and is not a performer—learned Onoda'gega traditions from his father, who learned and practiced them, in part, in order to present them to non-Indian audiences. Because he was around his father while his father was doing these teachings and presentations, "I remember these things in much more detail than the folks on the reservation." Today, he said, he and his family don't dance or perform for the public. Although they're sometimes asked, "We're not going to put on a performance for non-Indians," he said, noting that they will do other kinds of educational presentations. Yet, he said, today there are "One or two of the faithkeepers, staunch upholders of traditionality," in his family. "They took a greater pride in their heritage" because of the work his father did and some have since become "part of the hierarchy and leadership of the tribe," he said (telephone conversation, April 9, 2003). His comments suggest that Two Arrows used his performances of an Indian identity fundable in the 1950s as a space in which to explore and develop artistic and cultural practices vital to his specific community today.

Dorsey, discussing his father's dance presentations with fifty years' hindsight, called what his father did "chronologically correct." "Nowadays, we would resist having non-Indians take over our dances," he said. "At that time, you were getting away with doing those things for the public. Now, it's a different world than the 1950s," Dorsey said. "Now, we resist the YMCA Indian Guides," he said. "But my dad worked for them." He called his father's work "something that was appropriate in its time."[49]

In the arena of dance history, the State Department's termination agenda seems to have worked: Tom Two Arrows, promoted and produced as an ethnically authentic Indian dancer—and not as an Onoda'gega choreographer who was actively exploring and improvising his relation to complex, changing, Native American histories and politics—has subsequently dropped out of virtually all discussion of American dance history. Meanwhile, the State Department's promotion of Limón as emissary of American dance while they searched for appropriate Native American dancers to send abroad continues to be reflected in the ways Limón is usually interpreted today. In the 1960s, as claiming an Indian identity became more fashionable and readable, Limón's connection to Native dance and a Native heritage did become more frequently mentioned. The Capezio Dance Award Limón received in 1964 recognized him as a man who has "introduced the great values of his Latin American heritage into the contemporary American dance theatre and who, as a descendent of the earliest Americans, has linked, through his dance art, our ancient past with our adventuresome present."[50] His piece *The Unsung,* an explicit paean to eight specific American Indian leaders including Tecumseh, Black Hawk, and Sitting Bull, premiered as a work in progress at Julliard in May 1970, at the end of Jones's and Morsette's fellowship year.[51] Daystar suggested that his work with Native dancers, through the auspices of the fellowship program supporting her, "may have been what inspired him to create *The Unsung,*" which brought Native identity and politics more to the forefront of his choreography. In parts of this piece, the eight male dancers, dressed in black tights, move together on stage, stamping rhythms on the stage as musical accompaniment. Critic Deborah Jowitt described how *The Unsung* "doesn't show us the doom of the Indians, but rather the vitality and beauty of a group of young men dancing."[52] Toward the end of his life and career, then, recognition of this connection to Native politics and peoples began to emerge. For the most part, though, his use of the tools of the modern dance stage, including improvisation and journeys into one's interior, have obscured readings of him as an important Native stage choreographer who has influenced contemporary Native American dancers and choreographers.

On the one hand, this history calls out for acknowledgment of the self-awareness and interiority, the self-conscious improvisational abilities, of both José Limón and Tom Two Arrows. Limón lay insistent claim to these, but as improvisation and self-aware self-exploration was at the time seen as antithetical to Indian identity, they obscured readings of his relation to Indigenous dance and Indigenous history. Two Arrows was consciously inventive, using the dance forms and forums available to him to both educate an audience in a period of intensive racism, and also to educate Indian peoples themselves in a period of cultural loss, but his billing as Indian obscured critics' awareness of his creative resiliency.

The point here, though, is not exactly to argue for Limón's and Two Arrows's centrality in Native American dance history based on this evaluation of their self-conscious inventiveness. In some ways, their careers show how the act of dancing, the practice of performing, is a ritual act with repercussions beyond itself, even beyond the self-conscious control or intentions of the dancers and choreographers. Tom Two Arrows's teachings of traditional Onoda'gega dance to audiences at Jacob's Pillow and to students at the 92nd Street Y, produced for and received by one audience, were part of what, fifty years later, had propelled tribal leaders' pride in their heritage. Limón's dances were received and conceived by him at the time as about universal ideas of "the human spirit," yet they read and speak today not only to the human condition, but also to contemporary Native choreographers investigating the specificity of an Indigenous movement process and practice, using the modern dance stage. Both dancers used the tools, stages, funding possibilities, and audiences that were out there and available to them. It is the fact of this dedicated dance practice, not their politicized self-awareness or the way particular performance events in the 1950s were or were not read, that affected future generations of Native people.

Instead of (only) suggesting that both dancers are important figures in the history of Native American stage dance, my interest here is in the awareness the histories of these two dancers bring to the different ways Native American dance wasn't readable as part of American modern dance in the 1950s, and by and large hasn't been since. Both have figured the absence of Indianness in this history: Limón, in being seen as not *really* Indian because of his Mexican American identity and because he didn't dance like viewers (at the time and largely still) expect Indians to dance; Two Arrows, in being seen as simply demonstrating authentic American Indian dances, not astutely, politically, creatively engaging with them in "chronologically correct" ways (and thereby registering more in a Natural History Museum archive than in the annals of dance history). It would be another twenty years before American Indian dancing, read as such, emerged visibly on concert dance stages.

III.

INDIGENOUS CHOREOGRAPHERS TODAY

The Emergence of a Visible
Native American Stage Dance

Traditional Native dance established, secure, strong as a
rock, will serve this new breed of dance and music artists as
a training ground and launching pad for the journey toward
forging a flexible, tensile dance performance.

> ▸ *Hanay Geiogamah, director,*
> *American Indian Dance Theatre*

Over the past thirty years, Native dance, choreographed and directed by Native
peoples, has emerged more visibly on concert dance stages. These dances include
performances by powwow-based Native American stage dance troupes like
Louis Mofsie's Thunderbird American Indian Dancers and the American Indian
Dance Theatre, founded in 1987 and today directed by Hanay Geiogamah, as well
as modern dance–based companies like Rosalie Jones's Daystar: Contemporary
Dance-Drama of Indian America, formed in 1978, and that produced by choreographers working at the Aboriginal Dance Program, established at the Banff
Centre for the Arts in Alberta, Canada, in 1996.

This chapter discusses the beginnings of this burgeoning of Aboriginal and
Native American stage dance. The political climate in which it emerged is complex and includes the "Red power" movement and the counterculturalism of
the 1960s and 1970s, as well as discussions of identity politics and multiculturalism of the 1980s.[1] The focus here will be the influence of the passage of the
American Indian Religious Freedom Act in 1978 on its emergence in the United
States.[2] The chapter looks in particular at the relations between stage dance and
ceremonial practice as engaged by Native stage choreographers in this period.
It also looks at policies in Canada that aided the emergence of Aboriginal stage
dance by bringing greater visibility to Native people, but that also, unlike in
the United States, led to greater funding for Aboriginal Peoples and to land

claims agreements that have since led to the return to Aboriginal control of land and resources. It suggests that these differences, with religious freedom and explorations of identity supported in both countries, but much greater funding resources and more active and effective land claims policies in Canada, have contributed to different dance scenes today.

By 1970, in the United States, the climate for American Indian policy had begun to change yet again. In the political climate of the 1960s, the American Indian Movement (AIM) and other legal and political challenges to prevailing policy brought Indian presence, power, politics, and religious freedom more into the public eye. This activism created a climate of pride and solidarity for Indian Peoples, as well as a more visible presence of Native peoples very much still alive, despite centuries of genocidal attempts and policies. "In the hothouse growth of the late sixties came a strong move towards pan-Indianism, more cohesion as a group, and an upsurge in ethnic pride and a sense of cultural uniqueness. A number of intellectuals and political activists began to rethink and redefine what it meant 'to be Indian,'" writes Geiogamah.[3] Coincident with this emergence of a more visible, rather than vanishing, rhetoric of Indianness in America was the increasing emergence of Native American dance companies on public stages.

In 1963, not long after Tom Two Arrows presented solo pieces on the Jacob's Pillow stage, Louis Mofsie, who is Winnebago and Hopi and has lived his whole life in the New York metropolitan area, incorporated the Thunderbird American Indian Dancers, a New York City–based intertribal dance troupe. Mofsie explained that the Thunderbird dance company had its roots in the Mohawk community in Boerum Hill, Brooklyn. "We lived in a community of Mohawk people on Pacific Street," he said. "Many of us went to the Cuyler Church, which held services in the Mohawk language."[4] Mofsie noted that the group first formed at this church as a kind of youth group activity. "Reverend [David Munroe] Cory asked us teenagers if we wanted to start a dance troupe. He would give us space to practice. We thought it was a great idea. We had a Sioux teacher from Pine Ridge who named us The Little Eagles." The group eventually became the Thunderbird American Indian Dancers, named for the clan of Mofsie's mother, a Second Mesa Hopi. For the past four decades and continuing today, the troupe presents intertribal and powwow-based educational programs to audiences throughout the New York area.

The creation of a dance troupe in a church, encouraged by a minister, suggests a sea change in attitude about Native American dance and Christian religious practices. This minister, who spoke Mohawk and had connections to the community he served, clearly did not see American Indian dance as threatening to his ministry. While his encouragement of this teenage dance troupe could hardly be seen as intended to support the free exercise of Indian religious or ceremonial practices, it nonetheless suggests a space within organized Christian religious practices in which American Indian dance practices were enabled and fostered, rather than shunned and discouraged.

Indeed, a complex relation to religion and religious practice emerges in the increasingly visible emergence of American Indian dance in public arenas and on public stages in this period more generally. AIM members marching on Washington in 1972 included among their demands that "Indian religious freedom and cultural integrity [be] protected."[5] Legal changes leading up to this march, and in the decade following, included legislation that attempted to do just this. In July 1970, U.S. President Richard Nixon formally renounced termination. In December 1970, Congress passed a bill restoring Blue Lake to the Taos Pueblo, after the pueblo argued that control and access to it were essential to the free exercise of Taos religion.[6] In 1978, the secretary of the interior amended the Bald and Golden Eagle Protection Act so that federally recognized Indians could take eagles "for the religious purposes of Indian tribes" (Vecsey, *Handbook*, 17). And in 1978, Congress passed the American Indian Religious Freedom Act (AIRFA), stating:

> On and after August 11, 1978, it shall be the policy of the United
> States to protect and preserve for American Indians their inherent
> right of freedom to believe, express, and exercise the traditional
> religions of the American Indian, Eskimo, Aleut, and Native
> Hawaiians, including but not limited to access to sites, use and
> possession of sacred objects, and the freedom to worship through
> ceremonials and traditional rites.[7]

The act sought to address numerous situations in which Indians have found their religious practices endangered, including access to sacred lands and sites.[8]

AIRFA, like so much federal legislation on Indian affairs, has been rife with problems since its passage and deemed inadequate and ineffectual in numerous ways. It applied only to "federally recognized" Indians; it has not been upheld in the courts, especially in cases involving access to land, and land development and exploitation cases. In the years since its passage, scholars and activists have argued that AIRFA has contributed little to promoting Indian religious freedom. The act was amended in 1994 to better spell out protection of the ceremonial use of peyote as "religious sacrament" by Indian peoples, which again did nothing to support its applicability to land access and land development cases.[9] Yet despite its lack of legal teeth, AIRFA nonetheless signaled a shift in federal rhetoric regarding Indian religious practices and sent a message that, however indirectly, reverberated among some Native American dancers.

The Native American stage dancing emerging during this same time period, in one sense, had little to do with this rhetorical and legislative push for protection of American Indian religious freedom. All the Native American dancers, company directors, and choreographers discussed here have noted that what they are presenting is most definitely *not* religious practice put on stage; all are fully aware of and attuned to the issues and negotiations involved in working publicly with particular tribal stories, ceremonies, and dance practices and would make no claim for their stage dances being religious acts (and therefore needing freedom of religion protection). At the same time, emerging Native American directors, choreographers, and dancers didn't experience the stage as *entirely* separate from a space of spiritual, religious practice, as this chapter explores. Nor did critics and viewers of this new American Indian stage dance, who were sometimes troubled by the connections they thought they understood between American Indian religious practice and the American Indian stage dancing they saw emerging. Some fretted over the way, as they saw it, staging drains American Indian dance of its religious and ceremonial import, rendering it inauthentic; others, alternatively, saw the stage as an inappropriate place to present ceremonial dances that do retain sacred elements. This public anxiety about the religious aspects of Native stage dancing suggests that AIRFA, even if not actually needed to protect the dances, helped create an atmosphere that enabled more public explorations of Native dancing—explorations that, in a climate hostile to Indian religious practices, might have been thwarted or kept hidden. The American Indian Dance Theatre (AIDT), in particular, has engendered discussion of these issues over the years and provides a useful site for their examination.

AMERICAN INDIAN DANCE THEATRE

The AIDT was formed in 1986 when Kiowa theater director Geiogamah brought dance to the forefront of his theatrical explorations.[10] Twenty-four gifted dancers and singers came together to form what Apache/Ute/French Canadian/Latino Raoul Trujillo, AIDT's initial co-director and choreographer, called "the first attempt to create a Native dance company."[11] Since then, the company has toured regularly and widely and has performed throughout the United States, Canada, Europe, the Middle East, Australia, Africa, and Asia. In 1989, it was the subject of a PBS *Dance in America* hour-long television special, "Finding the Circle," and in 1993 the second public television special about the company, "Dances for the New Generation," was nominated for an Emmy Award. Tapes of these programs have since become publicly distributed, and a 1996 CD of the music from the company is widely available. AIDT is usually the first (and often the only) Native American dance company many people have had some exposure to over the past decade.

One common understanding of this company, as *New York Times* dance critic Anna Kisselgoff writes, is that they "present authentic dances in distilled form in a theatrical setting."[12] "The same people who enact the works' meanings participate, as members of a culture, in their delineation," another dance critic writes. "There is with AIDT, in that sense, no drama at all, no gap between dancer and character."[13] These responses suggest parallels between the way viewers have seen the AIDT dancers and the way viewers of *Buffalo Bill's Wild West* a century earlier presumed the Indian performers in those arenas to be not so much performing an act as acting out a real version of themselves.[14]

Proceeding from this perspective has led some critics of AIDT to argue that, because AIDT performs these authentic Indian dances in a theater, on a stage, mediated by a paying audience, this theatrical staging intervenes in the authenticity of the dancing. Indeed the flip side to this belief in Buffalo Bill's day was that the theatrical setting circumscribed and contained any ritual, ceremonial, or religious effects the dancing might have—a perspective echoed by contemporary dance critics. In 1995, for example, dance historian and critic Lynn Garafola responded to an American Indian Dance Theatre performance at Jacob's Pillow by calling the dancing "ultimately disappointing." "However closely the theatrical version of a dance may approximate its ceremonial or social original, the very act of representing it onstage militates against its authenticity," she writes. "Inevitably, something is lost in the transfer to the stage." Garafola goes on to explain the inadequacy of this stage dancing by comparing it to the dancing she witnessed in a Pueblo village:

> Many years ago I witnessed an Easter dance in a Pueblo village
> outside Santa Fe. Lines of men and women snaked across a plaza,
> a vast space bounded by houses and dotted with spectators
> huddled under blankets chatting and eating. The dancing began
> in the morning and went on until lunch, and the sense of limitless
> space and unlimited time was as visceral as the sense of commu-
> nity. Although the dancing I saw at the Pillow was infinitely more
> expert, it traded more on superficial folklore than mystery.[15]

In Garafola's and others' responses, the stage is seen not only as reflecting but also as detracting from the authenticity of the American Indian dancers.[16]

This is not to say that AIDT itself holds to this reception. The company's approach, like that of various other contemporary American Indian dance companies, instead plays with these presumptions, consciously maintaining a separate sphere between what is read as traditional and modern even as it complicates these definitions. On the one hand, many contemporary Native choreographers and dance companies such as AIDT steadfastly uphold a clear separation between certain ritual practices and publicly presented stage dance. Henry Smith, the non-Indian director of the Solaris Lakota Sioux Indian Dance Theatre, explained how when he first became interested in staging Native American dances over thirty years ago, he had to learn this difference. He said he saw a play in the Bronx where they had a Sun Dance on stage. "And I, you know, came in the same way, thinking, 'Wow. Wouldn't it be great to do Sun Dance on stage?'"[17] When he began working with Native dancers, though, he learned quickly that "that was totally verboten, totally not allowed. They said, 'Well, would you want to do the Eucharist on stage?'" The stage, he learned, would be an inappropriate place to perform this kind of religious ritual practice. Louis Mofsie explains similarly that the Thunderbird dancers are careful to distinguish the social dances they stage from ceremonial dances. "For non-Native people, we explain the difference between social and ceremonial dancing, and make it clear that we are performing social dances," Mofsie said (Garcia, "Company Funds Students").

Yet at the same time, Geiogamah noted that the boundary between what is sacred and what is public is often a lot more fluid than many non-Indian viewers realize. He remarked that people's (often non-Indians') sense that Indian things should be kept hidden or secret—the "aren't you supposed to not be showing us all that?" kinds of responses he's gotten to AIDT—serve non-Indians' desires to be in control and function as a kind of continuing romanticization of Indians. He noted how many secrecy restrictions came out of a particular historical context, where people who had come to watch Hopi dances were behaving inappropriately. All the AIDT dancers and he himself, he explained, have a very strong sense of what is to be kept at home, and what doesn't need to be, and so don't have any trouble negotiating these issues. Non-Indian people's ideas about the treatment of what is sacred and to be kept at home are often romanticized, Geiogamah added. For example, he described his family's relation to his Kiowa tribe's Ten Grandmothers medicine bundles, one of which his father is entrusted with keeping. They are sacred medicine bundles, and they are kept at home, he said, but they are not secret or to be kept hidden away. You can visit with them. You can come and talk with them, pray with them, tell them about what is going on, ask for advice. They are actually very social, he said, and interested in the world around and in what is happening in it, and like to be visited with. He's brought non-Indian people to visit with them. So even this most sacred part of his Kiowa background, while protected, is not secret or to be kept from outsiders or non-Indians. All the dancers know this and know what, in their traditions, is appropriate to do and not to do (Geiogamah, interview).

Steeped in this understanding, AIDT's staging and self-presentation stress not the separation between authentic and staged that some critics bemoan, but more the connections remarked by viewers who see the AIDT dancers performing as themselves. The American Indian Dance Theatre presents itself in a way that emphasizes the correlation between the dances practiced within American Indian communities and those presented on the theater stage. Publicity material from the company stresses how "The dances and music are authentic and traditional. They have been given a new focus, possibly a new energy, by placing them in a theatrical setting."[18] Members are chosen from prestigious Native American festivals, ceremonials, and powwow competitions throughout North America and perform a variety of dances with roots in various tribes' social and ceremonial dance, especially powwow dancing.[19] The pieces are theatrical in their dramatic lighting, evocative stage sets, short length, and blocking, yet remain renditions of powwow or other community dances. Dancers in resplendent regalia perform in the women's *Fancy Shawl Dance* and the men's *Fancy Dance Suite* in ways similar to how they would in a powwow competition, with some variations in staging. (For example, the women dance in sync, in a line facing the audience, rather than with variation in their movements and with multidirectional fronts as they most likely would in a powwow arena.) This dancing "never was just straight powwow," Geiogamah explained. "From the beginning, we had to edit, shorten, extend, delete, use ellipses, we had to do regroupings, convert from form into form, we had to heighten and diminish accordingly, all of these artistic things that are part of the process of transferring powwow to the stage" (Geiogamah, interview).

Camera work in AIDT's first television special, "Finding the Circle," underscores this relationship between the stage dances and versions of the dances practiced off stage. The special opens with scenes of a powwow that fade to scenes of the company performing on stage. Later in the program, the camera pans from dancers at a pueblo dancing a Zuni Rainbow Dance to the sky, where an eagle flies, and then fades to the stage, where smoke from dry ice creates a cloud-like atmosphere and six eagle dancers with long feathered wings move together, in synchronized formation, at times mirroring each other in groups of three, at times weaving in and out among each other. Next, a rendition of the *San Carlos Apache Crown Dance* begins as three dancers run out onto the stage before a fire, wearing intricate flat fan-shaped crowns and bells around their waists that shake as they move, and step in rhythmic beats, looking around, clearing the space with their dancing, and calling out, at times moving together in a circle, at times circling around themselves, then in a line following the back and forth actions of the front dancer as he faces out and dances from stage left to right. As they dance, a somber, serious voice explains how "the good spirits that live up in the mountains help us San Carlos Apache to drive away the bad spirits, to chase them back into darkness. . . . When the dancers call out, they are helping those spirits." These words serve to explain aspects of the dance, but they also more subtly imply, with the words "us San Carlos Apache" and with the indication that dancers in this stage version must maintain proper relation to the spirits and that these dancers' calling out helps them, that what viewers are seeing is a version of the "Apache Crown Dance" with relations to the spirits itself.

Both the project's showcase focus and its relation to the traditional have come under pressure. Geiogamah notes that some see the troupe reinscribing a troublesome understanding of Indian identity as always in the past, rather than contemporary and, like all vibrant contemporary cultures, ever changing. "These danced stories, wonderful and inspiring and often highly personalized, are, in the opinion of some, focused toward a more traditional, in-the-past, the-cultural-legacy-we-have-inherited-from-our-ancestors context," he writes ("Old Circles, New Circles," 284). This understanding leads in turn to a belief in the need to preserve a culture that might otherwise tragically disappear. Indeed aspects of the company's self-presentation, especially in its early days and the first television special about it, tread close to romanticized stereotypes of a stoic Indian speaking in monotone of spirits and nature.

Yet in some ways, AIDT's early insistence on the close connections between the dances it presents and vibrant, continuing, traditional Indian communities could be seen as a corrective response to federally funded endeavors of the day that attempted, paradoxically, to promote American Indian arts, artists, and artistic practices, but primarily only insofar as these endeavors could be enfolded into a mainstream modernist art world. AIDT's initial lack of interest in investigating the relation between Native American stories, rituals, and dance forms and modern dance forms, in other words, could be read as a refusal to participate in the kind of artistic economy, for example, promoted through the founding of the Institute of American Indian Arts (IAIA) in Santa Fe in 1962. According to Joy L. Gritton's astute history and analysis of the IAIA, the institute fed on and nourished both a colonialist and a modernist agenda, ultimately encouraging students to leave behind their tribal histories and cultures for "an enlightened and more promising artistic milieu" (Gritton, *Institute of American Indian Arts*, 154). As Gritton notes, the rhetoric surrounding this institution sought to recognize but then to enfold young Indian artists, as natural primitives, within the rhetoric of modernism. Rather than stressing the return of Native artists to Native communities and the strength the promotion of tribal arts would bring to these communities, as the Collier era's promotion of Indian artistic practices had done in the 1920s and 1930s, this arts promotion agenda sought to teach Indian artists how to make it in a competitive modern art market. The rhetoric shafted those traditional arts and instead sought to, like modernism, "make it new"—use these as raw materials in the making of art forms more common in studio galleries, like paintings and sculptures. This system, Gritton explains, recognized and rewarded Indian artists and artistic material most fervently when it was translated from the context of traditional values, beliefs, and art forms—what a *New Yorker* writer called "the dreary round of basketry, ceramics, rug- and blanket-weaving, and all the other small skills that have been for so long set aside as the traditional provinces of the Indian" (Gritton, *Institute of American Indian Arts*, 143)—into "modern international techniques." Gritton traces how response to the young artists' work implied that "drawing on tradition in some limited respect—keeping that which was useful and appropriate to 'life in space-age America'—was to be encouraged. To participate in that tradition in its totality, that is to return to the Native community" was not (129). Gritton's analysis suggests that IAIA funders and promoters—and she herself—understood this modernist art to be largely removed from traditional contexts and practices.

The American Indian Dance Theatre was founded in the wake of this subtle (and not so subtle) disdain for the "small skills that have been for so long set aside as the traditional provinces of the Indian," and the promotion of, instead, the use of elements of Indian art in culture in more modernist and universal artistic endeavors. In light of this rhetoric, a promotion of traditional dance with connections to community practice seems an astute rhetorical and politically resistant move.

AIDT's insistence on a strong relation between the staged dancing and dance practiced in the community carries over to the company's relation to ceremony, as well. Geiogamah noted that "ceremony" is not intrinsically separate from the stage or staged dancing. "Everything Indian people do is ceremonial," he said, explaining how the staged dancing AIDT performs does function as a kind of ceremony. "The ceremony involves not just the people," but also the audience, also the cosmos, the water and air and all the creatures, all the elements. One of the effects of the ceremony of the staged danced performance, he said, is "to create a sense of a tribe, a unit of people connected and working together." He added, "Dance is ceremonial literature, it's just not written down." Geiogamah drew a distinction between ceremony and ritual, which he described as "more goal intensive," and yet also noted that aspects of AIDT performances do have specific ritual intent. For example, he said, the Shaman who opens AIDT concerts is there "to ceremonialize the experience, the show itself." The purpose is "not to provide an exotic shaman," he said. Rather, "it actually has some effect on what the audience is experiencing." "Once this happens, then you feel like you've been welcomed, you can smell the sage (or the sweet grass—we alternate between sage and sweet grass), you've been brought in." The Grass Dance has a similar function, to prepare the dance space. It's a stylized Grass Dance, in a stylized dance performance, but it still has this purpose. And it does have an effect on the audience. When people leave, "you see people who are happy, you see people who are connecting," you see things have changed. "It's being done for a purpose," he said.[20]

Other dancers, directors, and choreographers likewise describe ways that the act of presenting Native dance on stages has ceremonial and spiritual effects for performers and audience members alike. Smith explains that, in the dances the Solaris Lakota Sioux Indian Dance Theater performs, "The overall effect is of a ceremony." He adds that he hopes audience members will approach it as such

Early poster of "DAYSTAR: Classical Dance-Drama of Indian America," circa 1980. Courtesy Daystar/Rosalie Jones.

and will come to the theater knowing "that this is a ceremony, and you're going to be involved in different levels of this little journey, of this little ceremony. . . . That's how you should go view it." He adds further that this is quite different from the way most viewers are trained to understand stage dance. "Like critics who try to say, well the footwork was so dazzling and reminded me of when this dancer was doing her step dancing and, you know, they're going on, without any understanding at all, what Indian dance is about, or why they do dances" (interview).

DAYSTAR: CONTEMPORARY DANCE–DRAMA OF INDIAN AMERICA

Daystar/Rosalie Jones, who founded Daystar: Classical Dance-Drama of Indian America in 1980 (changing the "Classical" to "Contemporary" around 1986), likewise described how her stage explorations of Indian stories and themes, over time, became a site in which she could approach aspects of Native American spirituality and ceremony that were kept underground by her family when she was growing up.[21] Jones was born on the Blackfeet reservation in Montana and was raised about sixty miles from the reservation. Her Blackfeet/Chippewa/Cree mother, Jones explained, "very much wanted to be just a middle-class person.

She certainly continued to be an Indian person inside, and we had lots of relatives and friends on the Blackfeet reservation . . . so there was a constant interplay there. But as far as anybody else who was not Indian who knew her, she was a typical middle-class person." Jones said that for her mother, "the whole Indian thing" at the time—the 1940s—was "under wraps." "It was what we talked about in the family, and with relatives, but not outside." She said, "My mother was Indian. My grandfather was Indian, my grandmother. And I had an uncle and aunt who were both Indian. And these Indian dialects were being spoken in the family, but there wasn't an over-acknowledgement of the whole thing, of 'We are Indian and we're going to tell the world. We're going to practice our Indianness in front of the whole world, and we don't care what they think.' That was not the attitude at all. It was, 'This is who we are, for us, but save yourself a lot of grief and don't bring it out in the open.'" Jones explained that this was the era of "the cowboy and Indian movies where the Indians get killed, and they're the savages, and we have to protect ourselves. That was so prevalent. It was so real, at that time." She added, "It was really how people were living at that time, and it influenced absolutely everything that you did, particularly if you had left the reservation, which my parents had."

For Jones, beginning to work with Native American dance was a point at which she began to really think about what "this connection to Indian things and to Indian people, somewhere over there," really meant to her. "Once I got started on it, it was a process of really reidentifying myself with the Native American part of the family," she said. "The whole dance thing was really bringing it out into the open." The modern dance stage, she said, became a way for her to explore this part of her as a visible, public identity. "There was some sort of stamp of approval on it, because it was an art form, and it was on stage," she said. "In a sense, the modern dance gave validity to what I was doing." Jones explained, "It was a great adventure to say, okay, I really can express Indianness, and being Indian."

As she began working in this way, Jones says the mission of her choreography became not technical display, like showing what a fabulous Shawl dancer or Fancy dancer does, but rather exploration of stories, legends, and vision behind Native American dances. "When I formed the company in 1980, I felt that it was not about being a big, flashy company, but it was about showing some of the soul, some of the secrets, maybe, underneath the dances or underneath the tribal belief," she said. "I wanted to show, really, the spirituality behind Native American dance and culture."

She was drawn to both dance-drama and Native American culture's relation to story. "I gravitated toward mythology and legend," she said. "And the mythology is so theatrical. That's probably the other reason that I gravitated toward dance-drama, so that there's always a story involved, some sort of a story and characters, rather than abstraction." In 1966, the Institute of American Indian

Arts in Santa Fe hired Jones to choreograph a piece for students at the Institute, based on Coyote stories.[22] She then joined the faculty there and, working with students from many different nations, though predominantly the Southwest Pueblo and Navajo peoples, began to develop a dance form based in Native American dance—an exploration that she was to continue for more than the next four decades.[23]

Jones's more "Native modern dance"–based approach fit with IAIA's modernizing mission, yet at the same time, she developed the modern dance space as one in which not to distance herself from but rather to connect with American Indian practices and worldviews from which she had been separated growing up. For Jones, the stage thus became a space in which to explore both the increasing acceptance of a politically visible Indianness as well as to engage with aspects of Native American ceremony and spirituality. Jones explained how, through her dance work with children and young adults on reservations and in Native communities in the late 1960s and early 1970s, she was invited to ceremonies and drawn to the way they create and strengthen community. Jones's experience with ceremony drew her to story cycles and to mask work. Stage pieces like *Wolf: A Transformation* eventually developed out of these explorations. This mask dance enacts the Anishinaabe story of "how the Creator gave the Wolf as a First Companion to the First Man." In it, a male dancer in wolf head and fur moves, watchful, crouching, head turning, through states of change, between wolf and human, shedding the wolf head and fur, transforming into man—and then reinhabiting the wolf skin, repeating the crouching, arching, and turning moves, blurring and connecting relations between man and wolf and between wolf dancer and wolf.[24] *Wolf* "has a shamanistic feel to it because it's pure transformation, from beginning to end," Jones explained (Magill, "Guiding Light of Daystar," 65). Mary Kay Conway notes that Jones described how important it is to her to stage this and other pieces in a way that puts "the audience in a receptive state so that they will be open to receive the messages conveyed by the stories" ("Staging Animal Dances," 49). With awareness shifted in this way, the stories and legends can do some of the work for the theater-going audience that they do in Native communities. Jones noted that these stagings worked on multiple levels to create connections similar to those enacted by ceremony (55). One effect was to inform non-Indian audiences about Native American culture, but in doing so, "to go a step farther than what they would see either at the powwow or even at the Pueblo dances which is—come in and you are looking at the dances" (56). Instead of a distanced, tourist, visual relation to the dancing, audience members at these performances, having settled in and shifted their awareness, would experience the stories as active witnesses to them, more akin to the way witnesses at a ceremony participate.

Another effect of engaging these stories and story cycles in her choreography was to help her make a connection herself to the spirit and animal world.

She explained that *Wolf: A Transformation* "came out of thinking that there is a spirit in everything, in Native people as well as other peoples, that human beings can connect to the natural world at another level other than strictly physical" (45). Jones discussed *Wolf* as a choreographic exploration of "a person attempting to make this connection and in fact could . . . communicate with animals and could talk to them and could learn from them and in a sense embody them . . . there could be these transfers back and forth." For her, choreographing became "another way of experiencing it." Jones explained, "Because I never had a personal experience with that kind of a, say, shaman growing up, although I knew they existed, this was a way for me as an individual, as an artist, to make that connection for myself."

While AIRFA had no legal effect on any of this stage dancing, in some instances their visible, publicly presented work did directly engage with shifts in religious freedom policy. The second television program about AIDT, "Dances for the New Generation," filmed in 1992, implies ways a history of federal Indian policy restricting religious practice—and the legislated end to this policy—continue to be part of the context of Indian dance practices off, as well as on, the theater stage. Its depiction of company members learning the Red Cedar Bark Ceremony, a ceremonial dance belonging to the Kwakiutl people of Alert Bay, British Columbia, underscores this history of religious persecution at the same time as it stresses connection between the AIDT stage dances and the community-based dances from which they are drawn.

The television production shows AIDT dancers arriving in British Columbia, touring the area, being shown totem poles, speaking with tribal leaders, visiting the cultural center. Intercut with these are excerpts of footage from earlier in the century, showing the potlatch practices that the Canadian government forcibly outlawed in the late nineteenth century, and interviews with Kwakiutl people about the effect of this policy on their elders and community. The camera cuts to an interview with one (unidentified) woman, who talks about the history of the potlatch, and recounts how in 1921 her father gave a potlatch "and forty-five people were arrested for really criminal activity like singing and dancing and giving speeches, distributing gifts, accepting gifts." She adds, "And the shame and the shock that people felt, for some of our old people remains today. But in spite of that, people didn't stop potlatching. They went even further underground. And one of the things we pride ourselves on here is that for us it never disappeared." These comments frame the dances the AIDT performers are there to learn and to translate to the stage. Their staging in turn testifies to an era in which ceremonial dance masks, and other regalia the government tried to procure and museumify, are still being shared, still being used, still being lovingly and laboriously handmade (a young man notes that one mask they are providing AIDT took one hundred hours to make). In the face of this history, the plan to overtly and explicitly present dances from these formerly prohibited events to paying public audiences, on stages across the continent and beyond, reads like a triumphant act of Indigenous resilience. It underscores the failure of the parliamentary ban on potlatching and ways the continuation of the ceremonial practices refused and refuted its presumptions. At the same time, the Kwakiutl people imply, in their welcoming of the AIDT dancers and their teaching of these dances to them, that they expect the sacred aspects of the practices to be respected and reflected in the stage dancing. A tribal leader presents them with a ceremonial mask, explaining, "This is a very sacred part of our ceremonies and we trust that you will be treating these as such." Geiogamah notes that AIDT's performance of the staged ceremony has ceremonial effects as well. "The Hamatsa (initiate) is experiencing something—not in a ritualistic sense," he said, but the ceremony, the excitement, the fear are having an effect on that person. Performing in that staged ceremony is "an identity transformative process" for the AIDT dancer, he explained. These comments reinforce ways that stage dance, including its use of ceremonial regalia and items, is understood as related to, and carrying some of the effects and responsibilities of, ceremonial dances practiced off the stage.

The AIDT stage dance *Red Cedar Bark Ceremony* can thus be seen as testimony of the failure of this history of religious and ethnic persecution to disappear the peoples and practices it targeted. While clearly the U.S.-based AIRFA had no legal effect on these Canadian practices (the ban on which had been taken off the books in Canada in 1951), and the AIDT would make no claim for its staged version to need such protection, the atmosphere of religious freedom it legislated is nonetheless itself part of the vibrant story that the AIDT's staging of still-vibrant First Nations and Native American ceremonial practices tells.

This direct engagement with ceremony has created some controversy regarding AIDT. Some viewers have taken issue with the company, not because they think the stage somehow mitigates against the dances' authenticity (as the dance critics quoted earlier contended), but rather precisely because the stage *doesn't* do this. They argue that the stage presentation of what they understand to be ceremonial and sacred material that is just showcased and not passed through a creative reenvisioning is itself the problem. "They're taking sacred material and turning it into vaudeville. And I really frown upon that," San Juan Pueblo choreographer Belinda James argued.[25] Yet, Geiogamah reiterated that he and his performers are well grounded in their communities' traditions and know what is appropriate and what is not. "We are all well aware of our responsibilities," he said, noting the company has performed for tens of thousands of Indian people and has never (or only once) received specific complaints about ways the dancing they present is inappropriate or disrespectful.

At the same time, Geiogamah noted that AIDT's approach to staging traditional material has changed in the years since it began and has been moving more toward creative reworking and reenvisioning of American Indian dance forms and practices. He described how, since the beginnings of his theater work, he's been "slowly, calmly . . . trying to present Indian dance in new contexts."[26] A decade after it was formed, the AIDT experimented with more directly bridging the two worlds of powwow-based traditional American Indian dance and modern dance. Starting around 1995, Geiogamah said, he noticed a trend in the media response to the company that made him start to question the company's program. "I was really starting to get frustrated with 'the costumes are fabulous,' 'it's a feast for the eyes' kind of response," he said. So in 1995, he brought in Mashpee choreographer and classically trained dancer Marla Bingham to work with him on a piece designed "to let the audience see the real dance" by focusing more on the movement and less on the outfits (dancers in this piece wore tights). The piece the company worked on with Bingham, he said, slowed down the movement and "deconstructed the fancy dance." "It really was radical," he said, for its time especially. "The slowing and paring down of the dance—called 'Modern Fancy' at the time—meant that you get to see the most danced dance, without it being beautifully disguised."

Bingham had danced with Alvin Ailey and in 1996 would found her own Southern California–based dance company, Marla Bingham Contemporary Ballet, for which she choreographed works that drew on both ballet vocabulary and Native American dance.[27] She described the challenge of working with AIDT, explaining that as a choreographer she had a very different dance education and training than the AIDT dancers in the outside world (interview). Most of the AIDT dancers, she said, were "powwow dancers who've lived on their land or on their reservation, and have been with their own tribe," and not trained "in the Western world, where you're learning dance in a formal environment." When she arrived to work with them, the dancers were initially protective and suspicious of her, she said, "like, 'Oh, so you're going to bring this European style to us,' and 'What do you think you're going to do?' And, so it took a while." She explained that in part because of her own powwow training ("I can look at Grass Dance, and I would be able to do Grass Dance with the guys") and in part because of her intense ballet and modern training ("I could memorize something very quickly, and then I can duplicate it and show them what they actually did") she impressed the dancers and won them over. "Being older and in such good shape, some of the men couldn't believe what I was able to do," she explained. "Then it started to come a conversation and we were able do an exchange, and then they were able to trust me," Bingham said. "I asked a lot of questions. I was very interested, genuinely interested. You know, 'Well, in your tribe, what did you do here, or how did you learn this, and how did you learn that?'" From here, she worked with the dancers on memorizing the moves they had improvised, and on formulating patterns, setting entrance cues, and maintaining consistency, all of which she acknowledged to be "tricky" because "in powwow you want to improvise and be free, but when you're on stage you only have a limited amount of time."

A second such endeavor occurred when Jacob's Pillow Dance Festival commissioned the troupe, together with white modern dance choreographer Laura Dean, to make a piece together.[28] This attempt at collaboration underscored not the bridging of their approaches but rather the differences between them. *New York Times* critic Christopher Reardon describes how, during a week-long residency at the National Arts Center in Ottawa, "tensions mounted steadily as Mr. Geiogamah and Ms. Dean realized how differently they viewed the conception, creation, casting and cost of the commissioned dance." He reports that dancers pointed to the differences between Dean's approach, which "regards movement as an end in itself," and Geiogamah's, which "sees it as part of a larger whole." Different rehearsal requirements and contested working approaches threatened to unravel the project. In the end a compromise was reached and a piece was staged, billed as *New Dance,* with scaled-down choreography by Dean. "Wearing just a few ribbons and feathers over plain black clothes, the dancers revealed the mechanics of the tribal dances and presented them as a new modern esthetic," Reardon writes of Dean's section.

Modern Fancy Dance and *New Dance,* versions of the pieces developed with Bingham and Dean, have remained in AIDT's repertoire, often closing the show.[29] In them the dancers dance much as they have been dancing throughout the program, showcasing staged versions of powwow dances. Yet in *Modern Fancy,* the dancers wear not resplendent regalia, but black exercise clothes—T-shirts, bike shorts—and do slowed-down Fancy Dance movements, at times incorporating break dance and hip hop moves. In *New Dance,* some dancers wear regalia but most are again in black workout clothes, moving together in and out of formations, sometimes dancing and kicking high just as they had done in the renditions of *Men's Fancy Dance* earlier in the program. The absence of full regalia, alongside moves that have at this point in the program become familiar, is striking. The pieces effectively deexotify the evening, showing the dancers as contemporary performers (they look like the kids, college students, young adults that they are) and calling on the audience to question assumptions about who and what American Indian dance includes.

These shifts suggest a different political climate for American Indian dance in the 1990s. When it began, AIDT's approach more directly promoted maintaining a separate sphere, where dancers, trained by their extended families and drawn from powwows and community festivals, retained and reinforced strong relations to traditional Native American art making and to their tribal communities. This approach served and continues to serve a vital function. AIDT has dramatically contributed to a public awareness of American Indian dance and theater, and for many audiences today has legitimized it as a theater art form. It has brought this awareness, and this legitimization, into an international arena. It creates community among its dancers and provides a forum for young American Indian dancers to come together; it continues to launch new American Indian dancers and dance artists. More recently, however, Geiogamah

American Indian Dance Theatre, Modern Fancy, *2005. Back: Marla Mahkimetas, Isaiah Bob, Tawny Hale. Front: Doug Scholfield and Jason Whitehouse. Courtesy Hanay Geiogamah.*

has described how now, in a new political climate, some American Indian artists have pushed for an expansion of this relation to tradition:

> [F]or some younger performing artists, there is a strong desire to expand the picture to include Indians in leotards performing the steps of classical ballet, modern dance styles, jazz, tap, and show dance. Traditional Native dance established, secure, strong as a rock, will serve this new breed of dance and music artists as a training ground and launching pad for the journey toward forging a flexible, tensile dance performance that can present the images and stories of the contemporary cultural, social, and political realities of 1990s Indian life. ("Old Circles, New Circles," 283)

Geiogamah goes on to support these desires, calling this "a critical transitional period in Indian performing arts." He writes, "By uniting the creative energy and styles of the past with the impulses of modern American Indian imagination, these Native artists of the dance will quickly join the vanguard of an artistic renaissance that promises to thoroughly reinvigorate American Indian arts" (284).

ABORIGINAL DANCE IN CANADA

Changing federal policies regarding American Indian and Aboriginal peoples, arts, and religious practices, of course, were far from the only force affecting the emergence of American Indian and Aboriginal stage dance companies in the 1980s. Yet the profound effect that federal Indian policy can itself have on dance history is nonetheless dramatized by the counterexample of Canada.

In Canada, federal Indian policy also began to change in the 1970s, but in different ways and for different reasons than it did in the United States. Up until then, Canadian federal Indian policy mirrored that of the United States, though policies in Canada remained more consistently assimilationist throughout the century. "As in the United States, Canadian Indian policy was inspired by the assumptions of nineteenth century Christianity, by cultural imperialism of the dominant non-native society, and by faith in marketplace economics," writes C. E. S. Frank in a comparison of the two nations' Indian policies ("Indian Policy," 238). Yet, Frank notes, Canadian Indian policy didn't deviate from assimilation and custodianship, the way U.S. policy did in the early twentieth century (244); there was no Canadian counterpart to the Indian Reorganization Act of 1934 that repealed the antidance resolutions, nor was there a counterpart to termination in the 1950s (241). Policies in Canada "scarcely changed from 1890 to 1970," he writes. In general, Frank suggests, "The Canadian government exercised more control over Indian bands, allowed them less autonomy in administration and religion, maintained residential schools longer, and articulated the policy of assimilation more consistently than did the Americans" (244). While restrictions on American Indian dance were taken off the books in the United States in 1934, in Canada, the Indian Act with its antidance clauses wasn't repealed until 1951, and Parliament didn't enfranchise Indians with the right to vote in federal elections until 1958.

In the late 1960s, the Canadian government began to examine Indian issues with an eye to addressing problems with existing policies. Yet the federal government's proposals, made public in 1966, shocked First Nations people in Canada by suggesting Canada follow a termination-type policy ending all special treatment for Indians, just as the United States was abandoning this approach. This proposal "aroused a tremendous and hostile outcry and stimulated Canadian Indians to organize and take political action in a way they never had before," Frank writes ("Indian Policy," 243). This response led to new federal policies centered more on culture and group rights, and in 1973, the Canadian federal government announced its willingness to negotiate comprehensive land claims agreements in parts of Canada where Aboriginal people had not signed treaties.[30] These negotiations have been slow and fraught, and the legal policy surrounding them troublesomely grounded in narrow parliamentary presumptions frequently at odds with Aboriginal views of rights and title. Nonetheless, they have led to the settlements of numerous agreements.[31] Implementation of these agreements has likewise been drawn out and bitterly disputed, and dozens more are still in process. Yet after the federal government announced a new comprehensive land claims policy in 1986, abandoning previous requirements that settlements include "extinguishment" of all other claims (Frank, "Indian Policy," 251), doors opened a bit wider. Land claims settlements remain active political struggles in Canada today, with tangible results affecting tens of thousands of Aboriginal peoples, kilometers of land, and billions of dollars.

Concurrent with this activity, according to C. E. S. Frank's analysis, has been a marked difference in the amount of federal funding accorded U.S. and Canadian Aboriginal/Native American programs since 1970. Frank writes how, in 1975, "Canada's dollar figure per Indian was about 15 percent higher than the U.S. figure" ("Indian Policy," 257). Since then, he suggests, budget provisions have "diverged enormously," with Canadian expenditures increasing steadily and U.S. expenditures decreasing, especially during social program cuts of the Reagan era. "This analysis of budgets shows a profound and growing difference between the two countries in real policies since the mid-1970s, despite the similarity in stated policies," he writes. "Aboriginal issues in Canada have grown increasingly important and prominent on the political agenda, while in the United States, along with other disadvantaged people, Indians have become less important" (258). Despite Canadian budget cuts and shifts in expenditures over the years, Frank concludes that "expenditures on Canada's Aboriginal peoples continue to be high and remain well above those of the United States" (259).

Since the late 1960s and early 1970s, land claims have been settled in the United States.[32] And U.S. Indian activism has circulated around questions of land claims and title, as the occupation of Alcatraz Island perhaps most dramatically demonstrated. Yet despite the Alcatraz occupation's important symbolic effect, it and the aggregate of other land claims arguments launched in both political and legal arenas in the United States have had nowhere near the tangible outcome in terms of land claims as they have in Canada.

It seems that as Canadian policy moved toward recognizing land claims and negotiating settlements, and toward increasing federal funding for Aboriginal peoples and programs, political activity and legislation in the United States circulated around more abstract issues such as religious freedom, addressed in AIRFA, Indian identity and artistic production, addressed in the revised Indian Arts and Crafts Act of 1990, and repatriation, addressed in the Native American Graves Protection and Repatriation Act (NAGPRA). While land claims legislation is undoubtedly active in the United States, the Native American issues most prominent in legal, scholarly, and popular discussions of Indian politics circulate around the identity question, peyote usage, and the more abstract aspects of religious freedom that dealt not with resources but with moral questions.[33]

Perhaps this history helps explain the development of American Indian stage dance in the United States. Legislated guarantees of religious freedom, and growing social acceptance of Indian identity and political activity around it, have opened the field and enabled some artists to explore this arena. As they explored the stage not as a site of religious ritual, but nonetheless as a space in which to access the spiritual and ceremonial aspects of Native American dance practices, this legislated religious freedom served to help foster an atmosphere in which they could freely engage with these ideas. But even as this opening up of explorations of Native American spiritual and ceremonial practices found space on U.S. stages, the lack of substantial financial support for Indian peoples—including resources that would lead to land claims, and thus to real economic and spiritual rights to those lands and their resources—mean that American Indian stage dance has *not* been that abundant in the United States, even after Indian activism of the 1970s and passage of AIRFA in 1978. There has been some, but those Native American dance artists who have dedicated themselves to a career as choreographers in the United States have by and large struggled, with tenacity and integrity, to support themselves while doing so.

On the other hand, this combination of increased funding for Aboriginal peoples and artists and effective land claims policies have helped contribute to a vibrant, active, Aboriginal dance scene in Canada. Institutionally, this includes the founding of the Native Theatre School (later the Centre for Indigenous Theatre) in Toronto in 1974, to the development of the Aboriginal Dance Project (later Program) at Banff Centre for the Arts in Alberta in 1996, through the semiannual Aboriginal Dance Symposium, which has fostered dialogue and discussion about the development of Aboriginal dance in Canada. The 2001 "Nimitohtak! We Dance!" symposium, for example, brought together Aboriginal dance artists and administrators to share ideas and create alliances and to discuss issues of concern in the Aboriginal dance community.[34] Today, relatively substantial funding from the Canada Council is available to support Aboriginal dancers.

Once again, in other words, access to land and federal policies regarding Aboriginal and Native American lands have been intricately interwoven with Aboriginal and Native American dance history—including stage dance history. Just as nineteenth-century landgrabs led to curtailed dance practices, land claims settlements and the possibility of more in Canada helped spawn and support contemporary Aboriginal stage dance practices in Canada, and these burgeoning practices likewise supported land claims efforts. The absence of these in the United States can be seen reflected in the comparatively less active dance scene in the United States. What follows more specifically supports the idea of dance and land-policy histories as not only coincident, but also politically and spiritually interconnected.

EIGHT

Aboriginal Land Claims and Aboriginal Dance at the End of the Twentieth Century

———

We can feel the land, and we can feel the beat, and we can feel the vibration, and that is the connection. So, when I begin to feel that, I begin to believe it is possible to make a movement.

> *Pablo Palma, dancer, Aboriginal*
> *Dance Program*

From 1987 to 1991, the Gitxsan and Wet'suwet'en people presented their claim to over 22,400 square miles of land in British Columbia to the British Columbia Supreme Court. Arguing that they are descendents of people who have lived in the territory since time immemorial, and that their claim to the land has never been extinguished through treaty or warfare, the Gitxsan and Wet'suwet'en argued for legal recognition of their ownership and jurisdiction over the land and its resources. In support of their claim, Gitxsan and Wet'suwet'en chiefs and elders described and presented to the court not only totem poles, house crests, and regalia, but also oral histories: Gitxsan *adaawk*—sacred reminiscences about ancestors, histories, and territories—and Wet'suwet'en *kungax*—spiritual songs, dances, and performances about trials between territories, all tying them to the land.

According to anthropologist Dara Culhane's lengthy and incisive analysis of the *Delgamuukw v. Regina* trial, the trial judge took exception to the material, particularly to witnesses singing in court. "'This is a trial,'" he reproached an elder at one point, "'not a performance,'" Culhane reports him saying.[1] In his ruling, the judge largely dismissed the material as evidence. "I am not able to accept *adaawk*, *kungax* and oral traditions as reliable bases for detailed history," he wrote, admitting oral tradition only when used "'to fill in the gaps' left at the end of a purely scientific investigation" (Culhane, *Pleasure of the*

Crown, 257). Instead, the judge concluded that "The evidence suggests that the Indians of the territory were, by historical standards, a primitive people without any form of writing, horses, or wheeled wagons" (247), and ruled in favor of the Crown. The case was appealed to the British Columbia Court of Appeal, and then to the Supreme Court of Canada.

In declaring *kungax* to be antithetical to a trial, as a trial "is not a performance" (and *kungax* implicitly are), the judge rehearsed familiar attitudes about the relation between performances and legal enactments. His annoyance with the elders' "performance" in a courtroom trial, and subsequent dismissal of the performance material they presented as evidence, is based on his assumption that performance is in a different category than documents or declarations carrying legal weight or consequence. Unlike, say, a treaty, or a letter, or a bill of sale, a performance doesn't actually prove anything, make anything actual, or serve as official record of having made anything actual in the past. It is just a performance, and by (his) definition outside of what is legally admissible as factual. Although it may be interesting or amusing, it is superfluous and inappropriate to the decorum of a courtroom where facts are adjudicated and a judge's trial pronouncements (because a trial is *not* a performance) create law, reflected in documents, which then *do* carry the factual weight of official history and memory.

The conception of the lack of legal weight carried by *adaawk* and *kungax* performance echoes that of J. L. Austin's seminal proclamation, in *How to Do Things with Words,* about performative utterances. Austin writes that certain performative utterances do carry legal weight in a court of law or sanctioned legal setting, but when those same words are spoken as part of a stage performance, they do not. For example, according to Austin's oft-cited example, when a heterosexual couple says "I do" and a justice of the peace declares them husband and wife, this creates them as such, but these same words are "in a peculiar way hollow or void if said by an actor on the stage."[2] Both Austin and this judge thus imply that a performance doesn't actually *do* anything, at least not in the way a bill of sale, or a performative utterance, does; it is a performance, an act—not a performative.

While *Delgamuukw* was under appeal, public Aboriginal song and dance performance continued to gain momentum in Canada. In 1993, Aboriginal artists and storytellers initiated a working partnership with the Banff Centre for the Arts in Alberta, Canada. This led to the creation of the Aboriginal Arts Program at Banff in 1994. In 1995, a residency for Aboriginal Women's Voices brought Aboriginal women together to share songs and create new works. In the summer of 1996, the Aboriginal Arts Program introduced a summer dance residency in conjunction with the Banff Arts Festival, which became the first annual Chinook Winds Aboriginal Dance Project. Also in 1993, the Parliament of Canada, the Northwest Territories, and the Inuit of Nunavut signed the

Nunavut Final Land Claim Agreement. The agreement established Inuit control of more than 350,000 square kilometers of land in northern Quebec, over a tenth of which includes mineral rights. The agreement followed over thirty years of Inuit organizing and study of unextinguished Inuit Aboriginal title in the Arctic.

Then, in December 1997—after the Nunavut Agreement was underway, while Aboriginal music and dance in Canada were gaining increasing support and visibility—the Supreme Court of Canada rejected the British Columbia judge's ruling in the *Delgamuukw* land claim case. This appellate judge argued the earlier ruling was faulty due in large part to the first judge's rejection of oral tradition. "The Gitxsan Houses have an *adaawk* which is a collection of sacred oral tradition about their ancestors, histories, and territories. The Wet'suwet'en each have a *kungax* which is a spiritual song or dance or performance which ties them to their land. Both of these were entered as evidence on behalf of the appellants," the appellate judge noted.[3] "The oral histories were used in an attempt to establish occupation and use of the disputed territory which is an essential requirement for aboriginal title," he added. "Had the oral histories been correctly assessed, the conclusions on these issues of fact may have been very different" (*Delgamuukw,* 29).

In coming to this decision, the Canada Supreme Court ruling noted a 1996 commission report that states, "The Aboriginal historical tradition is an oral one, involving legends, stories and accounts handed down through the generations in oral form. It is less focused on establishing objective truth and assumes that the teller of the story is so much a part of the event being described that it would be arrogant to presume to classify or categorize the event exactly or for all time" (*Delgamuukw,* 75). It concludes, "The laws of evidence must be adapted in order that this type of evidence can be accommodated and placed on an equal footing with the types of historical evidence that courts are familiar with, which largely consists of historical documents" (76).

The Supreme Court found the lower courts' errors to be so "palpable and overriding" as to warrant a new trial, but advised instead that the issues of Aboriginal title be settled through negotiations and not future litigation. On the one hand, the decision was celebrated as a landmark victory that changed the legal landscape for Aboriginal title and rights litigation in Canada (Culhane, *Pleasure of the Crown,* 370). On the other, scholars have argued that the case was lost before the appeal decision because its terms had changed from the first case's claim for "ownership" of the territory and "jurisdiction" over it to the one appeal case's claim for, instead, Aboriginal title and self-government.[4]

On April 1, 1999, Nunavut—"our land" in Inuktitut—was inaugurated, becoming the largest land claim settlement in Canada's history. In celebration, the Canadian government issued a new 1999 two-dollar "twoonie" coin. As with previous twoonies, one side of the coin carries Elizabeth II's profile, contained neatly in the gold-colored circular center, surrounded by a silver-colored rim. Embossed on the other side, new to this edition, is the image of an Inuit drum dancer, inscribed over and extending past the inner gold circle that, on the other side, circumscribes the crown.

One thing the Supreme Court decision on *Delgamuukw* has done is opened the way for oral histories to be admitted as evidence in Canadian courts, and not thrown out as hearsay. In this court case, the oral histories considered included dance—recognized as part of the Wet'suwet'en *kungax*—and thus the court decision recognized dance as not only a central and legally valid form of Aboriginal culture, but also a type of historical document tying Aboriginal peoples to the land. In this sense, the court decision echoed understandings Aboriginal peoples have long held about dance as connected to their relationship to land. At the same time, the *Delgamuukw* decision signals how much official Canadian governmental attitudes on both land claims and Aboriginal dance have changed in the past century. Participating in Aboriginal cultural practices like potlatching and sundancing and organizing for Aboriginal land title were outlawed and criminalized in 1884, according to Sections 140 and 141 of the Indian Act. In 1951, the Indian Act was amended and both Section 140 (the antipotlatch laws) and Section 141 (the ordinance against organizing for land claims) were dropped (though as Culhane notes, not repealed or acknowledged as wrong) (*Pleasure of the Crown,* 228). Yet, because they were added to the 1876 act together in 1884, and repealed at the same time in 1951, the Canadian government recognized and reinforced both a conceptual and a legal link between them—a recognition that Aboriginal peoples noted. "In Indian memories, section 141 is usually linked with the potlatch prohibition," Culhane writes (226). In other words, there has long been both an Aboriginal assertion of the link between dancing and relationship to land, and Canadian legal and historical, as well as rhetorical, connection between Aboriginal feasts and dances and Aboriginal land claims.

But admitting Aboriginal dances, and other forms of oral history previously dismissed as performance, into the courts as a form of historical document does more than just enter more evidence into legal consideration. It questions understandings that see performance as something with less truth and legal effect than, say, a written treatise or a courtroom trial. Admitting it into the halls of official memory forces a rethinking of how performance functions as historical document and suggests that performance such as dancing enacted, and continues to enact, effect on the world.

This echoes Native American and Aboriginal conceptions of dance, even as these conceptions extend understandings of enactment. "We dance to remember all our beloved ones," writes Leslie Marmon Silko in *Almanac of the Dead* (722). This relationship of dance and memory carries not only the physical sense of dance as something that is learned from others and held and remembered in one's body. It also carries a spiritual sense in which learning to dance, and the act of dancing, enacts a spiritual and physical connection to other beings, including those who have passed on, as well as to those who will come later. "Through the expression of dance, especially in Aboriginal cultures, a step into the past may be retained, explored, revived, or created," writes Inuit-Irish dancer Siobhán Arnatsiaq-Murphy in *Chinook Winds* ("Journal Entry," 90). Thus performance both records for the future and enacts relationship to the past even as it enacts for the future and records relationship to the past. This, in turn, raises questions for contemporary theorizings on performance as standing in for, and seeking in vain to replace, something that it is not—conceptions that harken back at least as far as the Platonic disdain for the arts as mimesis, or imitation.[5] Silko, in stating "we dance to remember our beloved ones," understands dancing as enactment of memory in the present, a memory that recognizes the past, and connection to ancestors and to land, by embodying it.

PROCESSES OF CREATION

In July 1999, I traveled to the Aboriginal Dance Project at Banff Centre for the Arts and started to get a sense of these understandings of dance's relation to time, memory, and spiritual connection. I had come to see that season's Chinook Winds Aboriginal Dance Project performances, watch videotapes of previous years' productions, and talk with the Aboriginal Dance Project dancers, choreographers, and program directors. On the plane there, I had read about *Delgamuukw* and had tried to get a handle on some Canadian land claims history. Then I arrived, ready to research the state of Aboriginal stage dance at the end of the twentieth century.

My first day I went over to Aboriginal Arts looking for Marrie Mumford, the program director, who was the only person there I'd met before. "You made it! You're here! C'mon over!" she said when we connect at last, and we talked for half an hour about how this year the preparation for the Aboriginal Arts Program began with a meeting of the Advisory Committee to revisit the intention of the program, how this began a process to restructure and set future directions.

She hinted at the difficulties the previous year, when they produced four new pieces in five weeks. She explained that the current year the program cut back production to two choreographies, rather than four, creating one new work and returning one choreography from repertoire. The program that year had also introduced a two-tiered program to balance the needs of training, creation, and production. The intention, she said, was to use production as a vehicle to build community by adopting cultural methodologies in the process of training, establishing an Aboriginal cultural framework, which includes Aboriginal values and principles in the process of creation and production. This intention guides the process and recognizes the need for identifying and affirming Aboriginal systems, and the need for translating these systems to contemporary practices, both Aboriginal and European. "Also part of the process is to identify the effect of colonization on people who come through the program. Colonization shifts you into a way of thinking, which then lives in your body. So, part of what we are doing is deconstructing that way of thinking and reclaiming Indigenous knowledge," she said. One change this two-tiered program has led to, she explains, is in the dance training that students undertake. "We used to have all our contemporary classes in the morning and our traditional classes in the afternoon. This year, we said, 'Let's not make that separation. Let's begin with the traditional dances,'" she said.[6]

Over the next several days I talked with the choreographers and choreographers' assistants and again with Mumford, and with as many of the dancers as I could, about the work going on at Banff. Many of the interviews started with qualifications. I was cautioned that dance, in an Aboriginal context, can't be separated out from other aspects of Aboriginal life. Mumford explained that even my focus on dance alone doesn't really fit. "Traditionally dance has both a cultural and spiritual significance. Dance, story, song and drumming are interrelated, they are not exclusive of one another," she said.

Santee Smith, a Mohawk woman who danced in the program for four years and is back this year as a choreographer's assistant, explained this as well. "Traditionally when we dance, it's a celebration," she said. "It's always been when people gathered. There's always been music, there's always been dancing, there's always the element of almost theater when somebody's speaking." Because of the way traditional Aboriginal dance is interwoven with story, song, music, and theater, what is labeled "dance" involves aspects beyond physical movement, and even beyond the focus of these other forms.

Smith contrasted the dance work at Banff with the years of ballet training she'd had. "Here it's focused on all three levels. It's not just the physical, it's not just the movement base," she said. "It's traditional, it's cultural, it's spiritual, and people are trying to make that come together in a way that I haven't experienced with any other place."

Other dancers also explained the sense of connection they felt, the sense of dance being more than just isolated physical movement. Penny Couchie, a Mohawk-Ojibway dancer from Toronto, explains how this understanding of dance as something more than physical training translates into the dance work going on at the Aboriginal Dance Program. "Here, there's less of a focus on, 'This is the shape that you're making with your body' and more of a focus on 'What shape does your body make when you're saying that?'" she said. "Approaching it from the inside out—but then understanding you don't stay on the inside. You understand your relationship. You understand your relationship to everything around you."

Shalan Joudry, a Mi'kmaq woman from Nova Scotia, echoed this focus on dancers' connection to the world around. She said, "I think that good dancers are very connected not only within themselves, but to everything around them, and they know what they're saying. There is a purpose that transcends their physical movement. And I think you can tell by watching someone if they have that greater connection."

At the base of the discussions was an understanding of connection between what might be called "traditional" Aboriginal dance, done within Aboriginal communities as part of ceremonies and celebrations, and the dance being choreographed and staged here at the Margaret Greenham Theatre, for primarily non-Aboriginal audiences.

Smith made brief mention of the potential controversies in staging some kinds of Aboriginal dance, but recognizing what's appropriate to stage, and what isn't, was more of a given than an issue she focused on. "There are controversial things about what we can take to the stage," she said. "There are certain things within everybody's nation that are not meant for public entertainment, stuff that is meant for the community." She added, "but we haven't had that problem here because everybody's respectful of that." The project's focus instead, she and others suggested, is on the relation between Aboriginal dance practices, as aspects of ceremony and celebration, and how the Aboriginal ways of understanding held in that dancing can be translated to the stage. The dancers implied they are tired of suggestions that their lives, including their dance lives, aren't sufficiently traditional.

"What is traditional?" asked Sid Bobb, a Sto:lo man from Vancouver. "Does that mean three hundred years ago? Does it mean a hundred years ago? Fifty years ago? Or does it mean a thousand years ago? To me, I keep intention, I keep the concepts the same. Dance is a reflection of that." He added, "It's a reflection of who you are. Your dance is a part of the way you envision things."

Again and again dancers mentioned relation between the dancers dancing there, that week, and other generations. "I envision myself as my ancestors," said Bobb. "We're not different. People ask today, well, you live in a city or you do this or you do that. I'm no different than I was a thousand years ago, because I'm the same person, reacting to things around me, making choices within things around me. So there's no difference with the man two thousand years ago." He explained, "The way you do things always changes—throughout your personal life, as well as your cultural life. Your culture has a history and it's still changing, it's going somewhere, same as your personal history is changing and going somewhere."

Smith explained this too. "We think that—a lot of people think here—that we have ancestral memories in our body, and we are just trying to awaken those. That memory is in our body and in who we are. So when we do our performances, and especially when we're talking about intention, about why we're moving in a certain way, what does that mean to us, as the individual performer, that's when we try to call upon that ancestral stuff or try to awaken that."

Joudry said something along the same lines. "My understanding is that as we go from one generation to the next a part of our spirit and body is passed on to our children, and they pass on a bit of their collected spirit, and so on. Therefore, within me is a piece of all my ancestors, and I have that memory within me somewhere. The challenge is to get in tune to that, to hear and feel it, respond to that kind of memory."

Intergenerational connection was more than a concept the dancers were attuned to; it was also part of the everyday comings and goings. The importance of this connection to children and grandmothers was visible all over the place. Couchie's almost five-year-old daughter, Nimikii, was there, everywhere, playing on the floor, coming over to show us her paper dolls while I interviewed choreographer Muriel Miguel and Smith in the Cultural Room. And Smith was there with her baby daughter, Semiah, and her mother Leigh had come along as well to help take care of Semiah, and (assistant program director) Cat Cayuga's daughter Zita was running around too, and (music and cultural director) Sadie Buck's son George, and Cat's mother showed up as well, toward the end.

When I asked Don Stein, in the Banff Centre administration, what effect the Aboriginal Arts Program has had on the Banff Centre for the Arts as a whole, I expected him to talk about awareness of Aboriginal issues or politics or culture. He did, but not in the way I expected him to. "Child care! Child care is better for everybody here now," he answered. "When we started working with the Aboriginal community, they brought their whole families with them. So there were enormous strides forward in terms of [the Banff Centre's] sensitivity and facilities and willingness to support family life. Ten years ago, this was one of the things that people often complained about. And now, ten years later, whenever somebody asks if they can bring their kids, we can say, 'Oh, the child care here is fabulous.'"

Connected with this relation to ancestors and to ancestral memory, the dancers suggested, are understandings of the body, and especially the dancing body, as holding and inhabiting histories and ways of understanding of which dancers might not even be fully aware. As Smith explained, "A lot of the work that we do is with taking ownership of our own bodies. There's a lot of things that, through colonization, we don't even realize [affects] the way that we think or the way that we view our own body and our own humanness. A lot of the work that Karla [Jessen Williamson, the Inuit mask instructor] did was very much of reclaiming our own bodies, feeling comfortable in who we are." She added, "We talk about this in the beginning—that we're going to be doing things that might spark something in you. We're working with our body and a lot of times issues will come up, because we're holding things in our body that we don't realize."

Inuit dancer Feliks Gower-Kappi talked about how in this way of understanding bodies, and connection to others through bodies that are danc-ing, ways of seeing what happens on the stage as merely representational—something acted or portrayed (but what Austin would call null or void in any real sense)—don't quite hold. "For these pieces here, you really have to be what you're portraying," Gower-Kappi said. "It's not just 'Okay, I'm told to be this, and I'll do it.' You have to learn to really become that. That's what Alejandro [Roncería, the choreographer Gower-Kappi was working with] wanted—us to really feel it, be a part of it, to really be that person or to really be that bird. And to think of it in that way, to have that focus, to exercise yourself to have that focus is really challenging," he said. "Because just playing it is not as genuine. It starts to have a feel of, 'Oh, just kind of get it over with.' But once you're being it, it's something. Because if you become it, and if there's something to stop it, it's in a sense a little part of you dying or something, so therefore you want to survive, you want to go on."

This sense of dancing as enactment, not portrayal, had come up again and again in the stated intentions behind the Aboriginal Dance Project productions over the years. In the video box description for the version of *Shaman's Journey* staged at the Aboriginal Dance Project in 1997, choreographer Raoul Trujillo wrote about how the piece is "about seeing into other worlds besides our own." He described the act of transformation the Shaman in the piece goes through: "He enters other worlds by learning the languages of his guides and even be-comes those animal forms." The Shaman's "arrival," said Trujillo, "is when he enters the spirit world and communicates with the ancient ones." Mohawk dancer Jerry Longboat described *Raven's Shadow,* a piece he choreographed after working at Banff with Trujillo, as "a contemporary investigation into the process of expanding oneself to experience the threshold between the living and the ancestral." He added, "I explore dance and movement as spiritual and ritual expression, sculpting a space of Indigenous culture in the contempo-rary world."

This understanding of dancing as becoming, rather than playing at, extended not just to the people or birds Gower-Kappi referred to in *Light and Shadow*. It also underscored the relationship to land that almost everyone mentioned to be part of what the dancing they were doing at Banff not only explores, but also enacts. *Light and Shadow,* one of two pieces on the 1999 program, is a dance for Nunavut that premiered during the 1997 season, before the Nunavut Land Claim Act came into effect. It was being restaged as a celebration of the land claim, and of the inauguration of Nunavut as an Inuit province in April. Pablo Palma, a Nahua dancer from Mexico, said he relates to the dance, a piece for Inuit land far from where he has always lived, because he can understand the relationship to land he is embodying in his dance movement in the piece. "This dance for Nunavut is for the return to the land of that people," he said. "We can feel the land, and we can feel the beat, and we can feel the vibration, and that is the connection. So, when I begin to feel that, I begin to believe it is possible to make a movement." Sid Bobb also said the connection to and embodiment of both animals and land is a central part of the two pieces they were staging that season. "In both pieces, there is a huge reference to the land. In Muriel [Miguel]'s piece *[Throw Away Kids]*, a lot of the connection and a lot of the characters' core is relationship to the land. And then in Alejandro [Roncería]'s piece, a lot of it is working with animals, seals," he said. "The seal-people are emulating that animal."

Joudry related this to what Aboriginal dance, including contemporary stage dance, offers. "For us, dance is deeply associated to the animals and land. That's our whole purpose of dancing," Joudry said. "It's all about how things are interconnected. Those relationships to earth being so important and that we never really disconnect from it. Dance then becomes a part of ceremony and a way of speaking, many things. We still view dance in that way. I think that a lot of contemporary kinds of dancers see their craft as a very distinct art. But then for us it's very connected to ceremony and to celebration."

Smith, like Palma, explained that this understanding of how dance relates to land—and how dancing is part of relationship to land, and enacts relationship to land—is what connects the dancers from so many different nations. "Even though we are all Aboriginal, we all come from our own communities, and we all come from a movement base which is different, and yet similar," she said. "So there's powwow style and there's the Iroquois dance we do and then there's Inuit people who come and teach us masking and drumming. But one common thread that's through everything is, Aboriginal dance is very much connected to the ground and to drum beats that are connected to the earth."

Gower-Kappi said the same thing. "We might be different, from different climates, landscapes, but we all believe we come from the land. That's our provider. We have the same similarities and respect for things." This, he says, is what he understands "collective memory" to be, this shared understanding, across Aboriginal communities. "Collective memory is memories of different people, from the different places they are from, coming together. And sharing what we have." Couchie agreed. "I think that all these stories that we're doing are very much collective memory, because our experience as Aboriginal people has been so similar. The loss of land and laws and social structures and way of life, our whole structure. It's something we have in common as Aboriginal people, all over the world." She added, "Dance is part of our families and a celebration of the people, and here it's part of political activism. It's part of us saying, 'We are the people who genocide has been performed upon.' It's our voice."

These comments suggest that what enables this "collective memory" to be shared across time and place is not a shared Indigenous bloodline or gene. Rather, what connects Aboriginal peoples from the Arctic to South America is a similar experience of colonialism and land loss, and a common relationship to and understanding of land and to the animals that share it. This relationship is passed from generation to generation. These articulations also focus on *connection* across history and geography, time and place. The relation to ancestors the dancers express is not one of surrogation or nostalgia, where a dancer replaces and stands in for a lost past or ancestor. As Bobb says, he envisions himself *as* his ancestors, not like them or replacing them. By way of his dancing, they *aren't* lost or gone.

In focusing on a "contemporary Aboriginal dance process" for the Banff program, which includes an emphasis on cultural process throughout each program area, Mumford explained, the process also maintains a connection to the land, the elements, and the natural world that surrounds us. "We always spend at least one day a week on the land," she said. "Being in contact with the earth gives us time to reflect, reminds us of who we are and where we come from, connecting us to the great mystery, ancestral roots, and ancient teachings, to guide us in creating new stories that contribute to defining our relationships." Being in contact with the land is part of the dance training, too. "As we were rehearsing we would take it outside," Joudry said. "I don't think you'd see many ballerinas outside to feel the trees and to be connected to the grass. We would take off our shoes to dance on the grass because that's what it's about. I think that it brings a lot more spirit to dance, something stronger to create a more enriched dance. I'm not saying that Western dancers are simply about physical movement because I understand that many of them must feel strongly about expressing themselves as powerfully as possible, but I think that our philosophies such as rehearsing on the grass bring a different kind of spirit." For the dancers and Aboriginal audience members, she added, this dancing provides inspiration and connection. "It's getting us back to our traditions and our stories," she said. "It's inspiring us to go and learn those dances and those stories and songs, all of them where there's no separation for us, and to bring it back and to put it into a contemporary context of what we see as dance or theater."

But always undergirding this connection to the land is a politicized awareness of Aboriginal land claim and land title issues. Mumford explained that part of the program includes connecting to the Aboriginal peoples whose territories are near, "to hear the stories of this land, of the waters and the sacred springs that are here, stories of these mountains." That year, for example, the company had been invited to Mii-stuks-koo-wa (Castle Mountain) to hear Siksika Elder Tom Crane Bear and former Chief Robert Breaker speak about their traditional territories and lands. Mumford explained that, as a term of the historic peace agreement known as Treaty 7, the Crown in Right of Canada set out in 1891 to survey and confirm twenty-six-and-a-half square miles to be set apart as a reserve of the Siksika Nation. The government informed the Siksika that this land was their reserve and encouraged the Siksika people to harvest timber and to hunt and gather for economic and subsistence purposes. Mii-stuks-koo-wa at Castle Mountain was eventually surveyed and recognized as a reserve by the federal government in 1893, before the creation of Banff National Park. The Crown relinquished the land without consent from, compensation to, and compliance with the Siksika Nation in 1908. Reserves were set aside for the Piegan and Blood Tribe in 1883 by the same surveyor, Ponton, for the same purposes and subject to the same treaty. The Siksika Nation are proactively pursuing the restoration of their rightful reserve title to the lands at Mii-stuks-koo-wa. "Sovereignty, legal, cultural and political issues all pertain to the land and are part of our spiritual connection to the earth," Mumford said.

All week, things Mumford had said echoed in my mind. At a conference at the University of Calgary earlier in the year, she had told one story about being invited to a community's ceremonies for the first time. She was unsure of the protocol and was afraid she would make many mistakes. Her grandmother told her to be respectful, to observe and listen. Then her grandmother laughed and said, "How are you going to learn if you are afraid to make mistakes?" At another point, a young woman in the audience had asked Mumford if she would teach them more about Aboriginal cultures or tell them where there were Native people who could teach them. Mumford had cautioned them that the quest for this knowledge is a journey. Although it is important that they become educated about Native issues and Native cultures so that they can become knowledgeable allies, it is her belief, she had said, that it is not the responsibility of Native people to educate non-Native people about Native cultures. Since Oka,[7] she has made the decision to work on behalf of Aboriginal people, to focus her work on building within Aboriginal communities. She had recommended that they learn about Aboriginal cultures through establishing relationships with Aboriginal students at the university, listening to them to gain awareness and understanding. She had recommended that they lobby the university to hire Native instructors who are knowledgeable of Native cultures, and that they lobby the university to establish an Indigenous Studies Program, so that cross-cultural work can begin.

On the third night I joined the Aboriginal dance people at a table in the dining hall. They were talking about these racist incidents with which they'd had to deal. Apparently the young ballet students at the ballet program also happening at the Banff Centre had been harassing a faculty member's eight-year-old son, teasing him and not letting him down the hallway, and making disparaging comments about the Aboriginal Dance Program in general. Someone had overheard one of them say something about how it smells in the Aboriginal Arts building and then add, "yeah well there's a bunch of Indians in there," or something like that. And other things they didn't really want to repeat. So there was a meeting scheduled to talk about it with the ballet students, two of the Aboriginal Arts Program administrators, and one of the ballet students' counselors.

After the Aboriginal Arts advisers left for the meeting, the rest of us stayed and chatted a bit, and then one of the waiters came by to offer us more coffee. He said to one of the choreographers, "Oh is your concert tonight? Cool—I'm going to try and see it. I saw an Aboriginal dance program up at Banff Springs Hotel last summer and it was cool."

We smiled at him, and one of the program coordinators asked, "Where did you say you'd seen Aboriginal dancing?"

"At Banff Springs."

"Where?" she said.

"It's that big tourist hotel," I said.

"Yeah it was cool," the young waiter said. "There was this guy with all these rings, you know? He had all these rings he was dancing with."

"Oh, the Hoop Dance," they said. "That's the Hoop Dance."

And he said, "Well, it was so cool! It was like it was getting all the evil spirits out—you could feel it! All the evil spirits coming out of you. And I was thinking, get back in there, I need you! It was great. So I'm going to try and come tonight."

"Oh," they said. The silence of their refusal to engage further with this young man echoed loud and clear. We watched as the waiter went off to some other table, and a sense of exhaustion hung heavy in the air at having constantly to deal with incidents like these—racist ballet students, waiters oblivious to the ignorance in the images they spout and to their right to spout them. It stayed quiet for a while.

Then one of the advisers came back from the meeting with the ballet students and said it had gone really well. The Aboriginal Arts people had given the ballet students an earful about teasing an eight-year-old boy—"What has he ever done to you?"

"But it gets tiring," they said to me. After that we mostly talked, and teased the resident adviser about a guy who seemed to be giving her the eye.

THE FOURTH CHINOOK WINDS ABORIGINAL DANCE PRODUCTION: *THROW AWAY KIDS* AND *LIGHT AND SHADOW*

I saw the performances four times, from different places in the theater. Wherever I sat, I was at ease, comfortable, and relaxed, watching from my place in the dark. I knew the role well. I had been in theaters like this one many times before. The first piece, Muriel Miguel's *Throw Away Kids,* tells the story of two women, Cosmos (danced by Penny Couchie) and her daughter Star Girl (danced by Teme/Augama/Anishnaabe dancer Sandra Laronde), and their struggles with life on a very present-day Earth. It interweaves three narratives: a portion of the Haudenosaunee creation story, *Sky Woman Falling;* contemporary fallout from the legacy of generations of stolen Aboriginal children; and a striving for cultural renewal, celebration, and laughter in a present-day world in which, in Canada, half the Aboriginal population is under twenty-five.

Each time I saw it I followed different threads through it and saw something I hadn't seen the night before. At first I found it frustrating and confusing and a bit all over the place—too ambitious, trying to do too much, needing more narrative drive. Yet each night, I was moved and intrigued, and more than once had those "ah, okay" moments, those glimpses when you connect and feel amazed. Each time I saw it, I wanted to see it again. In a way there was something about it being so raw that fit with the dancers, who were young and passionate and kind of raw as well, and with the concept of "throw away kids."

The piece opens to the sound of a heart beat, then a moaning wail from a woman on stage. "It was a long long long long long long time ago," Muriel says in a voice over, and then Cosmos dances like Janet Jackson, elbows out, to the heartbeat beat. These threads—a birth, a past that is also present, a dance that is, and isn't, the image that one might think of as Native or Aboriginal—run throughout the piece. The music works with these threads in fun and funny ways: The Beatles sing lines from "She's Leaving Home" and Cosmos pleads, "Don't go!" rubbing her belly, leaning forward and back, contracting, giving birth, it seems like, to Star Girl all over again. The Supremes sing "Baby love, my baby love," and she bops and twirls, her arm bent at the elbow and flicking out from her waist as she turns, a kind of Native-inflected hip hop move. But the story the piece tells is dead serious. After this opening section, the heartbeat starts again and Star Girl comes forward. "I had a three week old baby girl," she says. "I want her to be okay. But I do not want her."

This is the dark narrative running through *Throw Away Kids*: the cycles of abuse and abandonment that Aboriginal daughters who've been thrown away are caught up in and revisit on their children. This is where the Aboriginal sons enter, also caught up in these cycles.

A young man with long, dark hair, a bare torso, and a brightly beaded loin-cloth comes on stage, dancing in a skipping twirling kind of way, looking beautiful and angry. It is Carlos Rivera, a Mixteco dancer from Mexico. He is called Mean Thing in the program, but in my head I referred to him as "Peter Pan Indian" because the next moment, when he steps behind one of the screens and looms large, still dancing, his silhouette looks like a Disney stereotype. The image is stark and huge and familiar, and it's jarring to realize it's the same man who was just on the stage. It was like he had stepped into an image he now has to contend with. He emerges again from behind the screen, wearing a yellow tie, and romances Star Girl, enticing her into a nightclub partner dance and then back behind a screen again, where their silhouettes struggle with each other. Their shadows crouch down, and he hits her.

With this image of violence lingering, Cosmos returns and tells us a story. It's about a Miss South Dakota beauty pageant contestant who performed a

Carlos Rivera as Mean Thing in Throw Away Kids, *1999. Choreography by Muriel Miguel. Photograph by Donald Lee.*

Native American burial dance ritual for the talent part of her competition. "The lights shimmered off her short buckskin dress," Cosmos snarls, spitting each syllable in disdain and disgust.

Star Girl joins Cosmos. "A three-week-old Native baby dies in her sleep," Star Girl says.

"These events collide in my mind," Cosmos says. "Enough!"

"Enough!" the two women scream together. "Enough!"

And here the narrative starts to turn, slowly and with struggle, toward renewal. From behind the screen come two young men, Mean Thing and Mean Thing's Shadow (Sid Bobb), who looks just like him, but darker. They stomp out onto the stage together, crouched low, knees bent, stomping their feet to a fast double beat, looking like boys playing Indian as they move toward Cosmos. She engages with them in the dance, moving against them, then throwing herself onto them so they have to carry her. When she slides off they retreat, stomping out the way they came, and Cosmos turns to the audience and smirks, with a little shrug, to have gotten rid of them, and we chuckle with her. But pushing the men away isn't the answer either; Star Girl comes back, and when Lisa Loeb sings, "Let's Forget about It," Star Girl says, "I feel a cold in the lining of my heart."

The second man returns as Star Boy. He dances, by himself, off to one side. He dances with his legs apart, moving slowly, rhythmically, in place, his arms bent, his torso curving and twisting, lost in his own rhythm, his own thoughts. "Trying to weave the past with the future," he says. "Trying to connect." The music shifts to a stronger beat and he dances more intensely, though still alone. He is wearing a baseball hat with a feather tied on it.

"Babies came, babies went," says Cosmos. "Some drank, took drugs. Some did not." She and Star Girl dance separately, each in front of a screen.

"Some girls are like that," says Star Boy. "Some girls are like that," he repeats. "This is another beginning. This is where it stops and starts," says Cosmos. "And he stayed," says Star Girl. "Was there." Star Boy moves to center stage and stands behind Star Girl. "I am here," he says.

The theater fills with a sense that, with Cosmos, Star Girl, and Star Boy standing together, center stage, the process of healing has begun. "A three-week-old Native baby dies in her sleep," Star Girl tells us again. "Her mother, grandmother, and great-grandmother mourn her." "Young mothers and fathers grieve for her," Cosmos says. "It could have been one of theirs." They have a brightly colored felt blanket wrapped in a bundle and they toss it between them until it unbundles. Star Boy wraps his arms around Star Girl.

"We miss everyone we lose," says Cosmos. And together they face the audience and say, "We are the people who genocide has been performed upon." As the stage darkens, we see projected onto the three giant floor-to-ceiling screens, which have big hands printed on them, slides of dozens of smiling Native faces, young and old, one after the other. A voice-over reads the epigraph from the program: "Sovereignty is that wafting thread securing the component of a society. Sovereignty runs through the vertical strands and secures the entire pattern. That is the fabric of Native society."

One night I wrote in my notes, "I think in a way the piece is a lot about fathers." Other nights I tried to work through what I think the piece is saying about image and screens, and the stage. The disjunction is so striking between the silhouette of Mean Thing, whom we see dancing through the screen, and the colorfully, almost gaudily, dressed character of Mean Thing, who really looks very little like the image he projects, even though the dance movement is the same. It might suggest that the image is not true, that it's "just" a stereotype. And yet even more strongly, I find, it suggests just the opposite. This looming Indian image creates a truth that he then has to live in relation to; it has a power beyond itself in creating who and how he is. It is the Hollywood screen, the TV screen, as well as a screen of images and expectations between him and the audience. It registers both the pop image of "dancing Indian," stomping rhythmically, and the dance as having a function outside of the image it projects.

The last night I saw the piece, I thought I'd finally gotten it: the piece is really all about the beauty pageant story Cosmos tells. Cosmos describes how the Miss South Dakota beauty contestant performs a Native American bereavement dance. She puts it on as if it's a play, as if it were nothing but an act she can wear, a buckskin miniskirt that looks good in the lighting. The contestant doesn't seem to have any awareness that there may be a political aspect to representing bereavement and mourning practices on a public stage. She not only takes the dance and uses it inappropriately and for her own means, she also disconnects it (or at least thinks of it as disconnected) from its effect on people and the world, its relation to bereavement, the change it effects in dealing with death and loss and thrown-away Native children. She treats it as if it were just a performance. In the process, she suggests that her white, scantily clad body, moving in "Indian" motions in this contest for acclaim according to Western standards of beauty, is a substitute and surrogate for both the Native dead and the surviving Native mourner.

Her representation effaces the bodies of Native American peoples from the living (by embodying the old trope of the vanishing Indian and showing Native peoples as always already on the verge of disappearance) and from the stage, replacing them with her own. She seems oblivious to her performance's implication that South Dakota Native Americans are dead and missing, to the complexities of replacing a Native dancing body with hers, and to her relation (as a white woman living on land in South Dakota) to the erasure she represents and reinforces. No wonder Cosmos is beside herself.

The second dance on the program was the revival of Alejandro Roncería's *Light and Shadow,* first staged at Banff in 1997. It is "a contemporary work, inspired by the Arctic landscape and its profound role in shaping the life and spirit of the far northern culture," the advance release announced, and was presented that year in celebration of Nunavut. *Light and Shadow* also raises questions about stage dance in relation to Aboriginal history, culture, and politics. Unlike the Native dance that Miss South Dakota performed without any apparent understanding of its relation to and effect on present-day Native peoples and cultures, the dance of *Light and Shadow* suggests a performative relation between this dance on a stage in Alberta and the life and spirit of Nunavut.

From the start it's an eerie piece, the mood ponderous and breathtaking, the vocal music and drumming beautiful, rhythmic, and deep. The piece opens with two dancers (Carlos Rivera and Mohawk dancer Cheri Smith) hanging in harnesses, like bats in suspension, floating and curling and turning, and then lowering to the earth. Then Inuit drum dancers move in from the sides, each carrying a big round drum and a baton, swaying on bent legs as they drum, together, in slow rhythmic beats. Although the stage remains dark, they are all wearing white, and the light on the white makes them luminous. Behind them, the screen has the glow of a red sky, with one full moon, or sun, surrounded by two half orbs faintly shining. In the middle one dancer (Feliks Gower-Kappi) perches on a rock and slowly, like a bird being born, struggles to stand.

At other points the mood shifts as two dancers (Pablo Palma and Leslie Qammaniq, the other Inuit dancer at the program that summer), with reddish brown furry-rimmed green masks on their face and hands and fox heads hanging from their groins, wiggle on stage and cavort with each other, bumping butts and sparring for space on the rocks. The sky is now a luminous blue and purple. A huge silly statue, smiling in a rather subtle, bemused manner, peeks in from the wings. Then it is darker, the light only a faint orange glow, and then that fades too.

Throughout the piece, the music and sky keep changing. At one point, four dancers appear (Cheri Smith, Shalan Joudry, Carlos Rivera, Sid Bobb) with scrunched up faces as they bend forward, moving toward the audience, stamping their feet and swaying their heads back and forth like fish. Next come the seal people. Three dancers (Nakoda Sioux–Stoney Nation dancer Cherith Mark, Bobb, and Gower-Kappi), wearing masks on the sides of their heads, creep out on their bellies, moving behind and around the rocks, carrying what looks like giant claws or clubs. They stretch and walk on stage, knees bent deep, at times turning their heads so their faces, tongues out, in grotesque contortions, face us. One scratches himself with his claw club, his back, his leg, his groin, before walking off. Now the sky is crossed with lines of light as if through the mouth of a baleen whale. A physical and political relationship to land—the rocks, the animals, the climate—comes across clearly and compellingly in the dancers' physical involvement with the rocks, the darkness, the sky. The dancers' movements—the swaying drum dancing, the playfulness in darkness, the bodily

Felix Kappi, Cherith Mark, Sid Bobb in "Seal People" from Light and Shadow, *1999. Choreography by Alejandro Roncería. Photograph by Donald Lee.*

response to the light that starts to fill the stage toward the piece's end—convey a relationship to specific place. Of course, these are stage sets: the "rocks" are constructed, darkness and sky light are created through stage lighting, the dancers are on a stage in Alberta far from Nunavut land. The point is not to argue for the dance's immediate ability to mystically conjure Nunavut land on a stage in Alberta, or that certain dance movements caused the Nunavut land claim agreement to come into effect in any sort of "mechanical magic"[8] way. It is, though, to suggest that what the dancers enact, in dancing in celebration of Nunavut, is real and has real effect on the world.

In large part, this effect comes from the context of the piece. It is a production of the Chinook Winds Aboriginal Dance Program, engaged with Aboriginal politics, celebrating Nunavut at a time when Aboriginal dancing, as an element of oral history, has begun to be understood even in Canadian courts in legal (and therefore, again according to the viewpoint of the courts, actual or provable) relation to land and land claims. This concept of dancing thus echoes and strengthens a relationship to Nunavut as Inuit land, and celebrates governmental recognition of it as such. At the same time, the actual movement of the dancing, and the dancers' skill at embodying a connection to specific land, is itself part of this enactment. As a performance of continuing Inuit movement practices (drum dancing, masking, seal people) with much much longer histories, the dancing also performs and enacts relation to Nunavut land that is part of those practices. The celebration of Nunavut through this public dance performance thus underscores for the audience ways that, while this is a performance, not a parliamentary enactment, dance functions in a way similar to court documents and legal declarations that enact what they name. On the other hand, because the performance occurs outside of what the courts and legislature declare, it shows how governmental recognition merely reflects what the dance shows to have long been the case.

The two final sections of *Light and Shadow,* called "Nostalgia" and "Inukshuk," demonstrate this a bit more concretely. In "Nostalgia," the dancers move slowly on stage in pairs, some men with women, some women with women, some men with men. They lift one another and slide off, curling together, sex-like, in the dark. The dancers move apart curling and lifting, and then slowly they move together in the center and lift one dancer horizontally above them, turning her as she curls. In the next section, "Inukshuk," a voice-over tells a story in Inuktitut. The dancers sit on rocks and bring their hands to their faces, like they are washing or eating, and then push the rocks together, their hands over their ears. Moving apart again, they each lift a rock and creep slowly back, carrying the rocks, and piling them up so they make the "Inukshuk" rock formation that signals "Nunavut," with one long rock horizontal from a pillar.

Then the light comes up: daylight. Just at that moment, when after all those shades of darkness, day has come, Leslie Qammaniq reappears, down stage left, dressed in Inuit clothes, looking like a tourist poster of an Inuit woman. She holds a small airplane in her hand and flies it in swoops and swirls across the stage while we hear the sound of an airplane overhead. The tourists are arriving.

The end took my breath away each evening, that moment when after all that time in darkness, all that somberness and sex and silliness, that full life happening, the airplanes arrive, propelled by the Inuit image, who is also Qammaniq in *Light and Shadow,* dancing.

This piece, like *Throw Away Kids,* plays with the audience's relationship to the images of Aboriginal culture we hold, and their relation to what is real. Like the men in *Throw Away Kids,* whose silhouettes through the screens contrast so startlingly with their presence in front of the screens, Qammaniq, in her Inuit clothing, plays both herself and an image of herself playing a stereotype. Her startling transition from being one of the white-clad dancers, part of the *Light and Shadow* ensemble, to performing a tourist image of an Inuit woman underscores her distance from this image, her relation to it, and the image's continuing (tourist and ideological) effect on the Nunavut the dance piece celebrates. At the same time, it refigures a tourist relation to Nunavut by showing ways Qammaniq controls, or at least propels, that relation. If in one sense, the arriving airplane is propelled by what looks like the poster image of an Inuit woman, in another sense Qammaniq is holding it and directing it herself, swooping it up and down across the stage like a plaything.

This is not the nostalgia of lost and mourned and romanticized Inuit culture, a tourist image of an authentic Inuitness that's now gone and for which dance performance now provides a surrogate. The nostalgia in the title of the penultimate section of the piece references not a lost past, but young Aboriginal dancers lifting a young Inuit woman; Qammaniq, like 60 percent of the Inuit population of Nunavut, is under twenty-five years old. Her body, lifted horizontally, carries reference to the Inukshuk that signals both official Canadian sign of and guide and relation to land. This dancer at the end is active and present, wearing traditional regalia and propelling an airplane. She is not just an image, a representation, but has agency and effect. She is not just playing at what she's dancing. She is being it, as well as acting as it, and in so doing enacting herself as Inuit woman, with connection to Nunavut as Inuit land and to ancestors who had a relationship to the land and have passed that to her. This, in turn, is related to the return of Native land that the Nunavut Act marks. And these understandings of stage dancing as in fact enacting, rather than representing enactment, complicate contemporary theories that see what happens with actors during stage performances as "hollow or void" and thus distinctly separate from real life performative actions.

The first night, the dress rehearsal, I sat next to a fourteen- or fifteen-year-old young man. We talked a bit before the show started, and he told me he is from Montréal, at Banff this summer to participate in the ballet program. We both sat quietly through the performance, comfortable and at ease in the dark, in our theater seats, politely watching and applauding at the end. As we were leaving I asked him if he liked it and was it what he expected. And he said yes he liked it, but no, it wasn't what he thought it would be, it was a lot more modern. Out in the lobby I eavesdropped on other ballet students. The whole group of them had come to see the dress rehearsal. One young woman with a bouncy brown ponytail, tight pants, and chunky platform shoes was holding court, the other dancers gathered around her. "They looked so out of place!" she said. "It's like they feel so out of place in our society. Do you think that is how they feel in our society?" I wondered at her comments: the acceptance she presumes "our society" to accord her, a ballet student, on and off the stage, the implication that she and her fellow ballet dancers looked and felt "in place" against the "out of place" appearance that "they," the Aboriginal dancers, project. What effect would her reception of these dance pieces have, both her perceptions and her failures to perceive? I wondered to what extent her response mattered, or if the Aboriginal Dance Program would do what it does with or without whatever its audience members—mostly non-Native people like this young woman and me—take away.

The next day, after the opening-night performance, there was a reception. We gathered for food and drink and thank-you speeches. The ceremony opened with Elder Tom Crane Bear from the Siksika Nation, who welcomed us all to Siksika land and thanked the dancers for their dancing, and the program for the work it does, and everyone especially for that year's support of the return of Nunavut. He said it was an inspiration and that, as most of us probably knew, they too are fighting for the return, right there, of Siksika land. The dancers and choreographers spoke next, thanking the elder, and one another, and lots of other people who'd helped with the program. Then we ate and drank and mingled, and there was a video about Nunavut playing off to one side and a box full of information packets on Nunavut for us all to take home and keep.

PROCESSES OF CREATION II: QUESTIONS OF CURRENCY

In the fall of 1999, back at my desk in California, I sat in my swivel chair and turned the Nunavut "twoonie" I'd saved over and over in my hands, and riffled through the "Government of Canada" Nunavut packet, chock full of official documents printed in English and French (with a few sections in Inuktitut). There are chronologies and informational sheets and "fast facts" on Nunavut history and economy and the land claim settlement. There are big color maps and color prints of the Nunavut seal of arms and glossy "Welcome to Nunavut" brochures. There is a Nunavut "activities" sheet listing fourteen Inuktitut words for snow and suggesting that students draw them. The official documents inscribe Nunavut as real history, a geopolitical fact taught to children, grades 5 and 6. And this governmental recognition is cause for celebration, which is the spirit in which the Nunavut packets were handed out at the Aboriginal Dance reception. Of course, Nunavut has been here all along, recognized by practices, like dance, that legitimate and enact connection to it: it doesn't require a coin or coat of arms to be official, just to be seen as such. At the same time, it seems important not to discount this documentation or suggest that only oral and performance practices are authentic markers of Aboriginal relation to the land; instead, the official documents extend a recognition that Inuit peoples have long asserted and performed.

All the same, these documents call for an attentiveness to the histories of hegemony that have accompanied, and continue to accompany, official documents and sanctioned expert discourse on Native culture. At issue is the way that, in these documents and discourses, Aboriginal people themselves are often literally and figuratively displaced and discounted. This displacement is blatant when a non-Native like the Miss South Dakota contestant, invoking a disappeared Indian trope, performs herself as an "Indian" mourning her dead, deploying Native culture in a bid to gain the currency of a Miss America title. But it happens too easily in other arenas as well, including dance studies, when official dance histories and theories, dance conferences and essay collections, ignore Aboriginal dance or Aboriginal peoples' expertise on it. In a sense, the flip side of the "twoonie" with the drum dancer on it is a depiction of Aboriginal dance that circulates as commodity to legitimate the crown. Again, it seems important not to discount the agency that comes with commodification, the way that Qammaniq, dressed as Inuit Woman, plays with and propels the tourist economy she invokes. But even in this instance, it seems crucial to attend to the question of currency—who produces, and profits from, representing and documenting Aboriginal culture? And where are Native peoples and cultures in this document production and what it accrues? In other words, I struggle, given my position as a university scholar, complicit in systems of institutional racism that have long dismissed Native voices and rewarded outside experts that record, and edit, and themselves tell Native peoples' stories, with the place of the scholarly document I'm in the process of producing.

In *Chinook Winds*, Jerry Longboat writes about the role of the choreographers at the Aboriginal Dance Program:

> They recognize the need to train our own choreographers and writers. I think there's real danger in other people appropriating our stories and telling us who we are. We've begun to awaken to the effects of this through the telling of history and we are reclaiming our truth in our own words, in our ceremonies, through our stories. Dance is a prolific part of this healing and self determination. ("Interview," 79)

These words on Aboriginal self-determination, like the *Throw Away Kids* voice-over on sovereignty—"that wafting thread securing the component of a society"—need to resonate for dance studies, circa 1999 and beyond. To quote Cosmos, "This is where it stops and starts."

NINE

We're Dancing: Indigenous Stage Dance in the Twenty-first Century

Every time that Jonathan reads that letter, throughout the practices, being a Native person, just hearing him read it, sometimes it feels like there's something that falls over us—or myself—and I get very, I feel the words, and the only thought I ever really have is—*we're dancing*.

> ▸ *Siobhán Aratsiaq-Murphy, dancer, Aboriginal Dance Program*

In the first decade of the twenty-first century, stage dance productions by choreographers who identity as Indigenous, and who engage with Aboriginal stories, languages, processes, and understandings of the world in their dance making, have started to gain increasing prominence and recognition. Choreographers are forming companies that are funded, and drawing audiences, and awarded for the work they do (especially in Canada); magazines are featuring articles and cover stories on "contemporary Native dance";[1] academic institutions and conferences are supporting programs and discussions that foster its growing presence.[2] The dancing is raising awareness not just of the need to include discussion of Indigenous dance in modern dance history classes as well as in the multicultural mix often still taught as "world dance" in the United States. It is also articulating particular Indigenous understandings and ways of knowing, and in the process shifting understandings of the political and spiritual limits that staging has been seen to impose.

This chapter explores a few of these stage dance pieces, most of which I viewed live in performance between 1999 and 2004 on stages in the United States and Canada.[3] It looks at how they make visions of a multilayered, interconnected, cyclical, spiritually animated world clear through their staging and through the stories their choreography tells. It looks at how this dancing refutes the antidance circulars and other acts of colonization, and enacts the world-views and bodily understandings this colonization tried, but failed, to eradicate. It suggests ways these engagements with modern dance expand notions of the purpose, and possibilities, of the modern dance stage, first addressing some of the complexities of these interrelations.

INDIGENOUS APPROACHES, BODILY HISTORIES, MODERN DANCE: WE KNOW EXACTLY WHAT WE ARE DOING

Many contemporary Aboriginal choreographers and dancers, and the dance pieces they have made, have articulated understandings of the dance stage as a tool for Aboriginal peoples. For some, the stage is a space to address the interconnections of humans and other beings, the relations of generations across time, and the agency of an ever-present spirit world. Teme/Augama/Anishnaabe dancer Sandra Laronde, who established Red Sky Performance in Toronto in 2000, explained that her impetus to start the company stemmed from an interest in engaging, on the stage, with Aboriginal worldviews as she understands them. "Aboriginal people, when we create art, we're talking about a sprit-centeredness, as opposed to a human-centeredness. So we're not just talking about our relationship to other human beings only. We're really talking about our relationship, yes, to other human beings, but to the two legged, to the four legged, to the stars, to the moon, to the sun, to the earth, that the world is much bigger and moves beyond something that is human centered," she said. "I'm very interested in creating things that make people see the more-than-human world."[4]

Many of these contemporary Native American dance pieces also engage with the stage as a space in which to address a history of violent colonization. A notion of Aboriginal dancers' bodies as sites of investigation and connection to Native history, politics, and worldviews—connections ruptured by centuries of laws, treaties, and federal policies, and generations of genocide and removal—has emerged repeatedly in contemporary Aboriginal stage dance, and in dancers' and choreographers' discussions of it. This dancing not only recounts but also responds to this history, refusing its presumptions and refuting its stability and legal standing. Choreographers' comments and dances theorize ways that, just as these policies and documents have affected Aboriginal dancers' bodies and practices, the practice of dance making, of choreographically investigating tribal stories, of exploring their own bodies and using their bodies to explore whatever teachings they can locate and engage with, itself works as an act of empowerment. In other words, this dancing becomes not just a record of centuries of oppression and violence, but also a site of its redress. "The only way we can heal ourselves . . . is just through recovering our dances, our music, our ritual," said Zapotec choreographer Georgina Martinez, who choreographed

Miinigooweziwin . . . The Gift at the Aboriginal Dance Program in Alberta, Canada, in the summer of 2002.[5]

As they address these interrelations and histories, Aboriginal stage dances also trouble epistemologies of time that undergird understandings of history and historical analysis. "We don't put time on a linear plane," Laronde explained. "So it's not necessary to go from past to future, but I think we move around a lot more within that." She noted connections between this understanding of time and understandings of the body as not just a site of individual memory, but of collective, ancestral memory spanning thousands of years. "You remember something from a long time ago, or something, sometimes you have an image, but you don't know where it comes from. It's very, very old," she explained. "If we believe in something like blood memories—a term Martha Graham appropriated—that means something very immediate. It's in our blood, it's in our bodies at this point in time, and that recall can be instant, and that recall could be fifty years ago, could be a thousand years ago, two thousand years ago, it could be longer than that. The Teme/Augama/Anishnaabe, we've been around, according to archaeological evidence, for six thousand years." Martinez, too, talked about this recognition of relation across time, place, and generations. For her, the recognition came first through workshops in Butoh. "Those workshops were very, very demanding in terms of really getting in contact with one emotion. And for me, going through emotions, I discovered different layers of my body, physically. But also I discovered different layers of my mind," she said. Martinez explained that doing this work brought images into her mind that, at first, she didn't quite understand. "It was very old images, images of old people, people from, I guess now, ancient people," she said, explaining how she came to realize that the images had come from the Indigenous community in the highlands of Oaxaca, where she was born (although she was educated in the city). This attention to connections through and across time and place, and to time's cyclicality, informs Red Sky's and Martinez's work, as well as much of this contemporary choreography.

At the same time that Martinez and Laronde suggest that the particular memories they access through their bodily explorations are linked to their Indigenous heritage, they also imply that the practice of exploring history and memory in and through bodily exploration and observation, while tied to Native ways of approaching understanding, are not exclusive or available only to Native cultures and peoples, or inherent only to Native dance. Laronde noted that Noh and Kabuki theater, as well as Greek theater, all involved connection "to that bigger energy being part of the experience"—making space for and acknowledging gods or the creator. Martinez noted she has accessed these approaches through the practices of contact improvisation, Butoh, and Iyengar yoga.[6] It's rather, Laronde explained, that Native dance and dancers often have more of a connection to these understandings—perhaps in part from growing up, as Laronde did, with more immediate interaction with the land. The approach may be one taught in and reinforced by Aboriginal communities and worldviews, and accessing this approach part of the search for grounding in "Aboriginal process." But anyone can use it, and ways of accessing it are available from many directions.

Despite these and other Aboriginal choreographers' engagements with modern dance and background in it, many eventually come up against some conceptual limits of the practice, at least as it is understood along the trajectory of techniques codified by Graham, Limón, Horton, and their followers. For various reasons, many of these Aboriginal choreographers have eventually turned away from this training, seeing modern dance as too pedestrian, too abstract, too distanced from community connection and too invested in individualism to fit their purposes. Martinez explained that she started her training with all kinds of dance, from ballet to different styles of modern dance, including Graham, Limón, and contact improvisation. Yet throughout this training, she said, she "didn't feel comfortable dancing modern dance." She explained:

> For me it was, it was all the time the dilemma, "What am I saying
> with this?" Sometimes it was so abstract. And part of me, I mean,
> I really enjoy the aspect of using the rhythm, the space, the music
> and, you know, moving the body. It's something quite pleasur-
> able. But all the time it was for me like "What am I saying?"

"All Aboriginal dance is very specific. We know exactly what we are doing," she added. "There was an intention for every step, for every single movement of your hand, your arm. Or the way you move your eyes or the head."

Martinez and others noted a connection between this specific purpose and Indigenous modern dance's frequent grounding in story. Sometimes this choreography is based in a traditional myth or story.[7] Other times the dances tell family stories, or stories that connect tribally based mythic tales and visions as part of a larger narrative. This understanding of story's centrality, Martinez explained, was part of her choreographic approach from the start of her career, even before she quite understood its connection to her Indigenous heritage. "I never choreographed an abstract thing. For example I never choreographed only to music, or I never choreographed something like just an abstract idea, or an idea in general. All the time I had to create characters," she explained.

Classical ballet trained San Juan Pueblo dancer Belinda James, who has worked as a visual artist and as a ballet dancer in New York City since 1980, likewise expressed her dissatisfaction with much modern dance's lack of specific purpose. "The whole point of modern being so accessible means pedestrians can do it," she explained.[8] "To me it's very purposeless and pedestrian" (interview, August 28, 2001). In contrast, in her view, dance is crucial. "It's a way of life, it's a ritual, it's a manner of being. It isn't just a dance. It isn't entertainment. It isn't folly, you know. It's real and it's serious, where at the same time, it brings levity. But, you know, it's necessary, significant. It isn't just play. It's definitely purposeful" (interview, August 28, 2001). James connected her belief in the seriousness of dance, its importance, and the responsibility of those who do it to Pueblo rituals. "That's how the rituals are," she said, noting the honor, and the responsibility, of those who are called upon to perform them. "You don't decide [to be a dancer or dance leader]—the elders come up and say. You don't have a choice." When this happens, the understanding is that "you should be honored that you're going to be part of this whole universal responsibility." This understanding of dance's importance, she said, lies behind her attraction to the intense training required by ballet (although James took classes in Horton technique, and although his technique influenced her choreography, she remained committed to pointe work) and infuses her stage choreography. Martinez, too, explained how an understanding of dance as specific and intentional, with specific effects and responsibilities, informs her choreography. "It has to be the same when we are choreographing, what's behind each movement." She continued, "Because when you are on stage, you really know what you are doing with each single movement. So you don't get lost in the beauty of moving. For me, that's the most dangerous aspect of dance."

While James turned to ballet, Martinez turned to meditation and to Iyengar yoga as a movement practice that she explained doesn't have the abstraction of modern dance. "When you give instructions [in yoga], you don't give instructions like the instructions you give when you are teaching a specific technique," she said. "You really learn how to feel your body." She explained, "This way of observing the body is very related to what happens in meditation. In meditation when you have just attention in one single thing, such as your breathing, then you realize that you have more space in your mind and memories start coming. Memories from your childhood, or for some people memories from other lives, start to come." Martinez added, "It's the same with the body. You just observe the body, observe the body, without analyzing or without trying to explain things, but you just observe and feel. You release, many, many, many memories with your body. With yoga, we don't work with emotions, but then we become very emotional."

As these practitioners engage contemporary stage dance, investigating multiple training approaches, drawing on specific stories, seeking out and engaging connections across multiple realms, redressing the violent effects of colonization, they do continue to use elements of modern dance training and vocabulary. Yet the focus remains tied to choreographers' particular Indigenous worldviews and histories. In these approaches, this modern dance and this staging is not understood to automatically militate against the authenticity of real dance performed in more traditional spaces. It is instead another space, another context, in which the powerful tool of dance as it has been understood for generations can be engaged today, a space that does not just express an emotional, expressive, interiority, but accesses realms outside of the individual self. In engaging dance in these ways, the stage works of these contemporary Aboriginal and Native American choreographers acknowledge and redress not only centuries of physical and ideological colonization of Indigenous peoples, but also understandings of what modern dance—and the Western stage—can be. Similarly, the understandings of dance's transformative abilities, the ability to enact effect and change in the world through dance practice and performance, while drawn from Native cultural contexts, are available to transform understandings and histories of modern dance.

BONES: AN ABORIGINAL DANCE OPERA

One such vision of a cyclical, multidimensional world emerged in the summer of 2001, when the Aboriginal Dance Program at Banff Centre for the Arts in Canada premiered an inspired, full-fledged, breathtakingly ambitious "Aboriginal Dance Opera" called *BONES*. This project brought together the Chinook Winds Aboriginal Dance Program and the Aboriginal Women's Voices Program to create an evening-length opera (three acts with a total of seventeen scenes) with original choreography for sixteen dancers and original music and songs, all performed live. The codirectors of the piece, Suesca/Sogamoso choreographer Alejandro Roncería and Seneca composer Sadie Buck, write that they "wanted to bring these two separate entities back to the reality of song and dance as it exists in our own communities—music and dance exist as one."[9] To tell the story the piece tells, Buck worked to create an entire new language. "In the spirit of Indigenous ideology of inclusiveness, sounds of many languages have been incorporated into a language based on sound," she writes.[10] The twenty-one songs that tell the story of this opera are all written and sung in this "Language of the World," though a Spirit Woman, Kuna/Rappahannock performer Muriel Miguel, speaks to the audience in English throughout, commenting jokingly and bawdily, philosophizing, and cajoling from her own space on the sides, or as she watches over the Humans from a platform in back where the Spirits dwell, or as she roves about among the Humans as they dance on stage.

BONES presents an overarching vision of the world structured in cyclical rhythms, large to small, planting to harvest, day to night, baby to mother to grandmother to spirit world. It is a creation story that opens when the "earth calls to the people," the people respond and revel in earth's bounty, strength, and knowledge, and onto the earth First Woman, First Man, First Earthbaby are born. It tells a story of these humans and how they play, die, connect to one another, build, dwell. It incorporates a story of the seven brothers, who become Pleiades, and "pass along their knowledge from the heavens." Throughout, the

Bones: An Aboriginal Dance Opera, *2001. Codirectors Sadie Buck and Alejandro Roncería. Joel Te Maro, A. Blake Tailfeathers, Jody Gaskin, Carlos Rivera, Faron John, Kalani Queypo, Brandon Oakes, Jeremy Proulx. Photograph by Donald Lee.*

Spirits are both part of the stories and also part of the staging. As the Humans dance on stage, the Spirits move in between and above, on a raised platform, with the musicians, swaying and singing and observing—or ignoring—the goings-on below.

This vision underscores a cyclical notion of time in which the pleasures and sorrows of a specific present, as well as the relation of these happenings to an overarching, much larger, understanding of events in the world, are equally present. In one of the most powerful scenes, the People play a stick game. As they sing and dance, hunched over, clacking their sticks, intently engaged with each other, a rhythm builds, and a sense of love and joy and well-being permeates the theater, rising up and filling the space, swelling it with an intensity that borders on euphoria. "I love this game," says Miguel as Spirit Woman. Three times the stage darkens and faces flash on ceiling-height side panels of three figures. The dancers form two circles, passing sticks between them. One group wins at first, and then the second time the other group does. "Life's game is on," Spirit Woman says as the dancers build on and with the rhythm, making it with and moving it through their bodies, passing the sticks between them, intense, driven, fully present. "I love this game," she repeats.

Bones: An Aboriginal Dance Opera, *2001. Codirectors Sadie Buck and Alejandro Roncería.*
Back: Soni Moreno. Front: Carlos Rivera, Kalani Queypo, Santee Smith, Jody Gaskin.
Photograph by Donald Lee.

Yet the scene segues from this one, of such intense life, into death scenes in which the Grandmother passes on and the Spirits come to greet her, and to supervise the Humans as they prepare her way. The stage empties and Grandmother stands alone, until the people and dancers return, coming from the sides, carrying giant bones on their backs, bent forward, creeping slowly on stage. Grandmother sings in the "Language of the World"—"Mes machiema, me nem se manema, Me spa no miks . . . Mes doa do nilu"—but they hold their ears, refusing to hear, and then slowly take off the giant bones, standing on them, looking up, moving their arms out and forward. Over to the side, Spirit Woman braids a multicolored braid. Then one bone is lifted up on a stick, and they are all lifted, as the dancers move around the stage holding them up, bringing the bones of the title into being, and at the very last minute they lift the bones together and form the skeleton of a person. Grandmother switches to English: "My grandchildren, I love you much." The giant figure made of bones moves and dances off in a silly, oversized, comical way. "My time is near." Spirit Woman and Earth Woman come on and stand near her and Spirit Woman speaks, "Grandmother, your time is here." Light fades as she walks off, repeating, "My time is here." A funeral procession follows, in which the Spirits greet the Grandmother and give her the braid, and then watch and hover around the Humans as they build a house for the community, prepare food, carry on.

Intertwined in this intense narration of life and death, joy and sorrow, is both a recognition of these events and emotions and an understanding of them as part of cycles and forces greater than themselves. Instead of foregrounding the events themselves, what emerges most viscerally in this "Aboriginal Dance Opera" is a sense of grounding in physicality—in the earth, bones, bodies— that continues over time even as its particularities shift and change. The recognition of this physicality, in and through a dance piece, swelled by the physical presence and rhythms and movements of dancers and musicians, imparted a vision in which both the present and the ever-present exist together.

The piece's use of language made space for clarity and understanding and a recognition of the gift of communication, but also of the need to suspend desires to know all and understand all. The singers were communicating so clearly, but you can't understand their words. You aren't supposed to be able to understand. The language was invented; no one in the audience, at least no one not intimately involved with *BONES*'s production, knew just from hearing what the songs' words meant (though they were both transliterated and translated in the program, to pore over later). In the meantime, the "Language of the World" created a powerful sense of surrender, of the need to accept both your understanding in the flickers in which it came and your not-understanding, and give in to both.

In these ways, *BONES: An Aboriginal Dance Opera* depicts a vision of the world that foregrounds its cyclical continuity, a vision of time in which a story

of the creation of the earth and the people on it is also part of the story of dancers and humans now and the lives they create and deaths they accept, a world
in which the dead pass on to the spirit world and remain on stage, however
much more in the background.

I FEEL THE WORDS, AND THE ONLY THOUGHT
I EVER REALLY HAVE IS—WE'RE DANCING

In this temporal landscape, where linear notions of history have been layered
by these engagements with the presence of beings from what history would
call the past, the fetishes of historical belief—written documents, legislation,
letters—are themselves rendered spectral. This is not to say that they hold no
force or aren't real; in these landscapes specters are crucial and forceful. Rather,
they are presented in a realm in which the act of dancing over and against them
also holds force, a force that, over time, through its very continuation, replaces
the document—and its violent effects—with the fact of its own continuation.
Dance thus becomes a form of Indigenous writing over of the legal, historical
documents of North American colonialism.

Five years before premiering *BONES*, the Aboriginal Dance Project at Banff
inaugurated its program with a direct invocation of how continuing Aboriginal
dance practices, despite decades of Canadian policy attempting to suppress and
eradicate them, have overwritten, and continue to overwrite, these very attempts at containment.[11] The opening Chinook Winds Aboriginal Dance Project
(later Program) included several pieces, choreographed by Roncería, that directly address this history. Roncería had trained in classical ballet in Colombia,
the Soviet Union, and New York and danced with the Karen Jamieson Dance
Company in Vancouver before moving to Toronto and collaborating for several
intense years in the 1980s with Raoul Trujillo and Cree dancer René Highway.
After Highway's death in 1990, Trujillo left Toronto to work in the film industry, and Roncería felt the next step for him was to train Aboriginal dancers
(Roncería, interview, November 11, 2005.). He continued to choreograph work
in Canada and Mexico, directed several short films, and spent time in different
Indigenous communities in South America with his camera, learning and sharing dances. In 1996, he helped found the Chinook Winds Aboriginal Dance
Project at Banff.

One of Roncería's pieces from the program's first year, *Buffalo Spirit*, is literally danced alongside and against the echoes of a historical document attempting to contain Indian dancing in Canada. The piece opens to a darkened stage
onto which—moving slowly, deliberately, first an elbow, and the glint of a
long staff light on the stage, then a slightly hunched figure, bare chested with
skirted sash wrapped around his waist, covering trousers, with long braided
hair trailing behind him—the Buffalo Spirit emerges into the light. His steps

Jonathan Fisher in Buffalo Spirit, *1996. Choreography by Alejandro Roncería. Photograph by Heather Elton.*

are halting, jerking, stiff, difficult, but he emerges. As Ojibway/Odawa dancer Jonathan Fisher, the Buffalo Spirit, crosses the stage, he recites a circular sent by Canadian Deputy Superintendent General Duncan Campbell Scott to Indian affairs officials in 1921, directing them "to use your utmost endeavors to dissuade the Indians from excessive indulgence in the practice of dancing." Scott writes that "the Indians . . . should not be allowed to dissipate their energies and abandon themselves to demoralizing amusements." He claims that "by the use of tact and firmness you can obtain control and keep it, and this obstacle to continued progress will then disappear" (Elton, *Chinook Winds,* 12). Writer Heather Elton comments on the effect of the piece and the dancer's movements: "Jonathan Fisher moves like a ghost dragging the spirits of his culture across the stage." Roncería responds, "In a sense, he is dragging all that history and what happened to the people. He represents the past and the visions many of the elders had about what would happen. He is an ancient character with the voice of the present time. He knows what happened to the people. . . . Many of these dances were prohibited by the Canadian government and were not performed publicly for a long time."[12] The Chinook Winds Aboriginal Dance Project dance piece thus literally presents the dancing both of the Buffalo Spirit and of Fisher, a young Aboriginal dancer, as a defiant response to this official historical document and projections of the disappearance of both the buffalo and Aboriginal dance. By invoking this Buffalo Spirit on a dance stage, as an act of contemporary Aboriginal dance and an inauguration of a new Aboriginal Dance Project, this staging speaks back to a violently suppressed dance history even as it signals the continued, ever-present, and ever-effective practice of Aboriginal dancing.

Both a publication and a video documentary that grew out of the Chinook Winds Aboriginal Dance Project's first year underscore this connection. The book reprints the Scott letter on one page, with a photograph of Fisher as Buffalo Spirit beside it. The letter's presence is there, stark on the page, but so too is the Buffalo Spirit dancer, who, his back to it on the page, is walking away from it, directing the reader's eye instead toward the rest of the book and the story it tells. The Chinook Winds First Aboriginal Dance Project documentary similarly frames its representation of its contemporary stage dance with this historical document. The video begins with the voice-over reading the Scott letter, as the camera cuts from dance piece to dance piece in an overview of the summer's program. Later, as we see excerpts from *Buffalo Spirit*, Fisher discusses what it felt like to read the Scott letter, and Inuit dancer Siobhán Aratsiaq-Murphy explains what she felt hearing it:

> Every time that Jonathan reads that letter, throughout the prac-
> tices, being a Native person, just hearing him read it, sometimes
> it feels like there's something that falls over us—or myself—and
> I get very, I feel the words, and the only thought I ever really
> have is—*we're dancing*.

Aratsiaq-Murphy's comments underscore the force of the official circular's words. But at the same time, she explains how the continuing practice of dance, the continuing participation in this Aboriginal stage dance program, by her and the other program participants, has been part of what is successfully thwarting this document's intended oppressive effect.

Other pieces from this Aboriginal Dance Project's first year's program theorize ways that contemporary dance redresses not only antidance policies but also other oppressive federal Indian policies. *Residential School for Boys*, choreographed by Roncería, presents the act of its own dancing as both record and response to the oppressive official Canadian Residential School system for Aboriginal children. In this piece, three boys in stiff high-collared shirts walk on their knees on the stage, their hands in prayer positions, while a giant cross of light is projected over them. The residential school history reflected in the piece is an incredibly painful, and relatively recent, one; in Canada's residential schools, which were not all closed until the late 1960s, Aboriginal children were frequently forcibly separated from their families and communities, and the

Canadian government is now in the process of grappling with ways of acknowledging and redressing the rampant physical, emotional, and sexual abuses that occurred at them. The trauma of this history is a subtle, pervasive, palpable part of the piece, with its stark lighting, the dancers' confining clothes, and the melancholy, understated, achingly gentle music—composed by Stla'limx musician Russell Wallace based on songs his mother sang in residential school when the nuns weren't around.[13] Yet the choreography, in the frame of this overarching history, is surprisingly playful. Within and around the stretches of light, the boys find each other and play together, rolling and somersaulting and romping around, finding spaces of joy and comfort in their physical motion and engagement with each other in which to resist the somber oppression imposed upon them by the cross of light—before falling back into line and walking off stage on their knees, hands folded as in a prayer. The playful movement, the dancing, the community the three boys find together provide a counterforce to the violence enacted by residential school policy even as the dance piece recounts that history.

STAGING TRANSFORMATION

Other contemporary pieces engage even more directly with the stage space as a site that enacts change, often by engaging with transformative practices. Raoul Trujillo's 1988 classic, *Shaman's Journey,* the subject of a 1989 *Alive from Off Center* public television series, explores a Shaman's transformation into Raven and Lizard, and his entrance into the spirit world. Camera work in the special—filmed on sand in what looks like a beachside cave, with a crevice entrance filtering light in—emphasizes the intense, eerie, transcendent process as the Shaman awakens to feel the spirits, summons his animal spirit guides, transforms into those animal forms, and arrives, entering the spirit world. Trujillo embodies all these states and beings, starting as "contrary man," facing backwards and moving in hip-swinging jerky moves beside a fire, then unmasking and, beating a hand-held drum, dancing along the white lines of a circle drawn on the ground, bent kneed, shoulders moving rhythmically up and down in time to the beats with increasing speed until the screen whites out and he emerges as a black-winged raven with long arching wings reaching high, then looks at himself in a body of water that has appeared, seeing himself as a lizard in that reflection, becoming that lizard and moving with jerking quick moves until the scene whites out and he appears nearly naked, moving slowly, contorted, in white body paint with Butoh-like intensity, as if floating on or under water, until he emerges from the water onto land and creeps off, creature like, fading completely as he moves through the crevice of light. The piece was re-created at Banff in 1997 for six dancers inhabiting different stages in this journey, and different animal forms; a video recording of it pronounces the piece to be "about seeing into other worlds besides our own."[14]

Transformative connection between human and animal beings or spirits recurs through numerous other contemporary Aboriginal and Native American stage dance pieces as well. Dancers and choreographers comment, often in passing, on the way this transformation is not only depicted but also enacted on stage. "I believe in transformation on stage, for sure. The most exciting stuff on stage is transformation," said Laronde, noting as an example how Mixteco dancer Carlos Rivera's experience as a Deer Dancer in Mexico contributed to "his ability to transform into a caribou, which is so close to a deer" in Red Sky's *Caribou Song,* so that audiences could see "the Caribou spirit in Carlos, as opposed to a human being playing an animal."

Metamorphosis, a 1990 dance by Belinda James, also engages with acts of transformation on stage. James based this work on the Deer Dance of San Juan Pueblo and in the program notes to a 2001 performance of the piece in Brooklyn, New York, explains:

> In the original traditional dance, men come from the hills at sunrise, singing for the lives of all creatures. Led by an elder, dancers enter the center of the pueblo. The dance ends with a stampede. The deer dancers run and are pursued by women of the tribe, whose families will be blessed with successful hunts and general good fortune if they catch a deer dancer. Legend has it, however, that if a dancer is not caught and does not return by sunset, he is transformed into an actual deer. As no one has ever stayed out past sunset, this piece depicts what might happen if one were to challenge the legend of the Deer Dance.[15]

Her piece is based in this legend yet "takes it to another place, to another level," she explained (James, interview, August 28, 2001). *Metamorphosis* opens when a bare-torsoed man hurls himself onto stage right, looking lost and bewildered, as the stage is lit in a dusky orange glow. As the light fades through purple and deep blue to darkness, he lies on the ground and lifts his arched, ballet-slippered foot at an angle, turns two sticks he's holding into walking sticks that elongate his forearms, pulls himself to standing, and steps a few steps on all fours, before rolling again on the floor. The dancer continues to move with identifiably ballet moves—his leg extended straight behind him as he spins, the lights coming up and down around him in murky, purplish blotches, he falling and catching himself with his arms bent at the elbows and his legs extended long and straight to the side, or falling into a split, with his head curved forward and his elbows lifted behind him, fingers splayed, then again upright, his legs stiff, straight, as he turns in a penchée turn, and hurls again to the floor. Something is overtaking him. As his legs pull him from the floor straight up onto his shoulders, another figure emerges into the shadows on stage left, quietly watching. He looks similar, this figure, but wears a deer head and antlers, and the slightly longer sticks he holds in front make his back straighter, stiffer. His rear feet are arched like the first dancer's, but are harder, firmer, and they click, click, more as he slowly moves onto the stage, mimicking the motions of the first dancer, who has seen the deer and is walking across the stage, away from him, yet whose motions morph more and more with those of the deer as both move, and the echoes between them become all the more inescapable. There is a moment first of panic, and then of utter calm, as we sense the connection between these beings, as the flickers of deer-like aspects that were implied in the first dancer's movements and actions—his dark pointed foot, his extended forearms, his graceful straight legs—become literalized in the second's black pointe shoe hooves and antlered head. The second deer turns aside for a moment, so the two now mirror each other, and then again they turn and, single file (they are both more deer than human now), saunter off the stage.

Part of what this dance theorizes is a metamorphosis of man and deer dancer, and the role of dance in the act of ritual transformation. *Metamorphosis* stages this connection between animal and human and draws from and presents a worldview that understands the crucial importance of keeping this connection in mind and in balance. At the same time, it also explores the connection between this San Juan Pueblo traditional Deer Dance and the ballet form, as itself a kind of "metamorphosis." The deer's hooves, after all, are also black pointe shoes—and vice versa. "I liked the way the pointe shoe looked. It looked like a deer hoof," James said, noting how this attraction to the pointe shoe was part of what drew her to ballet.[16] It's not that the second dancer's deer-ness is simply represented in a ballet form, like a balletic rendition of the San Juan Pueblo Deer Dance story inserted in Clara's *Nutcracker* dream. Nor is it that the first dancer's ballet moves are taken over and erased from the stage by the second deer's more Native American, down to earth, deer-like movements. Rather, these aspects, the Deer Dance story and the relations it explores and lessons it teaches, and the act and practice of ballet come together in this piece. The ballet slipper and pointe shoe morph into the deer hoof; the straight, graceful, extended legs of the ballet dancer become the deer's legs.

Metamorphosis theorizes this understanding of dance exploring, and ultimately reinforcing, the levels of evolution available in Pueblo dance ritual, through ballet. On the one hand, as James's program notes explain, the piece challenges the Pueblo Deer Dance legend on which it is based. It pushes the story past where it usually ends and depicts what would happen if a deer dancer doesn't get caught, and thus bring successful hunts and good fortune to families in the tribe—if he runs off or stays out longer than anyone else ever has; it tests the story. On the other hand, *Metamorphosis* enacts a story where, although the traditional San Juan Pueblo Deer Dance's specific teachings aren't heeded (these deer dancers don't return), the piece nonetheless does adhere to, respect, and reinforce the story's broader messages and the worldviews it underscores—

the intimate, interdependent relations between animal and human beings, the consequences that will ensue if the dances aren't performed correctly, the crucial power of dance to help humans survive and negotiate a place in this ever-changing world. Its effects are still reinforced and respected, and still shown to be true: what it says will happen does happen, even far away, even when these deer are inhabited and animated through ballet, that prototypically Western dance form. Part of what makes seeing this change, this transformation, this merger of dancer and deer that the traditional story predicts, so breathtaking is seeing it happen in and through ballet, on a stage in Brooklyn. It's thus the connections between ballet and "the traditional Deer Dance of San Juan Pueblo," and the animating power of dance in both, that *Metamorphosis* so powerfully enacts.

I BELIEVE THAT IN THE BODY OF EVERY HUMAN BEING WE CAN READ BOTH AN INDIVIDUAL HISTORY AND THAT OF AN ENTIRE CULTURE: *MIINIGOOWEZIWIN . . . THE GIFT*

While James, in *Metamorphosis,* sought to bring ballet training and Native stories and context into relation with one another, in choreographing *Miinigooweziwin . . . The Gift,* Georgina Martinez sought to develop a contemporary stage dance that was grounded not in modern dance training, but rather in ancient bodily practices such as yoga and in contemporary Indigenous dance forms. While *No Home but the Heart, Buffalo Spirit,* and *Residential School for Boys* address the continuing effects that a history of colonization has had on generations of Native people, *Miinigooweziwin* is based on a traditional story and tells of hardships prior to contact. The four-act, evening-length stage dance is grounded in a traditional Anishnaabe story about a period of very long winter when food was scarce and the people were starving. It also narrates and enacts ways of redressing the destruction this hardship has wrought, plunging deeply into explorations of the Aboriginal dancing body, and the practice of Aboriginal bodies dancing, as forces that, when accessed, can redress centuries of physical and spiritual hardship and loss—including that of colonization.

Miinigooweziwin was created through a process that took place over three summers, from 2000 to 2002. The piece is woven around an ancient story from Lake of the Woods that Anishnaabe performer Don Kavanaugh brought to the Aboriginal Dance Training Program after consulting with an elder storyteller from his community. In 2000, under Martinez's program direction and Kavanaugh's production coordination, those involved with the Aboriginal Dance Training Program (which had just been revised from the Chinook Winds Aboriginal Dance Program) formed the first story ideas for the piece. This first phase was performed as a studio showing with the title *Pawaachige,* a word in Anishinaabemowin that translates as "he who dreams" or "he who visions" (and from which some say the word "powwow" comes). In the summer of 2001, artistic director Marrie Mumford organized a symposium, "Oral Tradition as Choreographic Source," codirected by Martinez and Daystar/Rosalie Jones, that brought together senior and emerging Aboriginal choreographers and eight elders and storytellers from a diversity of Indigenous nations. The symposium included presentations from the elders and storytellers and many in-depth discussions regarding protocols and process around Indigenous communities' intellectual properties and oral traditions as they vary from nation to nation and from community to community within nations.[17] Symposium participants gave the company direction as they were working toward a workshop presentation shown later that summer. Because the story included what some might consider controversial elements, those involved with the Aboriginal Dance Training Program were particularly careful to make sure respected and knowledgeable elders from diverse communities were invited to the showing, as a way of inviting feedback, respecting protocol, and honoring the responsibility that comes from being given someone else's story. Afterwards, Mumford made sure someone known to the elders, to whom they would have felt comfortable saying what they really thought, went back to listen for commentary and critique about the piece. With reassurances from this and from *Miinigooweziwin* Anishnaabe cultural director Edna Manitowabi that the elders were comfortable with the piece—indeed, that they wanted to see it staged, that the staging of it comprised one way of communicating it from one generation to the next, in line with the renewing of Anishnaabeg culture through the oral tradition of storytelling—the dance piece continued.[18]

Miinigooweziwin . . . The Gift is a dance of renewal and strength. It depicts Indigenous peoples' journey into relation with ancestors and the spirit world. The piece opens with an immense "Tree of Life" (a floor to almost ceiling ladder-like fixture) on stage right while on stage left, a group of youth, the Kids from the City appear; they stand together and see into that other world. The program synopsis explains, "Through the words of the ancient ones, the youth are able to see the Spirit world and follow Wabano Manito [the Spirit of the East] to Manitowatig—The Tree of Life." As the youth touch Manitowatig, they begin to remember the life of their ancestors. They watch as the Eagle and Spirit of the East are moving through the branches of the Tree of Life; at the top of the Tree of Life is an eagle's nest on which is perched Miigizi, Eagle (Rulan Tangen), with a feather head piece, a line drawn down her face, feathered body suit, and skirt with black tights, and Wabano Manito—Spirit of the East (Hawaiian/Blackfeet Kalani Queypo)—bent forward so the back of his torso shows. The Kids wear fleece shirts and sweats over loose pants, and at first the smoke swirling around them lends an eerie, mystical feel, but when the sound track shifts to sounds of traffic, cars, horns blowing, the smoke reads instead as exhaust. They dance together at first, holding one arm up, then moving in jerky moves, then hunched

Rulan Tangen, Yvonne Chartrand, Penny Couchie from Miinigooweziwin . . . The Gift. *Choreography by Georgina Martinez. Photograph by Donald Lee.*

over, running in place, then incorporating movement from various powwow dance forms, with their arms down, strong, looking intensely out to the audience, as they move in unison, then break as a group, moving hands to head like they're listening to cell phones, moving from hunched down positions and popping up, with gasps, faces aghast, moving closer in toward one another and huddling together. The Grandfather, Mishomis (played by Kavanaugh), walks onto the stage and speaks to them in Anishinaabemowin "Sagaakwa— The Journey is hard and difficult—there are many obstacles." He adds in both Anishinaabemowin and English, "Who lives today is lost, He has to go back, To take back what was given." He then continues, as an invocation, asking for help, "They are hungry, have pity on them, Guide us, On what to do."

Miinigooweziwin then tells a story of how the Young Boy, Gwiizehns (Mestizo/Mexican Francisco Carrera), dreams of the ancestors as they lived prior to contact and shows the dancers transported into the dream. Gwiizehns sees the women in the Dance of the Red Willows on a beautiful morning at dawn—the stage bathed in iridescent pinks and oranges—by the water where the red willows grow, and the men come to gather the willows. He dreams of Manito Memengwahn—Spirit of the Butterfly (danced by Sheshegwaning First

Miskwabiiminigohns Niimiwin—The Dance of the Red Willows, from Miinigooweziwin . . . The Gift. *Yvonne Chartrand, Kalani Queypo, Penny Couchie, Tracey Lloyd. Choreography by Georgina Martinez. Photograph by Donald Lee.*

Nation/Ojibway powwow dancer Celina Cada-Matasawagon)—who, dressed in full Fancy-Dance regalia, dances out onto the stage while a feeling of joy and happiness pervades, and the dancers smile at each other. He also sees the hardship, suffering, starvation, and illness that come upon the people: more ominous music starts, and all stop dancing, look down, around, start to shiver, huddle together, scared, nervous. They shiver and sway, and a Young Woman, Oshikiikwe (Iyaxe Nakoda dancer Cherith Mark), falls as the others watch in horror. A Helper, Ishkabewis (Mohawk Brandon Oakes), carries her off stage. Later in the piece, she is treated by the collective actions and medicine dance sent to the people in a dream.

It is a strengthening journey for these youths and also for the Grandfather, who seems bewildered and lost at times, and yet keeps watching, trying, attempting things—and sometimes conjures the Spirits without quite meaning to. The piece tells the story of his journey into increasing awareness of the teachings of Spirits of the East, West, North, and South, and of the Grandmother, the Bear Spirit, who enter at different points in the journey, when invited, imagined, and dreamed onto the stage. The piece particularly explores how this journey strengthens the Young Boy, Gwiizhens, who watches the Grandfather throughout. In the final scene, as the Spirits watch from the Tree of Life, the Grandfather and Young Boy enter and crouch in the middle of four long branches that have been placed on the stage, in the four directions, so they form an arch, and sit quietly there.

As this dance recounts this story of renewal, it also acts as a strengthening dance for the performers themselves, the "seventh generation" of "Kids from the City." These Kids from the City don't return to the stage as characters after the opening scenes, but do fill it as the dancers themselves. Their presence, dressed in sweats, like contemporary dancers, like the kids from the city many of them are, positions them as participants in this journey of reconnection to Aboriginal worldviews and approaches through the journey of making this stage dance. In other words, the piece both narrates and enacts the mending of Aboriginal peoples from generations of hardship.

Throughout the piece, this mending comes, in part, from people feeling their way, watching and remembering and finding a path without necessarily knowing exactly what to do or how to do it or what effects it will have. The program explains how the Grandfather remembers that he was given instructions for what he needs to do. As the Grandfather begins a song with a shaker, "the Spirit of the East, the Spirit of New Life appears, bringing a new cycle—spring—to Bemaadizijiig—the people." Yet at other points, his actions bring effects without his intentions or awareness of them. When he makes a hoop from the fallen willow branch, the Spirit of the Butterfly appears and he is "reminded that the mending of our communities begins with the mending of the sacred hoop." This is something his actions remind him of, rather than an effect he deliberately intended. Later, he drums inadvertently on the Earth, as he thinks of what he should do next. We read (and the dancers act out) how, "Without knowing, he summons Ningabiyano Manito, the Spirit of the West" (Ojibwe Jeremy Proulx)—a trickster spirit who teaches about laughter—with feather bustle on butt and head, and face paint, who grins and grimaces and taunts and teases the Grandfather, shaking his butt and feather bustle at him, chasing him, mimicking him, moving his butt bustle to the front, near his groin, and shaking it at Grandfather and at the women, sitting and watching from the back, with a wild yell. "Trickster brings the gift of laughter—to teach the people to laugh at themselves as they approach adulthood when life—work becomes too hard," the program describes (8). When the Grandfather touches the stone to his heart in thanks for this teaching, "unknowingly he invites the Grandmothers, who bring the gift of wisdom, bringing healing for the people in the winter of their lives." The Grandfather thus summons the Spirit of the North, a woman in a white dress and long white rope hair who swoops her hands over the Grandfather, the bangles on her wrists jangling. Her presence and actions in turn summon Nokomis, Makwa Manito: Grandmother, Bear Spirit (Manitowabi) who dreams of Zhiibashkayiigan Niimiwin, the Jingle Dress dance, "a medicine dance, a healing dance for Oshikiikwe—and for all women in the future," bringing on a Jingle Dress dancer (Anishnaabe/Odawa Karen Pheasant). It is at this point that the Young Woman who fell earlier reenters the stage, herself Jingle dancing. This renewal and reconnection, then, comes in part because the Grandfather is told what to do, but also in part because he does things in the right place (in the space formed by the rocks), and in the right frame of mind (seeking a way of strength and renewal), and because of how his body remembers what to do (touch the rock to his heart) even without his conscious intent. These actions bring the Spirits, who come to teach and aid him, and who enable the healing and strengthening that comes to the people.

As the Grandfather follows this kind of remembrance, this watch, try, and trust approach, so too do the other dancers, both in the dance piece and also in the Aboriginal Dance Program itself with its careful exploring of the staging of this story. The piece depicts the dancers observing the spirits who are summoned, carefully watching them and imitating them, slowly starting to mimic, mirror, remember, and move like them. The dance students in the program, under the choreographic direction of Martinez and cultural direction of Kavanaugh and Manitowabi, work similarly—watching and observing, having been given some teachings and otherwise finding their way by trying and remembering and seeing what they summon. Mumford and Manitowabi, for their part, feel their way into appropriate ways of putting elements of this story on stage.

The program suggests that the piece offers "audiences a rare opportunity to experience the power of authentic Aboriginal Dance grounded in Indigenous knowledge, history, traditions, and ancestral memories, presented in a contemporary context" (4). The "authentic Aboriginal Dance" the piece offers, though, is not tied to some anthropologically determined notion of authenticity. Rather, what is authentic is a process where movement and ritual come from the teachings of cultural leaders, but also from lots of watching others and oneself, from trying out movement, from practicing and through that practice remembering teachings that perhaps have been muted or half-forgotten, from learning and trusting that what one learns, what develops from this process, is connected to one's cultural past. This process of seeking an effective and appropriate approach, the piece suggests, is "authentic Aboriginal Dance." Martinez writes in the program, "I believe that in the body of every human being we can read both an individual history and that of an entire culture: we can read our past, present and even find in the blood and flesh the seeds for a better future. Our bodies reflect our individuality as people living in the 21st century directly linked to an ancestral history full of knowledge and wisdom" (13).

The various dance backgrounds of the choreographers and dancers are visible in their movement. In training the dancers, Martinez combined the observational approach of yoga with training in contemporary Indigenous dance forms. A modern dance training and aesthetic are still visible in parts through-out, especially in the use of stage space in the "Kids from the City" scene, and in the sections with torso-initiated arm movements, and lifts and arches, or where swooping arms and barrel turns signal a modern dance vocabulary. The Eagle Dance section, especially the performances of Couchie and Tangen, seem particularly modern with their arabesque steps, lifted leaps, and torso undula-tions. Yet equally visible is its base in yoga, from breath-initiated movements to the "Eagle pose" legs the eagles hold. And throughout, a rhythmic relation to powwow dance is clear. At times, what starts out as walking in place or shift-ing weight builds quickly into a more clearly powwow rhythm, with an up-down weighted movement. In the "Kids from the City" section, for example, the dancers are at one point hunched over, running in place, and as they do so, the running becomes more rhythmic, with arms down; both the steps and the torso movement—held more stable, less the initiator of arm or leg movement and more a base for it—signal powwow training and aesthetic. The third eagle dancer, Cherith Mark, who enters when the music shifts to include a drum beat, dances more in this powwow-based way, signaling, even within the Eagle dance section, a shift from a more modern aesthetic to a drum-initiated, pow-wow one.

The dance piece is grounded in narrative, yet also has a mesmeric, abstract, feel. Some audience members struggled to read the program notes, with names in Anishinaabemowin and a complicated story line, and gave up half way through, deciding to settle in and just watch, turning their questions instead to whether there would be an intermission (there would not). A young French Canadian boy asked his mom repeatedly to explain what was going on, why certain things were happening, who the figures were (except for the Trickster section, with its tongue-wagging and butt-shaking, which he understood per-fectly), and she shushed him and said she didn't know. Some audience mem-bers, then, even as they recognized the dance had a narrative, followed it as they would any modern dance performance, looking not for the story but for the sense or effect the movement had on them. Yet the piece is inextricably grounded in the very specific story brought to the program by Kavanaugh and further developed in collaboration with Martinez, Manitowabi, Mumford, and the dancers.

As the piece explores Indigenous history, knowledge, traditions, and ances-tral memories in a contemporary dance context, it also reframes a standard stage dance relation to audience. Each night, the audience erupted in applause and shouted as the piece ended. On the second night of the performance, as the au-dience applauded, the voice of a Maori woman in the audience could be heard, her voice rising through and out of the clapping and yelling, and eventually the audience quieted to listen to her finish. A man in the audience had a guitar and another came up on stage and spoke in Maori, gesturing toward the woman who had chanted, and then explained in English that the Maori people wished to thank the Aboriginal people from Canada for this dance performance, and to offer their thanks would sing. About twenty people came from the audience onto the stage, to join them on stage and sing them an exit song. The man explained that the song was written to unify the Maori tribes; they sing it now to unify Indigenous people worldwide. After they sang the song and left the stage, another group—from Hawai'i, also in town for the World Indigenous Peoples Conference on Education that was about to start—came up and sang, with a ukulele and guitar, then one young woman, wearing jeans and with a pair of sunglasses tucked in the neck of her sweatshirt, danced a hula. They ended by singing a chant of thanks to all of us for being there, then the dancers on stage sang again and the audience members joined in. Even within this proscenium theater, with its purchased tickets and rows of comfortable seats designed to enable docile viewing, the stage dance production and the audience it drew created a space of reciprocity and interconnection between performers and viewers.

These brief discussions touch on only a small fraction of the dance pieces staged recently by Indigenous choreographers. Many, many of the dancers and choreographers mentioned throughout this work or involved with the programs and productions described, as well as those inspired by them, have continued making work, teaching and building dance companies and programs. Here are just a few of the names to plug into your Internet search engine and follow over the next few decades. Mohawk dancer and choreographer **Santee Smith** (www.santeesmithdance.com), whose work "infuses the techniques of ancient movement and music with the full-bodied movement of modern dance," toured her evening-length production *Kaha:wi* to international critical acclaim in 2004 and 2005. In 2005, Smith incorporated and launched **Kaha:wi Dance Theatre** in Toronto, an innovative Aboriginal dance company whose vision is to create and promote contemporary artistic expression that reflects the integrity of Indigenous cultural aesthetics and worldview and continues to make and tour highly acclaimed work. **Red Sky Performance** (www.redskyperformance .com), the Toronto-based company directed by **Sandra Laronde** that creates, develops, and produces original Aboriginal performance works, has since its founding in 2000 presented numerous performances, lectures, and workshops all over the world and won a myriad of awards for the work it does. **Dancing Earth** (www.dancingearth.org), a collaborative ensemble of Indigenous contemporary dance artists directed by **Rulan Tangen** out of Santa Fe, and including **Raoul Trujillo** and **Kalani Queypo** among its members, continues to create and produce experimental dances that draw from sources including hip-hop, modern, and powwow, reflect its members' rich cultural heritages, and "explore identity as contemporary Native peoples." **Earth in Motion Indigenous**

World Dance, co-directed by **Penny Couchie** and **Alejandro Roncería** in Toronto, choreographs and presents new work and runs choreography workshops and laboratories, helping younger choreographers develop work and producing their pieces. The company toured *Agua* to Mexico City in fall 2005. **Daystar/Rosalie Jones's** company, **Daystar: Contemporary Dance-Drama of Indian America** (www.daystardance.com), continues to produce new work, such as *Between the Earth and the Moon: Voices from the Great Circle*, which premiered at Ohio State University in 2005. Daystar currently teaches dance in the Indigenous Studies program at Trent University in Ontario, Canada, where along with Marrie Mumford and Edna Manitowabi, who are also on the faculty, she is assisting in the development of an Indigenous Performing Arts curricula. **Raven Spirit Dance** (ravenspiritdance.com) was established in 1999 in Vancouver. Led by Artistic Director **Michelle Olson**, its mandate is to create, develop, and produce contemporary dance that is rooted in traditional and contemporary Aboriginal worldviews. It has coproduced work with the Tr'ondëk Hwëch'in First Nation, and in spring 2006 premiered a new dance/theatre piece at Trent University, *Evening in Paris*, created with **Muriel Miguel** and inspired by Penobscot dancer Molly Spotted Elk and by Olson's grandmother. The **American Indian Dance Theatre** (www.americanindiandancetheatre.com), currently relocating to Los Angeles, under the direction of **Hanay Geiogamah**, tours regularly. In summer 2006, Geiogamah collaborated with choreographer **Marla Bingham** on a major remake of *Unto These Hills*, an outdoor dance-drama about the history of the Cherokee people staged for fifty-seven years in North Carolina. The new version includes mostly Cherokee performers and focuses on the Eastern Band's survival. The **Marla Bingham Contemporary Ballet** (www.marlabingham.com), based in La Jolla, California, has a dozen pieces in its repertory. **Sylvia Ipirautaq Cloutier** returned home to Nunavut from Banff in 1997 to produce a new dance piece with **Siobhán Arnatsiaq-Murphy**, *Nunattinni* (in our land). A professional Throat Singer, her company **Aqsarniit** (Northern Lights; www.aqsarniit.com) continues to give workshops and perform. Métis choreographer **Yvonne Chartrand** is artistic director of *Compaigni V'ni Dansi* (meaning "Come and Dance" in Michif-French), a Métis traditional and contemporary dance company in Vancouver. A recent work, *Gabriel's Crossing*, tells the story of the Métis Resistance from the hearts of Gabriel and Madeleine Dumont. Iroquois-Mohawk choreographer **Gaétan Gingras** has been choreographing since 1993 and in 2005 performed *Manitowapan* as part of a cross-Canada "Indigenous Dancelands" tour. Plains Cree actor and dancer **Michael Greyeyes** choreographed and created a number of theatre works and is currently part of the full-time faculty in the Theatre Department at York University. San Juan Pueblo ballet dancer **Belinda James** continues to make new work and showed a new piece, *MDCXXC*, in 2005 in New York. Aluutiq dancer/choreographer **Tanya Lukin-Linklater**, from Alaska and currently based in Edmonton, premiered *Woman and Water* in May 2006. **Geraldine Manossa**, a member of the Bigstone Cree Nation in Northern Alberta, choreographed and danced *ISKWEW* at Trent in 2006. **Byron Chief-Moon**, a member of the Blackfoot Confederacy, Blood Band, founded the *Coyote Arts Percussive Performance Association/CAPPA* in 1999, a multimedia dance-theatre company incorporating Blackfoot language, song, dance, and story, infusing traditional Plains Indian style music with contemporary music techniques and initiating new media into the performances. His dance work includes *Possessed, Dancing Voices, Voices,* and *Quest*. **Julia Jamieson** (Mohawk/Cayuga) presented *My Baby You'll Be: Ankewi:raenkenhake* at "Weesageechak Begins to Dance XVIII: A Festival of New Works by Native Artists," held by Native Earth Performing Arts in 2005. **Christine Friday Keeshig**, who choreographed *Misabi* at the Aboriginal Dance Program in 1997, presented three contemporary works, *Metamorphosis, Notchemowwaning,* and a collaboration with British Columbia hiphop artist Manik 1derful in 2005.

All across the Americas, on large and small stages of many sorts, the People Have Never Stopped Dancing, in multiple ever-expanding ways.

Acknowledgments

So many beings have helped bring this book about, I hardly know where to start.

Thank you to the People who've never stopped dancing: the dancers, choreographers, and program administrators who have helped fuel this project. Thank you for creating such inspiring dances, for spending time talking with and e-mailing me, for your openness, trust, and good-hearted bemusement at my fumblings. Thank you Daystar/Rosalie Jones, who sparked this project over a decade ago, and whose voice weaves so fully through it; Rulan Tangen, whose kindness, generosity, and brave and beautiful work continue to awe me; Alejandro Roncería, whose chorography opened my heart to this field and whose teaching has been a joy to witness; Georgina Martinez, whose words and presence of spirit still reverberate with me; Raoul Trujillo, whose breathtaking performances glimpse into how forces manifest; Muriel Miguel, whose sharp work makes me laugh and ponder; Santee Smith, whose deep-rooted understandings infuse such stunning dances; Penny Couchie, whose movement has always riveted me; Tanya Lukin-Linklater, whose brightness shines with passion and integrity; Michelle Olson, whose gifts seem to keep unfolding; Sandra Laronde, who has done so much to put this field on the map; Jerry Longboat, whose questions and support have enriched this book; and the many others whose dancing has filled and energized me, and who have generously shared their time, work, expertise, and insights, including Geraldine Manossa, Marla Bingham, Kalani Queypo, Carlos Rivera, Belinda James, Gaétan Gingras. And finally, Marrie Mumford, can you possibly not know how much you have meant to this project, and to me? On the hardest, most uncertain days I'd somehow always find my message machine blinking full, and hear your warm voice gently prodding me. Thank you for in-depth feedback (especially on chapters 6, 8, and 9), for the time and care with which you read and answered questions and helped rephrase, for the strong wing you extended out to me.

I am enormously grateful to the scholars who have worked so passionately to make dance studies the vibrant field it is today. Thank you Susan Foster, with love and admiration, for giving and sharing so much with me, including in-depth response to this project at many stops along the way, and the nourishment of good food, discussion, and focused consideration of our upper outer deltoids. This book would not exist, in so many ways, without your vision, energies, and support. Thank you Susan Manning, for propelling this project since before it was formed, for supporting it and me over many years in many ways, for the clarity of your words and insights, and for bringing so many of us together in fruitful ways. I have had the good fortune to work on this project while surrounded by a dazzling group of people at the dance department at the University of California, Riverside: Anthea Kraut, Priya Srinivasan, Susan Rose, Anna Beatrice Scott, Linda Tomko, Wendy Rogers, Sally Ann Ness, Derek Burrill, and Fred Strickler have been invigorating, supportive colleagues. Very special thanks to Tommy DeFrantz, whose breaks and beauty-musings have long inspired me, and whose generous official readings of this project in several forms have been so helpful. Thank you to Mark Franko for incisive scholarship, and for helpful comments on chapters 4 and 5. Many other dance studies scholars have given to this project by inspiring me with their ideas and by providing insights and leads and invitations as well as the greatest offering of all, their own interest and enthusiasm. Thanks especially to Anne Flynn, Lisa Doolittle, Rachel Fensham, Jens Richard Giersdorf, Rebekah Kowal, Brenda Dixon Gottschild, Ann Cooper Albright, Ananya Chatterjee, Marta Savigliano, Katherine Mezur.

I am thankful for the Native Studies scholars whose insights have nurtured this project from near and far. Special thanks to Tharon Weighill, whose brilliant provocations infuse this project, for all he's given it and me, including helpful comments on chapters 1–3. Thanks to Philip Deloria for warmth, encouragement, and ready support; to my UC Riverside Native American Studies colleagues Michelle Hermann Raheja for inspiring conversations, ideas, and multiple readings of several chapters, and Clifford Trafzer and Rebecca "Monte" Kugel, for mentoring, support, and thorough readings of the first three chapters; to Hanay Geiogamah for insights and support; and to my Native Studies teachers at UC Berkeley, Hertha Dawn Sweet Wong (who introduced me to the field) and Gerald Vizenor, whose teachings continue to reverberate. Other Native Studies scholars and writers—some friends, some whom I've never met—likewise have inspired and enriched this project and helped bring it into being; thank you Leslie Marmon Silko, Vine Deloria, Craig Womack, Tara Browner, Jill Sweet, Paula Gunn Allen, Greg Sarris, Linda Hogan, Jace Weaver, Linda Tuhiwai Smith, Audra Simpson, Michael Tsosie, A. J. (Annette Jaimes) Guerrero, Leisy Thornton Wyman, Robert Allen Warrior, Chadwick Allen.

I would like to thank the dancers, scholars, and strangers who gave generously of their time and expertise to help me research and write this book: Norton Owen of Jacob's Pillow, for archive searching and helpful corrections; Larry Warren, for many gracious and generous e-mail exchanges about Lester Horton; Thomas Dorsey, for sharing information about his father; Henry Smith, for discussion of Solaris Lakota Sioux Indian Dance Theatre; Ellen Graff, for putting me in touch with May O'Donnell; Naomi Jackson, for pointing me toward information on Tom Two Arrows, and Steve Siegel of the 92nd Street Y for research about him; May O'Donnell and Helen McGehee, for perspectives on working with Martha Graham; Bridget Murnane, for pointing me toward Bella Lewitzky's autobiography; Diane Shewchuk, for guidance at the Albany Institute of History and Art; Hershini Bhana Young, for insights into presence and absence; and Parijat Desai for editing help. I've tested versions of this book for many audiences, and would also like to thank the many people who have offered feedback, corrections, leads, insights, and excitement; their response has been invaluable. This project departs (in both senses of the term) from my dissertation research, and I thank my advisor, Carolyn Porter, for her belief in the way I see.

I owe a special debt to the UCR Dance department's fabulous graduate students, whose creativity, passions, hard work, questions, and feedback make my job so much more enriching. Two in particular deserve special mention for work on this book: Roxane Fenton, who transcribed nearly all the interviews, and Alison Bory, who chased down most of the photos and permissions with tenacity and grace. Thanks also to the many others who have helped along the way: Shakina Nayfack and Ramie Becker as research assistants, the students in my "Dance Literatures" and "Choreographing Writing" seminars, and my PhD advisees for the ways their work keeps stretching me.

Thanks to the teachers who have strengthened and enlightened me, body and spirit, in ways that have informed and infused this project: Cynthia Jean (Novack) Cohen Bull, for fueling my love to dance while at Barnard College; Sue Li-Jue, for keeping me dancing through grad school and into this field; and my yoga teacher Manouso Manos and his teacher B. K. S. Iyengar, for their passion, clarity, and demanding insistence on the subtleties of awareness that bodies can teach.

I am grateful for the research and funding support I received to pursue this project, including yearly research grants from the University of California Senate and Regents' offices; without this travel funding, this would have been an immeasurably weaker book. I am thankful for a UC President's Research Fellowship in the Humanities that gave me much of a year to write; to the UCR Center for Ideas and Society for a fruitful residence quarter; to former UCR Dean Patricia O'Brien for support; and to the Huntington Library for a W. M. Keck Foundation and Mayers Fellowship. Gratitude as well to Elizabeth Theobald Richards of the Ford Foundation for her generous support of the field of American Indian contemporary dance. And much thanks to everyone at the University of Minnesota Press, whose hard work made this book real; special thanks to Carrie Mullen, for her excitement about and initial support of this project, and to Jason Weidemann, for his hard work and generous care in shepherding it through.

I am particularly thankful for the sustaining friendships that have filled my life with love and lightness as I've been working on this book. Cindy Franklin has read more versions of more of these chapters than anyone else, with lightning-fast turnover and the keenest eye imaginable; thank you for the joys of our friendship and the tenacity of your care for me. Michelle Raheja, co-conspirator, what would I do without you, besides go insane? Thank you and yours for opening your hearts, home, bookshelves, closets, refrigerator, computer, car, and everything else to me and mine, and for making my crazy life a little more laughable. Thank you Irene Tucker, for the complex voyage of a long deep friendship; Kim Sargent-Wishart, for sparkle, laughter, and healing intuition; Francesca Royster, for filling the world with bright spaces and me with glee; Theresa Tensuan, for warmth, faith, and cleansing immersions; Bruce Burgett, for making it fun, and keeping me up on what's hot and what's not; Lauren Muller, for steadfast connection in love and struggle; Lori Merish, for knowing when times were hard and swimming along beside me; Tiffany Ana Lopez, for grounding generosity and fashion advice; Kathleen McHugh, for feisty outrage and wise council; Cynthia Schrager, for articulate insights; Anya Grundmann, Nancy Lipsitz, Colleen Keenan, Judy Berman, Tom Hoopes, Rob Zeiger, Joan and Scott Warren, and Sue Rosenthal, for enriching my life from way back and far away.

I balk when I think of the multitudes of people whose help cleared time and space for me to write. Special thanks to Liliana Lobos Ferreira for loving, creative, sustaining support during a fellowship year that was also my son's first; and to Max Berk-Wakeman (and parents) for hours of fort-building sessions and other elaborate schemes.

This book is dedicated to Richard J. Shea, my father, who died shortly after I was born, whose sparkle, wit, and passion for words lit a fire inside me, and who has been with me in spirit my whole life—though never more palpably than while I've been writing this book. Deepest thanks to my parents Caroline Shea Murphy and Jim Murphy, for the example of their intelligence, dedicated tendings of earth, plants, and creatures, and steadfast faith in me, and for crossing the continent so many times to help catch me in the juggle; my beautiful, strong, and gifted sisters Wendy Shea Murphy and Bridget Murphy Brown, for knowing me so well even when I think they don't; Lois and Herman Dinkin, Judy Benson and Jerry Dinkin, Marc Dinkin and Beth Dinkin, for countless meals, hours of child care, and boundless warmth; my nieces and nephews, miracles each: Christopher, Miranda, Colby, Toby, Max, and Joelle, and Noah, in loving memory; my elders Judith Hill, Shirley Dinkin, and Herman and Arnoldine Berlin for friendship and connection across generations; and my beloved *famille du monde,* Sirio *et* Anne-Marie Rossi, *et* Françoise Cognard *et famille: je vous embrasse très fort.*

Finally, thanks to Casey Shea Dinkin, my darling rascal of delight, for his bright joy, his love of stories, and for never having stopped dancing himself, in our kitchen and in my heart; and to my campañero Kenny, for taking this journey with me, with all its peaks and meadows, and for filling my life with song.

Notes

—————

INTRODUCTION

1. Leslie Marmon Silko, *Almanac of the Dead* (New York: Penguin, 1991).

2. See Jacqueline Shea Murphy, "Drawing Blood: Prophesy and Performativity in Leslie Marmon Silko's *Almanac of the Dead*," in "'Words Like Bones': Narrative, Performance, and the Reconfiguring of U.S. Literatures" (PhD diss., University of California, Berkeley, 1996), 197–209.

3. See Martha Graham, "Seeking an American Art of the Dance," in Oliver Martin Sayler, *Revolt in the Arts* (New York: Brentano's, 1930), 254. Cited in Amy Koritz, "American Gesture: Martha Graham's Narratives of Self and Nation," presented at the American Studies Association annual meeting, Nashville, 1994. See also Merle Armitage, *Martha Graham: The Early Years* (New York: Da Capo Press, 1937), in which Graham wrote further of "Our two forms of indigenous dance, the Negro and the Indian" (99). Graham was not the only early modern dance choreographer to call on these sources. In 1926, dancer/choreographer Ted Shawn wrote, "The obvious themes which first come to mind when one thinks of American art production of any kind are the Indian and the Negro." Ted Shawn, *The American Ballet* (New York: Henry Holt, 1926), 15.

4. Over the past several decades, scholars have been tracing the careers and accomplishments of previously neglected Black dancers and choreographers, noting the difficulties of African American entrance into the concert dance arena in the 1920s and 1930s, analyzing the work of contemporary African American dancers and choreographers, and tracing the economies of race, gender, sexuality, and political identity negotiated in their work. The many important books in this field include Lynne Fauley Emery, *Black Dance from 1619 to Today* (Princeton: Dance Horizons, 1972); Katrina Hazzard-Gordon, *Jookin': The Rise of Social Dance Formations in African American Culture* (Philadelphia: Temple University Press, 1992); Jacqui Malone, *Steppin' on the Blues: The Visible Rhythms of African American Dance* (Chicago: University of Illinois Press, 1996); Brenda Dixon Gottschild, *Digging the Africanist Presence in American Performance: Dance and Other Contexts* (Westport: Praeger, 1996); John O. Perpener III, *African-American Concert Dance: The Harlem Renaissance and Beyond* (Chicago: University of Illinois Press, 2001); Thomas DeFrantz, ed., *Dancing Many Drums: Excavations in African American Dance* (Madison: University of Wisconsin Press, 2001); Brenda Dixon Gottschild, *Waltzing in the Dark: African American Vaudeville and Politics in the Swing Era* (New York: Palgrave Macmillan, 2002); Brenda Dixon Gottschild, *The Black Dancing Body: A Geography from Coon to Cool* (New York: Palgrave Macmillan,

2003); Thomas F. DeFrantz, *Dancing Revelations: Alvin Ailey's Embodiment of African American Culture* (New York: Oxford University Press, 2004); Susan Manning, *Modern Dance, Negro Dance: Race in Motion* (Minneapolis: University of Minnesota Press, 2004); and Ananya Chatterjea, *Butting Out: Reading Resistive Choreographies through Works by Jawole Willa Jo Zollar and Chandralekha* (Middleton: Wesleyan University Press, 2004). Symposiums like the American Dance Festival's "The Black Tradition in American Modern Dance" (1988–90) and "Black Choreographers Moving Toward the 21st Century" (1991–92) also brought together scholars, teachers, and dancers interested in these issues, practices, and histories. Scholars have also insisted that the influence of African American dancers, choreographers, and dance practices on white practitioners be accounted for. See, for example, Dixon Gottschild's discussion of George Balanchine's and others' interest in and debt to African American dance *(Digging the Africanist Presence)*. For discussion of Gene Kelly's uncredited borrowing from African American tap and African American performance sources in *Singin' in the Rain,* and of tap's relation to race more generally, see Carol J. Clover, "Dancin' in the Rain," *Critical Inquiry* 21 (Summer 1995), 722–47. Others were noting how white choreographers of the 1920s and 1930s saw their own staging of African American dance forms as central to their development of a distinctly American dance, and were launching incisive inquiries into these choreographers' blatant appropriations and embodiments of African American dance in asserting an American identity for modern dance. Susan Manning, for example, looked critically at Helen Tamaris's staging of Negro spirituals on white bodies, and analyzes the minstrel frame of Martha Graham's 1938 *American Document,* noting how the piece "reiterated minstrelsy's paradoxical staging of race." Susan Manning, "*American Document* and American Minstrelsy," in *Moving Words, Re-Writing Dance,* ed. Gay Morris (New York: Routledge, 1996), 192. See also Susan Manning, "Black Voices, White Bodies: The Performance of Race and Gender in *How Long Brethren,*" *American Quarterly* 50, no. 1 (March 1998), 24–46. Versions of these articles were later included in Manning, *Modern Dance, Negro Dance.*

5. Throughout this book, I deliberately vary my use of the terms "Native American," "American Indian," "Indian," "Native," "Indigenous," and "Aboriginal." I adhere to some generalized guidelines. For example, I usually use "Aboriginal" when referring to Canadian First Nations, Métis, or Inuit peoples as a category; I mostly use "Native American" when referring to scholarship or academic discussion of primarily U.S.-based peoples and issues. My intention with this variance, however, is to destabilize all of these constructed and contested terms, and to use the term I feel is most appropriate given the context of my writing.

6. See Maria Tallchief with Larry Kaplan, *Tallchief: America's Prima Ballerina* (New York: Henry Holt, 1997); Lili Cockerille Livingston, *American Indian Ballerinas* (Norman: University of Oklahoma Press, 1997); Bunny McBride, *Molly Spotted Elk: A Penobscot in Paris* (Norman: University of Oklahoma Press, 1995). See also Jacqueline Shea Murphy, "Far From the Powwow," *Women's Review of Books,* June 1997.

7. See, for example, James Mooney, *The Ghost-Dance Religion and the Sioux Outbreak of 1890* (Lincoln: University of Nebraska, 1896; repr. 1991); James H. Howard and Victoria Lindsay Levine, *Choctaw Music and Dance* (Norman: University of Oklahoma Press, 1990); John Q. Bourke, *Snake Dance of the Moquis* (Tucson: University of

Arizona Press, 1884; repr. 1994). William K. Powers, *War Dance: Plains Indian Musical Performance* (Tucson: University of Arizona Press, 1990); Alexander Lesser, *The Pawnee Ghost Dance Hand Game: Ghost Dance Revival and Ethnic Identity* (Lincoln: University of Nebraska Press, 1933; repr. 1996); Michael Grummett, *Sundance: The 50th Anniversary Crow Indian Sun Dance* (Helena: Falcon Press, 1993); Fred W. Voget, *The Shoshoni-Crow Sun Dance* (Norman: University of Oklahoma Press, 1984); Charlotte J. Frisbie, ed., *Southwestern Indian Ritual Drama* (Albuquerque: University of New Mexico Press, 1980); Clyde Holler, *Black Elk's Religion: The Sun Dance and Lakota Catholicism* (Syracuse: Syracuse University Press, 1995). Jill D. Sweet, *Dances of the Tewa Pueblo Indians: Expressions of New Life* (Santa Fe: School of American Research Press, 1985).

8. Charlotte Heth, ed., *Native American Dance: Ceremonies and Social Traditions* (Washington, D.C.: Smithsonian Institution, 1992).

9. Reginald Laubin and Gladys Laubin, *Indian Dances of North America: Their Importance to Indian Life* (Norman: University of Oklahoma Press, 1977).

10. Philip Deloria, *Playing Indian* (New Haven: Yale University Press, 1998), 190.

11. The "Footsteps and Foothills: New Research in Dance Studies" conference organized by Lisa Doolittle and Anne Flynn, the University of Calgary, January 1999.

12. The Congress on Research in Dance 30th Anniversary Conference, "Dance, Myth and Ritual in the Americas," November 2–5, 1995, Miami, Florida.

13. The issue of identifying ethnicity has a particularly fraught history in the context of American Indian dance, both in the way Plains Indian cultures (tipis, headdresses, horses, feathers, drums) have come to signify "Indian" despite the enormous diversity of Native peoples in North American, and in the way Indian identity has and has not been acknowledged in this country. Consider the differing laws and ideas about racial construction between antebellum Negro/Black/African American identity (the "one-drop rule," where any small amount of African American "blood" could make one legally enslavable) and American Indian identity (where inadequate levels of blood quantum make one legally unrecognizable as Indian—and therefore ineligible for treaty and other rights).

Throughout this study, I have largely refrained from any direct discussion of the stability and instability of particular performers' Indigenous identities. The politics that would attend my judgment of dancers' claims of Native identity and their apparent acceptance by their communities—identities determined by those communities, and not by me—as well as my desire to help construct this history within dance studies (and sense that deconstructing it at the same time is premature) are primary factors in this absence. So too is the widespread discussion of the controversies and politics of Native American identity available elsewhere: many Native studies scholars, especially over the past decade or two, have queried the degree, depth, adoption, and construction of Native American identities. These discussions have been crucial and have led to important scholarship about the invention of Indian identity and its relation to troublesome histories: removal and allotment policies, education and forced assimilation, blood quantum requirements and intermarriage, relocation policies and their creation of pan-Indian and urban Indian identities, and how all of these relate to both federal recognition and tribal recognition, and to the self-presentation of writers, scholars, activists, and performers as Indians. See, for example, Jana Sequoya, "How (!) Is an Indian? A Contest of Stories," in *New Voices in Native American Literary Criticism,* ed. Arnold Krupat (Washington, D.C.: Smithsonian Institution Press, 1993), 453–73. C. Mattew Snipp, "Some Observations about Racial Boundaries and the Experiences of American Indians," *Ethnic and Racial Studies,* October 1997. And Michelle H. Raheja, who writes on Iron Eyes Cody and the representational economy of the Indian in "Screening Identity: Beads, Buckskins and Redface in Autobiography and Film" (PhD diss., University of Chicago, 2002).

14. Exceptions include citations from Georgina Martinez and Pablo Palma, whom I was unable to locate after our discussions, and from May O'Donnell (who died in 2004 at the age of 97).

15. At a 2004 conference on "Red Rhythms: Contemporary Methodologies in American Indian Dance" held in Riverside, California, Andrew Brother Elk cited the discomfort of young Native contemporary hip hop dancers at the Sherman Indian High School, formerly the Sherman Institute—one of the largest boarding schools deployed by the U.S. government.

16. Materials in the Mary Austin files held at the Huntington Library also proved helpful (see chapter 3). Francis Paul Prucha's *The Great Father: The United States Government and the American Indian,* vols. 1 and 2, continuously paginated (Lincoln: University of Nebraska Press, 1984) has been a helpful initial reference throughout.

17. For discussion of blood memory, indigenous racial identity, and essentialism, see Chadwick Allen, *Blood Narrative: Indigenous Identity in American Indian and Maori Literary and Activist Texts* (Durham, N.C.: Duke University Press, 2002).

18. See especially Susan Leigh Foster, "Choreographing History," in *Choreographing History,* ed. Susan Leigh Foster (Bloomington: Indiana University Press, 1995), 3–21, and Susan Leigh Foster, ed., *Corporealities: Dancing Knowledge, Culture and Power* (New York: Routledge, 1996). These as well as Foster's many other publications all explore dance's theorizing capacities.

19. In *The Archive and the Repertoire: Performing Cultural Memory in the Americas* (Durham: Duke Univeristy Press, 2003), Diana Taylor makes a similar argument: "Embodied practice, along with and bound up with other cultural practices, offers a way of knowing" (3). Taylor's important study, developed through her interactions with, in part, Indigenous performance traditions in Latin America, argues for the archival validity of what she calls "the so-called ephemeral repertoire of embodied practice/ knowledge (i.e. spoken language, dance, sports, ritual)" (19).

20. For example, one young choreographer from the Tr'ondëk Hwëch'in (Han) First Nation in Canada, Michelle Olson, at the conference on "Red Rhythms: Contemporary Methodologies in American Indian Dance" (Riverside, California, 2004) spoke about the way her people don't have a continuous, unbroken dance practice, because in the face of colonization their chief (Chief Isaac) sent their dances and songs to communities in Alaska where elders now hold them for safekeeping. She explained how, while the songs have started to return over the past thirty-five years, there's very little dancing at all for her and other young dancers to learn and learn from. For her, as a contemporary dancer trained in modern dance, raised away from but with some connection to her community, she has to investigate Han dance practices using any tools she can find—which include photos, stories, anthropological snippets, but also her modern

dance training. Yet, she notes this bricolage form of investigation provides a way of accessing a sense of identity and community. "I think in our own community we're using contemporary expression to really define who we are," Olson said. "I bring the language into my contemporary dance; I bring in images and stories, and that is a way of generating a pride in our own community, that we can start working together. And I don't know how it's going to turn out. Like the kids are really, the young ones just love it. And I'm trying to train them to be the next group of dancers. And I'm interested to see what's going to be traditional Han dancing in ten, twenty years." She is not, in other words, interested in providing a narrative of historical continuity and stability that researching through dance can provide, but rather in the moments of connection, and in purpose—ways this contemporary dancing can generate community identity and pride, making it function traditionally.

21. Jace Weaver, "Losing My Religion: Native American Religious Traditions and American Religious Freedom," in *Native American Religious Identity: Unforgotten Gods,* ed. Jace Weaver (Maryknoll, N.Y.: Orbis Press, 2002), 219.

22. Arnoldo C. Vento, "Rediscovering the Sacred: From the Secular to a Postmodern Sense of the Sacred," *Wicazo Sa Review,* Spring 2000, 183–206.

23. For example, Benedict Anderson, *Imagined Communities: Reflections on the Origin and Spread of Nationalism* (London: Verso, 1983), argues that secular simultaneity, "a temporal coincidence . . . measured by clock and calendar" (30) (what he via Benjamin calls "empty, homogenous time," 28), was a fundamental shift from premodern religious temporality of prophecy and fulfillment (28). Other contemporary philosophers, including Johannes Fabien, *Time and the Other: How Anthropology Makes its Object* (New York: Columbia University Press, 1983), and Giorgio Agamben, "Time and History: Critique of the Instant and the Continuum," in *Infancy and History: Essays on the Destruction of Experience,* trans. Liz Heron (New York: Verso, 1978; repr. 1993), have written compellingly of the Christian conceptualizations undergirding linear notions of time as something that "develops irreversibly from the Creation to the end, and has a central point of reference in the incarnation of Christ, which shapes its development as a progression from the initial fall to the final redemption," as Agamben writes. He continues, "The modern concept of time is a secularization of rectilinear, irreversible Christian time, albeit sundered from any notion of end and emptied of any other meaning but that of a structured process in terms of before and after" (96). I find this essay helpful for a few reasons: because it makes a link between what are called secular and Christian worldviews; because it doesn't posit an easy opposition between "linear" (modern, secular) and "circular" (primitive, religious) understandings of time, but instead sees all understandings of time as linked to religious/philosophic understandings and explores them; and because I find its turn to pleasure as a possible site for founding "a new concept of time" intriguing and resonant.

24. Dipesh Chakrabarty, *Provincializing Europe: Postcolonial Thought and His-torical Difference* (Princeton: Princeton University Press, 2000), 106. See also Dipesh Chakrabarky, "The Time of History and the Times of Gods," in *The Politics of Culture in the Shadow of Capital,* ed. Lisa Lowe and David Lloyd (Durham: Duke University Press, 1997), 35–60.

25. Paula Gunn Allen, *The Sacred Hoop: Recovering the Feminine in American Indian Traditions* (Boston: Beacon Press, 1986), 149.

26. Ibid. In "The Ceremonial Motion of Indian Time: Long Ago, So Far" (*The Sacred Hoop,* 147–54), Gunn Allen explains that "Achronicity is the kind of time in which the individual and the universe are 'tight.' The sense of time that the term refers to is not ignorant of the future any more than it is unconscious of the past. It is a sense of time that connects pain and praise through timely movement, knitting person and surroundings into one" (150).

27. Script for this performance, "No Home but the Heart (An Assembly of Memories)," by Daystar (Rosalie M. Jones) copyright 1998. Reprinted in *Keepers of the Morning Star: An Anthology of Native Women's Theater,* ed. Stephanie Fitzgerald and Jaye T. Darby (Los Angeles: UCLA American Indian Center Press, 2003).

28. For a story of the origins of the Jingle Dress Dance, and how it continues to be performed as a prayer of healing, see Tara Browner, *Heartbeat of the People: Music and Dance of the Northern Pow-Wow* (Chicago: University of Illinois Press, 2002), 53–57. Browner writes, "One of the most profound elements of Jingle Dress dancing is its spiritual power, which originates as an energy generated from the sound of the cones that sing out to the spirits when dancers lift their feet in time with the drum. The very act of dancing in this dress constitutes a prayer for healing, and often spectators, musicians, and other dancers will make gifts of tobacco to a dancer and request that she pray for an ill family member while she dances." Browner calls the Jingle Dress Dance "an example of hidden spirituality and ritual within a public forum" (53).

29. I adhere to this structuring device, which makes this project more accessible to dance students and scholars—and serves after all as a marker of my own position and training—even as I hope and trust the holes in its trajectory and the resonances between chapters across time will trouble its linearity For discussion of this kind of "methodological and epistemological questioning of what the very business of writing history is all about" (107), see Chakrabarty, *Provincializing Europe.* He suggests that we write in such a way that "the scandalous aspects of our unavoidable translations . . . reverberate through what we write" (90).

1. HAVE THEY A RIGHT?

1. These state attempts to control Native bodies through institutional and discursive "discipline and punish" methods anticipate the influential theories of French philosopher Michel Foucault, developed a century later through analysis of the history of French medical clinics, prisons, and discourses on sexuality.

2. In the United States, this period marked the end of overt Indian warfare and the beginning of a rhetorical policy shift from "the only good Indian is a dead Indian" to "kill the Indian in him, and save the man." Richard H. Pratt, *Official Report of the Nineteenth Annual Conference of Charities and Correction,* 1892. This move was articulated in monetary terms. In 1881, Secretary of the Interior Carl Schurz estimated it cost nearly a million dollars to kill an Indian in warfare, whereas it cost only $1,200 to give him or her eight years of schooling. Charles Schurz, "Present Aspects of the Indian Problem," *North American Review* 13 (July 1881); quoted in David Wallace Adams, *Education for*

Extinction: American Indians and the Boarding School Experience, 1875–1928 (Lawrence: University Press of Kansas, 1995), 20.

3. The enforcement of wage-labor systems was imposed, though Native peoples have of course long been involved in capitalist commercial exchange involving monetary exchange. Thanks to Tharon Weighill for this clarification.

4. Ronald Niezen, *Spirit Wars: Native North American Religions in the Age of Nation Building* (Berkeley: University of California Press, 2000). See especially the chapter on "Medical Evangelism," where Neizen notes the relation between the imposition of biomedical beliefs and Christianity.

5. For descriptions of corporally imposed and enforced boarding school policies, see Adams, *Education for Extinction*. The 1928 "Merriam Report" outlined the malnutrition, unsanitary kitchen facilities, insufficient sleeping room, inadequate toilet and bathing facilities, heavy work demanded of Indian students, and inadequate hospital facilities in government-run boarding schools. Other reports told of brutal physical punishment inflicted on boarding school children; see John Collier, "Grave Charges of Mistreating the Indians," *Literary Digest*, January 26, 1929. Another 1929 pamphlet reporting the "Remarks of Hon. Burton K. Wheeler of Montana in the Senate of the United States" (U.S. Government Printing Office, 1929; Huntington Library, Mary Austin files [AU Box 128]) describes beatings, abuses of U.S. child labor laws, insufficient health care, rampant tuberculosis and trachoma, and inadequate nutrition. The federal boarding school at Carlisle, Pennsylvania, had dungeons designed to hold students in isolation.

6. In the 1880s, Indian reservations in the U.S. West were still sizable and held by the people in common. Christian reformers from the Indian Rights Association believed in individualism as a tool for "civilization," and believed that without individually owned parcels of land, the Indians would soon lose everything. They agitated for and led Congress to pass the Dawes Act, which legislated assimilation by breaking up communally held tribal lands and allotting portions to individual Indians. The act stipulated how, after Indian land had been allotted to individual Indians, the United States could then purchase "surplus" lands and resell them to white homesteaders. See Prucha, *Great Father,* 666–71; and C. E. S. Franks, "Indian Policy: Canada and the United States Compared," in *Aboriginal Rights and Self-Government: The Canadian and Mexican Experience in North American Perspective,* ed. Curtis Cook and Juan D. Lindau (Montreal: McGill–Queen's University Press, 2000), 228.

7. This included, on the one hand, the strategic neglect of Indians decimated by starvation and disease, considered a dying race and relegated to isolated reserves where they were largely left alone. On the other, the government pursued the active assimilation of those Indians seen as more advanced and capable of joining non-Native civilization. For a helpful and astute comparative analysis of U.S. and Canadian Indian policy, see Franks, "Indian Policy." He explains how in Canada, there was no major nineteenth-century Canadian policy separating Native peoples from Native land, as the Dawes Act had in the United States. Instead, perhaps because Canadian reserves were generally already small, other policies sought to alienate Indians from their lands by enfranchising Indians as Canadian and disenfranchising them as Indians. This included the disenfranchisement of Indian women who married non-Indian men and (ultimately

unsuccessful) attempts at disenfranchising all Indians who joined the armed services, became a member of a profession, received a university degree, or otherwise were deemed fit to join Euro-Canadian society (238). He suggests that white dominion over the land was assumed to be an inevitable outcome of Canada's integral role in the great civilizing mission of the British Empire (241).

8. Christopher Bracken, *The Potlatch Papers: A Colonial Case History* (Chicago: University of Chicago Press, 1997).

9. For example, the 1884 Commissioner of Indian Affairs (CIA), in the Report of Agents in Indian Territory, writing on "Cheyennes," notes how "They make medicine several times during the season, which occupies several months of their valueless time," and also how some "dance until they drop from sheer exhaustion; not many stand it for more than a day or two without food or water." The agent then concludes, "Their endurance is worthy of a better cause." *Annual Report of the Commissioner of Indian Affairs* (congressional serial) (Washington, D.C.: G.P.O., 1884), 73. All subsequent references to these volumes given as "CIA Report," followed by year and page.

10. For discussion of Chief Illiniwek as the University of Illinois mascot, and the effect the mascot has on Native American peoples, see the video *In Whose Honor?* written and produced by Jay Rosenstein (Ho-ho-kus, N.J.: New Day Films, 1997). For just one example of how children's media represent Indians through dance, see Peggy Parish, *Key to the Treasure* (New York: Yearling, 1966). In this young adult mystery, Bill, the young protagonist, tries on an "Indian bonnet" his grandparents keep displayed in a glass case. The text then reads, "'Say, I make a pretty good Indian,' said Bill. He began to dance around in front of the mirror" (37).

11. Joseph E. Marks III, *The Mathers on Dancing,* including Increase Mather, *An Arrow Against Profane and Promiscuous Dancing Drawn out of the Quiver of the Scriptures (1685)* (Brooklyn: Dance Horizons, 1975), 50.

12. Thanks to Michelle Raheja for this insight.

13. See Weaver, "Losing My Religion."

14. See Thomas Gage, *The English-American His Travail by Sea and Land; or A New Survey of the West Indias* (London: Printed by R. Cotes and are to be sold by Humphrey Blanden and Thomas Williams, 1648). In this treatise designed to encourage the English, instead of the Spanish, to control the Americas, Gage describes Indian dances he has seen in Guatemala in such terms, 154–56.

15. Francis Paul Prucha, *American Indian Policy in Crisis: Christian Reformers and the Indian, 1865–1900* (Norman: University of Oklahoma Press, 1976), 32. Robert H. Keller Jr., *American Protestantism and United States Indian Policy, 1869–82* (Lincoln: University of Nebraska Press), 18.

16. The peace policy included church control of agents on reservations, the creation of a board of Indian commissioners, and a greatly expanded and intensified program of federal aid to Indian education and missions (Keller, *American Protestantism,* 17). Keller notes that Jews, Moravians, and Mormons were excluded from participation, while Methodists, Catholics, Presbyterians, Episcopalians, and Congregationalists were entrenched, and other Protestant denominations participated to a lesser extent (36 and 184). See also Francis Paul Prucha, "Indian Policy Reform and American Protestantism, 1880–1900," in Prucha, *Indian Policy in the United States: Historical Essays* (Lincoln:

University of Nebraska Press, 1981), 229–51. Prucha notes that during the last decades of the nineteenth century, evangelical Protestantism brought about an "almost complete identification of Protestantism with Americanism" (241). See also Jon Butler, *Awash in a Sea of Faith: Christianizing the American People* (Cambridge: Harvard University Press, 1990).

17. See Keller, *American Protestantism,* 214; Holler, *Black Elk's Religion,* 113; Prucha, *Indian Policy in the United States,* 247 and 253.

18. Robert M. Kvasnicka and Herman J. Viola, eds., *The Commissioners of Indian Affairs, 1824–1977* (Lincoln: University of Nebraska Press, 1979), 176.

19. Francis Paul Prucha, *Documents of United States Indian Policy,* 2nd ed. (Lincoln: University of Nebraska Press, 1975; repr. 1990), 160.

20. Tharon Weighill notes that "This practice of inventing Uncle Tommy Hawks to judge the non-civilized Indians was an intentional method of divide and conquer. It destabilized communities and broke many codes held important at the time." Personal communication, January 10, 2005.

21. Olive Patricia Dickason, *Canada's First Nations: A History of Founding Peoples from Earliest Times,* 2nd ed. (Don Mills, Ont.: Oxford University Press, 1997), 258.

22. Roger L. Nichols, *Indians in the United States and Canada: A Comparative History* (Lincoln: University of Nebraska Press, 1998), for example, writes, "Because of the continuing violence and bloodshed in the American West, churchmen, reformers, and other so-called friends of the Indian launched frequent movements to force the U.S. government to end the fighting, reform the operations of the Indian Office, and give them more say in the way tribal people were being treated. No direct parallel existed in Canada at the time" (207). Nichols writes how while church and missionary activity had a large role in both countries during this period, in Canada the churches actually operated many Indian schools (270, 227). (While there were Catholic boarding schools in the United States, the number of church-operated schools was substantially larger in Canada.)

23. Holler writes that Fool's Crow was required to obtain official permission to pierce eight men in 1952. "Since sacrifice is essential to the Lakota form of the dance, it seems best to consider that the ban on the Lakota Sun Dance ended with the first public Sun Dance performed with piercing, whenever it is deemed to have occurred, not with Collier's directive," Holler writes (*Black Elk's Religion,* 138). The first open Sun Dance in the United States after this period was in 1978 at Leonard Crow Dog's arbor in Pine Ridge, South Dakota.

24. For discussion of how Native people in the Sonoran part of Mexico did continue to dance to empower themselves for their own protection against colonizing forces, see Robert Cristian Perez, "Indian Rebellions in Northwestern New Spain: A Comparative Analysis, 1695–1750" (PhD diss., University of California Riverside, 2003).

25. Regulations of the Indian Office, UCLA law library

26. The problem, the agent suggests, is that the dance is too effective in maintaining political and cultural agency among practitioners. He writes, in reference to a twelve-year-old boy initiated at the dance, "I have no doubt this ceremony at his age will have a stronger influence on him in later life than all his schooling" (CIA Report, 1903, 9).

27. The 1911 CIA Report, for example, makes reference to "exercises which the

Indians consider of a religious nature"—phrasing that implies that others may not consider it so.

28. E. Brian Titley, *A Narrow Vision: Duncan Campbell Scott and the Administration of Indian Affairs in Canada* (Vancouver: University of British Columbia Press, 1986), 164.

29. Adolph Hungry Wolf, *The Blood People* (New York: Harper and Row, 1977), 301. Quoted in Titley, *Narrow Vision,* 165.

30. Chapter 3's discussion of U.S. Southwest Indian dance in the 1920s takes this up more fully.

31. PAC, RG 10, vol. 3825, file 60, 511–12, 23 November 1903. Quoted in Titley, *Narrow Vision,* 169.

32. Andrew Brother Elk, personal conversation, January 16, 2004.

33. Clyde Ellis, in his insightful study *A Dancing People: Powwow Culture on the Southern Plains* (Lawrence: University of Kansas Press, 2003), recounts examples of this "clandestine" dancing in "remote locales . . . beyond the immediate reach of agents." He notes how "Along with the Kiowa Ton'konga, and Tiah-Piah societies, O-ho-mah members continued to meet and dance despite intense pressure" (18).

34. In this the Ghost Dance was far from unique: the Indian Shaker religion, promoted in the Puget Sound region by the prophet Squsachtun (John Slocum), combined tribal religious practices with Christian teachings he learned from the missionaries (Nichols, *Indians in the United States and Canada,* 241).

35. This practice of dancing on July 4 was hardly unique to this instance; other tribes' engagements with patriotic rhetoric and celebrations of July 4 appear throughout the CIA Reports; see 1895, 198; 1896, 203, 300; 1899, 332.

36. Paula Gunn Allen. "'Indians,' Solipsisms, and Archetypal Holocausts," in *Off the Reservation: Reflections on Boundary-Busting, Border-Crossing, Loose Canons* (Boston: Beacon Press: 1998), 97.

37. For examples, see Crow Creek Dakota Agent V. T. McGillycuddy's 1882 report: "Dancing is diminishing, and the heathenish annual ceremony, termed the 'sun dance,' will, I trust, from the way it is looking ground, soon be a thing of the past" (CIA Report, 39); the agent in Dakota's 1883 report: "excepting one locality, dancing and other superstitious habits have been almost entirely abandoned" (22); the Northern Cheyenne Agent Jas. G. Wright's 1883 report that "the barbarous festival known as the sun dance has lost ground" (43); the Dakota agent's 1884 report that the Sun Dance "for the first time in the history of the Ogalalla Sioux and Northern Cheyennes was not held" (37); Rosebud Agent James C. Wright's 1884 report: "The aboriginal festival of the sun dance was not held here this year. . . . I do not expect it will again be revived" (48); and Indian agent in Nebraska S. E. Snider's 1884 report: "The Sun Dance is a thing of the past" (117).

2. THEATRICALIZING DANCING AND POLICING AUTHENTICITY

1. See Nancy Chalfa Ruyter, *Reformers and Visionaries: The Americanization of the Art of Dance* (New York: Dance Horizons, 1979), 18, 27.

2. Ted Shawn, *Every Little Movement* (Pittsfield: Eagle Printing and Binding, 1954), 15.

3. Delsarte's base in Christian thought has been well noted. Ruyter describes how "underlying Delsarte's technical system was an elaborate and mystical sense of esthetics deriving from his personal interpretation of the Christian Trinity" (*Reformers and Visionaries*, 17). Ted Shawn notes "Delsarte could not have evolved this system had he not been a deeply religious man," quoting Delsarte's statement, "'Man carries in his body, as in his substance, the sacred stamp of the adorable trinity'" (*Every Little Movement*, 210, 27). Shawn further explains how Delsarte's teachings were promoted in the United States by the Reverend William R. Alger, a Unitarian clergyman who wanted to call the system "Religious Culture" (21). For more on Alger, see William Rounseville Alger, *Life of Edwin Forrest, the American Tragedian* (Philadelphia: J. B. Lippincott, 1877), vol. 1, which includes sketches of the "Scalp Dance of the Dacotahs," John White's "A Dance of the Carolina Indians," and "Dances of the Mandan Indians," and which adroitly expresses the tensions in this period regarding Native dance's relation to theatrical drama.

4. Ruyter argues that although Stebbins deemphasized Mackaye's influence on her, "Her practical system owes a great deal to Mackaye, since everything is based on relations (or decomposing, as it was often called) and poise (equilibruim), two of Mackaye's major concepts. In addition, her exercises for various parts of the body and her 'gamuts of expression' (series of formulas for expressing any given emotion) derived at least in part from Mackaye" (*Reformers and Visionaries*, 21).

5. See picture of "Grief," "a Delsartian tableau," from Elsie M. Wilbor, *Delsarte Recitation Book*, 4th ed. enl. (New York: E. S. Werner, 1905); reprinted in Ruyter, *Reformers and Visionaries*, 16.

6. Genevieve Stebbins, *The Delsarte System of Expression* (New York: E. S. Werner, 1885).

7. Ruth St. Denis, *An Unfinished Life: An Autobiography* (New York: Harper and Brothers, 1939), 16–17; quoted in Ruyter, *Reformers and Visionaries*, 23–24.

8. Makaye, on the other hand, does seem to have more frequently situated these movement practices within dramatic narrative contexts.

9. Randy Martin, *Critical Moves: Dance Studies in Theory and Politics* (Durham: Duke University Press, 1998), 169.

10. For example, in 1901–2, Indian Commissioner William A. Jones wrote, "Indian dances and so-called Indian feasts should be prohibited. In many cases these dances and feasts are simply subterfuges to cover degrading acts and to disguise immoral purposes"; CIA Report, 1901, 14. Quoted in Prucha, *Great Father*, 764–65.

11. Gideon H. Pond, "Power and Influence of Dakota Mecicine-Men," in *Information Respecting the History, Conditions and Prospects of the Indian Tribes of the United States,* ed. Henry R. Schoolcraft (Philadelphia: Lipincott, Grombo, 1853–57), 4:641–51. Quoted in Holler, *Black Elk's Religion*, 113–14.

12. Quoted in both Prucha, *American Indian Policy in Crisis,* 187, and Holler, *Black Elk's Religion,* 120.

13. See Holler, *Black Elk's Religion,* for history and discussion of the Sun Dance.

14. Stephen E. Feraca, *Wakinyan: Contemporary Teton Dakota Religion. Studies in Plains Anthropology and History* (Browning, Mont.: Museum of the Plains Indian, 1963),

2. Quoted in Holler, *Black Elk's Religion,* 154. Feraca is referencing the statements of one of his "informants," Gilbert Bad Wound.

15. Indian commissioners sent "Instructions to Indian Agents in Regard to Wild West Shows" (Prucha, *Great Father,* 712–15), and at times, those working on reservations made reference to the phenomenon in their annual reports. In 1899, a Miss Mary C. Collins, a missionary from Standing Rock, decried "Let us have no more 'Wild West' Fourth of July," arguing that "Agents should be required to forbid dancing and painting faces" (CIA Report, 1899, 332). Whether or not they themselves were in the show's audiences, the show's hype, publicity, and depictions of "real Indians" influenced agents and other reservation officials.

16. See Paul Reddin, *Wild West Shows* (Chicago: University of Illinois Press, 1999), 55.

17. A number of recent scholars have documented and analyzed the fantastically popular phenomenon of *Buffalo Bill's Wild West* and its influence in constructing the myth of the Plains warrior as prototypical American Indian. See L. G. Moses, *Wild West Shows and the Images of American Indians, 1883–1933* (Albuquerque: University of New Mexico Press, 1996), 22.

18. Sarah J. Blackstone, *Buckskins, Bullets, and Business: A History of Buffalo Bill's Wild West* (New York: Greenwood Press, 1986), 17, 69.

19. Richard Slotkin argues that the "Buffalo Bill signature appears clearly in its characteristic confusion of the theatrical and the historical or political." I suggest that this apparent confusion instead banks on a stark separation between the two. See Richard Slotkin, "Buffalo Bill's 'Wild West' and the Mythologization of the American Empire," in *Cultures of U.S. Imperialism,* ed. Amy Kaplan and Donald Pease (Durham: Duke University Press, 1993), 168.

20. Percy Mackaye, *Epoch: The Life of Steele Mackaye, Genius of the Theatre, In Relation to His Times and Contemporaries* (New York: Boni and Liveright, 1927), 2:85.

21. These federal prohibitions of certain dances, when practiced outside the arena, continued to be referenced, even as impresarios staged some of them as part of their shows. For example, in 1889, Commissioner W. A. Jones repeated the dance restrictions in his "conditions" for which Indians might be "obtained for attendance" at the "Greater America Exposition" in Omaha, Nebraska. "The company must agree that the Indian camp shall be kept in a good sanitary condition and every precaution taken to preserve the health of the Indians. The ghost dance, sun dance, scalp dance, war dance, and other so called 'feasts' of a similar nature interdicted by the rules of this office must be prohibited" (CIA Report, 39).

22. Nebraska Ned, *Buffalo Bill and His Daring Adventures in the Romantic Wild West* (Baltimore: L. and M. Ottenheimer, 1913), 174–75; Quoted in Blackstone, *Buckskins, Bullets, and Business,* 12.

23. Quoted in Richard J. Walsh in collaboration with Milton S. Salsbury, *The Making of Buffalo Bill: A Study in Heroics* (Indianapolis: Bobbs-Merrill, 1928), 262.

24. From Queen Victoria's Journal, May 11, 1887, The Royal Archives, Windsor Castle; quoted in Joseph G. Rosa and Robin May, *Buffalo Bill and His Wild West: A Pictorial Biography* (Lawrence: University Press of Kansas, 1989), 120–21; and in Moses, *Wild West Shows,* 55.

25. Comments of Col. Tom Ochiltree. Mackaye, *Epoch,* 83.

26. Mackaye, *Epoch,* 79. Quoted from Louis E. Cooke, "Reminiscences of a Showman," *Newark Evening Star,* July 1, 1915.

27. Mackaye, *Epoch,* 83–84. Mackaye notes only that the press report appeared November 20, 1886, under the caption "The Great Playwright Teaching Indians," not where or by whom.

28. Jane Goodall, "Acting Savage," in *Body Show/s: Australian Viewings of Live Performance,* ed. Peta Tait (Amsterdam: Rodopi, 2000), 16.

29. Moses's text tells the story of the Indian participants in Wild West shows, focusing not only on the stereotypes they created, but also on the performers' roles, words, and perspectives. I follow Moses's lead in further exploring the agency invoked by these performers and involved in these performances. Other recent critics also suggest spaces of agency engaged by participants in both historical and contemporary exhibitions. See Nancy J. Parezo and John W. Troutman's "The 'Shy' Cocopa Go to the Fair," and Katie N. Johnson and Tamara Underiner's "Command Performances: Staging Native Americans at Tillicum Village," both in *Selling the Indian: Commercializing & Appropriating Indian Cultures,* ed. Carter Jones Meyer and Diana Royer (Tucson: University of Arizona Press, 2001), 3–43 and 44–61.

30. Implicit in my argument is an awareness that many of the Show Indians working with Buffalo Bill suffered from disease, loneliness, and differing degrees of exploitation during the tours, and that more than a handful died, some after leaving the show and/or being abandoned by it in Europe. Moses notes how some showmen remarked that "the travel, the tumult of cities, the going rapidly from place to place disoriented them. They felt betwitched at times" (*Wild West Shows,* 33, cited from Walsh, *Making of Buffalo Bill,* 257). The hope here is to nuance this well-known argument of Indians' exploitation with a focus on the agency that at least some of the performers also experienced.

31. In the Buffalo Bill context, these positions date back as far as Christian reformers' and missionaries' outcries at the shows' hiring of Indians, calling the shows "immoral," "unchristianizing," and "demoralizing," claiming the impresarios mistreated the Indians and that touring led to disease and exploitation (though the reformers' agenda was primarily to contain any celebration of Indianness and instead promote Christian assimiliation). For discussion of these protests, see Moses, *Wild West Shows,* especially 65–79.

Clearly, the Show Indians performed within an arena circumscribed by the desires and expectations of Cody, Salsbury, and other impresarios. Theater directors such as Steel Mackaye dictated—or at least attempted to dictate—what their performances as Indians should look like. Undoubtedly, the performers' choices of what to wear and how to act or dance were at least in part suggested by those directing the show, and likely influenced the performances themselves. However, when these requests for Indian dance or performance seemed inappropriate, the performers did place limits on what they would and would not do. For example, Moses reports how in 1887 some Sioux performers who visited a public school in New York City and sang for the children "refused to perform a 'war dance' requested by the principal of P.S. 40" (ibid., 37). Reports such as this suggest the performers were not mindlessly following the commands of those around them, but also making choices about what they would and would not perform publicly, and at times pushing back on audiences' or directors' expectations. The Indian actors and performers both worked within the theatrical structures presented them, and yet also made choices about and within those structures, themselves exploiting them for their own uses and agendas.

32. Raymond J. DeMallie, ed., *The Sixth Grandfather: Black Elk's Teachings Given to John G. Neihardt* (Lincoln: University of Nebraska Press, 1984), 246.

33. William K. Powers explains: "Among the Lakota on the Pine Ridge and Rosebud reservations, [the 'war dance'] is called 'Omaha dance,' because the dance was historically learned from the Omaha tribe." He adds, "The popularity of the term ['war dance'] probably originated with the advent of Wild West shows when non-Indian impresarios were coining promotional slogans to attract the imaginations of the general public." Powers, *War Dance*, 30. Tara Browner adds, "In the early 1840s, the Omaha sold the right to perform the dance and its songs to the Yanktonai Dakota, who soon after gave performance rights to the Teton Lakota. Both nations called the ceremony 'Omaha Dance' in honor of the people from whom they had bought it." Browner, *Heartbeat of the People,* 21. As a Lakota man dancing a dance bought from the Omaha, Black Elk was already, it seems, performing a version of Indian identity that acknowledged interrelation with other peoples, rather than any kind of pure Lakota heritage.

34. Browner, *Heartbeat of the People,* 19. Browner stresses, however, that not all experts on Grass and Omaha dancing see them as the same thing with different names. Browner points out that accounts based on Lakota oral tradition suggest that "the ancestral forms of Grass and Omaha Dances were distinct and had a single, overlapping musical style, generically referred to as 'Omaha' or War Dance songs." "Indian terminology can sometimes be deceptive to outsiders, with a single word having multiple and hidden meanings," she writes (ibid., 21).

35. Rita G. Napier, "Across the Big Water: American Indians' Perceptions of Europe and Europeans, 1887–1906," in *Indians and Europe: An Interdisciplinary Collection of Essays,* ed. Christian F. Feest (Aachen: Alano Verlag/edition herodot, 1989), 389.

36. Kills Enemy Alone to Little Whirlwind, 1889, MS 31, John L. Champe Collection, Manuscript division, Nebraska State Historical Society, Lincoln, Nebraska. Quoted in Napier, "Across the Big Water," 385.

37. *Newcastle* (England) *Daily Chronicle,* April 4, 1887. Quoted in Napier, "Across the Big Water," 386.

38. Newspaper clipping, *Daily Post,* May 8, 1887. Quoted in Napier, "Across the Big Water," 392, and Moses, *Wild West Shows,* 49.

39. "Examination of the Indians Traveling with Cody and Salsbury's Wild West Show by the Acting Commissioner of Indian Affairs," contained in Belt to Secretary of the Interior, November 18, 1890, Records of the CIA, Correspondence Land Division, LS, Vol. 104, Nov. 11–Dec. 20, 1890, Letter Book 207, 191–204, RG 74, NA. Quoted in Moses, *Wild West Shows,* 103.

40. From Seventeenth Annual Report of the Executive Committee of the Indian Rights Association (1899), 25–27; Francis Paul Prucha, *Americanizing the American Indians: Writings by "Friends of the Indian," 1880–1900* (Lincoln: University of Nebraska Press, 1978), 314.

41. Thomas J. Morgan, from Report of September 5, 1890, in House Executive Document No. 1, part 5, vol. II, 51 Congress, 2 session, serial 2841, lvii–lix. Quoted in Prucha, *Americanizing the American Indians,* 311.

42. From Eighteenth Annual Report of the Executive Committee of the Indian Rights Association (1900), 18–20. Quoted in Prucha, *Americanizing the American Indians,* 315–16.

43. McLaughlin to Burke, April 16, 1886, Maj. James McLaughlin Papers, Correspondence and Miscellaneous Papers, 1855–1937, microfilm edition, roll 20, frames 479–80, Assumption Abbey Archives (AAA), Richardton, North Dakota. Quoted in Moses, *Wild West Shows,* 31.

44. Contract, Cody and Salsbury, April 21, 1886, sent to Washington in McGillycuddy to CIA, May 1, 1886, Records of the CIA, LR, No 13400–1998, RG 75, NA. In Moses, *Wild West Shows,* 33.

45. In 1889, Commissioner of Indian Affairs John H. Oberly decried the "immoral and unchristianizing surroundings incident to such a life" of theatrical shows, further bemoaning how "the effect of traveling all over the country . . . creates a roaming and unsettled disposition and educates him in a manner entirely foreign and antagonistic to that which has been and now is the policy of the Government, as well as the aim of all good christian people who are doing so much for the welfare and benefit of the Indian" (quoted in Prucha, *Great Father,* 712). Oberly's successor, Thomas J. Morgan, sent an official circular asking Indian agents to report on the moral and physical effect of the shows.

46. J. R. Miller includes a photo of a "group of Bella Coola, who went to Germany in 1885." J. R. Miller, *Skyscrapers Hide the Heavens: A History of Indian-White Relations in Canada* (Toronto: University of Toronto Press, 1989; rev. 1991).

47. PAG, RG 10, vol. 3825, file 60, 511–12, J. A. Markle to D. Laird, September 9, 1907. Quoted in Titley, *Narrow Vision,* 172.

48. The *Globe,* September 4, 1912. Quoted in Titley, *Narrow Vision,* 174.

49. Most comprehensive among these is Mooney, *Ghost-Dance Religion,* originally published 1892–93 as Part 2 of the Fourteenth Annual Report of the Bureau of Ethnology, by the Government Printing Office. See also Prucha, *Great Father,* 726–33, and DeMallie, *Sixth Grandfather,* 269–76. For an insightful analysis of Mooney's and Black Elk's narrations, see Carlton Smith, *Coyote Kills John Wayne: Postmodernism and Contemporary Fictions of the Transcultural Frontier* (Hanover, N.H.: University of New England Press, 2000), 39–47.

50. In a post to the ASAIL listserve on Monday, September 24, 2001, Joyzelle Godfrey writes: "I think for my tribe the equivalent of the WTC massacre would be the famous, or infamous, Wounded Knee massacre. The people of the Big Foot Band were unaware of the politics of the American 'perpetrators' (another word may be more appropriate but I can't think what it would be). The reality of our history is that most of the Sioux people didn't know anything about the Ghost Dance. It's historical fact that the 'Craze' was manufactured by reporters to stir the emotions of the people in the east and of course to have something to report to their editors. Big Foot and his people were related to Sitting Bull and ran from Standing Rock in North Dakota in the middle of the winter, December, because they were afraid of being killed as Sitting Bull was killed

in their midst that day. Their intent was to escape to relatives on the Pine Ridge Reservation for safety, not to join a Craze they were most likely unaware of. The American military was responding to a manufactured threat." Cited with permission.

51. See Tharon Weighill, "The 2-Step Tales of Hahashka and Pullack'ak: Expressions of Corporeality in Aboriginal California" (PhD diss., University of California, Riverside, 2004).

52. See DeMallie, *Sixth Grandfather,* 251–56.

53. On November 15, 1890, the brand new agent at Pine Ridge, Daniel F. Royer—an inexperienced patronage appointee the Lakota called Young-Man-Afraid-Of-Indians—telegraphed Commissioner Belt: "Indians are dancing in the snow and are wild and crazy. . . . *We need protection and we need it now.*" Royer to R. V. Belt, November 15, 1890, quoted in Robert M. Utley, *Last Days of the Sioux Nation* (New Haven: Yale University Press, 1963), 111, and in Prucha, *Great Father,* 728.

54. Letters Received by the Commissioner of Indian Affairs, Ghost Dance Special Case 188, Doc. No. 1890–37076, Record Group 75, National Archives and Records Service. Quoted in DeMallie, *Sixth Grandfather,* 268.

55. The exact numbers of killed and wounded are difficult to know, as sources differ widely. These follow Mooney, *Ghost-Dance Religion,* and represent the most frequently cited numbers. Prucha, *Great Father,* 729, lists 153 Indians killed and 25 whites.

56. Mooney writes, "There can be no question that the pursuit was simply a massacre, where fleeing women, with infants in their arms, were shot down after resistance had ceased and when almost every warrior was stretched dead or dying on the ground" (*Ghost-Dance Religion,* 869).

57. Officials also tried to use the show Indians' return as a chance to dissuade interest in the Ghost Dance. On November 18, 1890, Commissioner Belt warned the nearly one hundred show Indians returning to Pine Ridge that they would find "some little excitement growing out of your religion" about the coming of a new messiah when they returned to their reservations, and told them he hoped that they would use the knowledge they'd learned on their travels to encourage loyalty among their people to the government. "Examination of the Indians Traveling with Cody and Salsbury's Wild West Show by the Acting Commissioner of Indian Affairs," contained in Belt to Secretary of the Interior, November 18, 1890, Records of the CIA, Correspondence Land Division, LS, Vol. 104, Nov. 11–Dec. 20, 1890, Letter Book 207, 204, RG 75, NA. Quoted in Moses, *Wild West Shows,* 103.

58. Cody to CIA, February 26, 1891, Records of the CIA, LR No. 7678–1891, RG 75, NA. Quoted in Moses, *Wild West Shows,* 109.

59. Morgan to Secretary of the Interior, January 2, 1891, SC 188. Quoted in Moses, *Wild West Shows,* 107.

60. Prucha writes, "In March, 1891, the partners were permitted to enroll one hundred Indians for a new European tour, including a number of Sioux who were prisoners of war at Fort Sheridan as a result of the Ghost Dance disturbances" (*American Indian Policy in Crisis,* 324).

61. From *Oakland Tribune,* August 30, 1962. Quoted in Moses, *Wild West Shows,* 125. *Dr. W. F. Carver's Wild America* performed from 1889 to 1893. Don Russell, *The*

Wild West: A History of the Wild West Shows (Fort Worth: Amon Carter Museum of Western Art, 1970), 122.

62. For example, Agent J. P. Woolsy, of the Otoe Subagency in Oklahoma, reported in 1894, "The greatest evil we have to contend with at Otoe is the insatiable desire of nearly every member of the tribe for dancing. It would not be so bad if they would indulge in harmless dances, but they have what they term the 'hand game,' and claim it to be their worship of the 'Great Spirit,' which in reality is a form of the 'ghost dance'" (CIA Report, 250). In 1895, the acting agent at Tongue River, Montana, Captain Third Infantry, George W. H. Stouch, reports triumphantly that several prominent "ghost dancers" had given up the dance. He writes, "Porcupine, who had been the representative of the so-called Messiah to the Cheyennes, a prophet and leader of the ghost dancers, was, after repeated interviews, convinced that his Messiah was a false god and said he would take my advice and make a white man of himself" (CIA Report, 198). Five years later, however, the new agent at Tongue River, J. L.Clifford, writes how among his charges, "quite a good many neglected their gardens, as they were engaged in messiah or ghost dancing." He adds: "The police have been unable entirely to stop this dancing. Porcupine and eight others are now off the reservation without authority; they are reported by their followers who are here that they have gone to be at the resurrection of the Indians and then the whites will be swept from the earth" (CIA Report, 1900, 273).

63. "Fancy Dance regalia has evolved from the older, Omaha style dance outfit," notes the narrator of a video on the history of Fancy Dance. "The older bustle was worn at the hip," the narrator continues. "The first Fancy dancers took this tradition and made it more colorful and showy." Fancy Dance, the video makes clear, is constantly evolving in relation to changing times and contexts, requiring innovation, creativity, flexibility, endurance, and strength as well as pride in and connection to Indian identity. See *Fancy Dance*, vol. 1 of the Native American Dance Series, produced by Scott Swearingen and Sandy Rhodes (Tulsa: Full Circle Videos, 1997). Browner explains that most other styles of men's powwow dancing, including those popular in competitions today, likewise have roots in the Omaha Dance—and likewise provide dancers with opportunities to explore the strength, pride, and agency in performing Indian identity.

64. See, for example, Mark Mattern, "The Pow-wow as a Public Arena for Negotiating Unity and Diversity in American Indian Life," and Luke E. Lassiter, "Southwestern Oklahoma, the Gourd Dance, and 'Charlie Brown,'" both in *Contemporary Native American Cultural Issues*, ed. Duane Champagne (Walnut Creek, Calif.: AltaMira Press, 1999), 129–44 and 145–66. For a helpful overview of the literature on powwow, see Vincent H. Whipple Jr.,"Perspectives on Identity in the Lakota Ceremony of Hunkapi and the American Indian Pow-wow" (master's thesis, UCLA, 2001).

65. Browner summarizes Joan Weibel-Orlando's argument characterizing powwows as "inauthentic renditions of a glorified past, simulations without internal cultural referents, and elaborate ethnic theaters where Indians construct an idealized identity and present it to outsiders" (*Heartbeat of the People*, 2). See Joan Weibel-Orlando, *Indian Country L.A.: Maintaining Ethnic Community in a Complex Society* (Urbana: University of Illinois Press, 1991).

66. Tharon Weighill, PhD qualifying exam, University of California, Riverside, 5.

67. Ibid., 10–11.

68. Sherman Alexie, "Powwow," from *The Business of Fancydancing* (New York: Hanging Loose Press, 1992), 52.

69. In Canada, where Christianity as state policy remained steadfast, no such turn to theatricality was needed.

3. ANTIDANCE RHETORIC AND AMERICAN INDIAN ARTS IN THE 1920S

1. Leah Dilworth, *Imagining Indians in the Southwest: Persistent Visions of a Primitive Past* (Washington, D.C.: Smithsonian Institution Press, 1996), 82. Antonin Artaud, Rudolf Laban, D. H. Lawrence, Mary Austin, Georgia O'Keefe, and Willa Cather are among those for whom the Southwest provided artistic and intellectual fodder.

2. See Kathleen L. Howard and Diana F. Pardue, *Inventing the Southwest: The Fred Harvey Company and Native American Art* (Hong Kong: Northland Publishing, 1996).

3. In a 1928 article on the "Indian Detours," Austin describes viewing Indian dance as part of these excursions. Huntington Library, Mary Austin files (AU 244).

4. Arrell Morgan Gibson, *The Santa Fe and Taos Colonies: Age of the Muses, 1900–1942* (Norman: University of Oklahoma Press, 1983), 97.

5. May O'Donnell, interview with the author, March 29, 2002, New York City.

6. Sylvia Rodríguez, *The Matachines Dance: Ritual Symbolism and Interethnic Relations in the Upper Río Grande Valley* (Albuquerque: University of New Mexico Press, 1996), 110.

7. Jill D. Sweet, "Tewa Ceremonial Performances: The Effects of Tourism on an Ancient Pueblo Dance and Music Tradition" (PhD diss., Univeristy of New Mexico, 1981), 79.

8. For example, daily at the 1915 Painted Desert Exposition in San Diego. See Howard and Pardue, *Inventing the Southwest*, 73.

9. Luke Lyon, "History of Prohibition of Photography of Southwestern Indian Ceremonies," in *Reflections: Papers on Southwestern Culture History, in Honor of Charles H. Lange,* ed. Anne V. Poore (Santa Fe: Papers of the Archaeological Society of New Mexico, 1988), 238–72.

10. Sweet notes how "Secrecy has served the Tewa well as a device for protecting their ritual events from outside interference. Researchers and tourists quickly learn that most Tewa do not like to talk about their dances with outsiders and they consider direct questions to be rude. In fact, the most common complaint about the visitors who come to see dances is that they ask too many questions." Jill D. Sweet, "The Beauty, Humor, and Power of Tewa Pueblo Dance," in *Native American Dance,* ed. Heth, 89.

11. For more on the visual experience of Southwest tourism, and its symbolic fixation on Indians, see Sylvia Rodríguez, "The Tourist Gaze, Gentrification, and the Commodification of Subjetivity in Taos," in *Essays on the Changing Images of the Southwest,* ed. Richard Francaviglia and David Narrett (College Station: Texas A&M University Press, 1994), 105–26.

12. Cited in Prucha, *Great Father,* 801. Full text in BIA RG 75, Orders, Circulars, and Circular letters, Box no. &, PI-164, E–132, HM 1995, National Archives and Records Service. All further citations to Circular no. 1665 from this source.

13. See Titley, *Narrow Vision,* 176.

14. Titley cites PAC, RG 10, vol. 3826, file 60, 511–14A. He writes "An RCMP crime report dated 26 June, 1921 at For Francis, Ontario noted that Jim Kubinase was sent to Winnipeg jail for two months for organizing a sun dance at Buffalo Point, Manitoba. Another report in November 1921 announced that four Blood Indians were sent to Lethbridge jail for participating in a 'give away' dance" (*Narrow Vision,* 223, n. 67).

15. Letter reprinted in Heather Elton, ed., *Chinook Winds Aboriginal Dance Project* (Banff, Alberta: Banff Centre Press, 1997), 10.

16. In October 1922, a year and a half after Burke issued Circular no. 1665, a group of Christian missionaries working "in the Sioux country" issued their own series of recommendations to the U.S. Indian office. These included limiting Indian dancing to one day a month, during daylight hours, for seven of twelve months (excluding farming months); limits on the age of the dancers such that "none take part in the dances or be present who are under 50 years of age"; coordinated efforts to persuade fair managers "not to commercialize the Indian by soliciting his attendance in large numbers for show purposes"; and that the government cooperate closely with the missionaries "in those matters which affect the moral welfare of the Indians." In addition, the missionaries suggested "that a careful propaganda be undertaken to educate public opinion against the dance and to provide a healthy substitute." BIA files, RG 75, OIA CCF, General Service O63, 10429–1922. All subsequent citations to letters held in BIA files from this location.

17. Copy of letter in Huntington Library, Mary Austin files (AU 4918).

18. This is the same rhetoric employed in the Dawes Act of 1887, in which land was allotted to Indians to teach them private land ownership and farming, as otherwise the land they held was going to "waste."

19. Meritt continued to stress the central importance of their policy in the production of Indians as "competent citizens." The April 23, 1923, letter from Meritt to Gertrude Fly of Des Moines is typical: "Their prevailing nomadic and communal tendencies, and their traditional inclination to give much time to dances, ceremonies, and gatherings of various kinds are a very serious obstacle to the individualism and self-assertion they must learn and practice if they ever are to escape a state of dependence and become really competent citizens."

20. It reads, "The real objections to the dance are that it is reactionary, glorifies and makes prominent the more objectionable class of Indians, diminishes the interest of the Indians in their church work, discourages the missionaries, destroyes [sic] the interest of the Indians in industrial pursuits, isolates the Indians from the whites, is inimical to the educational efforts of the schools, and in fact has no place in the program we have to the Indian and to which he must subscribe if he is to survive."

21. Nebraska Agent F. T. Mann likewise reported difficulties. In a May 16, 1923, letter Mann writes, "I have spoken to a number of the more intelligent Indians in regard to their dances, etc., and have asked them to prepare statements but they are slow in

doing so and I am sending this report in the belief that it will furnish the Office the necessary information."

22. For a discussion of the Hopi Snake dance, see Dilworth, *Imagining Indians,* 21–75. Dilworth writes that although the dance "was not forbidden, it was not encouraged. It was not outlawed in part because it was such a big tourist attraction; the railroads promoted it and tourists demanded it" (62).

23. Burke wrote on April 4, 1924, to Senator James W. Wadsworth Jr., who had apparently questioned the commissioner's position on the Snake Dance: "The Indians by virtue of this recognized guardianship are in some sense legally and morally the children of the Government, and however religiously sincere they may be in performing with rattlesnakes in their mouths we would feel very neglectful of their spiritual welfare if we did not advise against such a dangerous and gruesome practice. It is hardly conceivable that your correspondent, if she has children, would permit them without a word of parental admonition to adopt the snake dance or some equally disgusting rite, however morbidly fascinated they might have become by it."

24. For example, the superintendent at the Sac and Fox Sanatorium in Toledo, Ohio, wrote to Burke on May 23 regarding the complaints that John Morgan (John Witonisee) and Sam Sissewln (Sam Lincoln) have lodged regarding the antidance circulars.

25. Prohibitions on "polygamy" and "immorality," previously listed separately from the antidance strictures, are in these circulars listed as part of them.

26. See Kenneth R. Philp, *John Collier's Crusade for Indian Reform, 1920–1934* (Tucson: University of Arizona Press, 1977), 59–60. Philp is quoting William E. Johnson, "Those Sacred Indian Ceremonials," *The Native American* 24 (September 20, 1924), 173–77.

27. Dominick Long Bull and Samuel White Eagle, who identified themselves as "full-blooded Indians of the Sioux nation" wrote to Burke on December 21, 1924, asking for help in upholding antidance restrictions, and noting the effects on marriage relations the dances have had. "Children are born outside of wedlock; this comes from Owl dancing. This Owl dancing is breaking up families where the marriage relation has been sacredly kept in the past," the letter they signed (again, possibly penned with the help of others) stated. BIA files.

28. Sharon O'Brien, *American Indian Tribal Governments* (Norman: University of Oklahoma Press, 1989), 166–68.

29. See ibid., 80.

30. Huntington Library, Mary Austin files (AU 4918).

31. Letters note how other Southwest Pueblo peoples also organized to protest the restrictions. R. J. Bauman, superintendent of Zuni Indian School of Blackrock, N.M., reported to Burke on April 20, 1923, "that the communication was received with considerable apprehension by the Indians of this jurisdiction." He writes, "The officers of the tribe came to me a couple of times for the letter to be explained to them. They held several councils on the matter. I am now in receipt of an unsigned copy of a letter purporting to be written by the officers of the tribe wherein they complain to a considerable extent about a move to deprive them of their old time dances and ceremonials (They claim all their dances are ceremonial) but in the letter they agree to in the future have no give away of any articles which they buy. They desire to be permitted to retain

the custom of giving away native corn and bread at one or two dances, as this is part of a ceremonial. They agree to make the dances shorter and less frequent. They assure me of their desire to conform to the wishes of 'Washington' in all matters." Bauman's letter is typical of those accompanying any letter of protest from an Indian. These letters, from the superintendent of the agency the letter comes from, give background on (often discounting the reputation of) the writer. For example, in May 1923 a man named White Pigeon apparently wrote to the Bureau, expressing his support for continuing the dances. While his letter is not in the files, included is a letter from the superintendent at Grand Rapids Agency, Wisconsin, W. E. Dunn. Dunn writes that White Pigeon, "a half breed Winnebago and Patawatomie, aged about 72 years, . . . is an intelligent person of the old non-progressive class and considers himself a leader, and does by promoting dances cause able bodied men to neglect their farm work." Dunn continues, "If these Indians are to become good useful citizens they must cease to live as old time Indians and leave behind their old customs and not put off their tasks until tomorrow, and strive to become producers instead of consumers."

32. O'Brien, *American Indian Tribal Governments,* 169; John Collier, "The Pueblos Last Stand: If the Arizona and New Mexico Tribes Lose Their Land, Their Ancient Civilization Dies," *Sunset Magazine,* February 1923, 19–22; 65–66.

33. As usual, the letter is accompanied by a letter from the superintendent at the Tongue River Agency, with background on Standing Elk. "In connection with the letter I will say that the writer, Eugene Standingelk, is one of our very best Indians and one on whom I can rely for a supporter in all progressive movements among his people. He was one of the Indian judges for a time and although his resignation was asked for by the Office because of criticism of one of his decisions, I will say that as a whole he was the best Indian Judge I have known in the service."

34. For discussion of how a kind of "modernist primitivism" gained currency in the 1920s among artists and writers who sought answers to the materialism, commercialization, and spiritual "weightlessness" of the modern by turning, especially, to "primitive" cultures, see Dilworth, *Imagining Indians,* 173–77. While Picasso, for example, turned to African masks, the American "modernist" artists I reference in what follows turned especially to Southwest Native American rituals, chants, and dances.

35. For more on Austin, see ibid., 174–82.

36. Hodge, chairman and director of the Museum of the American Indian, wrote these comments in response to a questionnaire Austin sent out in 1923 to prominent experts on Indian culture, asking about sexual impropriety and Indian dances. Huntington Library, Mary Austin files (AU 2767).

37. Huntington Library, Mary Austin files (AU 51).

38. See Deloria, *Playing Indian,* 122; 135–40. Deloria writes how between 1929 and 1931 Dakota linguist and novelist Ella Deloria taught Camp Fire Girls Native songs, dances, and philosophies. Other examples abound: a 1922 article announces a prize for Camp Fire Girls who "Dramatize an Indian Legend at Camp," noting that the legends "must be authentic." In the late 1920s, another Camp Fire Girls newsletter instructed leaders on what to do "If you give an Indian Party," noting that holding such a party "might be a fine opportunity for telling an interesting Indian legend, or giving your Indian song or dance." In another magazine article from the period, Bernard S. Mason

invited readers to "Learn to Indian Dance" and described "Indian dance" techniques and footwork, accompanied by diagrams of moccasined feet moving up and down. Concert recital presentations of Indian music flourished as well. Documents included in the Huntington Library, Mary Austin files (AU Box 128).

39. A June 11, 1923, editorial in the Arizona *Journal-Miner,* asking, "Shall the Snake Dance Go?" argues against Burke's decree because it would apply not only to the Hopis, but also to the Smokis. "While Commissioner Burke addressed his letter to all Indians, it is plain from his text that along with all the dances of the Pueblo settlements, the Hopi rituals upon which the dramatic ceremonies of the Smoki are based, will have to go." BIA files.

40. Mary Austin, "Native Drama in Our Southwest," *The Nation,* April 20, 1927, 437–40.

41. Mary Austin, "American Indian Dance-Drama," *Yale Review,* June 1930, 14; manuscript in Huntington Library, Mary Austin files (AU 7).

42. The letter continues, "And, above all, never put material in the hands of the child and allow him to draw according to his own inclinations. Direct him in all of his work and especially in drawing." Huntington Library, Mary Austin files (AU 4960).

43. Austin, "American Indian Dance-Drama," 13.

44. Austin apparently took this point up with the secretary of the interior, Ray Lyman Wilbur, in the fall of 1929, urging him to support a plan by which to "make the art work of the Indians profitable and go far to keep their art not only alive but growing." June 30, 1930, Letter from Ray Lyman Wilbur, the secretary of the interior, to Austin, Huntington Library, Mary Austin files (AU 5245).

4. AUTHENTIC THEMES

1. Jane Sherman writes, for example, of a 1924 book by Troy and Margaret West Kinney, *The Dance: Its Place in Art and Life,* 66–67, that exemplifies such attitudes about "the aboriginal savage" who "bounds through dances fitted to the limitations of muscles that can not be controlled by brain." Jane Sherman, "The American Indian Imagery of Ted Shawn," *Dance Chronicle,* 1989, 366–82.

2. Several nationally prominent choreographers spent winters in the area, teaching at the famous Taos and Santa Fe artist colonies (both colonies supported schools for instruction in ballet and modern dance) and giving private dance lessons. Gibson, *Santa Fe and Taos Colonies,* 96–97.

3. Sherman, "American Indian Imagery," 369. The piece was called "Dagger Dance."

4. Shawn's interest carried over to the dancers in his company as well. His principal dancer (and his lover from 1931 to 1948), Barton Mumaw, choreographed his own solo in 1939 based on Prescott's "The God of Lightening," and in 1947 danced as Wild Horse in Helen Tamaris's choreography for *Annie Get Your Gun.*

5. Erick Hawkins, *The Body Is a Clear Place and Other Statements on Dance* (Princeton: Princeton Book, 1992), 55.

6. New York Public Library [NYPL] Dance Collection, MGZB, Horton, Lester.

7. Larry Warren, *Lester Horton, Modern Dance Pioneer* (Princeton: Dance Horizons/ Princeton Book, 1977).

8. NYPL Dance Collection, MGZB, Horton, Lester.

9. Ted Shawn, *Gods Who Dance* (New York: E. P. Dutton, 1929), xiii.

10. Lester Horton, "American Indian Dancing," *American Dancer,* June 1929, 9, 31–32. Quoted in Warren, *Lester Horton,* 29.

11. Julia L. Foulkes, "Dance Is for American Men: Ted Shawn and the Intersection of Gender, Sexuality, and Nationalism in the 1930s," in *Dancing Desires: Choreographing Sexualities On & Off the Stage,* ed. Jane C. Desmond (Madison: Wisconsin University Press, 2001), 113–46.

12. Michaels has argued that in the mid-1920s, attempts to exclude American Indians from U.S. citizenship flip sided, and instead Indianness came to signal a true Americanness that was inheritable. "If identification with the Indian could function at the turn of the century as a *refusal* of American identity—in effect, as a refusal of American citizenship—it would come to function by the early 1920s as the *assertion* of an American identity that could be understood as going beyond citizenship." He argues this was a way of rhetorically discounting the rights to U.S. citizenship of the waves of newly arrived immigrants. Walter Benn Michaels, *Our America: Nativism, Modernism, and Pluralism* (Durham: Duke University Press, 1995), 30–32, 44.

13. Sharon O'Brien notes that Congress passed the Indian Citizenship Act of 1924 largely in response to the patriotic contribution of an estimated ten thousand young Indian men in World War I. O'Brien, *American Indian Tribal Governments,* 80. Prucha discusses ways the Citizenship Act pushed Indians into citizenship, and notes the Citizenship Act did not automatically bring with it voting rights for Indians, instead leaving voting rights up to individual states. "In fact Indians were prohibited from voting in a number of western states, and not until 1948 did Arizona and New Mexico extend the franchise to them," he writes. Prucha, *Great Father,* 794.

14. For more on the visual experience of Southwest tourism, and its symbolic fixation on Indians, see Rodríguez, "Tourist Gaze."

15. Erna Fergusson, *Dancing Gods: Indian Ceremonials of New Mexico and Arizona* (Albuquerque: University of New Mexico Press, 1931; repr. 1991), 46.

16. This marked the beginning of increasing restrictions on non-Indian observation and photography of Indian ritual practices, from the banning of photography at the Hopi Snake Dance at Walpi starting in 1913–15 to the prohibition of photography of all Hopi ceremonies in the late 1920s. Existing photos of the ceremony date until 1923, the same year Shawn staged his ballet. Lyon, "History of Prohibition of Photography."

17. In "The Case of the Hopi," James Willard Schultz (*Sunset Magazine,* October 1921) describes how missionary intrusion at Hopi villages in the late 1910s was resented (22).

18. Michelle Raheja, "Legalized Identities: Reading the Indian Arts and Crafts Act," presented at the California American Studies Association conference, Riverside, Calif., May 7, 2002.

19. This strain, in which American Indian dance serves the economic and spiritual needs of white Americans, continues not only in the work of early modern dancers, but also in more recent productions such as the Broadway production "Spirit."

20. Martha Graham, *Blood Memory* (New York: Doubleday, 1991), 176.

21. Ted Shawn, *Dance We Must* (New York: Haskell House, 1974), 117.

22. In 1934—the same year the U.S. ban on Indian ceremonial dancing was officially taken off the books—Shawn opened the company's second program with *Primitive Rhythms,* which began with another "Indian" piece, "Ponca Indian Dance," and continued with a revival of a 1923 Shawn solo called "Hopi Indian Eagle Dance." And in 1936, his solo "La Noche Triste de Moctezuma" was the opening act of an evening-length piece, *O, Libertad!*

23. Shawn reference in *American Ballet;* Fergusson, *Dancing Gods,* 54.

24. Rosalie Jones/Daystar, "Speaking Out," *Rochester Democrat and Chronicle,* March 30, 2000. Jones's comments follow her viewing of the Shawn *Eagle Dance* tape I lent her after our interview on June 13, 1999.

25. In this sense it shared much with the work of modernist modern dancers of the 1930s. Unlike left-wing radical dancers who sought to represent the needs of workers and who saw connections between their dancing and left-wing political reform, as scholar Mark Franko notes, Shawn's dance was inspired not by the position of those he represented, but by his own agenda. Mark Franko, *The Work of Dance: Labor, Movement, and Identity in the 1930s* (Middletown, Conn.: Wesleyan University Press, 2002).

26. This deployment of Indianness to further European American gender agendas has a long history as well. Recently, contemporary gay theorists have used the figure of the "berdache" (a term first used by French explorers to describe male Native Americans who specialized in the work of women and formed emotional and sexual relationships with other men) to provide a history of American homosexuality as a basis for promoting gay rights. Laguna/Sioux writer Paula Gunn Allen, for example, criticizes a 1986 book by Walter L. Williams for the way it "serves to bolster his sense of the acceptability of gayness." Once again, she writes, Native people's "attitudes, beliefs, and religious practices are used in greater America to authorize its own proclivities, and this use seldom redounds to the benefit of native people." See Paula Gunn Allen, review of Walter L. Williams, *The Spirit and the Flesh: Sexual Diversity in American Indian Culture, American Indian Quarterly* 13 (Winter 1989), 109–10.

27. Foulkes has outlined this rhetoric in depth, and her article, "Dance Is for American Men," provides a helpful analysis of Shawn's interests in promoting virile masculinity.

28. For example, for Shawn, "masculine" subject matter is "the 'magic' primitive dance," "religion, worship, etc.," "labour," "play," and dance as "pure art," and masculine music is "where the stress is on the time-beat or rhythmic pulse," in four-four or two-four time, slow and heavy and marked forte, and in which the phrasing is rough and abrupt. On the other hand, he says, "throughout the ages women's dances have been mainly romantic and sexual dances," where "women dances to display herself and arouse male desire," and in "feminine music" the stress is "on the melodic quality," in three-four, three-eight, or six-eight time, is light and fast, and with legato phrasing, and so forth (*Dance We Must,* 121–22).

29. Shawn was not alone in this endeavor. Erick Hawkins, too, used the Indian dancing he saw in the Southwest to negotiate a tenable masculinity for himself in the 1930s. "I had to see and feel whether a grown man could dance without being a fool,"

he writes. "That was a wonderful summer for me, for it set my soul at rest" (Hawkins, *The Body is a Clear Place,* 55).

30. Walter Terry, *Ted Shawn: Father of American Dance* (New York: Dial Press, 1976), 76.

31. Christina L. Schlundt, *Ted Shawn and His Men Dancers: A Chronology and an Index of Dances, 1933–1940* (New York: New York Public Library, 1967), 31.

32. Jane Sherman and Barton Mumaw, *Barton Mumaw, Dancer: From Denishawn to Jacob's Pillow and Beyond* (New York: Dance Horizons, 1986), 82.

33. Christina L. Schlundt, *Professional Appearances of Ted Shawn and His Men Dancers: A Chronolgy and Index of Dances 1933–1940* (New York: New York Public Library, Astor, Lenox and Tilden Foundation, 1967), 25.

34. Quoted in Foulkes, "Dance Is for American Men," 113, from "A Defense of the Male Dancer," *New York Dramatic Mirror,* May 13, 1916, 19.

35. André Marty, "Nijinsky as Narcisse," 1911. Published in *Comedia Illustré* (June 15, 1912) and in Ballet Russe souvenir programs, and in *Collection des Plus Beaux Numeros de Comedia Illustré,* 1921. Thanks to Tirza Latimer for bringing this print to my attention.

36. Susan Leigh Foster, "Closets Full of Dances: Modern Dance's Performance of Masculinity and Sexuality," in *Dancing Desires,* ed. Desmond, 166.

37. For example, the pop band The Village People, that 1970s and 1980s icon of gay culture, was formed, according to the band's official Web site, when "producer/composer Jacques Morali found Felipe [Rose] dancing in his Indian costume in a crowd in NY's Greenwich Village. Felipe's special visual attraction brought the idea to mind to put together a group of Village icons from various American social groups" (http://www.officialvillagepeople.com/History%20page.html). Thanks to Jens Richard Giersdorf for conversations on this topic.

38. Rosalie M. Jones, "Modern Native Dance: Beyond Tribe and Tradition," in *Native American Dance,* ed. Heth, 170.

39. Rosalie Jones, interview with the author, June 13, 1999, Santa Fe, New Mexico.

40. Shawn also promoted performances of American Indian material by non–Native American performers at Jacob's Pillow. These included Reginald and Gladys Laubin, who presented dances of the Plains Indians in 1947; La Meri, who presented Plains Indian Sign Talk Songs in 1950; and Shawn himself, who portrayed Saturiba, the Indian Chief, in a 1948 dance called "Minuet for Drums," based on Stefan Lorant's book *The New World.*

41. As numerous literary critics have noted, Longfellow's *Song of Hiawatha* "exemplifies the primitivist notion of the tragic but inevitable disappearance of Indigenous North American peoples and cultures in the march of progress and thus provided an 'enabling myth' for nineteenth-century British colonialism as well as American dispossession of Indian lands." See Hertha Wong, review of Helen Carr, *Inventing the American Primitive: Politics, Gender and the Representation of Native American Literary Traditions, 1789–1936, American Quarterly* 52, no. 1 (March 2000), 189–92. See also critiques by Henry Nash Smith, Roy Harvey Pearce, Richard Slotkin, Annette Kolodny, Robert Berkhofer, and others on this subject. Slotkin notes how Hiawatha "dies, and, in

dying, gives the land to the white man's keeping." He adds, "The newcome white men, by contrast, will live up to Hiawatha's teachings better than Hiawatha's own people." Richard Slotkin, *Regeneration through Violence: The Mythology of the American Frontier, 1600–1860* (Hanover: Wesleyan University Press, 1973), 366.

42. W. B. Seabrook, *The Magic Island* (New York: Harcourt Brace, 1929). Noted in Warren, *Lester Horton,* 37.

43. Larry Warren, "Starting from Indiana," *Dance Perspectives* 31 (Autumn 1967), 5–19.

44. See Warren, *Lester Horton,* 7–8, and Jana Frances-Fischer, "The Life and Work of Lester Horton," in Marjorie B. Perces, Ana Marie Forsythe, and Cheryl Bell, *The Dance Technique of Lester Horton* (Princeton: Dance Horizons, 1992), 4.

45. Dorothi Bock Pierre, "From Primitive to Modern," *American Dancer,* October 1937, 14.

46. Margaret Lloyd, "Modern Dance on the West Coast," in *The Borzoi Book of Modern Dance* (Princeton: Dance Horizons, 1949), 279.

47. Bella Lewitzky, "A Vision of Total Theater," *Dance Perspectives* 31 (Autumn 1967), 46.

48. Bella Lewitzky, Oral History, UCLA Research Library's Special Collections, URLSCRA-STAX 300/508, Tape Number: II, Side Two (June 18, 1991), 77–78. Thanks to Susan Rose, Bridget Murname, and University of Southern California Specialized Libraries & Archival Collections Librarian Melinda K. Hayes for help in locating this material.

49. *Lester Horton: Genius on the Wrong Coast,* directed by Lelia Goldoni (Hollywood: Green River Road/VDI, 1993).

50. Ibid.

51. Larry Warren, personal e-mail correspondence, November 3, 2002.

52. See, for example, Deidre Sklar, *Dancing with the Virgin: Body and Faith in the Fiesta of Tortugas, New Mexico* (Berkeley: University of California Press, 2001).

53. See the comments of Georgina Martinez, chapter 9.

54. Belinda James, interview with the author, December 27, 2000, New York City.

55. See *Lester Horton: Genius on the Wrong Coast* video; see also William Weaver, "Giant Step in the West: An Impression of Lester Horton's Career," *Dance Magazine,* January 1954, 34–37.

56. Warren *(Lester Horton)* notes, for example, how Horton's work is discussed under "The Black Dance" in Walter Terry's 1956 *The Dance in America* (53).

57. Alvin Ailey, "Foreword," in Perces, Forsythe, and Bell, *Dance Technique,* xiii.

58. Siobhán Arnatsiaq-Murphy, "Journal Entry," in *Chinook Winds,* ed. Elton, 40.

59. Warren *(Lester Horton)* notes an instance, during the "Choreo '52" season performance of "Prado de Pena," when James Truitte, playing the role of the lover, Victor, was about to make his entrance. "Horton stepped out of the shadows and whispered, 'Dance it with your balls,'" Warren writes (169).

60. Ailey, "Foreword," in Perces, Forsythe, and Bell, *Dance Technique,* xiii.

61. Thanks to Mark Franko for this observation. Franko notes these leftist dancers were also, like Native American dance and Horton (and unlike modernist dancers

interested in individual expression), dancing to effect change in the world. Personal correspondence, August 18, 2004.

5. HER POINT OF VIEW

1. "Copland Script," written between May 29, 1943, and July 10, 1943, held in the Music Division of the Library of Congress, Box 255, folder 22. Used by permission of the Aaron Copland Fund for Music, Inc., copyright owner of the works of Aaron Copland.

2. In the second version of the script, dated July 10, 1943, much of this remains the same, with only minor alterations in the language of the descriptions Graham uses. A major difference, however, lies in the ending. In the second script, rather than signaling the end of the piece, the Indian Girl is only part of the close; she "stands revealed in the shadows" as the town settles down for the night (6). Another difference is that in the second version, the description of the Indian Girl sitting at the mother's feet as if she were being told the story has been cut.

3. In a 1951 letter, Graham mentions the times how she and a friend "went on picnics and saw Indian dances." Graham, *Blood Memory*, 193.

4. Merle Armitage, ed., *Martha Graham: The Early Years* (New York: Da Capo Press, 1937; repr. 1985), 99.

5. O'Donnell, interview. May O'Donnell was ninety-six at the time of this interview and unclear as to the exact year of these trips.

6. Marie Marchowsky in *Martha Graham: The Evolution of Her Dance Theory and Training 1926–1991*, ed. Marian Horosko (Chicago: a cappella books, 1991).

7. Ernestine Stodell, *Deep Song: The Dance Story of Martha Graham* (New York: Schirmer, 1984), 74.

8. Tobi Tobias, "A Conversation with May O'Donnell," *Ballet Review* 9, no. 1 (Spring 1981), 74.

9. Critics both at the time and later equate this early work with a kind of adolescent provincialism. In 1931, John Martin wrote of *Primitive Mysteries*, "its simplicity of form and its evocation of the childlike religious elevation of a primitive people never falter for a moment" (Armitage, *Martha Graham*, 11). Lincoln Kirstein later bemoaned his own earlier failure to appreciate the "genuinely primitive expression" (26) of the first Graham works he had seen.

10. Agnes de Mille, *Martha: The Life and Work of Martha Graham* (New York: Vintage, 1956; repr. 1992), 181–82. Franko also discusses the way the piece "established an unhurried and deliberate rhythm, placing the spectator in an expectant, but likewise meditative, state of mind" (*Work of Dance*, 63) and discusses the response of its "cathartic opening-night audience" (65).

11. Ramsay Burt, *Alien Bodies: Representations of Modernity, "Race," and Nation in Early Modern Dance* (New York: Routledge, 1998), 186–87.

12. Burt, ibid., 182, writes that Betty Schoenberg says "Graham brought back 'Santos' from New Mexico—simple carved wooden saints made by Spanish-American Catholics—and that these were the inspiration for some of the stark, simple gestures

dancers take up in many of the tableaux." He is drawing from an interview with Schoenberg by Deborah Jowett, *Ballet Review* 9, no. 1 (Spring 1981), 31–63.

13. John Martin, *America Dancing* (New York: Dodge Publishing, 1936), 195–97.

14. See Tobias, "Conversation with May O'Donnell," 81.

15. Mark Franko, *Dancing Modernism/Performing Politics* (Indianapolis: University of Indiana Press, 1995), 47.

16. *Three Dances by Martha Graham,* with the Martha Graham Dance Company. Great Performances: Dance in America television series, aired December 28, 1992. Cámeras Continentales LA SEPT in association with Thirteen/WNET. Filmed Nov. 1991 at the Paris Opera Ballet.

17. Mentioned in Don McDonagh, *Martha Graham* (New York: Popular Library, 1975), 158–59, cited by Manning, *Modern Dance, Negro Dance,* 284.

18. See Wayne D. Shirley, "For Martha," *Ballet Review* 27, no. 4 (Winter 1999), 66–67. This article traces the correspondence between Graham, those commissioning *Appalachian Spring,* and the composers she was working with, including Aaron Copland. *Land Be Bright* was performed March 14, 1942, at the Chicago Civic Opera House (McDonagh, *Martha Graham,* 317); correspondence to Aaron Copland regarding the funding of what would become *Appalachian Spring* began July 23 of that year. By August 2, 1942, Graham had submitted a detailed script "of the idea and the action" to Copland.

19. Franko takes issue with Manning's characterization of modern dance of this period (referring to Helen Tamiris's 1937 *How Long Brethren*) as "metaphorical minstrelsy," and argues that at the time, "'speaking for' oppressed African Americans was not construed as appropriating identity from black subject positions," and calling such an argument "historically unwarranted revisionism" (Franko, *Work of Dance,* 93). Elsewhere, he suggests an alternative to Manning's analysis of Graham's *American Document,* arguing that the piece's aesthetic, understood in its historical moment, is rooted in international antifascism, not just domestic economic and racial issues. Mark Franko, "L'utopie antifasciste: American Document de Martha Graham," in *Etre ensemble: Figures de la communauté en danse depuis le XXe siècle,* ed. Claire Rousier (Paris: Centre national de la danse, 2003), 193–210.

20. John Martin, "Graham Group Offers Novelty," *New York Times,* May 10, 1944. Quoted in Manning, *Modern Dance, Negro Dance,* 140.

21. See Shirley, "For Martha," 91.

22. Hart Crane, "The Bridge," from the *Norton Anthology of American Literature,* ed. Nina Baym (New York: Norton, 1985), 2:1380.

23. See Annette Kolodny, *The Lay of the Land: Metaphor as Experience and History in American Life and Letters* (Chapel Hill: University of North Carolina Press, 1975).

24. Robert S. Tilton, *Pocahontas: The Evolution of an American Narrative* (New York: Cambridge University Press, 1994), 19.

25. In the 1976 video version produced for Nonesuch Dance Collection, the Bride is danced by Yuriko Kimura. Miki Orihara dances the Bride in the version photographed in the Fall 1999 *Ballet Review,* in the same company where Rika Okamoto dances the Virgin in *Primitive Mysteries.*

26. This hair arrangement appears in photos of the pioneer woman in a 1959

film version (see photo accompanying Arthur Knight, "Dance in the Movies," *Dance Magazine,* April 1959) and in a 1958 photo of Graham as the Bride; see Graham, *Blood Memory,* 239.

27. See, for example, McDonagh, *Martha Graham,* 180.

28. "Script for Aaron Copland—from Martha Graham," undated, in the Music Division of the Library of Congress, 3 and 2. Quoted in Peter M. Rutkoff and William B. Scott, "Appalachian Spring: A Collaboration and a Transition," *Prospects: An Annual of American Cultural Studies* 20 (1995), 216. In the second script, this is changed to "the Eve of this Genesis."

29. O'Donnell noted that Graham rarely discussed her visions or ideas for the pieces she was working on (interview). Graham dancer Helen McGehee's recollections were similar. "I don't remember any specific reference in rehearsals to Native American influence. I know she loved the art and dances—she owned some paintings and figures and rugs," McGehee wrote. McGehee explained further, "My work with Martha Graham started in 1942. The early 40s were when she began creating her 'Greek' pieces. But any artist, especially Martha, will not cast off previous influences—they become the property and the make-up of his culture and continue, however indefinitely, to be influences." Helen McGehee, personal communication, July 2002. Thanks to Karen W. Hubbard and Pam Risenboover for enabling this correspondence.

30. Chadwick Allen, "Blood (and) Memory," *American Literature* 71, no. 1 (March 1999), 94.

31. See M. Annette Jaimes, "Federal Indian Identification Policy: A Usurpation of Indigenous Sovereignty in North America," in *The State of Native America: Genocide, Colonization, and Resistance,* ed. M. Annette Jaimes (Boston: South End Press, 1992), 123–38.

32. See Juan Valenzuela, "Roots, Branches, and Blossoms," in *New Dimensions in Dance Research: Anthropology and Dance—The American Indian. CORD Research Annual VI,* The Proceedings of the Third Conference on Research in Dance, ed. Tamara Comstock (New York: Committee on Research in Dance, 1972), 299–306; see also *Dance On With Billie Mahoney,* "Special Guest: Juan Valenzuela" (video interview, March 25, 1986).

33. For a discussion of the term "blood memory," see Allen, "Blood (and) Memory." Graham's 1991 autobiography doesn't acknowledge the Native American inflection of the term "blood memory" as the signature trope of Kiowa writer N. Scott Momaday's 1968 Pulitzer Prize–winning novel *House Made of Dawn.*

34. The widespread and racist adopting-out of poor and underprivileged Indian children thought to be better off with non-Indian families led to the Indian Child Welfare Act of 1978, which recognized tribal rights to jurisdiction over such adoptions. For discussion of the Indian Child Welfare Act, see Prucha, *Great Father,* 1153–57.

35. Prucha notes that by April 1944 there were "21,756 Indians, exclusive of officers, in the fighting forces." *Great Father,* 1005–6.

36. Prucha notes that comments such as these made in 1944 by Secretary of the Interior Harold L. Ickes, about "the inherited talents of the Indian" as one with "endurance, rhythm, a feeling for timing, co-ordination, sense perception, an uncanny ability to get over any sort of terrain at night, and, better than all else, an enthusiasm for

fighting," were common at the time. Harold L. Ickes, "Indians Have a Name for Hitler," *Collier's* 113 (January 15, 1944), 58. Quoted in Prucha, *Great Father,* 1006.

37. Rebekah Kowal, "Dancing within the Margins: Martha Graham and American in the Mid-1940's" (paper presented at the American Studies Association annual meeting, 1994, Nashville), has discussed the dance's relation to the historical climate during which it premiered in May 1944, with the end of World War II in sight and a spirit of optimism and nationalism permeating the country. Kowal suggests the piece taps into a desire for "another brand of nationalism" (8) engendered by the war, and characterized in part by a "compulsion to search for meaning in universals" alongside "a desire to pull inward, to reflect" (3).

6. HELD IN RESERVE

1. Melinda Copel, "The 1954 Limón Company Tour to South America: Goodwill Tour or Cold War Cultural Propaganda?" in *José Limón: The Artist Re-Viewed,* ed. June Dunbar (Amsterdam: Harwood, 2000), 97–112.

2. Naima Prevots, *Dance for Export: Cultural Diplomacy and the Cold War* (Hanover: Wesleyan University Press, 1998), 111–25. For more on the Laubins, see Starr West Jones, *Reginald and Gladys Laubin, American Indian Dancers* (Urbana: University of Illinois Press, 2000).

3. He toured India, Indonesia, Burma (Myanmar), and Pakistan in the spring of 1956, and then returned to Japan, Korea, Formosa (Taiwan), Cambodia, Viet Nam, Thailand, Burma (Myanmar), and Malaya (Malaysia) later in the year and into February 1957.

4. The resolution targeted all Indian tribes within California, Florida, New York, and Texas, as well as the Flathead tribe of Montana, the Klamaths of Oregon, the Menominees of Wisconsin, the Potawatomis of Kansas and Nebraska, and the Turtle Mountain Chippewa of North Dakota. See Larry W. Burt, *Tribalism in Crisis: Federal Indian Policy, 1953–1961* (Albuquerque: University of New Mexico Press, 1982), 4–5. Quoted in Joy L. Gritton, *The Institute of American Indian Arts: Modernism and U.S. Indian Policy* (Albuquerque: University of New Mexico Press, 2000), 67, 69.

5. Although more than a third returned home within a few years (O'Brien, *American Indian Tribal Governments,* 86).

6. As Deloria notes, hobbyists did this even as, paradoxically, they valued the "traditional, reservation-based full-blood" Indian most highly (*Playing Indian,* 142).

7. José Limón, *An Unfinished Memoir,* ed. Lynn Garafola (Hanover, N.H.: Wesleyan University Press, 1999), 90–91.

8. *Mexican Suite:* excerpts, NYPL Dance Collection, MGZHB 2–2204.

9. Comments based on viewings of a 1962 production performed by Limón, Lola Huth, and Harlan McCallum, NYPL Dance Collection, *MGZIC 9–2009.

10. Items in quotations from program notes included in Limón, *Unfinished Memoir,* 140. Description from "José Limón, the Making of the 'Dialogues,'" *Dance Magazine,* August 1951, 15.

11. This piece even more directly explores male homoeroticism in relationships of power and betrayal than in *La Malinche,* the choreography here reprising some of the

very same, and very erotic, choreography from *The Exiles,* a heterosexual exploration of biblical banishment from Eden in which the two dancers climb onto each other, one lifting his groin from the floor almost into a backbend, the other lowering onto him.

12. Ann Vachon, "Limón in Mexico; Mexico in Limón," in *José Limón,* ed. Dunbar, 71.

13. Ann Murphy, "Lucas Hoving and José Limón: Radical Dancers," in *José Limón,* ed. Dunbar, 62. For mention of Limón's "Yaqui Indian ancestry," see also Barbara Pollack and Charles Humphrey Woodford, *Dance is a Moment: A Portrait of José Limón in Words and Pictures* (Pennington, N.J.: Princeton Book, 1993), 29.

14. Ernestine Stodelle, "José Limón, Poet-Painter of Dance," *New Haven Register,* 1967? Undated clipping in NYPL Dance Collection, MGZR, Limón, José.

15. Gordon L. Magill, "Rosalie Jones, Guiding Light of Daystar," *Dance Magazine,* August 1998, 67.

16. Rosalie Jones, "Inventing Native Modern Dance: A Tough Trip through Paradise," keynote speech given at the 23rd Annual American Indian Workshop, Dublin Ireland, March 26, 2002.

17. Alejandro Roncería, interview with the author, July 11, 1999, Banff Centre for the Arts, Alberta, Canada.

18. Alejandro Roncería, interview with the author, November 11, 2005, Toronto, Canada. Roncería explained that while living in New York, he would make weekly trips to Lincoln Center's Library for the Performing Arts to watch videos of dances by Limón and others.

19. According to the Pascua Yaqui Tribe official Web site, http://www.pascuayaquitribe .org/index.shtml.

20. In 1952, the same year Congress established its Voluntary Relocation Program, the Pascua Yaqui Indian tribe lost its land at Pascua Village, north of Tucson, when the City of Tucson annexed the community. In the decades since this period, Yaqui peoples fought for land and for tribal recognition. In 1960, Yaquis in Old Pascua initiated a request for land, and in 1964, Arizona Congressman Morris K. Udall—who would later become Commissioner of Indian Affairs, and whose wife Lee would later found the scholarship program that brought Rosalie Jones to study with José Limón at Julliard— successfully introduced a bill to transfer 202 acres of land southwest of Tucson to the Pascua Yaqui. The Pascua Yaqui Tribe of Arizona moved to this land base, and became federally recognized in 1978. In 1982, the tribe gained an additional 690 acres, and in 1988 the first constitution was created. Today, there are over eight thousand tribal members, two thousand of whom live on the Indian Land. For details see the West USA Realty Arizona Relocation Guide (http://arizonan.com/Indianlands/PascuaYaqui .html) and the U.S. Code Collection at Cornell Law School (http://www4.law.cornell .edu/uscode/25/1300f.html).

21. José Limón, "On Dance," in *The Vision of Modern Dance in the Words of Its Creators,* ed. Jean Morrison Brown et al. (Princeton: Princeton Book, 1979), 99.

22. Betty Jones, "Voices of the Body," in *José Limón,* ed. Dunbar, 37–44.

23. His other works from this period, even when not dealing with explicitly Native issues, likewise explored the complexity of racial struggles. For example, Limón's most famous work, *The Moor's Pavane,* which premiered along with *La Malinche* in 1949,

like the Shakespearean play on which it is based, is explicitly about race and the role of race in sexualized domination: Limón appears as the Moor, where the darkness of his body articulates against the fairness of Hoving's Iago. At the same time, Limón's signature piece places his exploration of race as part of European high culture and choreography, using Shakespeare as a reference and the pavane as a choreographic structure for the piece. In other words, Limón's choreography from this period explicitly addressed the issue of race as an integral part of present-day Western dance.

24. See Burt, *Alien Bodies*, 128.

25. Daystar/Rosalie Jones, e-mail correspondence, April 27, 2003.

26. "Dance with Indian Children," published by the Ford Foundation, Center for the Arts of Indian America, Washington, D.C., 1972, Coordinator: James McGrath; Consultants: Josephine Wapp—traditional Indian dance; Juan Valenzuela—Modern Dance. Part of an Educational Resource Development in American Indian Culture Heritage Education and the Arts for teachers of Indian children and teachers of dance. Thanks to Susan Cashion for sharing this material with me.

Information on Valenzuela's background from *Dance On* interview with Billie Mahoney (1986). In that interview, Valenzuela notes he was born in "old Mexico," brought to Arizona when he was six, and then moved to Salt Lake City when he was eight, where he grew up. Valenzuela notes that the desire to dance hit him as a lightening bolt: at a tap dance performance at his school in Utah: "I am part Indian—I am Aztec and Yaqui and Spanish, and therefore it has something to do with that particular kind of sign. The lightening bolt plays a big role in Indian culture and Indian stories and myths. That was my beginning." He goes on to discuss how an illness his mother faced later provided the opportunity "to learn about my Aztec heritage and my Yaqui heritage and all that, because when I was going to school they wanted us to learn English and to become an American."

27. His echoing of the treaty rhetoric of "time immemorial" in his words likewise recognizes American Indians' political identity.

28. Thomas Dorsey noted he seemed to recall stories about his father getting the name from a children's book, though that story may be "more anecdotal than factual." Telephone conversation, April 9, 2003. Dorsey added, "His Lenni-Lenape Native people had been exterminated by the European waves early on in our Eastern history so that Dad did not have his ancestral tribe to draw historical methodology from. . . . Fortunately, Six Nations, although suffering attempts at extermination, survived with vestiges of cultural history intact and regenerated what is today and was during the fifties a strong cultural base." Personal correspondence, September 2005.

For background on Delaware/Lenape people and history, see the Delaware Tribe of Indians home page (http://www.delawaretribeofindians.nsn.us/), the Nanticoke Lenni-Lenape Indian of New Jersey home page (http://www.nanticoke-lenape.org/), and Indian tribal records at http://www.accessgenealogy.com/native/tribes/delaware/delawarehist.htm. As these and other sources note, despite the incredible hardships they faced, Lenape people live today throughout the United States and Canada, including in Oklahoma, Kansas, Wisconsin, New York, and Maryland, near Allentown, Pennsylvania, as a State Recognized Tribe in New Jersey, and on two reserves in Ontario, Canada (the Delaware Nation at Moraviantown and the Munsee-Delaware Nation).

29. "I remember beating the drum at the Powwow out at Shinnecock when I was

very young for Louis [Mofsie] and Dad," recounts Dorsey. E-mail correspondence, September 24, 2001.

30. The Museum of the American Indian; Pilbrook Museum of Art and Gilcrease Museum, Tulsa, Oklahoma; Denver Art Museum; American Museum of Natural History; Montclair Art Museum, Montclair, New Jersey; the University at Albany, State University of New York; and the Albany Institute of History and Art.

31. See Camp Menatoma, http://home.att.net/~mk-de-peterson/photos.htm. "Several summers we all packed it up and stayed in a small log cabin near the camp," Dorsey explained.

32. These included "Contest Dance; Cut Dance; Eagle Dance; Partridge Dance; Girl's Shuffle Dance, to illustrate difference between girls' and boys' dances." Educational Catalog, 1950–51, 92nd Street Y Archives. Thanks to Steve Siegel for locating this reference for me, and to Naomi Jackson for pointing me toward it.

33. Monday, November 20, 1950, presentation on "Indian Dance in the Americas" at Henry Street Playhouse in New York City (program from NYPL Dance Collection); Friday, November 24, 1950, presentation at 92nd Street Y, first in a series of new children's dance and entertainment programs, "Rhythms of the Red Man," 481 tickets sold (house seated 800).

34. Dorsey, telephone conversation, April 9, 2003; personal correspondence, September 2005.

35. Obituary, "Thomas Dorsey, Jr.," dated "1993"; newspaper not noted but held in the clip files of the Albany Institute of History and Art.

36. Film 260, *Indian Dances,* copyright American Museum of Natural History.

37. On the tape credits, it is impossible to read the name of the music group providing this Indian music as it is written in white and falls on the screen over the white museum, effectively erasing the singers' and drummers' names from the record.

38. Later in the decade, reviews of the State Department presentations on his trips throughout Asia similarly stress educational aspects of his performances. A 1956 New York *Herald* account of Two Arrows's trip, for example, explained "Mr. Two Arrows has availed himself of every opportunity to discuss the dances, music and crafts of the Iroquois (and of the American Indian in general) with art leaders and simple villagers." New York *Herald Tribune,* December 30, 1956. NYPL Dance Collection, MGZR, Tom Two Arrows.

39. Dorsey, telephone conversation, April 9, 2003.

40. "The Iroquois Eagle Dance" presented in the Natural History museum film, for example, makes no explicit reference to the Eagle Dance legend referenced in the Jacob's Pillow program.

41. Hanay Geiogamah, interview with the author, October 28, 2004, UCLA.

42. Two Arrows's awareness of these issues is underscored by his 1942 writings accompanying the Albany Institute exhibit of his work, where he explains the privacy of many Longhouse ceremonies: "Most Haudenosaunee ceremonies, held on reservation in the special buildings called 'the Longhouse,' are not open to the public. Followers of the traditional religious rituals wish to remain private, conducting their special ceremonies only with others sharing their beliefs and language. Iroquois 'socials,' on the other hand, feature food, games and social dancing in a festive rather than ceremonial context. These activities can be performed for non-Indians."

43. One painting, *CA.NAN.DAI.GUA,* references the 1794 treaty that "established the precedent of sovereignty so important to the Haudenosaunee: the six nations of the Confederacy are separate and equal political entities, joined together in alliance, comparable in status to the United States and entitled to treatment as sovereign states." Notes Tom Two Arrows/Tom Dorsey wrote to accompany an exhibition of his artwork commissioned by the Albany Institute of History & Art in 1942, and reexhibited there in 2002. Thanks to Diane Shewchuk of the Albany Institute for providing me with copies of Two Arrows's exhibition notes, and for showing me paintings held in storage there.

44. His paintings depict primarily story or social dances, including *A.GOO.GWO. KA.O-WA.NA or Woman's Dance, Green Corn Dance, O-JUN.N-TA.O.WAN.NA or Fish Dance, GWEE SAS SE or War Dance,* and *GI.EO.A.O.WAN.NA or Partridge Dance.*

45. When Diane Shewchuk showed me these paintings in August 2002, held in storage, she also spoke of a box of materials that hadn't been displayed in the spring 2002 exhibit. These were paintings that depicted ceremonial masks and other objects that elders from the community had requested not be on display.

46. Termination-era legislation specifically affected Iroquois peoples and the sovereign rights they held to jurisdiction over their own lands. In July 1948, Congress passed legislation that authorized New York State to have criminal jurisdiction over Indians on state reservations, without Indian consent. This and an amended 1950 bill, conferring state control over civil law on New York reservations, were seen by members of the Iroquois Six Nations as part of a broader plan to destroy Indian rights. See Kenneth R. Philp, *Termination Revisited: American Indians on the Trail to Self-Determination, 1933–53* (Lincoln: University of Nebraska Press, 1999), 145.

47. Thanks to the audience at the 2000 American Studies Association conference in Detroit, Mich., for discussion on this issue.

48. His identity as an adopted Haudenosaunee dancer—billed as an authentic Iroquois—makes inroads into the more usual government tactic of turning to genetic blood-quantum, rather than tribally defined familial relations, as definitive of Indian authenticity. Recognition of him as Haudenosaunee (rather than any insistence that he be seen as Lenni-Lenape), in effect refuses essentialist attempts to contain an authentic Indian identity defined through genetics or bloodline alone. This was likely less a conscious political move on his part than just the way things worked when he married into a matrilineal society like the Haudenosaunee. By marrying a Haudenosaunee woman, and through Haudenosaunee adoption of him, he and his children were recognized as such. His practice of dance traditions other than those of the people he was born into likewise has a long tradition in Native American dance history, as the "Omaha dance" in powwow history (so named because it was learned from the Omaha), among many other examples, attests.

49. Dorsey explained that in the 1970s, his father was part of a resurgence of Indian Nationalism following Wounded Knee. "Now most eastern nations have made great steps in reestablishing the basics of Indian traditionality," he wrote. "In his decline he was still fairly active in this area. He taught and helped begin a great local summer day camp hosted by local educators. They, as many people do, remember his ability to connect with people and offer some of his knowledge and talent." E-mail correspondence, September 24, 2001.

50. Capezio Dance Award, March 11, 1964. Quoted in Daniel Lewis, *The Illustrated Dance Technique of José Limón* (New York: Harper and Row, 1984), 12.

51. "I would say that he was probably influenced to 'think' about the native heritage, and about the native people in the U.S.," Daystar/Rosalie Jones writes. Personal e-mail correspondence, April 27, 2003.

52. Deborah Jowitt, "Limón Pursues His Visions," *New York Times*, October 8, 1972, 9 and 38.

7. THE EMERGENCE OF A VISIBLE NATIVE AMERICAN STAGE DANCE

1. In addition to the Native American political activism of the 1960s and 1970s as well as other hugely influential political movements of the era (like civil rights), intellectual trends, themselves emerging in the wake of these politics, also undoubtedly contributed to the stage emergence of Native dance. These included a growing interest in identity politics and increased funding for ethnic studies programs and multicultural programming, with their recognition and promotion of cultural differences.

2. Thanks to Tharon Weighill for initially suggesting this connection.

3. Hanay Geiogamah, "The New American Indian Theater: An Introduction," in *American Indian Theater in Performance: A Reader,* ed. Hanay Geiogamah and Jaye T. Darby (Los Angeles: UCLA American Indian Studies Center, 2000), 160.

4. Quoted in Maria Garcia, Windspeaker Contributor, N.Y., "Company Funds Students," http://www.ammsa.com/guide/GIC02-Students.html (undated).

5. See the AIM Web site at http://www.aimovement.org/index.html.

6. See Frank, "Indian Policy," 233. See also Christopher Vecsey, "Prologue," to *Handbook of American Indian Religious Freedom,* ed. Christopher Vecsey (New York: Crossroad Press, 1996), 17.

7. The text of this act is available on various Web sites, including http://www .cr.nps.gov/local-law/FHPL_IndianRelFreAct.pdf, which includes federal historic preservation laws.

8. See Vescey, *Handbook,* 9.

9. See the 'Lectric Law Library's stacks at http://www.lectlaw.com/files/drg25.htm for the text of the amendment.

10. In the early 1970s, Geiogamah founded what he called the "first professional Indian theater in New York," the American Indian Theatre Ensemble. In 1974, the group, renamed the Native American Theater Ensemble, relocated to Oklahoma City where for two years it produced some successful plays and launched a number of Native American theater artists. For more on this history, see Geiogamah, "New American Indian Theater," 161. See also Jones, "Modern Native Dance," 174.

11. Raoul Trujillo, "Interview," in *Chinook Winds,* ed. Elton, 24.

12. Anna Kisselgoff, "Symbols and Bravura by American Indians," *New York Times*, September 19, 1991.

13. Bill Deresiewicz, review of September 17–October 6, 1991 AIDT performance at the Joyce Theater in New York, *Dance Magazine,* December 1991, 94.

14. This view of ethnic dancers (or actors) as just "being themselves" on stage, where audiences can catch a glimpse of them, rehearses familiar, ethnographic tropes. While European dancers such as Ruth St. Denis and Ted Shawn could inhabit multiple

ethnicities as artists, and could dance in ethnically unmarked modern forms without being read as having "no gap between dancer and performer," racially marked ethnic dancers have been allowed to represent only themselves.

15. Lynn Garafola, "Jacob's Pillow: A Sampler," *Ballet Review* 23, no. 4 (Winter 1995), 80.

16. Lillie F. Rosen similarly described her "unmistakable feeling that everything we were watching [on stage] was not quite authentic." See "American Indian Dance Theater," *Attitude: The Dancer's Magazine,* Winter 1992.

17. Henry Smith, Artistic Director, Lakota Sioux Indian Dance Theater, interview with the author, April 30, 1999, New York City.

18. Charlotte Heth, description/press packet, NYPL Dance Collection, MGZR, American Indian Dance Theater.

19. Hanay Geiogamah, "Old Circles, New Circles," in *American Indian Theater in Performance,* ed. Geioigamah and Darby, 284.

20. Citations in this paragraph from Geiogamah interview.

21. Jones, interview. Subsequent quotes in this section also from this interview unless otherwise specified.

22. See MaryKay Conway, "Staging Animal Dances: Contemporary Native American Modern Dance Choreographies" (master's thesis, UCLA, 2002), 43.

23. In 1969, she left the IAIA to study at Julliard with Limón, returning to the IAIA in the early 1990s to serve as chair of the Performing Arts faculty.

24. Quote from program March 25, 2000, in Brockport, New York. Comments based on my attendance at this production as well as a taped version of a performance from Greer Garson Theatre, Santa Fe, N.M.

25. Belinda James, interview, August 28, 2001, New York City.

26. Hanay Geiogamah, "Self-Interview," in *Here First: Autobiographical Essays by Native American Writers,* ed. Arnold Krupat and Brian Swann (New York: Modern Library, 2000), 149.

27. These include *Firebird: A Native American Vision,* which drew on Native American dance elements, and *Sanctuary,* which includes a section, "Amazing Grace" danced to a rendition of the song by Mixashawn that includes Native American drums and a Native American feel. Bingham explained how the piece references the musician's and other Native Americans' understanding of the Native American roots of "Amazing Grace." "When I dance, I think of prayer," Bingham explained, calling the piece an "expression of our religion." "It's a song that everyone knows, and then you flip on them, and you have this Native American piece, and then you start to listen to the words, and if you listen to the words carefully, the words are telling you something very powerful," she explained. "You're listening to your song, what you think is your religious song, and then you think, wait a minute, that's not what I'm expecting to hear." She added, "We've been here ten thousand years. It's all intertwined. It forces you to pay attention from another element." Marla Bingham, interview with the author, July 22, 2004, La Jolla, California. See also www.marlabingham.com.

28. Reardon writes that Geiogamah "envisioned folding Ms. Dean's work into his two-hour production," to be called *Kotuwokan,* which Reardon described as "a story ballet about a young Indian's journey to find his place in the modern world." Christo-

pher Reardon, "When Collaborators Find Themselves Out of Step," *New York Times,* August 30, 1998, Section 2, 24.

29. Comments based on a performance in Stockton, California, on November 7, 2004.

30. See Michael Asch and Norman Zlotkin, "Affirming Aboriginal Title: A New Basis for Comprehensive Claims Negotiations," in *Aboriginal and Treaty Rights in Canada: Essays on Law, Equality, and Respect for Difference,* ed. Michael Asch (Vancouver: University of British Columbia Press, 1997), 208–30.

31. These include the James Bay and Northern Quebec Agreement (1975); the Northeastern Quebec Agreement (1978); the Inuvialuit Final Agreement (1984); the Gwich'in Agreement (1992); the Nunavut Land Claims Agreement (1993); the Sahtu Dene and Metis Agreement (1993); six Yukon First Nation final agreements; and many others. For discussion of these issues, see Asch and Zlotkin, "Affirming Aboriginal Title," 270, n. 4.

32. These include the acknowledgment of Blue Lake as Taos land in 1970, the Alaska Native Claims Settlement Act of 1971 (Frank, "Indian Policy," 245–46), and a 1980 settlement in which the Penobscot and Passamaquoddy of Maine received $81.5 million for abandoning claims to land in the state, to name a few.

33. Of course, these questions of religious freedom, artistic production, and repatriation have concrete connection to political questions about land and access to land. For example, NAGPRA has addressed issues of ancestral burial grounds, and freedom of religion questions have hinged on Indian access to land on which to practice and perform religious ceremonies and on the protection of sacred lands from tourists and commercial development. But in implementing AIRFA, these issues of access to land have been the ones least upheld.

34. These were held in 2001 at the Morley Reserve near Calgary, Alberta, and in 2003 at the Eskasoni Reserve near Sydney, Nova Scotia. I attended the 2001 symposium, where discussion covered questions of ownership and rights to the dances, including media and photo control and cultural control, as well as the question of education outside the community. Participants also addressed community strategies, isolation, the relation between contemporary and traditional dancing, and questions of training, development, and collaborative exchanges. Funding issues, networking, and creating a service organization/national body were at issue as well.

8. ABORIGINAL LAND CLAIMS AND ABORIGINAL DANCE AT THE END OF THE TWENTIETH CENTURY

1. Dara Culhane, *The Pleasure of the Crown: Anthropology, Law, and First Nations* (Burnaby: Talon Books, 1998), 123.

2. J. L. Austin, *How to Do Things with Words,* ed. Marian Sbisa and J. O. Urmson (Cambridge: Harvard University Press, 1975), 22.

3. See the David Suzuki Foundation Series publication, *Delgamuukw: The Supreme Court of Canada Decision on Aboriginal Title,* Stan Persky, commentator (Vancouver: Greystone, 1998), 27.

4. For example, Native American Studies and Government professor Dale Turner

has argued that the *Delgamuukw* case was lost when Gitxsan and Wet'suwet'en claims for "ownership" were abandoned (conference presentation on "Indigenous Oral Histories, Political Sovereignty, and the Law in Canada and the U.S." on October 29, 1999, at the American Studies Association conference in Montreal, Canada). For discussion of the change in claims, see Persky in *Delgamuukw*, 26–27.

5. For a dazzling exploration of how an Indigenous context can inflect and reform Western philosophic conceptions of mimesis, see Michael Taussig, *Mimesis and Alterity: A Particular History of the Senses* (New York: Routledge, 1993).

6. All citations in this chapter are from conversations and interviews conducted July 2–11, 1999, at the Aboriginal Dance Program, Banff Centre for the Arts, Alberta, Canada. Most are transcribed from taped interviews; all citations were approved for publication by those cited (with the exception of Pablo Palma, who I was unable to locate after the dance program ended that summer).

7. Mumford is referring to July 1990, when "an historic confrontation propelled Native issues in Kanehsatake and the village of Oka, Quebec, into the international spotlight and into the Canadian conscience" (video jacket, *Kanehsatake*). For further reference, see *Kanehsatake: 270 Years of Resistance* (National Film Board of Canada, 1993), a film written and directed by Alanis Obomsawin, an Aboriginal filmmaker. The film provides "insight into the Mohawks' spiritual beliefs and fierce pride in their ancestry that governs the unyielding determination to protect their land." Obomsawin's portrayal of the Mohawk community places the Oka crisis within the larger context of Mohawk land rights, disregarded by white authorities for centuries and destined to culminate in the 1990 standoff. "The Oka crisis changed the lives of all Aboriginal people in this country," says Obomsawin. "We cannot go back."

8. See Vine Deloria, "Sacred Lands and Religious Freedom," in *For This Land: Writings on Religion in America* (New York: Routledge, 1999), 210.

9. WE'RE DANCING

1. See, for example, Hollis Walker, "Contemporary Dance," *Native Peoples*, September/October 2005, 30–37.

2. These include classes at Trent University in Indigenous performance; the "Red Rhythms: Contemporary Methodologies in American Indian Dance" conference held at UC Riverside in 2004 (see http://ideasandsociety.ucr.edu/redrhythms/); and the Living Ritual conference organized by Santee Smith in Toronto in 2006 (see www.livingritual.ca).

3. Exceptions include *Residential School for Boys* and *Buffalo Spirit*, choreographed by Alejandro Roncería in 1996, which I viewed on videotape while at the Aboriginal Dance Project, and Raoul Trujillo's *Shaman's Journey*, which I also saw on video, in two versions: the 1989 *Alive from Off Center* version as well as the version Trujillo restaged at Banff in 1996. The pieces discussed here represent only a sampling of those I have seen both live and on video since beginning this project; I hope to explore many more in later work.

4. Sandra Laronde, interview with the author, October 14, 2003, Toronto, Canada. All subsequent quotes from Laronde taken from this interview.

5. Georgina Martinez, interview with the author, August 4, 2002, "Gooseberry Deli" coffee shop, Banff Centre for the Arts, Banff, Canada. All quotes from this interview unless otherwise noted.

6. In some ways, this turn to Eastern movement practices is itself at the root of modern dance history, as scholar Priya Srinivasan discusses in her research on early modern dancers' appropriation of movement practices from India. Yet, the focus among contemporary Aboriginal dancers is not to use these movement practices to exotify or sexualize themselves within an upper-middle-class Christian-based Delsartian framework along the lines of Ruth St. Denis. Rather, it is to explore the way these practices disrupt the framework of modern dance, especially its abstraction.

7. These include Daystar's *The Corn Mother, Sky Woman,* and *Gift of the Pipe,* Belinda James's *Metamorphosis,* and Vancouver-based Raven Spirit Dance Company's *Raven Restores the Sun to the Sky,* a telling of a Yukon story from Artistic Director Michelle Olson's cultural heritage as a member of the Tr'ondëk Hwëch'in First Nation in Northern British Columbia. This piece was performed in Calgary, Alberta, Canada, on November 10, 2001, as part of the "Nimitohtak! We Dance!" First National Aboriginal Dance Symposium.

8. Belinda James, interview with the author, December 27, 2000, New York City. James explained that Graham technique "was too angular, not lyrical. It didn't appeal to me." She responded more to Horton technique, noting that while the Horton lines are also angular, "they seem more logical," she said. "They go into shapes that can come out of shapes."

9. Sadie Buck and Alejandro Roncería, "Directors' Statement," *BONES* Program, 8.

10. Sadie Buck, "The Language of the World," *BONES* Program, 9.

11. This program was presented at the Margaret Greenham Theatre at Banff Centre for the Arts on August 30 and 31 and September 1 and 2, 1996.

12. Heather Elton, "Alejandro Roncería," interview in *Chinook Winds,* ed. Elton, 34.

13. Wallace, drawing on stories his mother told about "being in residential school and when the nuns weren't around, they would teach each other songs," used a Lillooet song his mother sang, put it with Western music reminiscent of hymns, improvised on its melody, and layered her voice with his own. He recounts, "It was really powerful for me and I thought if I sampled one section it would be like a memory, like the residential school, where even though you were forced to speak another language that you had never heard before and you couldn't sing your songs anymore, and you couldn't do your dances anymore, the memory is still there . . . the very memory of the song, the memory of the language, even though you might not be using it, it's there on your tongue, it's there in your throat. . . . By taking a tradition and moving it, having the background of western music and incorporating my voice, it suggests that the culture is still there but changing. The language is changing, it's not static, it keeps moving." "Russell Wallace Interview," in *Chinook Winds,* ed. Elton, 54–55.

14. For an in-depth discussion of this piece, see Conway, "Staging Animal Dances." Conway explores transformative connections that occur between human and animal beings in several pieces: Trujillo's *Shaman's Journey,* Rosalie Jones/Daystar's *Wolf: A Transformation,* and Tlingit choreographer Denise Dovell's *Coho Salmon Life.* Conway explains ways that "Unspoken but inferred in [*Shaman's Journey* and *Wolf*] is a belief

that mystical entities or spirits surround us and that transactions are possible between animals and humans because our spirits possess the ability to transform" (83). By way of an extended exploration of these three pieces, Conway concludes that these and several other Native American choreographers she cites stress "the importance of embodying the past while reconfiguring the form in which it is expressed to promote an 'ongoing presence'" (126).

15. Program, "Color Pointes," a showcase of the works of classically trained choreographers who have created a new ballet idiom, curated by Marshall Swiney. Performed June 23–24, 2001, at Long Island University's Triangle Theater, Brooklyn, N.Y., and performed by Jonathan Phelps and Gregory Wolverton. *Metamorphosis,* choreographed in 1989 in New Jersey, was first performed on December 17, 1990, at the Mark Goodson Theatre in Manhattan's Columbus Circle.

16. Similarly, James explained that the crucial purposefulness of dance and the seriousness with which it must be approached and performed—familiar to her from Pueblo understandings of dance—overlap with the commitment, the intense dedication and training, required of those who dance ballet: "I respect the training. It's an honorable and amazing thing."

17. Marrie Mumford, personal communication, May 21, 2006.

18. Marrie Mumford, interview with the author, March 3, 2006, Peterbourough, Ontario.

Index

Aboriginal Dance Project/Program, 5–6, 24, 143, 177, 197, 216–18, 221–38, 245, 249, 251, 260; Aboriginal Dance Training Program, 255–56

absence: of funding for American Indian dance in U.S., 216; of Indians in Graham's choreography, 148–50, 157, 161–63, 166, 168; of Native American dance in modern dance history, 2, 7, 24–25, 147, 167, 185, 187, 194; of positive depictions of Native Americans, 185

African American dance, 2, 138, 176; dancers, 133–34; Horton's influence on, 136, 142, 294n56; representation in *American Document*, 156–57; scholarship on, 269n3, 270n4

Ailey, Alvin, 133, 142–44, 176, 211

Alarcon, Renaldo, 134

Albany Institute of History and Art, 184, 189

Alcatraz Island: occupation of, 215

Alexie, Sherman, 78

Allen, Chadwick, 164, 272n17

Allyellow, James, 81, 92

American Ballet, The (Shawn), 111, 115, 120, 126

American Document (Graham), 149, 155–57, 160, 270n4, 296n19

American Indian Dance Theatre (AIDT), 6, 24, 129, 188, 197, 200–206, 209, 211–12, 263, *Fancy Dance Suite*, 203; *Fancy Shawl Dance*, 203; *Men's Fancy Dance*, 212; *Modern Fancy*, 211–13; *New Dance*, 212; *Red Cedar Bark*

Ceremony, 210; *San Carlos Apache Crown Dance*, 203

American Indian Movement (AIM), 198–99

American Indian Religious Freedom Act (AIRFA). *See* religious freedom

American Museum of Natural History, 184–85, 188, 194

American Rhythm, The (Austin), 103

Apache Crown Dance, 203

Appalachian Spring (Graham), 24, 119, 148–50

Arnatsiaq-Murphy, Siobhán, 143, 221, 240, 251, 263; *Nunattinni,* 263

Arrow Maker, The (Austin), 103

art colonies: Taos and Santa Fe, 81–82, 112, 290n2

Arts and Crafts Act, American Indian, 113, 117–19, 147; Indian Arts and Crafts Board, 107; revised Act of 1990, 215; use–value of "art," 84, 104–7, 117

Asian American dancers: in Graham, 159, 296n25; in Horton, 129, 134–35

assimilation of American Indians, 29–32, 115; drives toward, 72, 88, 90, 167–68, 170, 275n6, 7; fantasy of, 113; in Limón, 170; and termination era, 187, 189, 214

Austin, J. L., 218, 225

Austin, Mary, 82, 103–7, 113, 286n2, 290n44; *The American Rhythm,* 103; *The Arrow Maker,* 103

authenticity, 3–4, 24–25, 79, 81, 83, 89, 112, 115, 132, 170, 189, 192, 194,

200, 260, 302n48, 304n16; "authentic themes," materials, as source of inspiration, 117–19, 141, 153, 185; and Camp Fire Girls, 289n38; dances as "fake," 54, 57–59; desire to record, 114; performance of "real" Indians, 59–62, 190; and Plains–sounding names, 188; and powwow hobbyists, 172, 298n6; and staging, 201–2, 210, 244; and women dancers, 80

Balanchine, George, 140
ballet, 55, 79, 115, 127, 237, 244, 249, 253, 308n16; American Indian ballerinas, 2; dedication required by, 140, 308n16; and masculinity, 143; Native American ballet, 3, 188; New York City Ballet, 3; pointe shoe as deer hoof; program at Banff, 228–29, 237; training, 139, 211, 222, 243, 249, 253–54; vocabulary and Native American dance, 211
Banff Centre, 5–6, 24, 143, 177, 197, 218, 222–24, 228–29, 252
Barnum, P. T., 64
Bauman, R. J., 288n31
Beck, William H., 49, 57
Belt, R. V., 69, 284n53, 284n57
Between the Earth and the Moon: Voices from the Great Circle (Daystar), 263
Big Foot, 283n50
Bingham, Marla, 211, 263; *Firebird: A Native American Vision*, 304n27; Marla Bingham Contemporary Ballet, 211, 263; *Sanctuary* ("Amazing Grace"), 304n27
Black Elk, 53, 65, 77–78; *Black Elk Speaks*, 65; in Buffalo Bill's Wild West, 66–68, 76; and Ghost Dance, 72, 74
Black Hawk, 193
Black Hawk, Peter, 91
Black Heart, 69
Black Lake (Hawkins), 113
blood memory, 9, 242, 297n33; ancestral

memories/ways of knowing accessed through dance, 10, 223, 225, 241, 244, 260, 272n20; *Blood Memory* (Graham), 148, 157, 161, 163, 167, 242, 272n17
blood quantum. *See* identity, Native American: and "blood quantum"
boarding schools, 30, 47, 85, 272n15, 275n5, 277n22
Bob, Isaiah, 213
Bobb, Sid, 13, 17, 223, 226–27, 232, 234
Boden, Herman, 144
BONES: An Aboriginal Dance Opera (Roncería/Buck) 11, 245–49
Bourke, John G., 116
Bowman, John H., 51
Bracken, Christopher, 30, 38, 41–42, 44, 46, 49
Breaker, Robert, 227
Brother Elk, Andrew, 43, 272n15
Browner, Tara, 66, 78, 282n34, 285n65
Buck, Sadie, 224, 245; *BONES: An Aboriginal Dance Opera*, 11, 245–49
Buffalo Bill. *See* Cody, William
Buffalo Bill's Wild West, 23, 53–54, 57, 60, 63, 65–66, 71–72, 75, 107, 281n30–31; Buffalo Bill performers, 23, 59–67, 77, 80; Ghost dancers hired into, 74–75; government relation to, 71–72; and invention of "Indian," 77; performers' agency within shows, 64–66, 71, 76–77; relation to early women modern dancers, 80; Wild West arena, 64, 76, 79; Wild West shows (general), 60, 69–70, 79–80, 280n15, 281n29, 282n33
Buffalo Spirit (Roncería), 8, 249–51, 255
Burke, Charles, 84–91, 93, 97, 103, 146, 287n16, 288n24, 288n27, 288n31, 290n39; "TO ALL INDIANS" letter/message, 87, 91, 96, 99–100, 102, 111, 114, 116, 290n39
Bursum Bill, 98–99, 103–4
Burt, Ramsey, 151, 153
Butoh, 7, 242, 252

Cada-Matasawagon, Celina, 258

Camp Menatoma, 184

Canada Council, 216

Caribou Song (Red Sky), 253

Carrera, Francisco, 257

Carver, Dr. W. F. (Doc), 60, 75, 80

Catholocism: in Canada, 38, 42, 46, 181, 277n22; in *El Penitente* and Southwest, 150, 153, 162–63, 295n12; fears of Catholic influence in U.S. policy, 36–37, 79; in *La Malinche*, 182

Cayuga, Cat, 224

Centre for Indigenous Theatre (Native Theatre School), 216

Ceremonials (Graham), 154

Chakrabarty, Dipesh, 11

Chartrand, Yvonne, 257–58; *Compaigni V'ni Dansi*, 263; *Gabriel's Crossing*, 263

Chief Illiniwek, 32

Chief-Moon, Byron, 264; *Coyote Arts Percussive Performance Association* (CAPPA), 264; *Possessed, Dancing Voices, Voices, Quest*, 264

Chinook Winds: Aboriginal Dance Project (book), 5–6, 8, 221, 239. *See also* Aboriginal Dance Project/Program

Circular no. 1665, 84, 287n16; supplement to, 86

citizenship: American Indian Citizenship Act, 94–95, 117, 291n13; Native American relation to U.S., 42, 48, 82, 85, 90, 102, 114–15, 167, 287n19, 289n31, 291n12

Cloutier, Sylvia Ipirautaq, 263; *Aqsarniit*, 263; *Nunattinni*, 263

Coconino Sun, 89, 91

Cody, William (Buffalo Bill), 60–61, 69, 71, 73, 79, 281n31; and Ghost Dance, 74–75

collective memory, 226, 242. *See also* blood memory

Collier, John, 39, 107, 116–17, 150, 167, 189, 204

contact improvisation, 242–43

Conway, Mary Kay, 208, 307n14

Cooper, James Fenimore, 156

Copland, Aaron, 148, 157, 296n18

Corn Dance, 82; *Corn Dance* (Horton), 113, "Corn Dance" (Shawn), 116; Green Corn Dance, 12; *Green Corn Dance* (Two Arrows), 302n44; Santo Domingo Corn Dance, 113, 150; at Zia Pueblo, 113

Cortez, Hernando, 173

Couchie, Penny, 15, 17, 222, 224, 226, 229, 257–58, 261, 263; *Earth in Motion Indigenous World Dance*, 262–63

Crane Bear, Tom, 227, 238

Crane, Hart, 158, 162

Culhane, Dara, 217

Cunningham, Merce, 156

Custer, George, 65, 74

Dale, Governor Thomas, 160

Dancing Earth, 262

Danzas Mexicanas (Limón), 172, 179–80, 182

Dawes Allotment Act, 30, 57, 92, 275n6, 287n18; allotment, 117, 271; and blood-quantum requirements, 164–65

Daystar/Rosalie Jones, 6, 13, 193, 206–9, 263; *Between the Earth and the Moon: Voices from the Great Circle*, 263; *The Corn Mother*, 307n7; Daystar: Contemporary Dance-Drama of Indian America, 24, 197, 206, 263; *Gift of the Pipe*, 307n7; and Limón, 176–77, 182–83, 299n20, 303n51, 304n23; *No Home but the Heart: An Assembly of Memories*, 8, 13–22, 255; and Shawn, 122, 128–29, 292n22; *Sky Woman*, 307n7; *Wolf: A Transformation*, 208–9, 307n14

Dean, Laura, 212

Deer Dance: San Juan Pueblo (James), 253–55; "Pueblo Deer Dance" (Two Arrows), 186

De Lavallade, Carmen, 134, 142

Delgamuukw case, 205, 217–21, 305–6n4

Deloria, Ella, 289n38

Deloria, Philip, 3–4, 6, 104, 115, 127–28, 130, 171–72, 289n38, 298n6

Delsarte, François, 23, 53–57, 59, 62, 79, 114, 146; Delsartian training/theatricality, 62–63, 78–79, 80; grounding in Christian thought, 23, 53–55, 78

DeMallie, Raymond J., 65, 67

De Mille, Agnes, 141, 166, 170

Denishawn, 112

Díalogos/Dialogues (Limón), 174, 182

Dilworth, Leah, 81, 83, 166

Dorsey, Thomas (father). *See* Two Arrows, Tom

Dorsey, Thomas (son), 184, 187–88, 192–93, 300n28, 301n29, 301n31, 302n49

Dovell, Denise: *Coho Salmon Life,* 307n14

Drama of Civilization, 61, 63, 65. *See also* *Buffalo Bill's Wild West*

Duncan, Isadora, 79–80, 145, 174

Dunham, Katherine, 183

Dunn, W. E., 289n31

Eagle Dance, 120, 128, 143, 188; Hopi, 5, 120; "Eagle Dance" (Shawn), 116, 121, 128, 292n22; *Eagle Dance* (Two Arrows), 187–88, 301n40; eagle dancers (AIDT), 203; in *Miinigooweziwin,* 261; *Pueblo Eagle Dance* (Horton), 113, 133, 137, 140, 142

Eagle Elk, 91

Earth in Motion Indigenous World Dance, 263

Easter Dance, 201

Edson, Casper, 47

Eisenhower, Dwight D., 169

Elk, 66–68

El Penitente (Graham), 149, 155–56, 161–62

Elton, Heather, 250

Fancy Dance, 77, 207, 211–12; *Fancy Dance Suite* (AIDT), 203; history of regalia, 285n63

Fancy Shawl Dance (AIDT), 203

Feather of the Dawn (Shawn), 112, 116, 118, 130

Fergusson, Erna, 116, 121, 128

Fisher, Jonathan, 250–51

Foster, Susan Leigh, 10, 126–27, 144

Foulkes, Julia L., 115, 127, 292n27

Frank, C. E. S., 214–15

Franko, Mark, 154, 292n25, 294n61, 296n19

Fred Harvey Company, 81

French jigging, 17; clogging, 21–22

Friday Keeshig, Christine, 264; *Misabi, Metamorphosis, Notchemowwaning,* 264

Frontier (Graham), 154–55

Garafola, Lynn, 201

Gaskin, Jody, 246–47

gaze, 8, 159; agency of performer vs. gazer, 64, 67, 69, 78; Indian as object of, 164; power of watching/witnessing dancing, 33, 84, 122, 127, 159; regulatory gaze, 38, 46; in relation to powwow, 77–78; theatrical gaze, 64, 69. *See also* visuality

Geiogamah, Hanay, 24, 188, 197–98, 200, 202–3, 205, 210–13, 263, 303n10, 304n28

Ghost Dance (rejuvenation dances), 1, 2, 47, 72–76, 88, 107, 278n37, 280n21, 283n49, 284n54–55, 284n57, 284n60, 285n62; billing in Wild West shows, 75, 80; and Christianity, 46–47, 278n34; as invented "craze," 73; Wild West hiring of Ghost dance prisoners as performers, 74–76, 107; "Zuni Ghost Dance" (Shawn), 112

Gibson, Arrell Morgan, 112–13

Gingras, Gaétan, 263; *Manitowapan,* 263

Godfrey, Joyzelle, 283n50

Gods Who Dance (Shawn), 114

Goodall, Jane, 64–65

Gower-Kappi, Feliks, 224–26, 234

Gunn Allen, Paula, 12, 50, 292n26

Graham, Martha, 1, 4, 23, 80, 118–19,

130, 137, 140, 145–46, 148–68, 174, 183, 242–43; *American Document*, 149, 155–57, 160, 296n19; *Appalachian Spring*, 24, 119, 148–150, 156–58, 161–64, 166–68, 295n2, 296n18, 298n37; *Blood Memory*, 148, 157, 161, 163, 242; *Ceremonials*, 154; *El Penitente*, 149, 155–56, 161–62; *Frontier*, 154–55; Graham technique, 307n8; and Indian dance in Southwest, 82, 112, 150, 295n12; *Land Be Bright*, 156, 295n18; *Lamentations*, 17; "Pocahontas: Notes for a Dance Never Choreographed," 159–61; *Primitive Mysteries*, 112, 151–54, 158, 162, 164, 295n9, 296n25

Graham, W. M., 86

Grant, Ulysses S., 36

Grass Dance, 47–48, 51, 66, 91, 205, 211; and Omaha and War Dance, 282n33, 282n34

Greyeyes, Michael, 263

Gritton, Joy L., 204

Grunn, Homer, 113

Hale, Tawny, 213

Harvey Company/Detours, 81, 83

Hawkins, Erick, 113, 143, 156, 163; *Black Lake*, 113; *Killer of Enemies*, 113; *Plains Daybreak*, 113; *Ritual of the Descent*, 113

Helms, James E., 47–48, 51

Heth, Charlotte, 3

Hiawatha, 293n41

High Horse, 89

Highway, René, 249

Hill, Martha, 177

History of the Conquest of Mexico, The (Prescott), 112

Hodge, Frederick Webb, 103

homosexuality, 119, 126–27; and "berdache," 292n26; homoeroticism in José Limón choreography, 298n11; and Horton, 144–45; and Indian costume/dancer in The Village People, 293n37

Hoop dance, 12, 20, 140, 229; *Hoop Dance* (Horton), 113, 137

Hopi Indian Eagle Dance (Shawn), 120–22

Horst, Louis, 150, 153, 167

Horton, Lester, 2, 23, 113–15, 129–146, 243, 294n59, 294n61; *Devil Dance*, 113; *Hoop Dance*, 113; Horton technique, 137, 244, 307n8; *Invocation to the Thunder God*, 139; *Kootenai War Dance (American Indian)*, 113, 129; Lester Horton Dance Theatre, 136; *Liberian Suite*, 142–44; *Mound Builders*, 113; *Painted Desert*, 113; *Prairie Chicken Dance*, 134, 136; *Pueblo Eagle Dance*, 133, 135; *Salome*, 143; *Song of Hiawatha*, 113, 129, 131–32, 137; *Takwish, the Star Maker*, 113; *Totem Incantation*, 113, 141–42; *Voodoo Ceremonial*, 129

House Made of Dawn (Momaday), 297n33

Hoving, Lucas, 173–75, 300n23

Humphrey, Doris, 145, 172, 174

Ickes, Harold L., 297n36

identity, Native American, 96, 171–72, 190, 194, 198, 207, 215–16, 240, 262, 271n13, 273n20, 291n12, 302n48; as always in the past, 204; and American identity, 3, 104, 115, 158, 167–68, 291n12; as appropriated, 132, 165; and "blood quantum," 16, 18, 128, 132, 164–65, 271n13; dance as central to definition of, 29–34; and Horton, 131–32; and identity politics, 164, 197, 303n1; and land, 22; and Limón, 169–70, 176, 179, 182–83; of Native American dance, 7; as performed, 59, 77, 127–28, 182, 193, 282n33, 285n63; and Two Arrows, 302n48

Indian Act (Canada), 38, 49, 72, 85–86, 214; Section 114 (149), 42, 86; Sections 140 and 141, 220; Subsection 2 of Indian Act, 72

Indian Child Welfare Act, 297n34

Indian Reorganization Act (Wheeler-Howard Act), 117, 214

Indian Rights Association, 70

individual: vs. collective memory, 242; as contrary to Southwest dance ideologies, 122; dances as obstacle to, 287n19; vs. group dancing, 138; heralding of individualism, 56, 82, 86, 275n6; individual expression, 114, 146; modern dance as invested in 243; and modernism, 119; in stage dancing, 79

Institute of American Indian Arts (IAIA), 204, 207, 304n23

Invocation to the Thunderbird (Shawn), 112, 120, 124

Invocation to the Thunder God (Horton), 139

Ito, Michio, 129

Jacob's Pillow, 129, 184, 188, 194, 198, 201, 283n40; Dance Festival, 174, 187, 211

Jaimes, M. Annette, 164

James, Belinda, 139–40, 210, 243–44, 253–55, 263, 307n8, 308n16; *MDCXXC,* 263; *Metamorphosis,* 253–55, 307n7

Jamieson, Julia, 264; *My Baby You'll Be: Ankewi:raenkenhake,* 264

Jingle Dress Dance, 16, 19, 21, 259–60, 274n28

John, Faron, 246

Johnson, William E. "Pussyfoot," 93–94

Jones, Rosalie. *See* Daystar

Jones, W. A., 40, 51

Joudry, Shalan, 223–27, 234

Jowitt, Deborah, 193, 296n12

Juarez, Benito, 174

Kaha:wi (Santee Smith), 262

Kahomini, 91

Kavanaugh, Don, 255, 260–61

Kawasumi, Misaye, 134

Keller, Robert H., Jr., 36

Kicking Bear, 73, 75

Kills Enemy Alone, 67

Killspotted, Claude, 81, 92

Kinney, Troy and Margaret West, 290n1

Kirstein, Lincoln, 295n9

Kisselgoff, Anna, 200

Kolodny, Annette, 158, 293n41

Kootenai War Dance (American Indian) (Horton), 113, 129

Kowal, Rebekah, 298n37

La Malinche (Limón), 169, 182

La Meri, 293n40

land: and AIRFA, 199, 305n33; in anti-dance legislation/rhetoric, 23, 29, 79, 83, 87–88, 97–99, 102–3; in assimilation policies, 31, 168, 170, 190; and Blue Lake, 199; centrality of relation to, 23–24, 29–30, 75–76, 182, 190, 216; dance as document of relation to, 21–22, 26, 220; and Indian Claims Commission, 171; and Indian Girl in *Appalachian Spring,* 163–64; and Indian identity, 182; land claims in Canada, 198, 214–21, 227–28, 235, 238, 305n31, 306n7; land loss as shared Indigenous experience, 7, 9, 226, 245; and *No Home but the Heart,* 13–15, 18, 21–22; and Nunavut, 225, 235–37; and stage dance, 14–15, 22, 226–27, 234–35, 237, 243; U.S. land, 171, 199, 215–16, 305n32. *See also* Dawes Allotment Act

Land Be Bright (Graham), 156

Laronde, Sandra, 229, 241, 253, 262

Laubin, Gladys and Reginald, 3, 170, 190, 293n40

Lewitzky, Bella, 137–41, 144

Liberian Suite (Horton), 142–44

Light and Shadow (Roncería), 225, 233–38

Limón, José, 24–25, 129, 145, 169–70, 172–183, 185–86, 193–94, 243, 299n18; *Danzas Mexicanas,* 172, 179–82; *Díalogos/Dialogues,* 174, 182; *The Exiles,* 299n11; *La Malinche,* 169, 182, 298n11, 299n23; Limón technique, 181–82; *Los Cuatro Soles,* 174; *The Moor's Pavane,* 169, 299n23; and racial struggles, 299n23; *The Unsung,* 193; Yaqui ancestry, 176, 178–9, 299n13

Lincoln, Sam (Sam Sissewln), 95, 288n24

Lloyd, Margaret, 131, 137

Lloyd, Tracey, 258

Lohah, 49

Lomavitu, Otto, 89–91, 102

Longboat, Jerry, 5–6, 225, 239; *Raven's Shadow,* 225

Long Bull, Dominick, 288n27

Longfellow, Henry W., 113, 293n41

Lopez, Antonio, 97

Lorant, Stefan: *The New World,* 293n40

Los Cuatro Soles (Limón), 174

Lost Bird (Zintka), 4

Lukin-Linklater, Tanya, 263; *Woman and Water,* 264

Mackaye, Percy, 61

Mackaye, Steele, 23, 55–57, 61–64, 67, 69, 79–80, 281n31; influence on Genevieve Stebbins, 279n4

Mahkimetas, Marla, 213

Mahoney, Billie, 300n26

Manitowabi, Edna, 256, 259–61, 263

Mann, Frank T., 87, 287n21

Manning, Susan, 2, 156, 270n4, 296n19

Manossa, Geraldine, 14–15, 264; *ISKWEW,* 264

Marble, H. P., 96

Marchowsky, Marie, 151

Mark, Cherith, 234, 258, 261

Martin, John, 153–54, 156, 295n9

Martin, Randy, 57

Martinez, Elsie "Pellie," 131

Martinez, Georgina, 241–43, 255, 260–61; *Miinigooweziwin . . . The Gift,* 11, 242, 255–62

masculinity, 4; in Horton 143–44; Indian dance as a way of asserting, 114; and manhood as sacred, 94; as negotiated through Indian dance, 119; and

Shawn, 120, 123–27, 146, 292n27; and Shawn and Hawkins, 143, 292n29

Mason, Bernard S., 289n38

Mather, Increase, 33, 35, 54, 77, 146

Maximillian, 174

McCormick, T. F., 97

McDonagh, Don, 156

McGehee, Helen, 297n29

McLaughlin, James, 71

Men Dancers. *See* Shawn, Ted: and Men Dancers

Men's Fancy Dance (AIDT), 212

Merrit, E. B., 87, 287n19

Metamorphosis (James), 253–55

Mexican Revolution, 178–79

Michaels, Walter Benn, 115, 291n12

Miguel, Muriel, 224, 226, 229–30, 245, 263; *Evening in Paris,* 263; *Throw Away Kids,* 226, 229–33, 236, 239

Miinigooweziwin . . . The Gift (Martinez), 11, 242, 255–62

Miles, Nelson A., 74

Mills College, 172

Modern Fancy (AIDT), 211–13

Mofsie, Louis, 24, 197–98, 301n29

Momaday, N. Scott: *House Made of Dawn,* 297n33

Montezuma, 174

Mooney, James, 73

Moor's Pavane, The (Limón), 169, 299–300n23

Moreno, Soni, 247

Morgan, Barbara, 153

Morgan, John (John Witonisee), 95, 288n24

Morgan, Thomas J., 40, 70, 74, 283n45

Morsette, Cordell, 176

Moses, L. G., 61, 65

Mossman, E. E., 88, 91

Mound Builders (Horton), 113

Mumaw, Barton, 124, 290n4

Mumford, Marrie, 5, 221–22, 227–28, 260–61, 263, 306n7

Murphy, Ann, 176

Napier, Rita G., 67, 69

Nation, The, 105

Native American Graves Protection and Repatriation Act (NAGPRA), 215, 305n33

Neihardt, John, 65

Nelson, Rose (Princess Blue Waters), 67

New Age, 1, 3, 132

New Dance (AIDT), 212

New Yorker, 204

Nichols, 48

Niezen, Ronald, 46

Nijinsky, Vaslav, 125–27

92nd Street Y, 184, 194, 301n32

Nixon, Richard, 199

No Home but the Heart: An Assembly of Memories (Daystar) 8, 13–22, 255

nudity/scant clothing: as complaint in Native dancing 42, 69, 72; in Horton's early career, 141, 145; as masculine ideal (Shawn), 124–27, 129; and white women's immodesty, 90

Oakes, Brandon, 246, 258

Oberly, John H., 283n45

Obomsawin, Alanis, 306n7

O'Brien, Sharon, 291n13

O'Donnell, May, 82, 150, 154, 163, 295n5, 297n29

Oka, 228, 306n7

Olson, Michelle, 263, 272n20; *Evening in Paris,* 263; *Raven Restores the Sun to the Sky,* 307n7; *Raven Spirit Dance,* 263

Omaha Dance, 51, 66, 70, 76–77, 282n33, 285n63, 302n48; Omaha Grass Dance, 66. *See also* Grass Dance

Osage-Pawnee Dance of Greeting (Shawn), 112, 120, 124

Owl dancing, 288n27

Painted Desert (Horton), 113

Palma, Pablo, 217, 225–26, 234

Pavlova, Anna, 122

Perpener John O., III, 136, 142

Pheasant, Karen, 260

photography: banning of, 84, 116, 291n16; Indigenous control of, 305n34

Picasso, Pablo, 127

Pierre, Dorothi Bock, 138

Pocahontas, 132, 167; in *Appalachian Spring,* 148, 158–60; in "The Bridge" (Crane) 158, 162

Ponca Indian Dance (Shawn), 123, 292n22

Pond, Gideon H., 58

Porcupine, 285n62

potlatch, 31, 38–39, 41, 43–44, 46, 49, 209–10, 220

Powers, William K., 66–7, 282n33

powwow, 4, 7, 17, 22, 24, 208, 211–12, 226, 256, 285n64–65, 302n48; and AIDT, 203, 212; intertribal powwows and termination, 171–72; movement incorporated in stage dances, 257, 261–62; "Powwow" (poem) 78; powwow-based stage dances, 197–98; "Powwow hobbyists," 3, 171–72, 190; and Tom Two Arrows, 184, 301n29; and Wild West shows, 66–67, 77–78. *See also* Fancy Dance

Prairie Chicken Dance (Horton), 134, 136

Pratt, A., 91

Prescott, William, 112, 290n4

Prevots, Naima, 169

Price, Hiriam, 37, 60

Primitive Mysteries (Graham), 112, 151–54, 158, 162, 164

Primitive Rhythms (Shawn), 124

Protestant policies/ideologies, 34–39, 71, 82, 85, 86, 95, 144, 146, 287n16; and Delsarte, 279n3; and "Peace Policy," 36, 276–77n16

protocol: questions of intellectual properties, 256, 305n34; in staging Native dance, 7, 20, 228

Proulx, Jeremy, 246, 259

Prucha, Francis Paul, 36, 167, 297n36

Pueblo Eagle Dance (Horton), 133, 135

Pueblo Indian Lands Act, 99

Qammaniq, Leslie, 234, 236–37, 239
Queen Elizabeth II, 219
Queen Victoria, 53, 62, 66–67, 69, 76–77
Queeny, Edgar Monsanto, 185
Queypo, Kalani, 246–47, 256, 258, 262

Raheja, Michelle, 118
rain, 51, 167; *Invocation to the Thunder-bird* (Shawn) as rain dance, 124; *Rain Quest* (Horton), 113; Zuni Rain Dance, 113, 167. *See also* water
Reardon, Christopher, 212, 304n28
Red Cedar Bark Ceremony, 209
Red Cedar Bark Ceremony (AIDT), 210
Red Shirt, 69
Red Sky Performance, 241–42, 262; *Caribou Song*, 253
religious freedom, 36, 58–59, 78–79, 90, 94–98, 102–3, 198–200, 215–16; American Indian Religious Freedom Act (AIRFA), 24, 197, 199, 200, 209–10, 215–16, 305n33; Circular no. 2970 "Indian Religious Freedom and Indian Culture," 107, 116–17
Residential School for Boys (Roncería), 8, 251–52, 255, 306n3
residential schools (Canada), 8, 214, 251–52, 306–7n13
Revelations (Ailey), 143
Riel, Louis, 13; "Riel Rebellion," 41
Rivera, Carlos, 230–31, 234, 246–47, 253
Rodríguez, Sylvia, 82
Rolfe, John, 158, 160, 167
Roncería, Alejandro, 8, 177, 183, 225–26, 233, 245, 249, 251, 263; *Agua*, 263; *BONES: An Aboriginal Dance Opera*, 11, 245–49; *Buffalo Spirit*, 8, 249–51, 255, 306n3; *Earth in Motion Indigenous World Dance*, 263; *Light and Shadow*, 225, 233–38; and Limón, 299n18; *Residential School for Boys*, 8, 251–52, 255, 306n3
Round Dance, 22
Royer, Daniel F., 284n53
Ruyter, Nancy, 55–57, 79

Sacre de Printemps (Horton), 143
Salome (Horton), 143
Salsbury, Nate, 60–62, 281n31
San Carlos Apache Crown Dance (AIDT), 203
Scalp Dances, 31, 37–40, 60, 75, 100–101, 279–80n21
Schoenberg, Betty, 295n12
Scholfield, Doug, 213
Scott, Duncan Campbell, 86, 250
Seabrook, W. B., 129
secrecy/privacy: as accusation, 93; Haudenosaunee ceremonies as, 301n42; as tactic, 84, 187, 202, 286n10, 302n45
Seger, John H., 58
sexuality: closeted/sequestered in Shawn's choreography, 114, 119, 126–27, 145; control of as part of assimilation policies, 30, 34; in dances seen as excessive/immoral, 35, 82, 84–85, 87, 93–94; in *El Penitente*, 156; in *La Malinche*, 173, 182; as overt in Horton's choreography, 143–44, 294n59; Pocahontas as available, 160; polygamy/immorality in dance restrictions, 38, 288n25; Shawn's definitions of in dances, 124, 292n28; trope of land and, 158; women's sexuality in Graham, 162. *See also* homosexuality; masculinity
Shaman's Journey (Trujillo), 225, 252
Shawn, Ted, 2, 4, 23, 53, 55–56, 111–15, 117, 119–129, 130, 132, 137, 141, 143, 145, 174, 290n4, 291n16, 293n40, 303n14; *The American Ballet*, 111, 115, 120, 126; "Basket Dance," 116; *Feather of the Dawn*, 112, 116, 118, 130; *Gods Who Dance*, 114; *Hopi Indian Eagle Dance*, 120, 121, 122, 292n22; *Invocation to the Thunderbird*, 112, 120, 124; and Men Dancers, 112, 114, 120, 124, 126–27; *O, Libertad!*, 292n22; *Osage-Pawnee Dance of Greeting*, 112, 120, 124; *Ponca*

Indian Dance, 123, 292n22; *Primitive Rhythms,* 124, 192n22; "Wolf Dance," 116; *Xochitl,* 113, 130; "Zuni Ghost Dance," 112

Sherman, Jane, 112

Short Bull, 73, 75

silence (as refusal), 93, 229

Silko, Leslie Marmon, 221; *Almanac of the Dead,* 1, 220; *Gardens in the Dunes,* 6

Sioux Falls Press, 91

Sissewln, Sam (Sam Lincoln), 95, 288n24

Sitting Bull (Tatanka Iyotake), 41, 60, 71, 283n50; assassination of 73–74; in *The Unsung,* 193

Sixth Grandfather, The (DeMallie), 65

Slotkin, Richard, 294n41

Smith, Captain John, 158–60

Smith, Cheri, 234

Smith, Henry, 201

Smith, Leigh, 224

Smith, Santee, 222–24, 226, 247, 262, 306n2; *Kaha:wi,* 262

Smith, Semiah, 224

"Smokis," 104, 290n39

Snake Dance, Hopi, 46, 51, 82, 89–90, 104, 116, 288n22–23, 290n39, 291n16

Solaris Lakota Sioux Indian Dance Theatre, 201, 205

Song of Hiawatha (Horton pageant), 113, 129, 131–32, 137

Soto, Jock, 3

Sousa, John Philip, 124

sovereignty, 182, 228, 233, 239; Haudenosaunee, 189, 302n43; and Limón, 182

spectacle, Indigenous dance as, 54, 60, 62, 73, 99–102, 106; vs. ceremonial, 103–4; staging, as disciplining institution, 75–77, 79

Spotted Elk, Molly, 2–4, 188, 263

Srinivasan, Priya, 307n6

Standing Elk, Eugene, 100–102, 289n33

St. Denis, Ruth, 56, 112, 120, 145, 174, 303n14, 307n6

Stebbins, Genevieve, 55–56, 279n4

Steele, Meade, 94

Stein, Don, 224

Stodelle, Ernestine, 151, 153, 176

story: and Daystar, 207–8; Delsartian shift away from, 56; and Horton, 139; and Martinez, 243; and Native American choreography, 6, 21–22, 222, 229–30, 236, 240, 243, 245, 254–55, 256–61, 273n20; and Two Arrows, 187–88

Sun Dance (medicine dance), 48–49, 58–59, 94, 277n23, 287n14; as "fake," 58; as morbid or "barbaric," 45–47, 50, 85; restrictions on, 31, 38–40, 42, 49, 85, 220, 280n21; on stage, 202

Sweet, Jill D., 83–84, 122, 127, 286n10

Tailfeathers, A. Blake, 246

Takwish, The Star Maker (Horton), 113

Talbot-Martin, Elizabeth, 143

Tallchief, Maria, 2–3, 129, 183, 187–88

Tallchief, Marjorie, 129

Tamanawas dances/rituals, 30, 38–39, 46

Tamiris, Helen, 270n4; *Annie Get Your Gun,* 290n4; *How Long Brethren,* 296n19

Tangen, Rulan, 256–57, 261, 262; *Dancing Earth,* 262

Taos and Santa Fe art colonies, 81–82, 112, 290n2

Tapia, 98

Tatanka Iyotake. *See* Sitting Bull

Taussig, Michael, 127, 306n5

Tecumseh, 193

Teller, Henry, 37, 39

Te Maro, Joel, 246

Ten Cent Treaty, 13–14, 21–22

Tenorio, Feliciano, 96

termination policies/era, 150, 170–72, 179, 184, 187, 189–90, 192, 199, 214, 299n20, 302n46

Terry, Walter, 124, 170, 188

Throw Away Kids (Miguel), 226, 229–33, 236, 239

Thunderbird American Indian Dancers, 24, 197–98

Tilton, Robert, 158–59

time: differing conceptions of, 1, 5, 11–12, 14–15, 25, 59, 105, 242, 246, 249, 273n23, 274n26; connections across, 21, 223, 307n14. *See also* waste, rhetoric of

Titley, E. Brian, 42–43, 72

Tomahawk, Red, 81, 92

Totem Incantation (Horton), 113, 141–42

transformation, 7, 9, 12, 21, 26, 84, 147; in dancing, 122, 128, 130; in Graham's "Pocahontas" 159–60; in Horton, 130, 139; in Shawn, 126–29, 146; in stage dance, 9, 210, 225, 245, 252–55; in *Shaman's Journey,* 225; in watching, 84, 122, 159; in *Wolf: A Transformation,* 208–10, 307n14

Treaty of Guadalupe Hidalgo, 95, 97

Truitte, James, 134, 137, 142, 294n59

Trujillo, Eufracio, 96

Trujillo, Raoul, 200, 225, 249, 252, 262; *Shaman's Journey,* 225, 252, 306n3, 307n14

Two Arrows, Tom (Thomas Dorsey Jr.), 24, 129, 170, 172, 183–94, 298n3, 301n29, 301n38, 302n43; *Hunter's Dance,* 187, 188; *Husk Face Dance,* 187, 190; on name choice, 300n28; on 92nd Street Y dances, 301n32

Udall, Lee, 176, 299n20

Udall, Morris, 176, 299n20

Unsung, The (Limón), 193

Vachon, Ann, 176

Valenzuela, Juan, 165, 183, 300n26

Vento, Arnoldo C., 11

visuality: acceptance of politically visible Indianness, 208; and commodification of Native culture, 33, 64, 77, 81, 164, 286n11, 291n14, 292n37; Indian as invisible presence (Graham), 149, 157–64; in other than visual terms, 132, 142, 165; privileging of vision, 8, 127–28; and rhetoric of disappearance, 83, 117, 128, 166, 233, 293n41

Voodoo Ceremonial (Horton), 129

Wadworth, James W., 288n23

Walker, Albert, 91

Walks Alone, Kuuks, 137

Wallace, Russell, 252, 307n13

War Dances, 37–40, 58, 60, 62–63, 66, 72, 75, 80, 280n21, 281n31, 282n33; *GWEE SAS ET* or *War Dance* (Two Arrows), 302n44; *Kootenai War Dance (American Indian)* (Horton), 113, 129. *See also* Omaha Dance: Omaha Grass Dance

Warren, Larry, 131–32, 138–41, 143

waste, rhetoric of, 23, 31, 38, 71, 82–84, 86–87, 92–94, 99, 102, 104, 107, 112–13; and Canada, 41, 42, 85–86; of land not owned/farmed, 287n18; of time, 23, 42, 84, 86–87, 116, 276n9; used in protest, 91–93

water, 12, 51, 83, 88, 97–99, 102, 205, 227; and medicine dance, 276n9; rain making and Tiswin Fiesta, 98; Zuni Rain Dance/Graham viewing of, 167. *See also* rain

Weaver, Jace, 11

Weidman, Charles, 145, 172, 174

Weighill, Tharon, 73, 77–78

Wheeler-Howard Act, 117, 214

White Eagle, Samuel, 288n27

Whitehouse, Jason, 213

White Pigeon, 289n31

Whitman, Walt, 124

Wilber, Ray Lyman, 290n44

Wilde, Oscar, 139

Wild West shows. *See Buffalo Bill's Wild West*

Williams, Walter L., 292n26

Williamson, Karla Jessen, 224

Wolf: A Transformation (Daystar), 208–9

"Wolf Dance" (Shawn), 116

women modern dancers, 123; middle-class white women and modern dance, 23, 54–56, 79–80, 146

Wong, Hertha Dawn Sweet, 293n41

Woolsy, J. P., 285n62

Wounded Knee massacre, 1, 73–75, 283n50, 294n55; survivor, 4; Wounded Knee (1973), 302n49

Work, Herbert, 95, 101

World War I, 72, 86, 95, 291n13

World War II, 167–68, 298n37; and cold war rhetoric, 168–70

Wovoka, 47, 73

Wright, James C., 50–51

Xochitl (Shawn), 113, 130

yoga, 7, 255, 260–61; Iyengar yoga, 242, 244

Zitkala-Sa (Gertrude Bonnin), 100, 102, 106,

Zuni Ghost Dance (Shawn), 112

Zuni Rainbow Dance, 203

Jacqueline Shea Murphy teaches dance studies at the University of California, Riverside.